Wrights & Wrongs

My life in dance

WRIGHTS & WRONGS

My life in dance

PETER WRIGHT
with
PAUL ARROWSMITH

First published in 2016 by Oberon Books Ltd
521 Caledonian Road, London N7 9RH
Tel: +44 (0) 20 7607 3637 / Fax: +44 (0) 20 7607 3629
e-mail: info@oberonbooks.com
www.oberonbooks.com

A catalogue record for this book is available from the British Library.

HB ISBN: 9781783193462
E ISBN: 9781783197194

Front cover: Peter Wright demonstrating at a summer school, Cologne, 1960s © Pieter Kooistra
Back cover: a design for The Nutcracker courtesy of the artist John Macfarlane
Author picture: Sir Peter Wright © Richard Farley

Visit www.oberonbooks.com to read more about all our books and to buy them.
You will also find features, author interviews and news of any author events, and you can
sign up for e-newsletters so that you're always first to hear about our new releases.

Front cover: Peter Wright demonstrating at a summer school, Cologne, 1960s
Back cover: A design for *The Nutcracker* courtesy of the artist John Macfarlane
Text designed and typeset by Caroline Waldron, Wirral, Cheshire

Printed, bound and converted by CPI Group (UK) Limited, Croydon, CR0 4YY

Contents

To Birmingham Royal Ballet –
and the many people who made it all happen

and

to the London Ballet Circle
whose untiring support and devotion to dance
celebrated its 70th anniversary
this year in 2016

List of Illustrations

Foreword

I participated as a 17-year-old in the Prix de Lausanne competition in 1983 which I was fortunate to win. I went to London that September and took part in a graduate class with the Royal Ballet School. Peter Wright, along with Desmond Kelly his ballet master, watched the class one day. There was a lot of tension in the room as it was an audition to join the company, but I could never imagine being part of it. At that time, Asian dancers had never really worked in this environment. That was my very first meeting with Peter, director of Sadler's Wells Royal Ballet, the person who gave me a chance.

I was not only Japanese, but also getting a working visa was a rare thing. I was only hoping to spend a year in London to gain some experience. Looking back now, I realise how amazing it was to be given this opportunity. I could say he was the one who made the way for Japanese dancers. When I joined Sadler's Wells Royal Ballet the following year, I quickly learned that Peter was – and is – incredibly kind. I got injured in my first year, and as I was dancing on a trial basis, I was really frightened that they might send me back to Japan, but Peter did not. He cared about me then and he still looks after me now.

The greatest thing about Peter's concern for me was that he took a long view of my career and artistic experience. He sees and thinks about dancers over time and believes in them, which in due course lets them grow. When he coached me in the major ballerina roles, he suddenly became a princess. It was very unique, 'Be like this,' he said, acting out and miming Aurora, Odette or Giselle in front of me. That helped me very much. As a young Japanese dancer I could not express my feelings easily, but Peter showed me how. It was a difficult process but I always appreciated his patience with me.

Peter was always very wise and very straightforward. He was honest in his advice, which could be upsetting sometimes, but I could tell he trusted in and cared about me so I trusted him. The greatest thing was that he never gave up on me. I started in the corps de ballet in Peter's production of *Swan Lake*. That really helped me understand Peter's wonderful production of ballets and his attention to detail. His productions of the classics made everything so realistic and natural, so this enables you, as a dancer, to find your way into these ballets and their major roles easily.

Giselle is another ballet that can be difficult, but Peter made it understandable and his productions always have a strong sense of theatre. Because Peter has worked with many companies, particularly with John Cranko in Stuttgart which I think had a big influence on him, he took the best from everywhere when he created his productions. His enormous contributions to Japanese audiences and ballet are worthy of high praise indeed.

It is difficult to now describe Peter as a friend. Of course he has been that for a long time, over 30 years in fact, but as I learned everything from him and his company, I really consider him more as a father-figure. It was amazing to be promoted to principal in 1988 by Peter. That made me feel respected as a dancer and changed my life. Peter has always said to me, 'You are my ballerina.' Those words have remained proudly in my mind, and always will.

Miyako Yoshida
Tokyo, December 2015

Prologue – an appreciation

This book is primarily an account of my working life, across nearly 75 years in the world of dance and theatre. It is not a conventional auto-biography, however. I do not detail much about my family or personal life. This is not to denigrate the love and support I have enjoyed from family, friends and colleagues throughout my life – but I fear that to mix them together would become far too complicated and overlong. However, it must be said I could not have had the career I did, without my beloved wife, Sonya Hana, and daughter Poppy.

Sonya and I had a blissful marriage which lasted 53 years. It would have continued to this day if she had not been snatched away from me by the dreaded Alzheimer's disease and brain cancer in 2007. I fell head over heels in love with her, a beautiful half-Japanese dancer, the first time we met in the summer of 1952 during a season of ballets that was being organised by John Cranko at Henley-on-Thames. It took some time for her to agree to marry me as she was also being courted by a rather high-powered suitor. This was Denholm Elliott, star of stage and screen, who would often visit her at Henley. Denholm, however, married Virginia McKenna, of *Born Free* fame.

This was a very traumatic time in my life. I poured my heart out to Clemence Dane, the playwright and novelist who was also a portrait painter, to whom I had been introduced by Richard Addinsell the composer who was a great friend of mine. Clemence, or Winifred as her friends called her, was a remarkable woman. Dick commissioned her to paint my portrait. As I was dabbling in painting at that time, and as a way of keeping my mind off Sonya, Winifred insisted that I should concurrently paint her portrait. This worked rather well. Her portrait of me is superb and now hangs in my flat. Mine of her is very inferior though it does capture her likeness quite well. The experience of painting with Winifred and learning from her wonderful tales she told gave me confidence. I decided to pursue Sonya again. I have to say I was helped too by the fact that John Cranko had created a duet for us, a paso doble, for the season in Henley. It was very amusing and very sexy. So during the following few months I persevered and finally managed to lure Sonya away from Denholm.

Sonya joined Sadler's Wells Theatre Ballet after Henley thanks to John's influence. We were together in July 1953 for a tour to Bulawayo in Rhodesia. Our repertoire included *Coppélia*, *Pineapple Poll* and *Les Sylphides* but I really do not recall much about what we danced. My excuse is that Sonya was with me. At the end of the Bulawayo season we went off to Victoria Falls for a few days' holiday. We stayed in a very simple shack of a hotel but we were very much in love. Kenneth MacMillan and Margaret Hill were due to come with us but at the last minute pulled out. We had planned to visit the Wankie game reserve before going on to Livingstone and Victoria. Kenneth and Margaret both had a terror of flying and decided it was better to go back to London direct. The falls were wonderful and our three-day visit turned out to be the most memorable three days of my life.

When we arrived back in London Sonya had to go straight into rehearsals at Drury Lane for *The King and I* alongside Herbert Lom and Valerie Hobson. Sonya was the principal dancer playing Eliza, in Jerry Robbins' ballet sequence about slavery, equality and intolerance, *The Small House of Uncle Thomas*. It was a wonderful role for her. After the excitements of Africa that autumn I was back to the normal touring round and the delights of Cardiff, Liverpool, Coventry and Peterborough, but another major overseas tour followed in the spring of 1954 to South Africa, this time without Sonya. I wrote to her every day and she did likewise to me from London. I begged her to marry me when I got back but she would not agree until I returned.

Sonya was there to meet me when finally I arrived after the two-week voyage. She agreed to marry me in August 1954 and I consider myself the luckiest man ever. We had a great carry-on to organise everything, for the wedding had to be on a Sunday as Sonya was performing eight shows, six days per week at Drury Lane. Wonderfully the management there decided to give Sonya a week off for a honeymoon while her understudy took over. We went to a little Cornish village called Mousehole. Sheer bliss! Unfortunately her pet dachshund, Yasha – or Ya-Ya – came too. He was the son of John Cranko's dog Clytie and shared his mother's tendency to eat everything in view. In Ya-Ya's jealousy he chewed up all Sonya's shoes and hat, as well as the coconut matting on the stairs.

John was best man at our wedding. Some 20 years later, after his premature death, Sonya and I were witnesses at Kenneth MacMillan's wedding to Deborah. When Sonya and I married, Winifred Dane gave us the most perfect wedding present. While she was working on the screenplay for one of Greta Garbo's films, she had given her a beautiful antique Japanese print. It is six feet wide and about 18 inches high and depicts a wedding procession with Mount Fuji in the background.

Sonya was always quick to defend me when she thought others had maligned me. A critic had given me great credit for a well-balanced triple-bill at the Birmingham Hippodrome, but when the same programme was repeated shortly afterwards in London he damned it. 'How could you? How could you change your mind?' she berated him in public. To which he replied, 'Consistency is the sign of a feeble mind.' This was a phrase I was to hear again later attributed to Ninette de Valois at a conference about her.

Sonya appears only at intervals in this book – always to speak sense, but that is what she did throughout our long and passionate marriage. I was always getting agitated about something. I used to get very stressed, particularly when I was staging a big new production. Once, when evidently I was stressing too much about something, Sonya turned and silenced me by saying, 'For goodness sake Pete. It's only a ballet! You die if you worry and you die if you don't. So why worry at all?' Then she gave me a big hug.

CHAPTER 1

Finding a footing

I RAN AWAY from school when I was 16. Bedales, at Petersfield in Hampshire, was a wonderful place in which to learn but I was angry and miserable because my father would not allow me to train as a dancer. I knew that 14 was usually the latest age for boys to start training for classical ballet so it was imperative that I began at once. I cannot say I was particularly drawn to classical ballet as I had never seen one. I just wanted to be a dancer.

Peggy Barnsley, a friend, absconded with me as she was fed up with how her life was dominated by the school. Her father Edward was one of the most important British cabinet-makers of the 20th century, inspired by the ideals of William Morris. His influence on design has been immense and the bespoke furniture business that carries the family name still exists. The company had worked on the construction of a new library at Bedales and Edward Barnsley was also a governor of the school, the first co-educational boarding school in Britain. The family lived close by so Peggy was a weekly boarder going home every weekend. School, however, dominated her life, meal times, conversations and holidays, even things that should not involve Peggy. Like me she was determined to get right away from Bedales. In fact six of us, including the headmaster's daughter, originally planned to make a run for it but the others chickened out so only Peggy and I made our bid for freedom. By then Peggy had already tried to leave home a couple of years before, moving to London as a 14-year-old at the height of the 1939–45 war. We were quite mad to try to escape. We got as far as Somerset and survived for two days in the freezing cold, sleeping in a cow field. Our dreams were shattered when we had to admit defeat and turned ourselves in to the police who sent us post haste back to our parents – after a night in the cells.

My elder sisters went to dancing classes because that was the sort of thing girls did. When I was about seven years old my mother took me along too in order to get rid of some of my excess energy. I was the only boy in the class but I think I must have impressed the teacher, a Miss Gayford. She suggested to my mother that I should go to a full-time dancing school. We went home and at tea my mother raised the subject. My father vetoed the idea immediately. He was a chartered accountant and a quaker. He had very particular ideas about what constituted entertainment and life in general. I suppose he had no experience of the arts or dance and was horrified. Odd really as he and my mother had met when she gave him ballroom dancing lessons at the little dancing school she shared with her mother. Miss Gayford's lessons ceased to be part of the family agenda, much to my sisters' delight. They had hated them.

Nor was I unhappy at Bedales. I went first to the prep school, Dunhurst. Life there was full of adventures so that I quickly forgot about dancing. I remember getting married to a little girl called Ali in a wedding ceremony behind the huge handicrafts' barn. We were both ten years old. The wedding ring consisted of a small corner piece of Meccano attached to her finger with a piece of orange ribbon. I remember it well because I made it. I think our marriage lasted for a couple of days. Then came the transfer to Bedales proper of which I have many wonderful memories. I adored the free life there and the friendly relationship the pupils had with the staff. We were even encouraged to call them by their first names. I found the liberal atmosphere positive. Family holidays in my childhood used to be spent at the Sport hotel in Grindelwald, in Switzerland, overlooking the Jungfrau. We were there when war was declared in September 1939. Although my father was prosperous he was sparing with the money but we went by car. Returning home that year we saw tanks, army lorries, huge guns and endless lines of troops being mobilised. At Calais we had to queue for a ferry as they were all full. It was foot passengers only. My father had to leave the car behind with the promise that it would be sent across when there was room on a ship. Fortunately we only had to wait in Dover for a day or so for its return. I always liked an adventure and some of the war I really enjoyed.

Bedales got a lot of German planes flying over and there were many air raids. My cousin from Ipswich came up to London, to Totteridge, where my family lived, and I remember we made model aeroplanes. There was an anti-aircraft installation near our house which vibrated so much that it cracked the walls of our house. My parents had an Irish maid, a big lump of a woman, absolutely dotty. During one raid she was left alone in the house, something that exacerbated her already excitable nature. To calm herself she helped herself to some of the holy water that my mother kept in a bottle in their bedroom. When they returned home they found a distinctly tipsy maid. 'I got the bottle of your holy water and shook it but that didn't help,' she explained. 'So I just had a little swig of it and that did help.' And presumably a second swig too, knowing full well that the holy water was in fact brandy. Instead of going abroad, during the early war years holidays from Bedales were spent at home. One year, although we had a coal cellar in our family home which had been reinforced as a shelter, it was considered too dangerous and upsetting to remain in London during the long summer school holidays. Along with my mother and sisters, we were all decamped to a farm in Somerset. There were already six evacuee children there. The farmers were very kind. I could ride, collect eggs and work with the farmhands whose tales of their conquests helped a lot with my adult education. My elder sister had a crush on one of them. There was a scandal when one of the male teachers responsible for the children was discovered with a boy in bed, half naked, reading poetry to him. I am sure it was all quite innocent but it gave everybody a lot to talk about.

Back at Bedales I hated football and cricket but I loved the swimming and tennis. I was captain of both. If I had not fought to become a dancer I would probably have gone into tennis, which I continued to play well into my seventies. I devoted my spare time to the arts and music for which Bedales had a strong tradition. It is where I learned to knit. Even now, some 80 years later, when my brain gets really scrambled I find that knitting complicated patterns is a way of relaxing. I also learned how to make pottery, which I adored. Later, after Sonya and I were married, we took pottery classes together and we set up our own studio which did rather well. While I was still a pupil I directed a production of Sheridan's *School for Scandal* and seemed to instinctively understand the artifice and style of the 18th century. In those days the school had a traditional proscenium theatre. Many years later I made myself unpopular with the planners of the new theatre that was to be built there. It was designed in-the-round. Kenneth and Deborah MacMillan's daughter Charlotte attended Bedales. I tend not to agree with Deborah on many things but we both thought that an open, round stage is too exposing for novice performers and directors. In-the-round is very rarely used these days and it is surely best to learn the rules of traditional proscenium theatre before tackling the art of other performance and direction styles. However, when I returned to Bedales in April 2015 to give a talk about my career, I was pleased to see Peggy Barnsley who was there too that day and I saw at a rehearsal that the configuration of the theatre could be adapted as a traditional proscenium stage. The rehearsal we witnessed there was very strong. Seeing Peggy again was a wonderful reunion.

It was also at Bedales that I could indulge my passion for horse riding. It had its own stables, only about five minutes away from the main premises. I loved it. Riding cost extra but it was something that my father enjoyed. He had learned to ride during the 1914 –18 war and continued with it, in his army breeches and puttees. I had initially learned when I was quite young from a Mrs Woodall, a large, sturdy quaker family friend, at a riding school in North Mymms in Hertfordshire. Along with her elderly husband, son and daughter, there was nobody kinder. Mrs Woodall had an American friend who used to stay with the family for long periods. She was always well turned out in her riding gear, boots, breeches, short jacket, tie and bowler hat. She even wore a watch chain and walked like a man, spoke like a man and rode like a man. I really thought she was a man but she was always called Mrs Crumm. One day I caught her kissing and cuddling Mrs Woodall in the stables which really confused me, then a naïve eight-year-old. At the Bedales stable I used to ride a spirited half-Arab pony called Kingfisher. We had a special connection and I was terribly upset when it was given to somebody else to ride. I became pretty good at dressage and bare-back jumping. Then to my horror, my father announced that he was going to send me to a quaker school in Reading to toughen me up. I thought I was tough enough, thank you very much. The new school was a disaster as academically it was much more advanced but musically it was very inferior. I lost the desire to play the piano. The teacher was a bit of a wimp. In fact I made such a fuss that after I had wasted a year I was returned to Bedales, now aged 15 or so. I was very happy to be back again. Unfortunately the riding stables had been abandoned as horses were requisitioned because of the war.

And so that is when I first got my passion for dance. Bedales had an excellent library and I discovered in it a lot of information about ballet. During one school holiday in the summer of 1943 my mother took me to the Lyric theatre in London to see a matinée of Mona Inglesby's International Ballet. This was a touring company established a couple of years before to entertain a public deprived of culture during wartime. That first triple bill I saw included Mikhail Fokine's *Carnaval* with Harold Turner as Harlequin, Anne Negus as Papillon, Nina Taraknova as Columbine and Rex Reid as Eusebius. Although I did not know it at the time, some ten years later Eusebius became one of my better roles with Sadler's Wells Theatre Ballet. I needed only to walk across the stage full of romantic love, a task I contrived to build up into something quite significant. The programme was completed by one of Inglesby's own ballets, *Planetomania*, which had music by Norman Demuth and Harold Turner, Britain's first and now forgotten virtuoso, leading the cast. But it was the opening ballet that really created an impression. When the curtain opened on *Les Sylphides* and its group of beautiful girls in lovely floating white dresses surrounding a handsome man, almost certainly Henry Danton who was partnering Inglesby then, I knew that this was what I wanted to do. I whispered to my mother, 'That's for me.' I told her afterwards just how serious I was. Henry went on to join Sadler's Wells Ballet and only three years later to be part of the original cast of Frederick Ashton's *Symphonic Variations* at the Royal Opera House, and was soon to become a colleague and lifelong friend.

As I quickly learned to appreciate, the repertoire of International Ballet included Nikolai Sergeyev's productions of classical ballets which Inglesby considered a vehicle for herself and her own rather limited talents as a dancer. Sergeyev's stagings were based on Marius Petipa's original productions for the imperial Mariinsky theatre where he had been a ballet master. After the communist revolutions in 1917 Sergeyev left Russia taking his notations of Petipa's ballets with him. Eventually he was invited by Ninette de Valois to stage the Russian classics for her young Vic-Wells company in London during the 1930s. However, Sergeyev soon became dissatisfied with de Valois' tendency to edit his original sources, which is how he came to work for Inglesby. She did not lack ambition. Inglesby choreographed herself. For *Amoras* she used music by Edward Elgar. *Endymion* was designed by Sophie Fedorovitch. I saw when I read a review in the library at Bedales of *Everyman*, which had music by Richard Strauss and designs by Rex Whistler, *The Times* complained that the medium of ballet was incapable of fully expressing a medieval play. Apparently the music and choreography were badly matched, not the sort of notice that any choreographer wants to receive. Even to my untutored eye I soon came to realise that Inglesby herself was rather dull. Claudia Algeranova was the company's second ballerina, in those days known as Claudie Leonard. She was a very strong technician with beautiful balances. Claudie, who has long been one of my greatest friends, told me that in Sergeyev's production of *The Sleeping Beauty*, designed by Alexander Schervashidze, at one point in the vision scene an arbour of roses was wheeled on by two elfin pages who also presented Aurora with a large rose. Framed by the arbour, she balanced, seemingly unaided, with one foot on pointe as the nymphs all gathered around her, forming a very pretty group. The prince then appeared and Aurora ran off followed by him. When I saw it – once with Inglesby and another time with Algeranova – getting the arbour on and off again was very clumsily done but the actual balance itself was very effective. I later learned that this was because of a little foot support concealed among the roses which made it easy for Inglesby to balance. Other Auroras, whom Inglesby considered a threat, Claudie included, were not allowed to use the device. They had to trust to their natural powers of balancing.

In later life I learned that Harold Turner, no great partner, found Mona difficult to lift. He pinned a notice to his dressing-room door, calling himself a haulage contractor. Harold in fact, although a brilliant virtuoso, was not good at partnering. Nor later, when he taught at the Royal Ballet School, was he a good teacher. He could not shape enchaînements to music at all. In my early days of ballet watching I also saw Anglo-Polish Ballet, which relied on such works as the second act of *Swan Lake* and *Le Spectre de la rose*. Rovi Pavinoff was their leading man. He considered himself to be rather good. I did not. Anglo-Polish Ballet included some national dances. Full of character work and beautifully done, I adored *Cracow Wedding* by Czeslaw Konarski. He and his wife, Alicia Halama, also performed a beautiful adagio number, full of lifts and swirling turns, not really ballet but it brought the house down. With the greater experience I gained as I saw more performances by different companies I came to recognise that Inglesby's were diluted versions of the classics without much excitement or style.

All of this was still in the future for me, of course. My own career had not yet started. My mother and I returned home from that performance of *Les Sylphides* that had so captivated me. During our evening meal, she told my father how much I had enjoyed the ballet and tried again to raise the subject of dance lessons. My father refused to discuss the matter. In vain I pleaded to be allowed to start training but was sent back to Bedales where the head was given strict instructions by my father as to who I could see and what I could do in my free time. Irene Spencer, wife of the biology teacher, had been a member of Anna Pavlova's company and she gave lessons unofficially to some of the girls, so that gave me a small window on the world of dance but really I felt thwarted. I confided in my music master, Harry Platts. He was a very inspiring teacher but had quashed my desire to learn the violin. Harry told me the piano, which my parents had made me learn, would be much more useful, which is probably true. He himself had been a rehearsal pianist for a dance school run by Kurt Jooss at Dartington hall near Totnes in Devon, that cradle for the arts that over the years has nurtured many dancers and actors, painters and potters, composers and musicians, philosophers, writers and poets. He told me a lot about Jooss and thought his company might be the right one for me as a late starter. I had seen some of Jooss' work for opera during my early days of theatre going. He directed *The Magic Flute* in 1942 and *The Marriage of Figaro* a year later for Sadler's Wells Opera at the New theatre. I recall queuing for stools at 6d, that is the equivalent of 2½ pence; or for 1s 9d, nearly nine pence now, you could go in the gallery. I thought it was marvellous how Jooss got the priests, normally very static in most productions, to move in formation. He could get a chorus to move extremely well. However, when Jooss himself visited Bedales to see if the school would be suitable for his daughter, I was forbidden to make contact with him. I saw him come into the dining-room – but I could not speak to him. I was completely shattered. This is what prompted me to abscond from school with Peggy in our mad bid for freedom. Peggy did not lose her independent spirit and immediately the war was over she crossed the Channel and established herself in France.

She later became a very talented artist and Contessa Karine Antonini as wife of Giacomo Antonini, an expatriate Italian writer and literary critic. However, my desperate behaviour had somehow done the trick with my father. My seriousness of purpose had evidently impressed him. He informed me that if I was determined to make a career in dance then I could go ahead and do it – but without any financial support from him. My mother had been in tears when I arrived back home and had made me my favourite soup for supper, Heinz tomato. I may not have had any financial backing but I did have the support of Harry Platts. Through him I was able to meet Jooss at the Arts theatre club in London. He seemed very keen to help me and asked me to go to Cambridge, where his company was currently based, to audition. I explained that I had not done any training but he said that did not matter. I duly arrived at the Red Lion hotel at Cambridge where the company rehearsed in an upstairs room with a horrible floor. Barefooted I put on my green gym shorts and vest. Jooss told me that the pianist would play different pieces of music to which I should improvise. I used to do that at school with a gramophone at weekends when the gym was empty, so I did some of the sort of movements I had invented. I was pretty unselfconscious in those days. The pianist was wonderful and I got quite carried away. Jooss seemed very pleased and then put me through some basic stretching exercises. He said he thought I had a lot of talent and would like me to go on tour as an apprentice. Imagine, joining a German company during the war. As I was only 16 Jooss explained he would need to have my father's agreement. I explained the problem about his attitude. Jooss said he would arrange to meet him with me and was quite sure he would be able to convince him. This happened. My father was impressed enough to give me his blessing but insisted that first I returned to Bedales to take my school certificate exams, which I did – and failed. No wonder, after all that carry on.

And so in autumn 1943 my father took me to Cambridge to settle me at 9 Adams Road where I was to stay in the care of Dr Alice Roughton whose house it was. Without quite knowing what I was letting myself in for, I was wildly excited to be able to start my training. It was not what my father wanted for me but the more I am prevented from doing something the more determined I am to achieve it. My father unbent enough to write out a cheque to Jooss from which he would pay me ten shillings – 50 pence – per week as pocket money. I would be required to work with the stage management when not doing training classes. Alice Roughton was notoriously eccentric. She had thrown open her house to war refugees. It did not matter to her where they came from. She and her husband, a distinguished professor, had led a life very much dominated by Cambridge society, which she loathed. She held the purse strings having inherited a large amount of money from her father. Her mother was a seventh child of a large family and Alice was the first of seven daughters, which was considered significant in some way. She was very much the boss, incredibly kind, and among the people to whom she gave support were members of the Ballets Jooss company. Alice adored Jooss and his form of modern dance.

Kurt Jooss was a German dancer, teacher and choreographer whose works shunned classical ballet technique but used a method of training that he developed with help from Rudolf Laban and Sigurd Leeder, both well known in Germany. Their work placed more emphasis on dramatic and modern dance styles. Jooss' most famous ballet, which 50 years later I was to introduce to the repertoire of Birmingham Royal Ballet, is *The Green Table*, about the futility of war and the failure of political diplomacy. It was created in 1932 when it won a major choreographic competition in Paris. Choreography and music were created in tandem by Jooss and composer Fritz Cohen. With the prize money, which was considerable, Jooss had been able to start his company. The company had many Jewish members, although Jooss himself was not, and the acclaim that *The Green Table* received made the company dangerous to Hitler, who had already started his purges of the population in Germany. Word got around that the SS intended to arrest Jooss and the company. They were expected to depart on a tour on a certain day but in fact Jooss secretly brought the departure forward by a day. Hitler's men were foiled and the company escaped to England. Once there, Dorothy Elmhirst, the daughter of multi-millionaire William Whitney and related by marriage to the Vanderbilts, but no relation to Elmhurst School for Dance now in Birmingham, took pity on the company. Being very interested in new departures in dance, she offered Jooss somewhere on part of her huge estate at Dartington where he could establish a base and school for the company. This was to be their home until 1940. Jooss himself lived in a modernist house designed for him by William Lescaze which

had its own dance studio and is now owned by Wayne McGregor. Rudolf
Laban, who had taught Jooss, was also resident at Dartington. Jooss and
his group flourished, undertaking tours across Britain, America, Holland,
Belgium and Switzerland until the aftermath of the battle of Dunkirk
in 1940 when Dartington became part of a protected area. Jooss, as a
German, and his compatriots were either interned or deported. Jooss was
sent to Chile to a camp there but managed to get back to England in
1942 with the intention of starting his group again in Cambridge, helped
enormously by Alice and Maynard Keynes who was then the chairman of
CEMA, the Council for the Encouragement of Music and the Arts, the
precursor of the Arts Council. Alice allowed Jooss the use of her big oak
ballroom as a studio for rehearsals and classes and liaised with the Arts
theatre at Cambridge to organise performances there and tours of Britain.

By 1942 they had become established enough again to undertake
a further tour to the USA. A year later, when Jooss took me on as an
apprentice and persuaded Alice to look after me, I was quite bowled over
by the other members of the household – French, Hungarian, Polish,
Austrian – mostly from the arts. They all talked at once in their own
language and I could not understand a single word. Hans Zullig, a Swiss
dancer, lived there too, as did Jooss and his wife. Hans, the star of the
company, was very kind to me but kept himself to himself and never
mixed with the others. Son of a Swiss sausage factory owner, he was the
most sensitive and totally dedicated dancer I have known. His portrayal
of roles such as a young workman in *Big City*, the mysterious companion
in Jooss' version of *The Prodigal Son* and the evil profiteer in *The Green
Table* were astonishing, riveting even. In particular, I also remember him
in *Ballade* as a courtier forced by a jealous queen to give his fiancée a
poisoned bouquet. Zullig also gave most of the daily company classes, a
task he shared with Sigurd Leeder. Zullig loved classical ballet and later
on, when the Jooss company closed in March 1947 following the withdrawal of its grant as it had been used for international touring rather
than UK tours, Zullig joined Sadler's Wells Theatre Ballet as a guest
principal, something which did not really work out. I was glad to coincide with him there but he was not happy and felt like a fish out of water.
Although we used to show him some classical steps he could not do
them properly and the ballets he appeared in did not show him off at all
well. His style of dance was just too different although Andrée Howard

tried very hard to adapt her choreography to suit him when she created *Selina*. Zullig soon returned to Germany where he taught successfully for some time. I learned so much from him about tension, relaxation, projection, focus and self-discipline as a dancer, teacher and choreographer. When Zullig died, a beautiful studio was built in his name at Essen-Werden, near the big folkwangschule, a college for music, theatre, dance and design which was the home of Ballets Jooss for many years.

After my initiation in Cambridge it was not long before I first went on tour as an apprentice. On 13 September 1943 I was given a ticket for Wolverhampton, the first venue of a 35-week tour, and told to check in at the stage door of the Grand theatre and ask for a list of digs. The doorkeeper was very helpful but warned me that it was very hard to find accommodation as there were many homeless caused by recent bombings. I duly trekked my way around the town to no avail and returned to the theatre very crestfallen. In the meantime the stage door man had made some enquiries and the company's stage manager said I could share his room – but I would have to share his bed as well. Luckily I had already met him and liked him well enough. What I did not know but soon discovered was that he had the most dreadfully smelly feet. Our landlady was more usually drunk than not. The walls ran with damp. There was one double bed, so tired that it dipped and sank into the middle. We were allowed five inches of bath water per day and one scuttle of coal for the week. I put it down to experience. I operated the follow spot. I acted as call boy, informing the dressing-rooms how much longer to curtain-up. I also had to help unload all the huge costume trunks and scenery. Besides theatres we also performed in factories engaged in producing supplies for the war. Audiences were small but hugely enthusiastic, cheering and shouting whenever *The Green Table* was performed. It was newly added to our repertoire having been specifically requested by theatres. The one thing I did not get much experience of was as a dancer. Jooss hardly ever had second casts. In any case what would I do onstage? I had no training and no experience and there was no time to rehearse understudies or alternate casts. My debut onstage turned out to be in *The Green Table* as a soldier required only to march across the stage and die, a cruel irony as it happened.

My career in theatre was interrupted by my military service. I should have been called up 18 months previously but this had been postponed due to an injury to my back I had sustained while fooling around. It had occurred when I was back at Bedales after my failed attempt to run away. The day before the annual tennis tournament between current pupils and Old Bedalians we had all been messing about in the dorm. We made a big pile of laundry baskets to dive over, landing on the other side with a somersault on a mattress. That was something I was quite good at but on one attempt I failed to tuck in my head sufficiently and as I landed I crashed sideways with an agonising pain in my lower spine and neck. The following day, as tennis captain, I had to play in a three-hour game in the tournament against some former pupils. I was still in great pain, really quite crippled. It has been the bane of my life ever since but I am convinced that having something you have to fight against makes you achieve much more. And fortunately it did defer my military call-up. I was perpetually dreading that this would catch up with me and prayed they would forget about me. But no, I was sent off to Ulster for six weeks' primary training. Having got this far and doing quite well, I really felt that my chances of making it as a dancer were now ruined. In the third week of training we had to go on an outdoor survival course during which we each had to carry another soldier over our shoulders down a steep incline about 20 feet in length. I got landed with a great lump of a man, much taller than me. Halfway down I tripped and fell, with him on top of me. I felt my back go with an agonising pain. In fact it later transpired that the cartilage between two vertebrae, where I had hurt my back previously, had now slipped out. I really thought that a higher power was telling me I was not meant to be a dancer. This really was the last straw. I was carted off on a stretcher to the army hospital in great pain and was surprised to be looked after with great kindness by the army nurses and doctors. I was, in fact, in that hospital for two months before they decided I would be a liability if I was returned to the ranks. Instead I would be honourably discharged with three months' pay. Actually, my back, once they had got the disc back in, was improving a lot, though I did not let the authorities know that of course. After another three months at Alice Roughton's house at Cambridge, where she enlisted the help of a wonderful orthopaedic surgeon from Addenbrooke's hospital, a Mr Butler, I was fit enough to start my apprenticeship with Jooss again.

I was certainly glad to return but my physical injuries had done nothing to help my already scant technical abilities. Jooss himself helped me a lot. He was an amazing man and I did much to make the most of the training that he and his staff were providing. He had rebelled against the classical ballet he had seen in German opera houses in the 1920s and 30s. The pointe work he had seen there was appalling, he said, and relied on hard blocked shoes which enabled the women to stay on their toes, but without lightness or expression in their feet. He did admit that he was reacting against something that was a gross misrepresentation of classical dance. Had Jooss been able to see great companies, like Sergei Diaghilev's Ballets Russes, he might have enlarged his vocabulary and style of choreography. But Jooss did not want to see much work by other companies as he was already intent on finding a new form of movement to make the body more expressive. Jooss' approach used the body's weight and strength to contrast with its lightness and speed. I recall when I was still an apprentice, along with two other boys, we had to develop some movements we had been working on into actual choreography in the studio. I performed what I thought was a very beautiful extended series of beaten and gliding steps. After Jooss had watched it he demanded to know what it signified. I replied that it was not about anything, it was just beautiful movement. 'Then forget it,' Jooss said. As far as he was concerned, movement for its own sake had no importance whatever. If you were performing for an audience, thought Jooss, you must have something to communicate. As I was later to discover too from Kenneth MacMillan, choreography is just as much about ideas as it is about steps.

Jooss' ballets always had a story or were an expression of such concepts as life, death, despair or hope. I remember him talking to me about Frederick Ashton's *Symphonic Variations*, only recently created. He told me it epitomised exactly what he was trying to achieve. He so loved the way Ashton's choreography flowed and how his dancers were so expressive of different emotions. Jooss wished he had seen more ballets like that when he was rebelling against the rigidity of classical ballet. If he had, Jooss admitted, then he would have used much more classical work in training his dancers and in his choreography. In fact, several of his ballets created in the 1950s and 60s, like *Columbinade* with music by Johann Strauss, *Nachtzug* (or *The Night Train*) and *Weg im Nebel* (*Journey in the Fog*) which both had scores by Alexandre Tansman, a protégé of Maurice

Ravel, and *Pandora* with music by Roberto Gerhard, did show evidence
of this, however. I learned so much from Jooss and Sigurd Leeder about
dynamics of movement. I was able to draw on that experience when,
later while I was teaching at the Royal Ballet School, Ninette de Valois
asked me to take over her plastique classes which she had devised to
help get students more aware of their relationship to space and get more
dynamic feeling in their work. ·

It was a strange experience to go back after the war to mainland Europe
with the Jooss company. The tour was partly funded by ENSA which had
been established in 1939 to provide entertainment for the British military. That post-war tour was also organised by Gabor Cossa, the Jooss
company's manager, a Hungarian who had a lot of connections. It was
my first time abroad with a ballet company. We went by ferry and started
in Oostende in Belgium. Compared to England, if you had the money,
you could get anything – fresh produce and food, sweets – but you had
to pay. In Holland we stayed in a very art nouveau establishment called
The American hotel where the whole company ate together. We all ate
boiled fish at practically every meal. If you could not pay black market
prices that is all there was – and there was a big black market. It was
incredibly exciting going over the Rhine. As all the main bridges had
been blown up we were on a temporary structure, under a very strong
moon. I could not believe we were entering Germany. We opened in
Lüneburg, south of Hamburg, and also performed in Hamelin, home of
the Pied Piper, which was undamaged and very beautiful in the snow. The
town had a nice feel about it, almost like being in a child's picture book,
and everybody spoke refined, high German or Hochdeutsche there. The
tour also took us to Braunschweig, Essen and Düsseldorf among many
places. I was shocked at all the devastation and mangled machinery
everywhere. We were largely performing to troops. The war was over but
there was an allied occupation force stationed in Germany. We toured
our normal repertoire – with the exception of *The Green Table* which
was not deemed to be suitable as army entertainment – and performed
in theatres and barracks, where we could. The reaction was pretty good.
When the troops saw what they were getting they did not object. We
performed *Big City*, about an upper-class libertine who seduces a working-
class girl before abandoning her. It was real, a dramatic and very good
work which included tangoes and other dances such as the charleston.

We also danced *Ball in Old Vienna* which was absolutely beautiful. Paris was also on the tour itinerary, the first time I had been to the city. It was cold but clean, I got up early and walked all day when we did not have any performances, looking at all the famous landmarks. I did not make it to Montmartre to any of the cabarets or sleazy bars but I did go to a play, Thornton Wilder's *Skin of our Teeth*. I fainted out of tiredness and excitement. Gabor Cossa took me home to the hotel in a fiacre, very concerned for my wellbeing, but I loved being in Paris. I was very impressionable in those days.

Although I enjoyed the opportunity to go abroad and the intellectual stimulation that I got from both Jooss and the company members, as well as his sort of ballets and sense of theatre, I realised that what modern dance technique I was managing to acquire was not really sufficient to develop the sort of technique and strength that would provide me with the skills with which to develop a career in other forms of dance. Hans Zullig helped me with the basics of classical technique but I knew he was right when he told me that I needed to get some proper training. It was good advice and I followed it. As a consequence of what Zullig told me I left the company.

I got jobs in musicals, reviews, films, modelling; anything in London so that I could pay for classes with Vera Volkova. I appeared as an extra in the Alexander Korda film *Anna Karenina*, starring Vivien Leigh. I was put at the front in one party scene as I could waltz rather well. Sadly most of that section ended up on the cutting-room floor. Such jobs were useful in gaining performing experience, but more importantly I used the money I earned to attend the classes taught by Volkova. She was a Soviet-era dancer from the then Kirov Ballet and teacher who greatly influenced Western ballet training. She had studied with Agrippina Vaganova, renowned for her beautiful style. At the time Volkova was teaching at Sadler's Wells school but also taught in the West Street studios near Covent Garden, giving classes for professionals. The dancers who attended her classes included some of the great pioneering names of British ballet, Margot Fonteyn, Henry Danton, Pamela May, Moira Shearer, Moyra Fraser, Brian Shaw and several more. During her career, Volkova also coached Alicia Alonso, Erik Bruhn, Eva Evdokimova and Peter Martins – among many others. Volkova recognised that I did not have much money but she did seem keen to teach me as there were not many boys around at that time. She said therefore that I could pay half fees per class, which amounted to 1s 9d in old money, and if I felt able to do two in a day, the second would be free. She also gave me a half-hour lesson on my own once per week, also free. She rightly said it was important that I paid something as I would want to feel I was getting my money's worth and work that much harder. In those days I was living on £4 per week and staying at home, for which I had to pay my father £1 per week to include supper and breakfast. Then there were fares and ballet shoes, lunches, union membership fees and visits to the ballet, in the gallery, so I had to keep myself employed.

I heard that a new ballet company was to be formed, with a famous Russian teacher, Victor Gsovsky, as ballet master. Henry Danton, who I knew now through Vera's classes, knew Gsovsky's work well and had at one time studied with him in Paris. He thought he would be an ideal teacher for me as more than anything I needed strength and stamina, and Gsovsky's classes were really tough. I managed to find out that auditions were to be held that day in a studio near the Windmill theatre in Soho. I got myself over there pretty quick, just in time in fact, for the boys' final audition which was about to start. I registered with a receptionist, found the dressing-room, hastily changed and dashed in as the music started for pliés. Gsovsky glared at me and pointed to a free place at the barre, shouting at me for being late. I managed to have a quick look around to see what the competition was like. Not much, I thought, and still panting from my rush to get there, proceeded to do the best class I have ever done, remembering everything that Vera had told me. At the end of the barre the rubbishy ones were thanked and asked politely to leave. Gsovsky looked at me and asked where I was studying. When I told him I was from Madame Volkova, his face lit up. He put me in the front row. Well, I loved that class and really worked my butt off. I was offered a contract there and then. I immediately went to find Volkova and tell her my good news. Well, she was not at all pleased and felt that I was not ready. But she did say that provided I took advantage of Gsovsky's classes and worked on my own as well – and most importantly promised always to come back to her whenever the company was in London – then she would give me her blessing. Henry was very supportive and as he and Vera were very close he convinced her that it was a good idea. Although we became great friends when we worked together he was very strict. He really helped me a lot. In fact Henry, now in his nineties and living in America, still corresponds with me regularly and occasionally we are able to meet up when he visits London. He was a superb dancer but also one of the few people who dared to speak out when he did not approve of the way a company was being run or how lessons were being taught.

So I now had a job to look forward to with Metropolitan Ballet. Despite its name, it was a touring company. Conditions were tough. After rehearsals in London we all moved down to Eastbourne. It was January 1947 and freezing cold. But the appeal of working with the company was ballet master Gsovsky. True, he had a rather forbidding glass eye and was a bit of a bully but somehow that contributed to him being a strong teacher and great disciplinarian. Before the 1939–45 war Gsovsky was ballet master of the company run by Alicia Markova and Anton Dolin and later taught in Paris. Nowadays his fame rests on his *Grand pas classique*, a showcase pas de deux still occasionally seen on gala programmes, but Gsovsky was yet to create that. Peggy Ayres was a corps de ballet dancer. She and I tagged ourselves onto Henry Danton who guided us through the tour. He evidently knew the ropes. Volkova, I discovered, had asked Henry to keep an eye on me, and the three of us became firm friends. The Metropolitan company was also where Svetlana Beriosova started her career, as her father Nicholas was one of the ballet masters but our paths did not coincide then. Metropolitan Ballet was to become a really good and exciting company but it had a really tough start. It began with a collaboration between Letty Littlewood's Anglo-Russian Ballet and Leon Hepner's Fortune Ballet, which had operated during the war under the auspices of ENSA but were now about to fold. It was Hepner who initially brought Victor Gsovsky to London who in turn introduced such good principals as Sonia Arova and Jeanne Artois, also Collette Marchand and Serge Perrault, her partner, both from the Paris Opéra.

The repertoire of Metropolitan Ballet included a number of ballets previously danced by the Anglo-Russian and Fortune companies. We opened in Eastbourne at the Devonshire Park theatre. The get-in for scenery and costumes began on the Sunday morning at 1am as soon as the previous show had moved out. The technical crew then worked right through Sunday and most of the night again getting the three ballets set and lit. The dancers were called for 10am on Monday for a barre and run-through of the programme which finished at 5pm. The curtain was due to go up at 7pm. Henry Danton, an absolute health fiend who never wore an overcoat, only a muffler and gloves, suggested us boys all go for a dip in the freezing sea. That January the weather was appalling. There were fuel shortages and endless power cuts. Electricity consumption was limited. The terrible weather actually lasted until May. Certainly the beach in Eastbourne was covered with snow that January. Well, Henry plunged in and actually swam quite a bit. I followed him into the water along with Peggy Ayres who joined in too. We immediately came out again, practically frozen through. But it worked, and having been in the theatre surrounded by chaos and bad tempers for hours all that day it really brought a bit of energy back into my tired and aching body. I was able to face dancing in all three ballets that night, though I must say the work for the men in those days was very mild compared with today. Our opening programme was a revival of Littlewood's *Caprice Viennois*, the second act of *Swan Lake* and Gsovsky's *Dances of Galanta*. It was a rather inauspicious opening. In those days there were very few ballet critics in London and none in the regions. In fact it was usually the local sports writer who would review ballet performances, which is who we got at Eastbourne. The other programme included Gsovsky's *Pygmalion*, *The Picnic* by Pauline Grant and Littlewood's *Marchaund's Tale* in which I had a small role as the troubadour, which had not much dancing but a lot of business. There was one moment when I had a grand jeté, a flying leap, across the centre of the stage. I made the most of it but still remember being reprimanded by Gsovsky saying that although I jumped high my feet were never pointed and my arms were still dreadful. That first tour was for six weeks, always doing eight shows per week. Pay was minimal with only half-pay for rehearsal weeks, none during holidays and no touring allowance. The worst things were the cold and the rationing which still continued after the war. We did not exactly have full houses but the company grew in size and standards got better. New ballets included *Designs for Strings* by John Taras and *The Lovers' Gallery* by Frank Staff. However, the company did not last long without Arts Council funding. The large amount of money that had been donated by Cecilia Blatch, a remarkable woman, to underwrite the company had dwindled. She was the wife of a Hampshire solicitor but was variously described in the programmes initially as secretary and later director-general. Whatever her title she put £300,000 into the company over the course of its existence. I think we all knew too that Leon Hepner, although doing his best, was a bit out of his depth. I do remember going to the last performance in London sometime after I had left in December 1949. They gave a superb performance of the Polotsvian dances from *Prince Igor*. I have never seen it done better.

In fact, although life was very tough in those days I did manage to improve. This was largely due to Gsovsky's rigorous training and Henry's encouragement and insistence that I lead a healthy life including taking a cold bath every morning. One important thing that dancing with Metropolitan Ballet did for me was learning how to look after myself and self-discipline. I think I grew up. In those early days there were several dancers from Copenhagen, including Frank Schaufuss as well as the brilliant dancer Paul Gnatt. He was previously a principal with Royal Danish Ballet. He had wonderful balon, a bouncing jump, was very good looking with quite an appetite for the ladies. When we were appearing in Southport he brought over a young Danish dancer with him who wanted to work with Gsovsky. This young god, with shining blond hair, wonderful physique, the most perfect legs and feet and a way of moving that made us all gasp, was Erik Bruhn, soon to become, in my opinion, the greatest male dancer who I was to see in my lifetime. The image of him executing a slow turn in arabesque, perfectly balanced and effortless, is still etched in my mind after all these years. He was not yet 20, utterly unspoiled. He never knew what an inspiration he was to us all. Our paths often crossed throughout his great career as dancer and director. He died aged only 57 from alcohol-related poisoning, tragically early like his lover Rudolf Nureyev, who died from Aids. So sad – but we should rejoice in the fact that these great stars, so different from each other, brought such passion, beauty and magic with them which changed our lives. While I was still with Metropolitan Ballet, Celia Franca, a principal dancer with Sadler's Wells Ballet, became our ballet mistress. She had been brought up in Mile End in east London. I first saw her dance in *The Nutcracker* when Sadler's Wells Ballet performed the second act only at the New theatre during wartime, part of my early days of watching ballet. She performed the Arabian dance, in those days a solo. With Franca's exoticism it seemed to go on for ever, wonderfully controlled and full of mystery. I also saw her as the prostitute in *Miracle in the Gorbals*, the queen in *Hamlet* and *Swan Lake*, the tango in *Façade* and the spider in *Le Festin de l'araignée*. She provided a wonderful contrast to the rather plain corps de ballet then, a superb artist. Celia did have pretty awful feet but also long black hair with a very distinctive, expressive and riveting face. I remember her in romantic roles too, the prelude in *Les Sylphides* being one of them. She had an ethereal quality and made you believe that her large feet were exquisitely petite. Celia would also stare into one of the stage lamps before her entrance, which made the pupils of her large blue eyes dilate as she stared out into the distance when she appeared. And she never made a sound, rather different from the clattering that you hear from some dancers today.

On returning to London for a three-week rehearsal break I at once made contact with Vera Volkova again. She welcomed me back but things were different. I was no longer her young protégé and had to pay full price for classes. She was really telling me that I had to cope on my own and could no longer rely on charity. This made me work even harder as I wanted to show her that I had benefited from Gsovsky's classes. However, when we were on tour again I realised that I was not improving enough, and as my contract was near its conclusion I decided to leave and I told the management I would not be renewing. I had heard that *Finian's Rainbow*, a Burton Lane musical, was coming to London with Michael Kidd's brilliant choreography, which he himself would be rehearsing. I found out where the auditions were being held, managed to get leave from the company for a couple of days, auditioned and was one of the lucky ones. There was, however, a slight problem in that I would have to finish my contract with Metropolitan Ballet which ended a week after the rehearsals for *Finian's* began. I was extremely chuffed when Kidd told the management I was worth waiting for. *Finian's Rainbow* ran for 725 performances when it premiered on Broadway. We survived for just 55 in the West End. It proved that if you are putting on big, expensive productions you need big, expensive stars. Apparently Emile Littler, the producer, wanted to save money and cast it without any star names: a big mistake as the bigger and better the show the bigger and better the stars need to be. A great shame because it was a really good musical and I loved being in it. Kidd's choreography was brilliant. In the show, Finian McLlonergan moves from Ireland to a fictional American state, an amalgamation of Kentucky and Mississippi, where he buries some stolen gold in the belief that it will magically grow. A leprechaun and a corrupt senator are involved and the score combines elements of Irish folk music, gospel, rhythm and blues. The cast included several from the Broadway production. I was thrilled too when I learned that Beryl Kaye, herself nearly deaf, would be playing the leading dance part of Susan. The big dance sequence to 'If this isn't love' stopped the show. The work was hard but Kidd's choreography was rewarding to dance. I had a two-minute spot with Beryl, the steps of which I can still remember today. At one performance that November, on my 21st birthday when there may have been some champagne flowing, I completely lost my balance during our duet, although I certainly had over-indulged. I tripped over myself and collapsed in the footlights while Beryl bravely went on without me. I just about got myself up to get back into the rest of the fabulous number. It was the worst thing ever. I have never been so ashamed and have never since had a sip of alcohol before or during a performance. These days you can be fired on the spot for such behaviour. During the run I remember another rather awful incident when Gracie Fields came to see the show. During the curtain calls a follow spot picked her out in the stalls and of course the audience was thrilled to see her there. The cast beckoned her up onto the stage, which she did. Rumour had it that she had wanted to appear in the leading role herself, and 'How are things in Glocca Morra?' was a favourite song of hers. Lo and behold, she gave a sign to the conductor who struck up the band in the opening chords of 'Glocca Morra'. She sang the principal lady's big song, something that was obviously pre-arranged as it was transposed to a different key to suit her voice and there were extra interpolations with some very high notes for which she was famous. I have to say she sang it beautifully and the audience went wild, but poor Beryl Seaton, whose song it was, was understandably upset. She had given it a good enough rendering and was devastated. She tried to smile and join in the applause but you could see how hurt she was. It is an unwritten rule of theatre that this sort of behaviour should never take place. The large white chrysanthemums – funeral flowers in any case – that arrived for Beryl from Gracie the next day were just that bit too large.

Even though I felt an outsider back taking classes with Volkova in my very tatty practice clothes I knew I cut an unlikely figure but I knew her training was excellent. I was building a classical technique. And I was in good company. I met Frederick Ashton, then resident choreographer of Sadler's Wells Ballet, recently installed at the Royal Opera House. He used to do class fairly regularly with Vera although he had stopped dancing except for character roles such as one of the ugly sisters in his new production of *Cinderella*, then in preparation. He put on weight fairly easily around the middle, which did not go so well with his beautifully small and delicately shaped feet and elegant hands. One day I found myself next to him at the barre. He kept going on about my arms and lack of co-ordination and for not using my hands properly. Somewhat boldly I asked him if he knew of any jobs going, rather hoping he might say that I should try for Sadler's Wells Ballet. No such luck but Ashton mentioned that William Chappell, always known as Billy, the former dancer turned stage designer and producer, was choreographing a new revue at the Savoy theatre. Billy had been the first male dancer to join up at the outbreak of war in 1939. On one occasion, during the Libyan campaign, Billy as a second lieutenant had no transport for his company and they had to march to their destination, nearly 20 miles distant. Then middle-aged, he arrived in better shape than men nearly half his age: testament, Billy argued, that a ballet regime was more demanding than army physical training. Billy also believed in the importance of maintaining ballet training, pointing out that male dancers in the Soviet Union were exempt from wartime military service, unlike in Britain. When I was introduced to him in June 1948 the show with which he was involved at the Savoy was to be called *À la Carte*. The Savoy of course had been built by Richard D'Oyly Carte to stage the operas of Gilbert and Sullivan. Then the theatre was run by his son Rupert. On Ashton's recommendation Billy gave me a job in the show. Billy adored Ashton – Fred – and designed several of his ballets and would always respect his judgment and vice versa. I was grateful that Billy took me on for that show at the Savoy and I began to feel like a confident performer. The writer was Alan Melville and it was directed by Norman Marshall. Hermione Baddeley and Henry Kendall were the stars. In one sketch, 'Restoration Piece', Hermione appeared as Lady Wanton Malpractice and Henry as Sir Solemnity Sourpuss. They pronounced all the 's' sounds of their words as 'f', in the way words were written at the time. It was hysterical and both Hermione and Henry had great difficulty in suppressing their giggles.

The credits listed décor, dresses and dances by William Chappell. Robert Helpmann and Roland Petit were also going to Volkova for training sessions then. Petit offered me a job in Paris, which I declined. I just felt that it was too early and a shame to stop benefiting from Vera's great teaching although there were some very good teachers in Paris at that time.

I rather enjoyed *À la Carte* and Henry Kendal tried very hard to persuade me to have my voice trained and become an actor. I had a few lines of dialogue in the show but I still had my passionate desire to be a dancer. I did try a few sessions with a very good voice teacher who used to look after the tenor Richard Tauber's voice, then near the end of his career, but my heart was not in it. I returned again to Volkova's classes for a spell. Alan Carter, a former principal with Sadler's Wells, came to watch. He had first attracted attention when Frederick Ashton cast him as Gemini in *Horoscope* for the Vic-Wells Ballet in 1938. In the post-war period Carter was starting to try his hand at choreography. He was also ballet master on such films of the day as *The Red Shoes*, *Tales of Hoffmann* and *Invitation to the Dance* and choreographer for *The Man Who Loved Redheads* starring Moira Shearer, based on a Terrence Rattigan play. By the late 1950s Alan was ballet director of the Munich Staatsoper, one of the largest opera houses in Europe, where he choreographed his own productions of *Ondine* and *The Prince of the Pagodas* and where much later I was to stage *Giselle*, *Swan Lake* and *The Sleeping Beauty*. At the time Alan was looking for dancers for a new company that was being formed. This was St James's Ballet, a small ensemble of 12 dancers, typical of one of many post-war companies, which did not survive long. It was launched by the newly formed Arts Council, then resident in St James's Square in London, to tour ballet to towns that had no theatres. The company largely performed new works by John Cranko, Pauline Grant, Angelo Andes and Alan himself. Lelia Russell was the main dancer, with whom Alan was in love I suspect. I do not know what happened to her but I thought she could have been a real star. Alan invited me to join the company and made it all sound incredibly exciting, stressing that I would be involved in many of the new works, which I jumped at. I accepted his offer and then began one of the toughest and most unrewarding periods of my life. St James's Ballet existed only between 1948 and 1950, and although there were a few new ballets they were mostly of doubtful quality. One that we performed was Alan's ballet, *The Catch*, about two brothers whose fishing expedition is interrupted by a girl, and which used music by Béla Bartók. I was the nuisance younger brother who nodded off, sitting on a stool with a fishing rod. Anne Woolliams was the girl. The repertoire also included the second act of *Coppélia* which Yvonne Cartier danced with Ken Russell as Dr Coppélius. He was not much of a dancer. His father had decreed that no son of his should be, could be or would be seen in tights. Russell's career in ballet was very short. He soon became a photographer and the provocative television and film director, on which his fame rests. I always enjoyed his programmes and films. Endless one-night stands with St James's Ballet in very small town halls, school halls and public buildings were difficult to perform in and very demoralising, however. A three-night booking was wonderful. We considered that a long engagement. I do believe that touring should be part of dancers' training. Dancers are generally very insecure and it can be very scary when you first go onstage. I am certainly glad I did all that touring. It helps to build confidence and I think it shows nowadays in the performances that such touring companies as Birmingham Royal Ballet and English National Ballet give.

It was while I was still working for Alan at St James's Ballet that I first met John Cranko, one of the most inspiring figures in my career. He gave me a lovely part in his new work and convinced me that to get on in ballet I really needed to be at the centre of things to keep up with modern trends. To achieve that, John organised an introduction for me with Ninette de Valois, the greatest force in British ballet. Both were to have an enormous impact on the future direction of my career.

CHAPTER 2

❧❧ ❧❧

Ninette de Valois – calling her Madam

W HEN MARILYN MONROE was in London in 1956 filming *The Prince and the Showgirl*, Colin Clark, whom I knew through his sister Colette, a great friend of Margot Fonteyn, landed his first job as an assistant director's assistant, really a gofer. Laurence Olivier, the film's star and director, was Clark's godfather. Although I had some experience of films by then, I was not involved personally. Richard Addinsell, whom I knew well, wrote the music, and Billy Chappell, with whom I had worked, arranged the dances for the film. Clark's responsibilities included everything that nobody else wanted to undertake, primarily ensuring that Monroe got from her rented house in Ascot to Pinewood studio on time. Whether Clark's role properly included keeping Monroe company while her husband, Arthur Miller, was away in Paris, was debatable. One evening, while Clark was entertaining Monroe, she experienced stomach pains and appeared to be seriously ill. Clark called a doctor who arrived to examine her. He diagnosed a miscarriage and eventually managed to sedate a distraught Monroe. So much is familiar from Clark's diaries, filmed as *My Week with Marilyn* with Eddie Redmayne and wonderfully Michelle Williams as Monroe. What was not recorded was the fact that, as the doctor was leaving, Clark remarked it must be unusual for him to have to deal with such temperamental women. 'Oh no,' he replied. 'I am married to a director of a ballet company.' The doctor was Arthur Connell, husband of the director of the Royal Ballet, Ninette de Valois.

When in 1943 my father saw that I was serious about a career in dance, considering joining the Ballets Jooss' school at Dartington in Devon, as well as thinking seriously about training at Sadler's Wells ballet school, I asked him to come with me to meet de Valois, founder director of Sadler's Wells Ballet. A very young Margot Fonteyn and the dynamic Robert Helpmann were its stars, surrounded by such greats as Pamela May. She was very glamorous I thought, but, I was to learn later, broke all the rules, loving a smoke and a goodly amount of gin and wine. The other leading lights were Beryl Grey, who always maintained her image as an English lady; Moira Shearer whom I always thought somewhat artificial; June Brae, wonderful though not a prima ballerina; the superbly exotic Celia Franca; Julia Farron, whom I adored for her strong personality; and Pauline Clayden, a real personality too, excellent onstage. The women were all in their prime, but good men were in short supply as most of them had been called up.

When we arrived to meet de Valois as arranged, my father and I were put in a poky little office right by the stage door at the New theatre, the company's temporary home, Sadler's Wells having been badly bombed. De Valois was not there; apparently she was busy rehearsing but would soon be along to see us. Her desk and chair dominated the room. Having recently injured my back in a nasty fall at Bedales, I needed to sit down but I did not dare sit in de Valois' seat. My father insisted that I should sit down in the only other chair in the room while he stood. We waited for two hours. Finally de Valois swept in, full of apologies to my father who I could see was quite smitten by her beautiful grey eyes. She turned on me and said, 'Get up at once and let your father sit down!' He interceded and said I had just had a deep injection against the pain in my back. 'Well! That's not a very good start is it?' She went on to say that it was late for me to start as a dancer but did add that I had quite a good face for the stage. She decided that she would allow me to go to her school at Sadler's Wells for a couple of years, saying, 'I might be able to make something of you – that is if we are all still alive then.' Then she burst out laughing before she informed us that I would have to pay. My father replied that this would not be possible. De Valois explained scholarships were not available because of wartime. And so we left. My father was obviously impressed by her strength of purpose combined with considerable charm. I, on the other hand, was not so impressed. I found her to be rather scary and hoped that Kurt Jooss, whom I was to see at the Arts theatre club the following day, might come up with a better solution for my future. That meeting did lead to the beginnings of my career.

Some five years later, in the hot summer of 1948, John Cranko, then an emerging choreographer, invited de Valois to see his latest ballet *School for Nightingales* when it was performed at St Albans by St James's Ballet, a small company established by the Arts Council. The music was by Louis Couperin and was set in a singing academy for young ladies during the 1700s. I was cast in the rather appealing role of a young man – Jacques, described in the cast list as a distraction – who broke into the school, the opposite of my actual experience in escaping from Bedales. My character Jacques was in search of pretty young girls, the nightingales of the title. Jacques, as impersonated by me, was meant to cause havoc, upsetting the teacher and his jealous wife. I managed to do that in more ways than were intended. With de Valois in the audience, this was going to be the greatest performance of my life. I had gone to great trouble to make sure I was properly turned out, including my 18th-century make-up. In those days, if necessary, we used soap to block out our eyebrows. Mine were rather bushy which I proceeded to hide with a coating of thick molten soap before I could apply make-up over them. But that warm evening I soon started to overheat. I sensed perspiration, full of soap, forming on my forehead. It got into my eyes. I could scarcely see a thing as I blundered around the stage causing havoc in quite the wrong way. I could just make out de Valois in the front row, ominously wearing black.

Next day I was determined enough to phone the Royal Opera House and asked to speak to Miss de Valois. Her secretary, the rather frightening Jane Edgeworth, took the call. She queried why I needed to speak to de Valois and I explained it was about the previous night's performance. Her tone of voice suggested it would not do much good trying to talk to de Valois and I was left to hold the line. Eventually she came back to the phone and informed me that there were no vacancies. In any case my standard was not sufficient to audition. I was devastated but determined not to accept that. I next phoned Peggy van Praagh, the company's ballet mistress whom I already knew as she happened to share a flat with John Arnold, a well-known film actor, and Ian Gibson-Smith, an excellent photographer, who were both at Bedales. They knew of my predicament trying to launch my career. Peggy had already given me some valuable insights into both Sadler's Wells Ballet and Ballets Jooss. Her advice to me, as a late starter of 16 years old, had been to take Kurt Jooss' offer but at the same time do all I could to get myself a strong classical technique and combine the two as she did not feel Jooss' company had much of a future. That is what I did. So now Peggy told me to come to company class on the following Thursday which was when de Valois usually attended. I went. No de Valois. I went again the next week. Again no de Valois, but Ursula Moreton, her assistant, was there. She told me she would report back to de Valois about me. The third Thursday I reported to do class yet again. De Valois was again absent but five other boys were there. They were all beautifully kitted out in dance gear, black tights and shoes, white vest and socks, with hairnets and head bands to stop their hair flapping around when they did pirouettes. I, on the other hand, was looking a bit scruffy. At least I was wearing tights and not my usual green gym shorts.

The class started but de Valois had still not arrived. Peggy, who was giving it, whispered to me that she was in the building and was certain to arrive soon. De Valois duly entered at the end of the barre work and I thought I must really push myself. This was finally my chance. I was determined to make her look at me, and by golly I did. I gave the full performance, even more than when I had auditioned for Victor Gsovsky. Following class we were asked to line up outside her office door. As a W in the alphabetical line-up I was the last. When you are a W you get used to being at the wrong end of the queue, right at the back. Many years later, when I was due to receive the Covent Garden silver medal for 25 years' service, I joked to John Tooley who was to make the presentations that no doubt he would keep me waiting until last, being a W. I still have the medal somewhere, somewhat tarnished nowadays, but that day John completely surprised me by calling me first. While waiting to know the worst from de Valois I watched each of the others go in – and quickly come out again, evidently declined. She did not want any of them. I was duly called in, full of trepidation.

De Valois was sitting at her desk, with Peggy in attendance. Fortunately she did not recognise me as the boy with soap in his eyes from St Albans. Almost laughing she said, 'Well, you certainly gave a performance.' Even more amazingly I was surprised to hear her telling me, 'You're just the sort of boy we need.' Her good news came with a caveat. Before any idea of joining the company I must join Sadler's Wells school as a student for six months. Attached to that was the promise of a vacancy when one arose. When I protested that I had professional experience already, having worked for two companies, de Valois' face hardened. Her words were equally resolute and insistent, 'Young man, I am offering you free classes. Your feet need a lot of work. Also I have promised you a contract within six months. You will find I always keep my promises. Take it or leave it.' I of course took it. Six weeks later a vacancy occurred and I was in. I was a very happy young man. My determination had once again paid off. I was a member of Sadler's Wells Theatre Ballet.

De Valois had established a company at Sadler's Wells theatre in Islington in the 1930s. After the war it was evident that it had outgrown its first home so plans were in progress for that company to become resident at the Royal Opera House, although it kept Sadler's Wells in its name until 1956 when it became the Royal Ballet. This was a move that de Valois apparently likened to being given a couple of dusters and told to clean Buckingham Palace. In comparison, it was an opportunity that Frederick Ashton was keen to seize. De Valois' reluctance stemmed, I think, from her essentially pragmatic nature. She was very shrewd, level headed and would never allow herself to get carried away by any proposal without getting all the facts. That, coupled with her extraordinary vision for the future, gave de Valois the reputation for being slow to make up her mind. But once she had, things rushed forward at a pace and nothing could stop her. There are conflicting opinions about how much at that time she foresaw as the destiny of a national company. Much later, when I once asked her about this, she insisted that all she was concerned about at that time was a permanent and secure home for dancers, staff and school. With the relocation to Covent Garden it was agreed another smaller company would be formed at Sadler's Wells theatre, mainly to perform in the operas being presented there. This honoured de Valois' promise to Lilian Baylis, managing director of the Wells, that if Sadler's Wells Ballet ever moved away from the theatre she would ensure that there would always be a ballet company based there. She persuaded the board of Sadler's Wells and Baylis to fund a new group of some 25 dancers. Called Sadler's Wells Opera Ballet, it made its first appearance in December 1945 in Bedřich Smetana's *The Bartered Bride*, an opera much performed at that time. Pamela May was frequently the leading dancer in the famous polka and national dances, one of her best roles I thought, and she was joined by Anne Heaton as the two ballerinas in the circus scene. Pamela danced all the big classical roles at Covent Garden, and Ashton used her a lot in his ballets as subsequently did Cranko and MacMillan. With that experience it was no surprise that she became an exceptional teacher. The choreography for *The Bartered Bride* was by Saša Machov who had escaped from Czechoslovakia to Greece during the war and had fought with the allies in Africa. Having contracted malaria he found his way to London where he became involved with Sadler's Wells. After the war he returned to Prague but committed suicide in 1951, the result of victimisation about his war record. Pamela performed the polka in *The Bartered Bride* with Saša, both dancing brilliantly. With that wonderful music they brought the house down. He was mad for her and she was mad for him, but Pamela insists their relationship never went further than dancing together.

This was the company that I was joining in January 1949, by then having been renamed Sadler's Wells Theatre Ballet. In its early days it performed one Saturday matinée each week and otherwise appeared in many operas. Charles Gounod's *Faust* had a big ballet by Pauline Grant, as did *Eugene Onegin* which was choreographed by Cranko, his first exposure to the story which was to become one of his most popular ballets. Sheilah O'Reilly and I shamelessly added a few of our own steps and some pieces of glittering jewellery in the ballroom scene. Cranko also did *Die Fledermaus* and David Poole did *Hansel and Gretel* which included the most beautiful floating Botticellian angels' dance.

Soon the company was strong and popular enough to be given a Tuesday evening performance as well. Its first all-ballet evening dated from April 1946, before my time as company member, when the programme included de Valois' *Promenade* with Anne Heaton and the premiere of Andrée Howard's *Assembly Ball*. She used a recently discovered youthful symphony by Georges Bizet. This was the same music adopted by George Balanchine for *Le Palais de cristal*, nowadays known as *Symphony in C*, which he created in Paris in 1947, a year after Howard. Completing the initial programme was the last act of *The Nutcracker* with Margaret Dale in the ballerina role. When I joined, other dancers included Kenneth MacMillan, Peter Darrell and June Brae. Rather cleverly, the company provided de Valois with a much-needed base where talented dancers could try their wings in principal roles before facing the much larger stage at Covent Garden. Over the years those who benefited from this included Elaine Fifield, Maryon Lane, Svetlana Beriosova, Stanley Holden, David Blair, Lynn Seymour, and later, when the company had grown into a large touring company, Anya Linden, Nadia Nerina, David Wall, Donald MacLeary – and later still, Miyako Yoshida and Darcey Bussell. Peggy van Praagh was the company's first ballet mistress. De Valois was keen also to have somewhere less forbidding than the Royal Opera House for new choreographers to be tried out. It was where John Cranko and Kenneth MacMillan first made their mark. At the Wells, John made *The Lady and the Fool*, *Pineapple Poll*, *Sea Change*, *Pastorale* and *Beauty and the Beast*; Kenneth created *Danses concertantes* and *House of Birds*. It was a path that David Bintley was later to follow.

One of the first things I went on in was *Etude* by Nancy McNaught. I was not impressed by it or her. There was a rostrum at the back of the set, and a line of six boys had to run down a flight of steps each carrying a girl in what we called the bluebird lift on our shoulders. We dreaded it. I had never done lifts like that before and it was always a near disaster. We could not look down and the girls used to jolt like sacks as we went down the steps. All McNaught could do was shout at us to go faster, faster. She had the most ridiculous counts in the ballet too, 23-And. Not 23 but 23-And. I somehow survived that, and over the years the company grew and grew, successfully developing into a really good group capable of undertaking small tours of the regions which, despite no star names, were quite successful. We performed many of Frederick Ashton ballets, *Valses nobles et sentimentales* created during the company's early days, with revivals of his *Les Rendezvous*, *Façade* and *Les Patineurs* regularly, as well as his version of the snowflakes' scene and second act of *The Nutcracker* made for our long tour to America in 1951. I loved being in the company at first and was so lucky to have Peggy van Praagh as ballet mistress, teacher and répetiteur. She really ran the company although Ursula Moreton, another of de Valois' disciples, was credited as assistant director. She was in fact rarely seen as, being second-in-command to de Valois, meant she was running Sadler's Wells school as well. Not that anybody saw very much of de Valois in those days. She was very much taken up preparing the Covent Garden company for its first visit to New York which was imminent, in 1949.

De Valois did appear on one occasion when we were rehearsing her ballet *The Prospect Before Us*. We were all having to do a particular step, and unusually, but because I was quite musical, I was the only one who really got it. 'That boy! That boy at the back! Come to the front and demonstrate!' she decreed. Needless to say, when singled out to demonstrate I messed it up good and proper. Although it did not have as much impact when the ballet was restaged as a 100th birthday tribute to de Valois in 1998, in those days I thought *The Prospect Before Us* was hilarious, particularly when Stanley Holden performed the drunken theatre manager, Mr O'Reilly. This was a role for which Robert Helpmann was famous but Holden was funnier. We arrived ten minutes late for a rehearsal one day as we invariably did. We had not learned that being on time for de Valois, with her father's army background, meant actually arriving five minutes early. That day we discovered Helpmann in full costume already waiting for us and an irate de Valois ready to read the riot act. She fined us for being late and told us that if Mr Helpmann, an established name, could be ready in time to rehearse, so we, at the start of our careers, could be so too. Actually it turned out to be a put-up job when Bobby revealed to us de Valois had purposely got him there early.

As a late starter technically – I was in my early twenties – and in terms of confidence, I was way behind all the other boys. I did manage to catch up but I knew, and I think everybody else knew too, that although I would go a certain distance, I would never be a topliner. That was despite the quality of some of our teachers. We were sometimes taught by Lydia Kyasht. Born in Russia, she had studied at the school of the St Petersburg Imperial Ballet and joined the Mariinsky theatre in 1902, reputedly being one of the tsar's mistresses, before joining the Bolshoi Ballet. She also appeared with the Ballets Russes during a couple of seasons. Later she settled in Britain, establishing a school which had recently moved to Cirencester when she taught us. I only remember the occasion when she needed to go to the toilet during class. When she returned the hem of her dress was caught in her waistband, revealing her red bloomers. None of us dared tell her or catch each other's eye. When you are working in large ballet mirrors you are not very conscious of your rear view. It was some time before her dress unhitched itself and Madame Kyasht's decorum was restored.

Of course we were all so lucky to have Peggy van Praagh as ballet mistress and a well-known Cecchetti inspired teacher. My arms were pretty terrible and I have to thank her for teaching me how to balance them in their different positions and how to use them with épaulement, how you carried and used your shoulders – so important but sadly lacking these days. I even took my Cecchetti intermediate exam. There is nothing like an exam for giving you an incentive to work hard. Peggy had been a superb Swanilda when I first saw *Coppélia* – full of charm, with faultless technique. I remember her too as one of the blue girls in *Les Patineurs*, just brilliant. Peggy worked widely too with Antony Tudor who featured her in many of his works, particularly *Dark Elegies*, *Gala Performance* and *Lilac Garden* with Ballet Rambert and The London Ballet, Tudor's own company. She was constructively critical of both Kenneth MacMillan's and John Cranko's early created works as she was particularly good at advising about the shape and construction of new ballets. She was incredibly encouraging to me too when I made *Under the Clock*, one of my first attempts at choreography for the Sunday Choreographers.

It was through Peggy that I first met Richard Addinsell, a composer famous for many film scores including the 'Warsaw concerto' he wrote for *Dangerous Moonlight*. Other films included *The Greengage Summer* and Noel Coward's *Blithe Spirit*, and he wrote music for many of Joyce Grenfell's songs. At one point Addinsell was MGM's highest paid composer, small wonder with films like *Goodbye Mr Chips* and *Beau Brummell*. He loved Sadler's Wells Theatre Ballet and used to come regularly to our Saturday matinées at the Wells. He also loved entertaining and asked Peggy if he might give a party for the company. In those days, around 1950, when rationing was still in full swing, that was something that was very difficult to do. In fact it was a lovely do to which some of his other friends were also invited. These included the actress Joyce Carey as well as Joyce Grenfell and others. During the evening I managed to speak to Dick, the name by which he was always known, aware that he was very knowledgeable about theatre music generally. I was desperately looking for a short piece of music for another early attempt at choreography for the experimental group, the Sunday Choreographers, which David Poole, a dancer from South Africa, organised at Sadler's Wells. I boldly asked Dick whether he had any suggestions. He said I was to give him a few days but he would look out some recordings and I could come round one afternoon and he would play them for me. He had the most fantastic and varied library of recordings. We listened to a few pieces and

Dick then played Wolf-Ferrari's overture to *Susanna's Secret* which I loved and used for a pas de quatre called *Piccolezza*, one of my earliest pieces of choreography. Everybody seemed to think it was not at all bad for an early effort and the audience loved it. Dick became one of my greatest friends and godfather to our daughter, Poppy.

With Sadler's Wells Theatre Ballet it was a joy to have proper facilities with regular daily classes. Training at Sadler's Wells school had been a taste of honey but I now had a new problem. Whereas with Jooss as well as in the St James's and Metropolitan companies I was among the youngest, with Theatre Ballet I was now one of the eldest but right at the bottom of the ladder. There was a lot of competition around which I had not experienced before. Young men like David Blair, Pirmin Trecu, Johaar Mosaval, Michael Boulton and Donald Britton were a huge challenge. That gave me the incentive to improve my technique. David Blair did the peasant pas de deux from *Giselle* as a divertissement with Maryon Lane, his future wife. He had a phenomenal technique but his line was not good and his feet were only average. He was strongly built; he could do clean double tours and finish in perfect fifth position. In those days that was something. Many of us could scarcely do a single turn. John Cranko used him a lot. David was marvellous in *Pineapple Poll*. He was a good partner too, the best ever Colas in *La Fille mal gardée*. He did it marvellously and of course we had not seen one-handed lifts in those days. David thought he was going to be Margot Fonteyn's partner when he joined the Covent Garden company but she did not warm to him. He was not sexy enough. Later, when David wanted to make a comeback, Kenneth MacMillan would not have him. He would not bring back a has-been when he had new dancers to develop.

Leo Kersley, who I had seen from my days watching Anglo-Polish Ballet, had been transferred to Sadler's Wells from the Covent Garden troupe. We understood de Valois wanted to have at least one masculine role model for the men. Leo was an experienced performer but was by then in his mid-thirties, never did class and did not have very good feet. Not the best example. However, he could fake his way through difficult solos as in *Les Rendezvous* and had an ability with pirouettes and beaten steps. There was also David Poole, just older than me. He was an unsung hero of British ballet, a superb artist with great presence onstage. He did not have much jump and could not turn for toffee. Still, he was a great partner, a brilliant actor dancer. John Cranko was a good friend of his and featured David heavily in his ballets. He rehearsed me as the man with the rope in de Valois' *Rake's Progress* when he practically killed me, but he did help me discover more strength and energy. David was passionate about music and getting dancers to learn to listen to understand how to feel and become the music rather than just using it as a background to steps. He had good qualities of leadership and was a great fighter, really becoming our spokesman.

Although based at Sadler's Wells, much of our time was spent on tour. My first destinations in 1949 were Stratford, Cambridge and Peterborough. It was on one now memorable day in May that year when I came up against the hard realities of touring. We were in Hanley. Rationing was still in force and, along with David Poole with whom I was sharing digs, we had gone into a butcher's shop to see what our coupons would buy. The butcher, a real joker, asked how we were going to perform that evening since the theatre had burned down during the previous night. We assumed he was pulling our legs but then we noticed there was a smell of burning hanging in the air. We went back out to the street and ran to the theatre. There was still plenty of smoke – but nothing left of it other than the proscenium arch silhouetted against the sky. Everything – sets, costumes, musical instruments and personal possessions – everything we possessed had been burned, apparently the result of the night watchman's lighted cigarette, left burning when he fell asleep. In a flurry of activity, telegrams were sent to other companies to see what costumes, props and scenery we could scrounge so we could fulfil the following week's booking in Hull. By some miracle we managed to open there with a different programme with borrowed sets and costumes. It was daunting but exciting in equal measure and certainly toughened us up.

I did gradually get a go in some roles for which I did not have to be perfectly turned out. I danced the male title role in Cranko's *Beauty and the Beast* and Captain Belaye in his *Pineapple Poll*. I was second cast as Leonardo in Alfred Rodrigues' *Blood Wedding* and the poet in Andrée Howard's *Selina*. This was a role that earned me an early review, from Clive Barnes, in those days writing in *Dance and Dancers*. While he detected that I lacked confidence when performing as a soloist, and he thought my mime lacked conviction, he considered the role of the poet was my best. *Selina* was a humorous ballet with Stanley Holden as a comedy witch among a cast of nymphs and assorted lovers. Really it was a send-up of the usual sort of ballet plot but I wanted to play the poet, a role created by Hans Zullig who did not have much classical technique, seriously without parodying it. I found it difficult to work with Andrée Howard who was terribly fussy and just-so in how she wanted things done. Her dog Pupo was often in attendance, often messily so. De Valois came to one of my performances where everything went wrong, which did not help, and wisely insisted that a double tour for the poet was a step that I should not attempt. Unwisely I did attempt it. I also did the second act of *Swan Lake* but never as Siegfried, always Benno his equerry. I only later learned from Anton Dolin's autobiography that he was apparently impressed by my noble looks and charming stage manners when he watched a performance, but that part was always a trial when Odette stood on my thigh – agony! – for the last pose in attitude at the end of the coda. In those days high lifts did not exist and there was no way that Siegfried would hold Odette high above his head in a similar position.

I knew, nevertheless, that I would never be able to achieve the things that dancers who had started earlier than me could. I felt my one advantage was that I could use my body in a very expressive way thanks to the training I received from Kurt Jooss, Sigurd Leeder and Zullig. In those days classical training for men was fairly rigid and upright. However, thanks to Ashton and MacMillan's choreography and a better understanding of Cecchetti training we were required to use the upper body much more, not just forward and back but sideways too. At the same time too it is important for a man to land from a big jump with one leg, in arabesque, while holding the upper body erect. Even Rudolf Nureyev, who did make a big difference to male dancing, had difficulty in keeping his back leg in position after one of his spectacular jumps.

I still found it hard to settle with Theatre Ballet. I really had felt part of the Jooss company, the people and intellectually with the sort of work they were producing. I got much more fulfilment out of the few performances I was in than from Theatre Ballet where I seemed always to be struggling with technique and line. Gradually, after a couple of years things began to get really difficult. I understood that my chances of getting much further in the art of classical ballet were pretty limited. I also knew that Sadler's Wells Theatre Ballet was not the only company – and that its style of performing was not the only way. I recall being on tour at the Manchester Palace while still with Metropolitan Ballet in April 1947 when the pre-London try-out of *Oklahoma!* was playing at the city's opera house. We managed to stand at the back for a matinée which happened not to coincide with our own. The performance had extraordinary impact. The men were so virile and strong. In those days men in English musicals sported handkerchiefs in their top pockets and were unfailingly nice. In *Oklahoma!* the way the entire male chorus lined up across the footlights singing their hearts out stunned the audience. My own experiences so far had been rather more frustrating. I heard that Ballets Jooss was reforming itself, and to be honest I was missing such works as *The Green Table*. I regard it as one of the great ballets of all time with its message about war and political diplomacy. There have been many productions of it around the world but de Valois professed not to like it. She felt too that Jooss was competition, certainly for Arts Council funding after the war. Although de Valois claimed not to like Jooss' choreography she did confide in me that she had used some of the moves the diplomats make in *The Green Table* in the gambling scene in her ballet *The Rake's Progress*. But that is what choreographers do. Frederick Ashton used to say there are no new steps – we choreographers all steal – but we have to make the things our own. It is all about how you use the steps.

Another of Jooss' ballets that impressed me at that time was *Weg im Nebel*, about the aftermath of war and people trying to adapt themselves after their experiences in a concentration camp or on rediscovering that a loved one you thought had been killed was still alive – after you had remarried. I got such satisfaction appearing in these sorts of ballets that was never matched in the classical repertoire. So, after two years, I decided to rejoin Jooss. I had just appeared in Peter Darrell's *The Telltale Heart* at the Mercury theatre. This was the first time I was really featured in *Dance and Dancers* magazine. Here I was, leaving Britain to rejoin Jooss in Germany instead of trying to consolidate my career in London on the back of that media exposure *The Telltale Heart* had given me. De Valois was understanding, telling me I needed to get this out of my system. She gave me a year's leave of absence but also said, 'You can do this once but don't make a habit of it.'

I was soon back in Essen-Werden, a medieval town outside Essen itself which was dominated by the huge folkwangschule, which post-war had become a college for music and the visual and performing arts, including dance. This is where Jooss had re-formed his company with offices, studios and a dance school in the centre of the town. I now felt much more confident. I could co-ordinate my legs and arms with style and focus, as well as use my feet properly as I had benefited hugely from the classical training I had by then received from Vera Volkova, Peggy van Praagh, George Goncharov and various other teachers. On my return, everybody was amazed at the way I had changed. I got some good roles including the standard bearer in *The Green Table*, the young man in *Columbinade* and in *Weg im Nebel* where I suffered intensely behind barbed wire in the concentration camp scene.

Pina Bausch was then with the company. At that time she seemed to be very withdrawn, totally disciplined, shy and incredibly polite. She moved in the most beautifully co-ordinated way. If the role she was playing was a young girl her body seemed to change and become young and innocent – and completely different from when she portrayed the old and tired refugee woman who appears in one of the most moving scenes in *The Green Table*. Whenever Pina and I met subsequently we always seemed to talk about Hans Zullig. I loved him as the wonderful artist he was and he adored her for the same reason. Although they were great friends she always treated him with the utmost respect, always addressing him as Herr Zullig and never speaking out of turn. What a difference from the wonderfully mature and imaginative woman she became, strong and masterful, inventing a completely new approach to dance with her own company. But with Jooss there were still no second casts, only understudies, so it was as hard as before to get performances. A British tour was planned, finishing at Sadler's Wells which I saw as a good opportunity to be seen by other companies as I certainly did not wish to make my career in Germany. However, after two weeks in England we learned that the city council in Essen had cancelled our funding. We were left high and dry. We had to survive on our box office income – which of course was practically nothing. We had to pool half of our salaries to cover our overheads and get us to London, but then Sadler's Wells pulled our season although it had been selling quite well. We just could not afford to cover our anticipated financial shortfall. With the loss of funding from Essen and the London season, it meant the closure of the company. We were completely broke. I had to go cap in hand back to de Valois. She welcomed me, for the second time, as she needed men for a big tour to America. In those days there were very few jobs in modern dance, so I was lucky to fall back on my classical training. Sol Hurok, the great impresario who had already presented Sadler's Wells Ballet three times on big New York seasons and tours, decided to take Sadler's Wells Theatre Ballet on a big seven-month, 72-city tour across Canada and the USA, beginning in October 1951. De Valois needed men for the tour – and she still did not recognise me from *School for Nightingales*. I did not disabuse her.

De Valois was with us until we opened in Quebec, our first venue, with a two-night stand. We stayed at the Fontignac hotel there, vast as a castle. We were all busy getting *Coppélia* ready, but de Valois for once in her life had nothing to do so she decided she would give classes for the principal women as she could never cope with doing nothing. I was to learn later from her husband Arthur, that at home during weekends de Valois would look longingly at the telephone in the hope it might ring. Those classes in Quebec proved to be disastrous. Her classes were notoriously fast and totally wrong for ballerinas preparing for big roles. Several of them were getting severe cramp and one of them was unable to perform as a result. She could be very tough on us, and when we played New York on our last date, seven months, many miles and many performances later, in March 1952, she was pretty beastly. We had arrived by bus from Boston at 1am that morning. We were utterly exhausted after so long a tour with many one-night stands. We had three days to get ready for our opening night at the Strand theatre, very near Times Square, which had recently been renamed the Warner and was principally used as a cinema and about to undergo renovation. De Valois had flown over for the New York season and was in the rehearsal room the following morning ready to watch us in our daily class at 10.30am. Only five dancers materialised. Nobody had known she was coming. When the rest of us finally straggled in for the rehearsal at 11.45am she cleaned us good and proper. David Poole, who was one of the few people who would speak up about problems, challenged her, pointing out that class was optional and we had only got into our hotel in the small hours of that morning. Not least, he told her that after six months on the road we were utterly exhausted. We had performed consecutive one-night stands in such places as Bakersfield, Waco, Shreveport, Little Rock, Springfield, Knoxville, Daytona, Greensboro, Raleigh, Troy and White Plains, towns where audiences were not exactly known for their connoisseurship of ballet. De Valois countered that was exactly why we should be doing our daily warm-up class before any rehearsals to avoid the possibility of any accidents or risks just before the most important opening night we had known. She had the last word of course but did thank us all after the first night. She realised she had been a bit harsh on us but she felt she needed to pull the whole company together as that New York season was so important to our future. She also changed most of the casting for the first night, upsetting many dancers who had been first cast for the whole tour and replacing them with young ones who had been allowed to perform only the occasional matinée performance in out of the way places. Again, de Valois was absolutely right of course and dismissed the complaints, insisting that it was the company as a whole that mattered and that fairness was secondary if it affected standards.

When Sadler's Wells Theatre Ballet got back from South Africa in the summer of 1954 we discovered again how tough de Valois could be, particularly when it affected the company as a whole. On our return from that three-month tour we were notified of our new contracts. Theatre Ballet dancers earned less than those at Covent Garden. Top salaries were £18 per week and the average was £8. Chorus dancers in West End shows were on £10 and we knew of former Theatre Ballet members earning £30 per week in revues and musicals. We felt justified in asking for an increase across the board of £2. De Valois refused to engage with the notion of collective bargaining. For her, any increases were based on an individual's merit. When we took exception to this approach de Valois told us we were getting too big for our boots. The company threatened to strike. Equity was involved. The opening performances of the season were cancelled. De Valois would not budge and threatened to close the company. Eventually an increase was agreed but not an all-round flat-rate rise. We capitulated. We wanted our jobs – and there was nowhere else to go except Festival Ballet, considered a real no-no in those days. Another case of take it or leave it from de Valois.

Touring in the 1950s meant playing eight shows per week for sometimes 14 weeks on the trot. That sort of thing is not really sustainable. By 1956 Sadler's Wells theatre itself was facing bankruptcy and was unable to support a large, touring ballet company any longer. Although de Valois was running the company it was Sadler's Wells theatre that was actually paying our salaries. After much deliberation the Royal Opera House took charge of us, paid us and from then on managed our tours. This was the beginning of an extraordinary existence. Covent Garden had only one tiny studio and the Royal Ballet's rehearsal base was at Baron's Court in west London. There was no room for the touring company. All our scenery, props and costumes were stored in various places across London, anywhere where there was space. Rehearsals took place in studios wherever they could be found, most of them unsuitable for classical ballet, with terrible floors and no heating. This coincided with the departure of Peggy van Praagh. She had led the American tour in 1951, subsequent ones to Africa in the following years as well as countless regional tours. She felt she should be formally recognised as assistant director. De Valois did not like strong women who stood up to her nor the way Peggy had failed to diffuse the salary dispute. Peggy left. She went on to become the founding artistic director of Australian Ballet in 1962. She suffered from the most terrible arthritis and had many operations on both her hip joints. Finally her doctors warned her that any more anaesthetics could affect her brain. Sadly she suffered another bad fall and had to take this risk. Shortly afterwards she died. I owe her a lot. I will always be grateful to her for helping me so much when I was still at Bedales. If I had not followed this advice I certainly would not have got into Sadler's Wells Theatre Ballet. Peggy was made a DBE in 1970. She certainly deserved the recognition for her services to dance, both here and in Australia.

De Valois decided to enlarge the company so that tours being planned for the future could incorporate productions like *Swan Lake* and *The Sleeping Beauty*. She thought it would need someone with the stature of John Field to achieve this. De Valois had known him since he was her student in the 1930s and it was John who did indeed take over. With Field's appointment the company's name was changed to the decidedly flat-footed sounding Touring Section of the Royal Ballet. It was enlarged so that we could perform the classics and still undertake long tours. I stuck it out for about eight weeks, sometimes travelling back to London on the last train on Saturday nights and returning early on Mondays. That is all right from Brighton but when it is from Stockton to Norwich, or from Morecambe to Swansea and from there to Southampton it is not such fun, although I do recall seeing my first beauty queen pageant at the municipal lido at Morecambe. In those days nobody co-ordinated the touring schedules and we often found that another company, usually London Festival Ballet, was playing the same towns at the same time. That today would be the equivalent of Birmingham Royal Ballet and English National Ballet playing the same week in Manchester. I decided that something had to change. It so happened that de Valois was going down to Plymouth to speak to members of the company about their futures. You always had to judge such opportunities carefully. With young female dancers, de Valois was known to say, 'You are having a baby? You want time off? But you won't be coming back will you. Next!' On another later occasion, Antoinette Sibley was due to dance with the touring company away from London midweek in a supporting role in *The Rake's Progress*, something that she did not much relish, as well as being scheduled to perform Aurora in *The Sleeping Beauty* at Covent Garden on the Saturday of the same week, something she did want to do. Antoinette went to de Valois with the intention of wriggling out of the performance on tour. Before she had made her case, de Valois interrupted Antoinette and said, 'I have got another Aurora ready to go on. It's really not a problem. Next!' Anyhow, I booked in to see de Valois in Plymouth and was duly summoned. I was pretty nervous as I explained why I wanted to see her. She had already told me I could leave once and return but not to make a habit of it. This would be my third time. She seemed in a good mood and said, 'Peter, come and sit down here', indicating the seat next to her on the settee, not the hard-backed chair placed opposite her. I knew she was being serious because she had never called me Peter before. De Valois asked me to explain my problem but interrupted my explanations. She announced she had just the job for me. She explained that because of financial problems at Sadler's Wells a new group of seven girls and five boys was to be established to dance in the opera productions there. She wanted me to take charge of it, take class every day, do any necessary choreography and organise all the rehearsals. De Valois had got it all worked out. I simply could not believe my ears. When I protested that I had never given a class in my life, she said I could go to her summer schoolteachers' course in my holidays. 'For goodness sake, get on with it and keep it moving. And keep it simple,' she said. Coming from her, that was a hoot considering her enchaînements, or sequences of different steps, often used to last for 16 bars. Then she would make you reverse them and then add beats.

One of de Valois' concerns was always how students related to the space around them. It was during the time I was responsible for Sadler's Wells Opera's dancers that de Valois asked me to work out a class to replace the one which she called plastique which she felt had become rather stale. From my experience with Kurt Jooss and Sigurd Leeder I had learned about dynamics of movement and using the weight of the body as a means of expression by either bringing it into the body's core or in a peripheral way by taking it away from the centre. I developed a class to teach this. Unfortunately there were too many students involved without enough time, studio space or pianists. With the resources we had it meant two classes with 40 students in each with only one lesson per week, which was ridiculous. I also wanted to teach improvisation which was out of the question. After two terms of getting nowhere, de Valois came to assess how we were getting along. She claimed she had always been a great admirer of the Jooss dancers and could see what I was trying to achieve but understood that unless there were fewer students and more time the classes were not effective. Some students responded extremely well, though not always those who were excelling in classical work. They were dropped but de Valois was very understanding and said, 'I now realise that this is not something that can be used to help just get a feel of this sort of work. I can see it really needs a daily lesson to have any effect.' With that she ended the classes. That was a great relief.

When de Valois took the Royal Ballet to the Soviet Union for the first time in 1961, for her it was the culmination of her work. To have a company of sufficient calibre to appear in such ballet capitals as Leningrad and Moscow, performing on the stages where the Kirov and Bolshoi companies had their homes, was the summation of everything she had striven for over the past 30 years. I heard that some extras were needed and thought I might go along. De Valois turned me down flat, 'For goodness sake, Wright. I have enough to worry about.' Somehow, though, David Poole did manage to get himself on that tour.

De Valois had a tremendous grasp of essentials but she could be forgetful. During one of many attempts to patch up the old Sadler's Wells theatre, a fundraising campaign, The Fonteyn Appeal, was launched to raise money for badly needed new seating. De Valois agreed to make a speech from the stage to celebrate the completion of the project. Several others were due to speak but it was agreed that none of us would reference Margot, leaving de Valois clear to make her own tribute. She was, however, then in her nineties and getting rather forgetful. She repeatedly checked with me that it was Margot that she was expected to talk about. I reassured her that this is what was wanted. Our cue came and I escorted de Valois onto the stage and the audience gave her a most wonderful welcome. She delivered a remarkable and moving speech, all about Lilian Baylis, much to the bemusement of everybody present. Margot's name was never mentioned at all.

Over the years I came to admire, respect, be infuriated by and finally love de Valois as the remarkable woman she was. I so remember conversations we had when I could tell that although she was speaking quite lucidly, her eyes and part of her brain were thinking about something completely different. I think this was something to do with her vision of the future. Her famous words – respect the past, herald the future but concentrate on the present – are apparently misattributed to her but she did quote them often, believing them worth remembering. It was amazing too that, long after she had retired, she was always a step ahead of us. When faced with a tricky problem I would often consider how de Valois would have solved it. I often went with various problems to see her at her home in Barnes, overlooking the Thames. Out would come the red wine, and great words of wisdom would pour forth, particularly if it was about casting. I never asked her to solve problems for me but it was invaluable to hear how she had approached difficult situations during her time as founder director. Well after her retirement, indeed after my own, she maintained a frequent correspondence with me about issues that concerned her – whether young choreographers were gaining sufficient opportunities for their work to be seen or the balance of repertoire being toured, for example – and her letters invariably ended with an apology for being a nuisance.

De Valois always gave the impression of being inscrutable. She appeared very strong both outwardly and inwardly, totally unaffected by adverse criticism or unfair situations. In fact this was far from the case and her often rather forbidding exterior shielded a very gentle and sensitive soul. She was sometimes deeply hurt but never cried, or so I thought until a special reception in 1976, held in the old crush bar at the Royal Opera

House to announce the publication of David Vaughan's book about the works of Frederick Ashton. Robert Helpmann had been invited to speak about Fred, and Marie Rambert was scheduled to present a copy of the book to Fred but not to speak. However, once Mim – Rambert – took up her position on the beautiful staircase that used to be the focal point of the room before it was removed during the redevelopment of Covent Garden, you could tell she was revelling being at last in this elevated position at the Royal Opera House with an audience at her feet. She obviously felt she must say something about Fred, whom, after all, she had discovered. Once she had started, she could not stop. I felt somebody tugging at my sleeve. It was de Valois, evidently upset and shaking with rage as Rambert continued on – and on. But for however much she said, Rambert never once mentioned de Valois. I tried to pacify her without much success. Finally, when Rambert finished I turned back to de Valois to see what I could do, but she had vanished. I searched around for her while the presentation was being made. I found Sergeant Martin, the rather outsized chief commissionaire who used to prevail over front of house in those days, and asked him whether he had seen de Valois. He most certainly had. He told me she had flown down the staircase at breakneck speed in quite a state.

I at once set off in hot pursuit and eventually caught up with her partway down Bow Street. I took her arm to steady her. She looked at me with tears streaming down her face. 'Peter, I have never been so insulted in all my life. How dare that woman treat me in that way,' she said. It was not the moment to remind her of another incident in the crush bar when Ashton had passed out on a couch. He told me that when he came to, he discovered 'those dreadful women' standing over him – de Valois and her assistant Ailne Phillips – obviously thinking he was about to expire. And so that evening in Bow Street I suggested to de Valois that I should buy her a drink. As luck would have it, we were right outside a pub. 'I Love Pubs' was the title of one of de Valois' poems. I sat her down in a quiet corner and got two glasses of red wine. She was very upset.

She and Marie Rambert had been friendly – and unfriendly – rivals for years and Mim had discovered Fred and given him his first opportunities to choreograph at the Mercury theatre where he was a member of her company, Britain's oldest. It was only when he was a member of de Valois' Sadler's Wells company, however, that he really established himself. Their partnership had continued then for nearly 50 years. No wonder de Valois was upset. On one occasion during the interval of a performance when I was director of Sadler's Wells Royal Ballet I informed de Valois, who was in the stalls, that Rambert was in the circle. 'How is the old cow?' de Valois asked me. I asked whether she would like to see her and whether I should bring Rambert down to see her. Instead she insisted she would go upstairs to see Rambert. I followed on. They kissed cheek to cheek but fortunately before anybody could say anything just at that moment the bell rang to herald the end of the interval. Everybody resumed their places without a word. Another relief!

That evening in the Bow Street pub, de Valois gradually quietened down. Out came a compact from her handbag and she tidied up her face. An extraordinary transformation took place. I could almost see her thinking that she had me captive and in her very beguiling way proceeded to ask me a favour. She used all her feminine wiles to explain that while she considered *Checkmate* was her best work choreographically, it was being neglected as we had performed *The Rake's Progress* too often recently. She really wanted us to do *Checkmate* as it was approaching its 40th anniversary. I could not believe my ears. I tried to explain that we were much too small a company, that to rehearse the production while we were out on tour with limited rehearsal facilities would be virtually impossible, that the cost would be enormous as students from the Royal Ballet School would be needed to make up the numbers and that they would have to be transported to our touring venues. That would mean paying them touring allowances, fees, hotel bills and fares. She brushed all this aside. I heard her say 'that Highwood girl' would be perfect for the black queen. By now she had completely forgotten about the insult she had just suffered. Well, she won of course. Finally de Valois got up from the table, thanked me for the wine and vanished into a taxi, leaving me utterly deflated and very apprehensive.

When *Checkmate* finally went on, it was a great success, staying in our repertoire for some time. As I feared we did have a few hiccups along the way, including the time when de Valois decided she needed to work on characterisation. She let it be known that she would be with us in Brighton where we were performing. I begged her not to come as we were way behind and suffering from many injuries, to which she replied she would be able to help. Also she had already booked her ticket and hoped that somebody would meet her at the station. I explained I would not be present until the end of the rehearsal as I had to be at the Royal Opera House for a board meeting. I warned Desmond Kelly as ballet master that de Valois' arrival was imminent. He nearly had a fit. De Valois duly did arrive and was met as requested. When she got to the rehearsal room Desmond was desperately trying to sort things out. More of the female dancers were sick, including some of the imported students. De Valois at once announced she would begin with the opening where characters representing love and death play a game of chess. Desmond explained this would not be possible as both were ill and in any case they had not finished learning it. 'Right then, we'll take it from the opening dance of the pawns,' she said. This was one of her favourite dances. Desmond was forced to explain that would not be possible either as the pawns were mostly sick or injured. And so it went on the whole afternoon. A nightmare! Desmond said he needed to finish one of the big scenes during which de Valois insisted on getting the style right before they had learned the very difficult steps. At that point I arrived, and de Valois went for me. She accused me of getting her, an elderly woman, all the way down from London when nothing was ready. Most of the cast had not even learned their parts – and on and on. I was really shocked that she could turn on me in this way. I managed to say that I had warned her right from the start that it was going to be difficult and well-nigh impossible, but that it was she who had insisted even though I had begged her not to come that day – but again she had insisted and now it was me who was being blamed. Big silence. Then de Valois slowly turned her head towards me and a glimmer of a smile appeared. She said, 'The fact is that I usually do this sort of thing to get everyone worked up. On this occasion, however, I seem to have got my timing wrong. I am so sorry, Peter.' Then, turning to the dancers and with a big arm gesture to include everyone, said it had been a very good rehearsal. 'We'll get there! Thank you Desmond. It's such a tricky ballet!' Then she grabbed my arm and said, 'Let's go and have a drink – I want to tell you all about . . .'

I remember a subsequent revival when we performed at the Royal Opera House where we celebrated the 50th anniversary of *Checkmate* in 1987. The first night really did go extremely well. De Valois was very pleased. The second night was a different matter. She had some very specific ideas about casting her ballets. She always insisted that the red

knight should be danced by a British dancer. It is a really demanding
role that has defeated many dancers over the years, including Rudolf
Nureyev. Your choice is already limited. I had winced when de Valois had
told me that she thought 'that Chinese boy' would be excellent. I pointed
out that David Yow was not British. 'Nonsense, he's from Liverpool!'
retorted de Valois and so he had done the first night – and extremely
well. I had cast a different dancer for the second performance, Petter
Jacobsson, as I had no other choice. He could sail through the choreography easily, almost too easily, which is partly why she did not care for
him in that role. During the interval I was having a drink in the crush
bar with Louise Browne, then director of the northern branch of the
Royal Academy of Dance. I felt somebody tugging at my sleeve. It was
de Valois, looking angry and asking to have a word with me. She led me
through the crowd to the top of the main staircase. She looked around
to make sure she had enough of an audience and then lammed into me
about me casting a dancer as the red knight who was Swedish. She said
he had completely the wrong training and that for this role you must
have an English dancer with English style, somebody with more attack,
épaulement and energy. She actually knew all about Jacobsson and that
he had trained at the school of the Royal Swedish Ballet, the Vaganova
Academy in Saint Petersburg and at Balanchine's school in New York. As
I reminded her of all of this she evidently did not think much of it. I said
what a wonderful solo it was but how difficult it was technically and that
we needed two casts at least. Until we could get enough money to afford
more dancers this was the best we could do. I also reminded her that she
had approved the casting when the ballet was being rehearsed. By then I
had learned that the odd glass of wine invariably lifted her spirits when
she experienced moments of stress. Before she could respond I managed
to steer her to the bar and buy her a glass of red wine. All hard feelings
vanished rapidly.

De Valois often said that she really wanted to be a writer. Judging by
her beautiful poetry and her prose works she would probably have been
as successful in this field as in ballet. She brought an understanding and
appreciation of great literature into the art of choreography. Her days
in Ireland in the late 1920s and subsequently working with W. B. Yeats
had a profound effect on her. He had asked de Valois to help him stage
his plays and to found a ballet school at the Abbey theatre in Dublin.

For Yeats, theatre was not solely a case of the words but it was about movement, shape and light. He and de Valois had met originally at the Festival theatre in Cambridge which was run by her cousin, Terence Gray, whose productions were noted for their expressionist style in terms of design and movement. She devised the choreography for them and Yeats encouraged her to develop a similar style in their work together. He encouraged her to find a style that bridged the disciplines of drama and dance. Together they created *Fighting the Waves, The Dreaming of the Bones, At the Hawk's Well* and *The King of the Great Clock Tower*, which was reconstructed by Richard Cave for a conference about de Valois at the Royal Ballet School held in 2011. As a result of de Valois' work with Yeats, most of her ballets have strong narrative themes that have helped them to endure. Her period as a dancer in the 1920s with Sergei Diaghilev's Ballets Russes also had an enormous effect on her. She readily admitted that anything she understood about creating and developing a company came from Diaghilev. She adored him although they never actually had a conversation together. I do wish I had seen de Valois dance a classical solo. She was famous for her pizzicato steps and moved at lightning speed. However, I did see her as Webster, the bossy and organising maid in Frederick Ashton's *A Wedding Bouquet*. She was 54 and had not danced for 13 years but it was the company's 21st birthday in 1952 and reluctantly she agreed to make a surprise appearance. The curtain rose to reveal her as Webster standing alone in the middle of the stage. The applause was tumultuous. It ceased the moment she raised her arm in one of her commanding gestures. With a nod of her head to the conductor and a twinkle in her eye, the performance began. She was witty, precise, very bold and bossy. My favourite moment came with a difficult diagonal step that Webster is supposed to execute. She looked out to the auditorium, wagged her finger in denial and marched down the diagonal with her nose in the air. She brought the house down.

In retrospect, I believe it was Sadler's Wells theatre more than any other that helped me find my way through my tangled career. It must never be forgotten that it was there that the foundations of our great national companies were laid – by de Valois, Frederick Ashton and Constant Lambert. She was always meticulous in acknowledging gifts on her birthday or the many tributes that were paid to her. When I retired as director of Birmingham Royal Ballet in 1995 she decided that a suitable present to mark the occasion would be the original set designs that John Piper had made for *Job* which I had recently revived. De Valois first made the work in 1931 for the Camargo Society during the earliest days of British ballet. Having designed Ashton's wartime ballet *The Quest*, Piper's involvement with *Job* dated from 1948 when it was restaged at the Royal Opera House. It was a work that I wanted to revive in 1993 to celebrate de Valois' 95th birthday. 'God help the poor company,' had been her reaction when I proposed it to her. She considered it one of the hardest pieces to restage as it has so little choreography. She called it a masque with dancing, and what steps there are have to convey an enormous amount. Satan's solo from this great work was one of the pieces danced in Westminster Abbey during the service of dedication in 2009 for a memorial stone commemorating the founders of the Royal Ballet. That was the occasion when behind the scenes a shower was made available so that the two dancers performing the solo – there were separate stages in the nave and between the transepts – could clean up afterwards. The part involves full body make-up. The shower was labelled with a notice, 'Reserved for Satan's use only'. I hope God was amused. But the real point was that de Valois knew how much I admired Piper. He had shown me his studio when I was involved with John Cranko's season at Henley some 40 years before. De Valois knew too I would recognise the historical significance of the designs, though she admitted that the empty space on her wall where they had hung did cause her a pang. They were, though, the perfect tribute for what she recognised as my devotion and loyalty to the company – though she did tease me about not originally having wanted to go to Birmingham.

De Valois had an intuitive understanding of people and she took great interest in how they developed. She fully approved of the choice of David Bintley as my successor as director of Birmingham Royal Ballet. She told me her 'voices' were quite loud about his appointment and hoped he was making the progress she believed he was capable of. She recognised that David was definitely not a 'Yes Madam' character and said to me she could never guess what was going on in his mind behind that grin of his. De Valois was still very much around after her retirement as director but she was better at keeping a distance than I expected. Of course she still exercised power as she was still a member of all the committees that mattered. 'For goodness sake, all of you, just stop all of these meetings and get on with it.' Those were de Valois' words to me during the many discussions about the move to Birmingham. She was the first to write to congratulate us after our first night as Birmingham Royal Ballet at the Hippodrome in October 1990 which she attended. She did not stay for the post-show party however, vigorously telling me that she did not queue up for a bus after performances in London and she had no intention of starting the habit in Birmingham. It had been the city's repertory theatre, however, that de Valois had first considered as a base for her company some 60 years before when Barry Jackson, the theatre's manager, had turned her down. Luckily, she told me, Lilian Baylis came into her life shortly afterwards, and the rest, as they say, is history.

Really de Valois had a gift of pushing you. Once when I was producing *The Sleeping Beauty* with Frederick Ashton at Covent Garden in 1968, rehearsals were not going well. There was a lot of resistance from Ashton's assistant directors to the changes I was intent on making. We were having a bad day and Fred would never fight for anything. De Valois saw me in a corridor later, 'Peter, I know it's difficult but I know that you will make it', and gave me a hug and a big kiss. On other days she could walk straight past you, totally preoccupied about something else. De Valois had vision. She was far-sighted, and talking to her I often had the sense that her mind was working on plans rather than actually listening to what you had to say. She was receptive but you always had to be careful if you wanted to make changes and lead her to believe those changes were her own idea. De Valois was one of the most brilliant women of the 20th century whose influence on the world of dance will certainly be appreciated for centuries to come. She was a born leader and although she could be contradictory, impatient and even ruthless, she was also a very compassionate and caring human being. During her last months I really grew to love her. I visited her every week, often with Pamela May. Mostly during that final period she did recognise her visitors but sometimes she treated us like students from the Royal Ballet School. But de Valois inspired loyalty and she was cared for by her many loyal disciples from her early days, among them Ailne Phillips, Ursula Moreton, Beryl Grey, Winifred Edwards, Joy Newton and Jill Gregory who helped her through thick and thin.

De Valois was plagued with ill health. She had polio when she was young and later arthritis which meant she needed to wear a neck brace.

She often had unrelenting migraines to which she rarely succumbed. During the last difficult years, months and days Pamela May, Graham Bowles, Peter Wilson and her loyal and devoted secretary Helen Quennel were her wonderfully patient, unofficial carers. Visiting de Valois a few weeks before she died at the age of 102 in 2001 I told her about the latest developments at the Birmingham Hippodrome. She interrupted me and told me I was speaking too slowly. By the time I had got to the end of a sentence she had forgotten how it had started. 'And I would like a little more rhythm please!' she insisted, thoroughly putting me in my place. So when I went back a few days later I did my best to respond to her criticism, only to be stopped again. Now I was told I was talking too quickly: 'I think you have rather a difficult voice.' Then she smiled in a very affectionate manner. I just wish I had had a third chance and I might have got it right. However, this little incident made me love her more than ever. She was my boss until her dying day and we parted the best of friends. I felt very privileged and close when I gave the eulogy to her at her memorial service at Westminster Abbey.

In all my long association with de Valois I always called her Madam, as most people did. Alicia Markova was one of the very few to call her Ninette. Margot Fonteyn always referred to her as Madam, Nureyev bowed to her; he knew at least how to be very courteous to Madam. When she formed the company, the need for respect was the reason why de Valois initially adopted the soubriquet of Madam. When she started out to build a company nobody seemed to know what discipline and respect meant, so de Valois said practically, 'Call me Madam.' That was long before the musical of the same name. Dancers need to show respect and the name stuck, particularly as she tended to terrify dancers in rehearsals and demonstrated that she could be ruthless and fierce. It was something that others adopted too, Marie Rambert for example. Board members and others were delighted to call de Valois Madam: it implied a certain closeness. But she was always single minded. And outside work, she was very different, a wonderful housewife and hostess. She enjoyed a glass of red wine and always made sure that you got something to eat or drink when you visited her. There was one occasion when I was unable to collect her from her home in Barnes to bring her into town for a performance and so I asked my wife Sonya. She was decidedly wary about undertaking the job and driving Madam across town, particularly as it was pouring with rain. In Sonya's agitation she arrived far too early and forgot to turn off the headlights as she parked the car. Despite Sonya being early, Madam, in her usual friendly and kind manner, invited her in to share a roast that she was cooking. While they ate, all the while the car lights were still on. When finally they did go out to the car it would not start: the battery was flat. It suited the ever practical Madam to go back inside to call for the AA's assistance, as a female motorist in need. None of us could really cope with calling her Miss de Valois, let alone later, Dame Ninette. It was easier just to call her Madam. Later on she did try to get me to call her Ninette but that was something I could not do. 'Right then, I will call you Sir Peter,' she countered with a twinkle in her eye, but we just went on as before.

Madam got to hear that Peter Clegg did a very good impersonation of her. Peter was a soloist with a wonderful feel for comedy. He became a very good teacher at the Royal Ballet School. Peter could see through dancers at once and tell instinctively when they were feigning injuries or faking their way through roles when they did not know the steps. He showed the same insight of character in his portrayal of Madam, which he sometimes did at parties but never when she was there. He was the company's unofficial impersonator of her, capturing exactly how she conducted class and brilliantly capturing the notes in her voice. Madam heard about this and decided she would rather like to see the impersonation. Peter was horrified when I told him. He could not possibly imitate Madam to her face, he replied. I told him he had to, Madam was demanding it. 'Oh yes, just let me see this,' Madam joined in. In front of the whole company Peter performed his imitation, brilliantly if slightly nervously. We all applauded – except Madam, whose face got harder and harder. It was too close for comfort. As she left the room Madam observed only, 'Very interesting Clegg. Good afternoon.'

CHAPTER 3

Television –
acquiring a director's eye

I SAW TELEVISION as a way to build a viable career. My daughter,
Poppy, was born in 1957 and my son, Jonathan, two years later. I
needed to be able to support them. When I was about 30 I began to
think seriously about what I could do to improve my finances and wondered whether television would be a way to augment my salary. This was
when I was running the opera-ballet at Sadler's Wells which, although
certainly good experience at the time, would not provide a lasting future.

Becoming ballet master of Sadler's Wells Opera in 1955 had been unexpected. Ninette de Valois asked me to look after a new group of dancers
who were to be part of Sadler's Wells Opera. The role, she told me, would
include rehearsing them in ballet scenes in existing productions and
producing new choreography as required. In addition I would teach the
young boys at White Lodge, the junior department of the Royal Ballet
School. I told Madam that although I was very interested in teaching
I had never given a class either at company or school level. That did not
faze her. She simply told me the sooner I started, the better. At that time I
was, at Ursula Morton's request, doing the rounds of the Royal Academy
of Dance's regional centres teaching choreographic studies and corps de
ballet dances for the academy's production club that Moreton had instigated. This was comprehensively organised and helped students become
aware of the basic principles of choreography and the different ingredients that went into putting on a ballet performance. John Cranko had
created four different studies using Felix Mendelssohn's *Songs without
Words* which I used to teach along with two pas de deux from John's

ballets at centres in Birmingham, Liverpool, Bristol and Manchester. As I remember them, the studies illustrated possibilities of how to use alternating movement, which could involve kneeling and standing, turning in opposite directions or lunging different ways before then mixing them all up. An expert in making tutus, both long and short, taught the girls the basic principles of this art. There were very few boys in those days whereas today sometimes there are more male applicants than females for the junior department of the Royal Ballet School. There would be a session on make-up generally as well as character make-up in particular. There was a class too on classical mime and on how to break up music into dance phrases with the use of counts.

The young boys from White Lodge were brought by bus from Richmond to Baron's Court studios near Hammersmith in west London for class that I was to teach at the start of each morning at 8.50am. The first consignment turned out to include Anthony Dowell, Geoffrey Cauley, Robert Mead, Austin Bennett, Michael Coleman and Ian Hamilton among others. Austin was a promising dancer but after injuries that stopped him dancing, in later life trained sheep dogs and became a sculptor. The bust he made of me is displayed inside the stage door entrance of Sadler's Wells theatre alongside the images of many notables from the development of British ballet. Chief of those, Ninette de Valois, in putting me in charge of the dancers of Sadler's Wells Opera, expected that I would have hot-footed it from the junior class at Baron's Court to be at Sadler's Wells by 11am in time to give class there, depending on the rehearsal schedule. In addition, on Fridays I was expected to take Harold Turner's senior boys' class. At 5pm I was on duty again supervising boys' make-up instruction. And – if all of that was not enough – Madam continued, I would be expected to dance in the operas if there was a leading dance role – and of course, produce any new choreography that was required.

I was soon called on in 1956 to redo Madam's choreography for a production of Tchaikovsky's *Queen of Spades* at Covent Garden. I found it terribly difficult working with the singers there. For the mock-Mozart masque I had Peter Brownlee as an archangel wearing gold wings, designed by Oliver Messel, standing on the shoulders of four boys. Peter got terribly cross with me as he was terrified of losing his balance. What I did was all right, nothing special. It did lead to another opera at Covent

Garden, *Ariadne on Naxos* and *Dido and Aeneas* at Sadler's Wells. Still in the repertory there was *The Bartered Bride*, and Pamela May, near the end of her dancing days, was performing as wonderfully as ever in it, but Madam had warned me of a lack of talent within Sadler's Wells school which should have been the feeding ground for the opera-ballet group so we would have to look outside. This meant auditioning. She promised to help – which she did indeed do. We needed three girls and a couple of boys to make up the numbers. We found them only with difficulty but everything came together and I had a really good group of dancers.

Of course for a young dancer being assigned to the opera-ballet at Sadler's Wells, not even the opera-ballet at Covent Garden, came low in the pecking order when it came to getting a contract. At the school there was always a sense that you were close to the exit door, and if you did not come up to standard it would be suggested that you might do better in the world of commercial dancing. I had about six months to get this all sorted. My recruits included Lynn Seymour, Elizabeth Anderton plus Clover Roope who later danced for Peter Darrell in his version of *Jeux*. She subsequently studied in America with Martha Graham, Merce Cunningham and Alwin Nikolais before joining Ballet Rambert. We also had Yemaiel Oved and Kathryn Beetham from Audrey de Vos' school, along with Ben Stevenson, John O'Brien, David Hymns and Christopher Gable. We ended up with a dozen really nice dancers. I did wonder whether this sort of talent was really too good for what I would be asking them to dance. I doubted that they would be satisfied appearing only in operas. Madam, however, insisted that this group of dancers would be looked after. She argued they represented the future. Practically, she had her eye on them for soloist and principal work with the Royal Ballet companies fairly soon.

I quickly got busy and found there were periods when the group had very little work because some of the operas in the repertoire did not require any dances. I was also aware that for a dancer, appearing in opera could appear seem to be something of a dead end. Lynn Seymour said how she appreciated not being made to feel like a reject thanks to the way in which I managed them. One of her earliest appearances, while still a teenager, was as one of the angels in *Hansel and Gretel* which still used lovely choreography by David Poole. Many years later she could still remember her gold silk costume and golden leaves that ornamented her hair. Lynn and Christopher Gable, as well as several others, appeared in a student production of Gluck's opera *Orfeo ed Euridice* at one of the Cambridge colleges which I was asked to choreograph during the 1956–57 season. Ursula Moreton came to see her former students who I was using for the corps de ballet. I created a duet for Lynn and Christopher as two blessed spirits. I recall a rather grudging Miss Moreton telling me that my choreography had flow – but it was not a patch on what Madam had done at Sadler's Wells. In fact I hated having to integrate my dancers with the singers who were a very undisciplined lot of students. They even had no feeling of how to walk properly. The dancers looked marvellous in comparison and were a great credit to the Royal Ballet School. I regretted doing the job but I was looking for any chance to choreograph. There were so few opportunities in those days. I have to say opera singers have changed a lot since then and most of them move really well.

When I learned that a gala was being organised at Sadler's Wells to support Hungarian refugees in December 1956 I was horrified to discover that the opera-ballet dancers were not part of the planned line-up. Instead dancers from the Covent Garden opera-ballet were scheduled to dance the polka from *The Bartered Bride*, an opera not even in their repertoire then. I soon put that right and my group of Sadler's Wells dancers appeared in an excerpt from *Eugene Onegin*. To create more opportunities for the group to perform, I got in touch with Barnardo's charity and arranged a few concerts in children's homes that had a piano and a space large enough for us to dance. By their reaction we could all see that the children adored our shows. Some of them had debilitating conditions, and seeing us dance was as if they were flying.

Arranging dances for the popular boogie-woogie and ragtime pianist Winnie Atwell's television shows was another of the ways I devised of keeping the dancers busy when there was nothing to do in the operas being performed. I contacted ITV when I heard that Atwell was to do a new series. I rang Dickie Leeman, the director of the show, whom I knew, and being aware that Winnie always included one classical piece in her show suggested that including a couple of dancers might help visually. Winnie loved the idea. As a result we did eight weekly shows where I would arrange a pas de deux or danced sequence. This proved successful and I became really interested in TV as a way of increasing the public's interest in dance. Dickie Leeman could see the potential of putting dance on television, which was then starting to become more widespread in people's homes, although as long ago as the 1930s the BBC had programmed performances by the Vic-Wells Ballet and works that Antony Tudor made for television. Unfortunately Atwell's husband, the comedian Lew Levisohn, did not like the idea and thought the dancers distracted too much from Winnie's playing. So, all of a sudden, despite the popularity of the programmes there was no more money to engage us. Our involvement with the series came to an end. No matter, these things all kept the dancers happy, and I was getting good practice choreographing, but importantly too, managing people and situations.

I started to explore possibilities of training for TV production and direction. Through this I was asked by Margaret Dale, along with Peter Darrell who was then fairly well established as a choreographer, to create two short ballets created especially for television, using dancers from the Royal and Festival Ballet companies. In 1937, while still a student, Margaret – Maggie – had appeared in several TV productions screened from Alexandra Palace in north London, from where the BBC had made its early broadcasts of ballet. These included versions of *Swan Lake* and *The Nutcracker*. Maggie joined Sadler's Wells Ballet in 1939. Her first appearance was in *The Emperor's New Clothes* by de Valois and she appeared in works by Frederick Ashton, Robert Helpmann and Léonide Massine. She was one of the fairies – as well as one of Aurora's friends and the white cat – in *The Sleeping Beauty* when the Royal Opera House reopened in February 1946. She was also the Sugar Plum fairy in *The Nutcracker* and Swanilda in *Coppélia*. In 1953 Maggie tried her hand at choreography, making a Sherlock Holmes ballet, *The Great Detective*, in which she cast the young Kenneth MacMillan in the double role of Holmes and Moriarty, going around with his magnifying glass, with Stanley Holden as Watson. It was rather ineffectual and difficult to understand thanks to its lack of choreography and too much action composed in the style of a TV treatment, shot after shot. It was an action piece, a ballet without steps. Maggie could see for herself that she did not have an aptitude for producing choreography but she did recognise that what she described as her nature might make her more suitable for producing people. As I was to learn, Maggie's experience of having been a dancer and her rather stubborn and bossy personality made her sometimes difficult to work with.

In the early 1950s Naomi Capon, a television producer who went on to direct Keith Michell in some episodes of *The Six Wives of Henry VIII* for the BBC in 1970, invited Maggie to help with the production of several short ballets for television. In those days programmes were broadcast live from Lime Grove studios in west London. Alongside an item about migrant butterflies and a presenter demonstrating printing patterns using leaves, one of the ballets to be broadcast in September 1952, after the Sunday night play, was John Cranko's *Dancing*. This had been part of the season he had created in Henley earlier that summer. Sonya and Kenneth MacMillan were the principals, supported by Yvonne Cartier, Margaret Scott, David Shields and Geoffrey Webb.

Later, in 1954, Naomi produced a series of educational dance programmes, *Steps into Ballet*, for children's television. These included *The Three Bears*, about a guardsman and two sisters who come to watch changing the guard. Sonya was one of the dancers along with Yvonne Cartier again, Michel de Lutry and Dominie Callaghan. *Steps into Ballet* was a monthly programme created by Felicity Gray that analysed ballet, showing, for example, how a character is created through dance and how a dancer is trained. The programmes included ballet excerpts arranged by Gilbert Vernon around such familiar stories as *Alice in Wonderland* and *Cinderella*. As I was later to discover when I worked with Naomi, she was good. She pushed for things to happen. I worked with her in a session when she was attempting to get BBC cameramen to understand how to film dancers in motion without cutting off their feet or other limbs. That was hard. We went over and over the same things on concrete floors while being filmed by ten cameras. I struggled through the bluebird solo from *The Sleeping Beauty*, never my best role, performing it again and again while the camera operator figured out how fast it needed to travel and how to avoid cutting off my hands and feet.

Thanks to the encouragement of Madam, Maggie Dale met George Barnes, the BBC's director-in-chief. As a result she decided to train as a television producer. Her first project under her own credit was to invite Kenneth MacMillan to create an original 30-minute ballet for television. This was *Turned Out Proud*, for the weekly *Music at Ten* programme in October 1955. This was already Kenneth's third experience of working for television. He had created *Punch and the Child* for the small screen the year before, and his first stage ballet, *Somnambulism*, had been adapted for television as *The Dreamers*. Kenneth was much interested in the process of filming, looking through the viewfinder and watching Maggie mark camera positions on the floor which at the time was an innovation for film crews. Altogether it was a process that always fascinated Kenneth and influenced his choreographic eye. With John Neville, the debonair star of the Old Vic, as a compere in top hat and tails, *Turned Out Proud* was more a revue than a ballet. Sonya featured in the cast alongside Gilbert Vernon, Ben Stevenson and Julia Farron as well as Violette Verdy who later married Colin Clark. She became one of George Balanchine's favourite ballerinas with New York City Ballet. At that time she was with Festival Ballet for a brief spell. Although we met on relatively few occasions subsequently, I have seen Violette dance, teach and talk many times. I feel I have known her all my life, and when we did meet it was like a grand reunion.

George Balanchine adored Violette. The combination of his musical choreography and her rich musicality and beautiful classical arms was utter perfection. I remember her with New York City Ballet, rehearsing the *Stars and Stripes* pas de deux at Covent Garden for a gala. The conductor simply could not get how Balanchine liked the music played for the solo. Violette boldly stopped the rehearsal, and standing down at the footlights she told the conductor, 'Non! Non! No!' She then proceeded to sing it for him in front of the entire orchestra, incredibly musically with every diminuendo and crescendo. The orchestra burst into applause, as did everybody else watching. The conductor understood what was needed and was impeccable as a result. I first met Violette in Stuttgart. She was so friendly when she watched a rehearsal for *The Mirror Walkers*, and very complimentary. We became great friends – something that proved beneficial when years later she came to Birmingham as part of an Arts Council assessment. She wrote the most comprehensive and encouraging report which I am sure made a big difference when future funding was decided. We last met at the Royal Ballet School when I presented her with a special award. I was quite overwhelmed by her generous words in reply. For me, Violette was one of the greatest exponents of classical ballet and its music that I know.

The critical reaction to *Turned Out Proud* was very positive. Putting dance on television was regarded as an experiment to be repeated, but the difficulties that Maggie and Kenneth had with *Turned Out Proud* illustrate the constraints of transferring ballet from the stage to the small screen. Both budgets and working conditions were constrained. Around £850, about £17,500 in today's terms, was a typical budget with which to screen a one-act ballet. As there was no money for new music or royalties, Kenneth was obliged to choose music from the BBC's record collection by a patchwork of composers, Einar Englund, father of the famous Danish dancer, Sorella, Sibelius and Françaix as well as several jazz and blues pieces, not so much for their suitability but because they did not attract any copyright fees. When the Musicians' Union objected to the use of recorded music Maggie managed to argue for the music to be performed by a live orchestra when Kenneth's next ballet, *House of Birds*, was broadcast in 1956. Typically that was a performance that went out live. Few programmes were recorded. A telerecording consisted of placing a film camera in front of a monitor and recording the pictures it displayed on film. This method was used until the advent of video which meant that many of the performances created for television in the 1950s have survived, whereas many programmes originated on video got wiped.

This was the world I was contemplating when Maggie asked me and Peter Darrell to create our television ballets in April 1957. Maggie had recently completed the BBC's television producers' course and set up a dance office in the music department. Peter decided very quickly that he wanted to create a zodiac inspired piece and created *Gemini Valse* for Anya Linden and David Blair. He pulled out of the other commission, I think because he was busy creating *The Prisoners*, for Western Theatre Ballet's forthcoming inaugural tour that June. That was the ballet that really established his reputation. I made the two, 15-minute ballets that Maggie asked me for which, along with Peter's, made up a programme entitled *Divertissements*, screened late on a Sunday evening. The music was performed by the BBC Concert Orchestra, conducted by Villem Tausky. I used Anya Linden in a dream piece about a young girl who finds a collection of puppets, including a high-kicking chorus girl and sailor, which come to life. You could not possibly do anything so banal now. I also used Benjamin Britten's *Soirées musicales*, Anya again with Blair and Merle Park, about people's fantasies while watching a concert. Of course that was not an original idea, Jerome Robbins had made *The Concert* in New York the year before, but I did not know that at the time and my little ballet was not a patch on Jerry's masterpiece.

Ballet on television in the late-1950s was not only a case of transferring contemporary British works to the screen. During the Bolshoi
Ballet's revelatory visit to London in 1956 Maggie organised a studio
recording of the second act of *Swan Lake*. In those days, film crews
were handicapped by cumbersome cameras and lighting equipment,
so justice could be done to major dance works only by bringing them
into one of the larger studios at Lime Grove, a warren of down-at-heel
facilities, or later to the Riverside studios in Hammersmith. Television
Centre at Shepherd's Bush did not open until 1960. Nearly ten million
people watched the *Swan Lake* broadcast, almost half the adult viewing
public with access to a television set. The figure was impressive as only a
decade earlier there were only around 20,000 households with a television, all within a 35-mile radius of Alexandra Palace. The screening was
significant too as Galina Ulanova, who appeared as Odette opposite the
Siegfried of Nikolai Fadeyechev, no longer performed the role onstage.
Given the reaction to the broadcast, Maggie saw an opportunity to film
complete ballets. She believed that the classics, as adapted by herself for
the small screen, were the way to popularise ballet. Ninette de Valois
was resistant to her companies being filmed, although in fact her *Job*
had been televised in 1936 and *Checkmate* a year later. She argued that
productions created for the stage should be seen in the theatre, not the
small screen. Later she changed her mind, accepting the logic of Maggie's
argument that television was a popularising force for dance. Maggie was
always quick to point out that the average audience for a ballet transmis-
sion was four million, the equivalent of 2,000 sold-out performances at
the Royal Opera House. Eventually this led to a series of studio-made
television broadcasts of Royal Ballet productions in the early 1960s. When
the dancers' Equity representative raised the issue of extra payment for
appearing on television, de Valois countered the demand, saying that as
everybody everywhere was a taxpayer, and as a publicly funded company,
the dancers had a duty to appear on television.

Coppélia was the first full-length classic that Maggie 'freely adapted'
for television, in October 1957. Nadia Nerina, Donald Britton and
Robert Helpmann led the cast. It began with an extreme close-up of
Helpmann's face as Dr Coppélius. The camera pulled back to reveal him
looking obsessively at the doll Coppélia he had made. Maggie asked me
to rearrange the mazurka, in which I also danced, and the dance of the

hours' divertissement. She managed to secure the London Symphony Orchestra conducted by John Lanchbery. Additionally from the Royal Ballet's repertoire, *Petrushka* with Alexander Grant, Nadia Nerina, Keith Rosson and Franklin White, *The Rake's Progress* with Donald Britton and Elizabeth Anderton, *Checkmate* with Beryl Grey and Robert Helpmann, *Les Rendezvous* with Doreen Wells, Brian Shaw, Merle Park, Graham Usher and Petrus Bosman, were all broadcast. *La Fille mal gardée*, *The Dream* and *Monotones* with their near original casts were all filmed. *Fille* was mostly filmed in long, unobtrusive takes, but one sequence, at the end of the farmyard scene, was rearranged for filming. Maggie insisted that her television productions expressed the feeling of the stage production as much as possible, and although her film of *Fille* captured many choreographic details that have altered over the years of stage performance, and was filmed with Frederick Ashton's supervision, Maggie did not think twice about asking for changes to the choreography in order to suit the camera. She was hard-headed about how ballet looked on television. The red chess pieces in *Checkmate* were problematic for monochrome studio cameras and so were remade in yellow to boost the colour contrast against the opposing black pieces.

Nadia Nerina featured in many of Maggie's filmed stagings but I always found her a distinctly unmusical dancer. Nadia herself was the only person who ever thought she was musical. 'You are just not listening properly,' she used to say to anybody who attempted to correct her phrasing. Several days in a TV studio being filmed from all angles by several cameras was a novel experience for dancers, but most did not enjoy it or having to dance on a concrete floor. They had to learn how to always be conscious of camera angles. It was easy to overdo a performance for film. Maggie was fussy about what how every shot looked and was very demanding but she would only allow the use of tiny marks on the floor to guide dancers. She really expected them to be exactly in position for each shot. As the broadcasts went out live this was very hard for dancers to achieve. I quite enjoyed the experience and the BBC was very organised when things like a camera failure occurred.

I really liked television and was interested in the craft of it. Studio-based recordings of *The Nutcracker* and *Giselle* were broadcast in March and May of 1959. Between the two I was ballet master for *Les Sylphides* with Nerina, Philip Chatfield and Rowena Jackson, broadcast on Easter

Sunday. *The Sleeping Beauty* followed in December. Notionally I was ballet master and responsible for producing some new choreography but really Maggie was in overall charge. The ballets had to be cut down a lot to fit the TV schedules and rearranged because of the cameras' limited field of vision. I did a new snowflakes' scene in *The Nutcracker* with Lucette Aldous as the snow fairy, with whom I enjoyed working, but it was not an inspired production choreographically except for the Arabian dance in which Sheila O'Neill, one of the most inspiring dancers I have worked with, was superb despite the music having been recorded much too fast.

Again, with *Giselle* I was ballet master and enjoyed working with Nikolai Fadeyechev as Albrecht. It had been extremely difficult to persuade the Home Office to issue an entry permit for him to appear on his own at the BBC and not as part of an official visit by the Bolshoi Ballet. Maggie won through, however, and the event became quite an historic occasion. He was great to work with and I learned a lot from him about partnering and mime while appearing as Wilfred, his squire. Fadeyechev was very masculine, and a strong partner, particularly when lifting Nadia Nerina in the title role, but in close-up on screen he tended to look rather ham. This was probably because Fadeyechev was used to projecting in the huge Bolshoi theatre where gestures and expressions had to be exaggerated in order to communicate.

Giselle was one of Nerina's better roles: she understood the contrasts of character between the acts, unlike some Giselles who tend to be too spiritual in the first act and so there is not enough difference with the second. Margaret Hill looked perfect as the evil Myrtha, queen of the wilis. She pretended to be upset when one of her solos was cut to keep the broadcast within schedule but she was in fact delighted not to be doing it, especially on the concrete floor. She was icy, evil. The famous Danish dancer, Niels Bjørn Larsen, was a disappointment as Hilarion. He found it hard to stick to Maggie's instructions and gave an old-fashioned portrayal of an older and sinister Hilarion which he would not change. It was nice to have Lydia Sokolova as Berthe, Giselle's mother, but she was not a particularly good mime, too exaggerated for the screen. With her pencilled eyebrows she looked rather odd. Frederick Ashton told me she had plucked them so often they would not regrow. Sokolova was very old school. She was shocked that the women of the corps de

ballet dared to talk during rehearsals. She criticised them for not concentrating and being terribly dressed for rehearsals.

Giselle was filmed at Riverside studios where there were two studios
connected by a huge door. That meant we could create a sense of distance
for the hunt's arrival in the first act, along with real wolf-hounds with
the duke, and for the wilis' scenes in the forest by following the action
through both studios. Maggie may not have been very adventurous but
she was very well organised and made the most of the spaces available.
In *Giselle* she made good use of the trees seen in the foreground with
dancers placed close to camera to allow viewers to see their reactions
to what was happening around them. Her filming scripts were meticulous. The only way she could work was to religiously learn the dancers'
counts of every piece that she did and then link the camera cuts to those
counts. That was her method and she expected everyone else to follow.
Maggie wanted to rehearse every single dance herself and I had to insist
that was my province as ballet master. In the context of a filmed performance, the ballet master takes class and puts things right during camera
rehearsals. It took a week to prepare and rehearse each ballet for transmis-
sion. Dancers were paid nothing compared to today's rates but the costs
quickly mounted up. The expense of filming dance meant that using a
permanent company was economically unfeasible but having an ad-hoc
ensemble did also give Maggie more control. There was never any shortage of dancers willing to participate.

One difficulty that Maggie experienced was that she found choreographers reluctant to think about television as a medium. One exception
was Peter Darrell, whose *Houseparty* Maggie produced in 1964. This was
a contemporary version of *Les Biches* using Francis Poulenc's score but
conceived in the style of Joseph Losey's film *The Servant* which had a
screenplay by Harold Pinter. He was asked to produce the scenario for
Houseparty but declined. The project went instead to John Hopkins. He
was one of the pioneers of TV drama who worked on *Z Cars*. Darrell's
Houseparty was a considerable success. It did not, however, lead to much
innovation in presenting modern choreography on television. The BBC
preferred to film known quantities, although Maggie did not think in
conventional terms, where ballet is traditionally framed by a proscenium
arch. In her film of *The Sleeping Beauty*, courtiers were seen walking
across the scene as in conversation and there was a lot of business for the

fairies around the crib. It was an approach that did not really work, in my opinion. *Beauty* needs the framing symmetry imposed by the proscenium in the theatre. The difficulty for me, as I made some new choreography including the garland dance, was that the set, designed by Guy Shephard under instruction from Maggie, was triangular in shape. That meant there was no diagonal, essential for classical ballet. For the bluebirds, Brian Shaw and Antoinette Sibley, this was extremely problematic.

As the production was already overspent there was no money to afford Frederick Ashton's choreography for the Florestan pas de trois and Maggie asked me to produce new choreography for it. Jelko Yuresha, who had just escaped from Yugoslavia and had no work permit, refused to dance the new male solo, telling me the choreography was not good enough for him. Really, if he was going to get a permit to stay in this country his future did depend on him performing that solo very well indeed. Later he married Belinda Wright, no relation, and became a very hard-working dancer and much more approachable. Yvonne Cartier was an evil and quite powerful Carabosse but her mime scenes with the Lilac fairy were much cut. The designs were conceived to register on a mono-chrome screen – this was before the days of colour – but there seemed to be no contrast, which had the effect of making everybody look rather grey. Still, it is one film that does capture something of the qualities that made Margot Fonteyn special – which is not always the case with her filmed performances. You see her musicality, her speed, her pirou-ettes and her concentration on every movement, though she was often filmed from the wrong angle. In fact, she had been working so hard, performing at Covent Garden, she was desperately tired and really did fall asleep during the filming of the awakening scene, only waking up when Michael Somes kissed her, which made it all look very realistic. She looked naturally surprised and lost. In retrospect, after nearly 60 years when the BBC screened the film in 2014, it does reveal how classi-cal ballet in this country has changed since that time; sometimes for the better, sometimes for the worse.

Maggie was keen for me to do the BBC television producers' course. Though she was not keen to have others to direct dance programmes, there were people like Colin Nears and John Drummond around at the time and both had aspirations to direct dance. John had the office next to me. A future director of the Edinburgh Festival and controller of Radio 3 and the BBC Proms, at that time John already revealed ambitions of doing things on a grand scale. I must say that he was very knowledgeable and incredibly erudite. He certainly had the gift of the gab and it was difficult to get a word in edgeways. He became a friend of Sonya and me but he did have some odd opinions about classical ballet. He understood contemporary dance well and I have to say he fought long and hard in the interests of all dance and music. Becoming director of the Royal Ballet was one of John's unrealised ambitions. Colin Nears became a very successful television director and producer and made many really good dance programmes including a recording of Frederick Ashton's *A Month in the Country* with Lynn Seymour, Anthony Dowell and nearly all the original cast. Colin was a highly respected instructor of TV producers and directors as well as being chairman of Birmingham Royal Ballet. He well deserved his CBE for his extraordinary contribution to dance and television. With this sort of competition I was lucky to be encouraged by the producer and presenter Huw Wheldon. I think too that Maggie was keen to build up her own people whom she thought she could influence, and that is why she chose me for the course. In fact it did not quite work out that way as I had pretty strong ideas of my own. When I was finally able to take up the contract I was offered I had quite a list of dance pieces from the repertoires of the Royal Ballet and Stuttgart that I was anxious to get on with. But I must say that Maggie did help and encourage me a great deal, as did Humphrey Burton, head of the music department.

The course offered no guarantees of a job afterwards. There were only ten of us and I felt something of an outsider as all the others were BBC employees. The course was two weeks long and I found a lot of it difficult to follow. It was full of TV jargon and much of it felt beyond me, but I took notes all the time and persevered. I learned a great deal about cameras, lenses and their characteristics and about cutting, composition, scripting and filming. It was all invaluable and I was glad to have done the course. Then there were wonderful lectures about television as a medium in its own right, not just as a filmed record. To the people who already worked at the BBC this was all familiar already but for me it was both fascinating and bewildering. We were all given £15 to make a 15-minute programme as the last part of the course. All the others made short documentaries but I decided to film John Cranko's ballet, *Beauty*

and the Beast, a 20-minute pas de deux. From my budget I had to pay
£2 each to two Australian dancers who were desperate to do some work,
and I managed to borrow some costumes from Sadler's Wells. By luck I
discovered that the studio next door had been set as a forest. As I knew
the floor manager for that programme I was able to persuade him to leave
some trees behind in my studio which would be ideal. I acquired some
rose bushes and other shrubbery from a gardening programme and it all
looked far better than when I did the ballet professionally for television
later on. In fact it went amazingly well. Luckily, just when I was getting
into difficulties with the ending, one of the cameras failed, which allowed
me time to work out how to shoot the sequence. When we all had to
show our programmes to each other, everybody deemed mine to be the
best. I had passed with flying colours. Mind you, I had gained quite a
bit of experience from having worked with Maggie. As a result, I was
offered a two-year contract with the BBC's music and arts department
there and then, but before I could discuss it with Sonya that evening at
home, the phone rang. It was John Cranko calling from Stuttgart where
he had recently become director of the ballet company at the opera house
there. 'Oh Pete, I'm in such a mess here, I'm having to do everything,
teaching, rehearsing, planning, choreography. Everything. I can't cope.
Come and be my ballet master.' I explained to John I had just had this
marvellous offer and needed to consider my family. Sonya had gone very
silent in fear. 'Oh don't give yourself to TV,' John pleaded. I knew the
opportunity with the BBC was the better offer financially but I turned
it down. The head of the contracts department was very understanding.
He said they would be quite happy for me to ring him at any time and
they would be very pleased to have me as a guest producer, which is what
happened. We went to Stuttgart, although I knew that Sonya was not
happy at the prospect of going there with two young children aged two
and four. When after five years we returned to London I did ring up the
BBC. Fortunately they still remembered me and honoured their promise
to employ me as a guest producer.

I played safe with my first production as a bona fide producer. I redid
Beauty and the Beast, this time with Doreen Wells and Richard Farley.
It was surprisingly hard. No free trees this time. I had to have a proper
set made, which was not easy working with a studio designer. I had to
abide by all the union agreements, and the technicians were a set of

toughies, clock-watching the entire time. Another familiar title I undertook was *The Telltale Heart*. I had appeared in Peter Darrell's ballet based on the same Edgar Alan Poe story at the choreographic workshop at the Mercury theatre in 1952. It is about a lodger's obsessive terror of his landlord's staring eye which ends in murder. I realised I had to make it completely different from Peter's version. I brought the story up to date and made it more realistic, with Nicolas Chagrin as the murderer. Although the programme is now lost it seemed to work well at the time but it was a pretty nasty story.

During my period as a guest producer I was asked by Maggie to use my experience as ballet master in Stuttgart to create a documentary with her about professional dancers' daily training which they do throughout their entire careers. This was *Ballet Class*, in 1964. It was intended to look like a normal daily training session, but with such a class you never know where anybody is going to move so it could not be rehearsed, certainly not for the cameras. That was difficult as it would be going out live. We gathered together a class of dancers, mostly principals from the Royal Ballet who had camera appeal, masculine-looking men and alluring women. It was the most tortuous thing I have ever been asked to do. The whole idea was that it should be spontaneous and completely unrehearsed, and as the public in those days knew little about dancers' working lives it would give them an insight into the hard work involved with their profession. It was up to me to get the right dancer in the right place at the right time for each sequence of steps. The dancers did not know what was going to happen until I set the steps and exercises. They had to perform as instructed, receiving corrections as they were dancing. It was hard to ensure they were positioned correctly and not moving too fast for the camera. When I announced that the next step would be something of a brain teaser, Maryon Lane countered, 'I don't come to class to think. I'm off.' She started to walk out. It was vital for continuity that the same dancers were seen at the end of it as at the beginning because of how the credits were arranged, so I chased her out of shot while the others were struggling with this difficult step. I grabbed her as she was about to disappear. I said, 'If you leave the set while shooting is in progress you will be blacklisted.' I insisted she continued, which thankfully she did. Maggie, brilliant as she was at directing cameras that had been rehearsed, was not the most spontaneous of people. She was having fits in the control room. Remember, this was all going out live. She managed to keep the cameras off Maryon until I got back on script and demonstrated the next step as if nothing had happened. The programme actually was a huge success. Even my greengrocer in Finchley said he enjoyed it when he saw me the next day, 'Saw you on the box last night mate. The girls were lovely! I'll watch more "bally" in future.' Actually it was one of the girls, Lynn Seymour, who gave problems. This was during one of those periods where she was struggling somewhat with her weight and was sensitive about her appearance. She demanded to see a recording from the broadcast, and, due to an oversight, she had not signed the release form that allowed the BBC to repeat a recorded programme. A legal battle started as Lynn thought she would stop the programme from being seen again. If she had looked bad I would have agreed with her. She was actually lovely to work with as she would try anything, but right from her early days she had a mind of her own. This all took about a year to resolve but she lost her case. The programme was repeated and there were no more complaints. It revealed Lynn's lovely line and she moved beautifully, like a dream. Although she was plagued with problems, soft corns being the least of them, she was ready to become a great ballerina.

I also produced *Las Hermanas* in March 1965 which Kenneth MacMillan had created in Stuttgart a couple of years before. It was a marvellous collaboration with a great cast combining dancers from Stuttgart and the Royal Ballet including Ray Barra as the man, Marcia Haydée as the eldest sister, Monica Mason as the jealous one and Georgina Parkinson as the youngest, with Ruth Papendick as the mother. Kenneth left me to direct the cameras but he was excellent in his understanding of working to the selective eye of the camera rather than a theatre audience. He would probably have made a very good film director. Still in black-and-white, Nicholas Georgiadis' set was expanded for television by a BBC designer. We developed the ballet to show scenes outside the sisters' house, which helped make more sense of the plot. You could compose scenes of the interior and exterior in the same sequence of shots. Of all my TV productions I think this was the one I really got right. When *Las Hermanas* was revived by the Royal Ballet in 2012 it was staged by Ray Barra and Monica Mason assisted with teaching various roles. It was still good theatre.

With the encouragement of Humphrey Burton, in 1966 Maggie Dale embarked on what was intended to be a year-long series entitled *Zodiac*.

Each of the star signs would provide the themes for an anthology of short ballets created for TV by leading choreographers, all danced in the vast arena of studio one at Television Centre in Shepherd's Bush. So in April that year I directed a ballet made for television, *Time Switch*, choreographed by Norman Morrice, that featured Elizabeth Anderton. It was paired with Samuel Beckett's play, *Act Without Words II*, which I also directed, similar in idea to *Waiting for Godot*. I had not seen the play on the stage. The actors were pretty good, found by Maggie's sister Elsa Bolam and her husband, a Canadian theatre director. Elsa and I directed the play together as Elsa knew about actors, and I, supposedly, knew about cameras. It was surprisingly very successful, I think possibly because the cameras can help actors by going in close at vital moments rather than them having to project unnaturally loudly to the back of a theatre. I rather enjoyed working with actors and think had I stayed in television I would have switched to drama or programmes featuring the spoken word. When telling a story in dance and mime the camera has to follow the dancer, often high in the air or changing direction at speed, but with plays there is so much more freedom in how the camera can be used, as actors are relatively static.

That September I also produced another ballet by Norman Morrice, *The Tribute*, which had been created for the Royal Ballet's touring company, including David Wall and Patricia Ruanne. Norman was then primarily associated as a choreographer with Ballet Rambert and was the principal architect that year of the company's return to producing new work rather than scaled-down versions of the classics. *The Tribute* was Norman's only ballet for the Royal Ballet. Madam apparently did not like it and did not commission him again. It was quite a big work in which a group of tourists find themselves caught up in a ritual sacrifice on a Mediterranean island. It ended with the strangled body of a tourist and the offstage screams of a woman in labour. Although it needed to be reset for television, it looked good on screen. The original designer, Ralph Koltai, worked with Clifford Hatts to recreate his set of a village square and café. It was a very good collaboration.

Another adaptation from the stage came in November 1966 when I directed a shortened, 35-minute version of John Cranko's ballet *Onegin* which had been created by Stuttgart Ballet in April the year before. When seen on television that Sunday evening it followed straight on from the 150th edition of *Billy Cotton's Music Hall* with a line-up that included Cilla Black, Leslie Crowther, Jimmy Edwards and the Tiller Girls. Clifford Hatts, who was one of the BBC's top designers, again redesigned the sets for television, with costumes for the principals coming from Stuttgart and for the others from the BBC wardrobe. It looked beautiful. John adapted his choreography himself. Peter Hawkins was the narrator and the programme was based on both Tchaikovsky's opera and Pushkin's poem. It was retitled *Eugene Onegin, a ballet for television*. Its focus was mainly on Onegin, played by Desmond Doyle, remembering his relationships with the other characters played by Marcia Haydée as Tatiana, Lynn Seymour as Olga and Egon Madsen as Lensky. As John and I were rearranging the ballet for the cameras it really was like a new version with much new choreography. John had great difficulty in feeling involved and slept his way through most of the two weeks of rehearsals before the actual recording. Once he could see the pictures all coming together during camera rehearsals in the studio he latched on to it 100 percent with the most wonderful ideas. Some of them were possible to achieve at that late stage, but once you are in the studio putting the shots together there is little that you can change in the amount of time available. However, all went extremely well in the end. The production gave a real sense of the characters and the BBC entered it for the Prix d'Italia award. All looked promising until one of the judges asked if the choreography had been performed before. When it was pointed out that it had, but in a completely different format, it was disqualified, unfairly I thought. Entries had to be completely original.

That year I also produced and directed a version of *Peter and the Wolf* which I choreographed myself. Some of the parts were played by children and it went out in a teatime slot in Christmas week. For this programme we had managed to get the English Chamber Orchestra. The bird, a mechanical flying one, flew round the head of the conductor, Dudley Simpson. He was very experienced with ballet and television, a real joy to work with. A ten-year-old Dorio Perez was outstanding as Peter, as was Eddie McMurray as the cat, who crawled through the legs of the orchestral players. It worked as TV but was not that strong choreographically. The musicians and cast performed wonderfully. The narrator was a dancer turned actor, Nicolas Chagrin, quite brilliant.

The following year, in March 1967, Maggie produced a 50-minute documentary called *Cranko's Castle*, about John's work in Stuttgart, and asked me to direct two sequences for it. *The Radio Times* listing described John as being in voluntary exile from the Royal Ballet and said, under John's leadership, that the Stuttgart company had become one of the best in the world. The programme was an opportunity to see Marcia Haydée, Birgit Keil, Egon Madsen and Richard Cragun being rehearsed by John in scenes from *Swan Lake*, *Giselle* and *Card Game*. It included too a performance of John's ballet, *Opus 1*, filmed on the stage in Stuttgart by me. This was one of his more abstract pieces about a journey through life. It is set to Anton Webern's *Passacaglia*, music that formed part of the score for MacMillan's *Different Drummer* almost 20 years later. *Opus 1* was premiered in Stuttgart in November 1965 on the same evening as Kenneth's *Song of the Earth* from which I also filmed two sections for the programme. Although Kenneth and John worked independently on their ballets, they both shared a similar concern for life, love and death. *Opus 1* is only 11 minutes long but the movement has an intense feel about it. The leading male dancer, Richard Cragun performing with Birgit Keil, carried with him the weight of an everyman. Working with a German crew in Stuttgart was quite an experience as I still had only a basic understanding of German and had never done an outside broadcast before with a foreign crew. They were incredibly helpful and I was pleased when they said they liked the way I directed cameras for dance.

A month later, in April 1967, I produced and directed a television production of Kurt Jooss' most famous work, *The Green Table*. Jooss came himself and brought with him members of his company from Essen. A young Pina Bausch was one of them and played the old woman. Pina seemed to have a magnetic ring around her when she was performing which drew your eyes to her and she seemed to make her movements speak. Her whole body seemed broken when the figure of death took her in his arms and bore her away to peace and rest. I wept. I have never seen another artist play this part so movingly. Winfried Kirsch played death. He was a well-known classical dancer in Munich but not really heavy or strong enough for that part. Overall *The Green Table* is an incredibly moving piece; you cannot relax when watching it. It affects you deeply. On television it could never have as strong an impact as on the stage. It is a stylised piece, incorporating masks and the use of a green spotlight narrowing in on death's skull as he claims his victims and slowly turns his head to face the viewers. However, even in black-and-white and when seen on the small screen, *The Green Table* still made a big impact.

Four months later, in August 1967, Kenneth MacMillan and I collaborated on *Albertine*, which he choreographed especially for the *Zodiac* series, with Lynn Seymour and Desmond Doyle in the leading roles. This was an occasion when Kenneth's nerves nearly got the better of him. Initial rehearsals were carried out behind closed doors – even I was not allowed in – and Kenneth was terrified by the time restrictions imposed when working for television. However, when the pas de deux was finished and I was allowed in I beheld the most passionate piece of dance that moved everyone deeply. It could not have been done any other way. It was perfection with the music. Later in the recording studio, when this particular section was being filmed, one of the rather bolshie stagehands, who thought that men in ballet were all poofs, turned to me with tears in his eyes and said, 'I didn't know that such love existed.' He became completely converted to dance. *Albertine* was inspired by a French film entitled *The Crimson Curtain*, itself based on a story by Barbey d'Aurevilly. The music Kenneth used was a harp concerto by Gabriel Pierné. The ballet tells the story of a young girl's passionate desire for a hussar who is billeted with her family deep in the French countryside. To get to his bedroom she must creep past her sleeping parents. In the middle of their lovemaking she dies in his arms. Somehow he must get the body back to her room without waking the parents. We are left with the final shot of him galloping on horseback into the distance, knowing that at any moment the parents will awaken. Lynn was wonderful, ravishingly beautiful and Desmond Doyle just right. It did not attract huge viewing figures; new works never do, so Maggie pushed for it to be repeated. However, the *Zodiac* series was cancelled because the audience numbers were too low. To my horror I discovered that although this MacMillan work was to be kept for possible inclusion in other programmes, all the *Zodiac* programmes got destroyed when the BBC was having a clear-out. Nobody bothered to check the content and this strange and romantically beautiful masterpiece was sadly lost for ever as there had not been time to have it notated. An enormous shame.

One of the people involved with *Zodiac* was Bob Lockyer who went on to become executive producer of dance at the BBC in a career spanning 40 years with the corporation. At the time he was writing some of the storylines for this series. He also created some short sequences on 16mm film for Maggie, including one about two people searching for each other in an empty concert hall, and another featuring a sword fight filmed on the last Underground train of the night ending at Westminster station. I commissioned Bob, who at that time was my assistant but who was looking after me as I was so new in the BBC, to write the scenario for *Corporal Jan*, broadcast as part of the *Omnibus* series in June 1968. This was a dramatic combination of witchcraft and mythology and featured Richard Farley in the title role with Elizabeth Anderton as his lover. During the apple-picking season, Jan, a poor soldier, returns home to a village obsessed with witchcraft. He dreams that the women in his life, mother, daughter, wife, become a goddess representing the different stages of a woman's life. He dreams that he is killed at the goddess' feet when presented with a sacred apple. Jan wakes from his dream to find his real lover accused of witchcraft, but it is he who meets his death, trying to protect her. This overheated story was credited to Bob Lockyer and Denis ApIvor who had composed successful scores for several ballets in the 1950s. These included Andrée Howard's *A Mirror for Witches* and Alfred Rodrigues' *Blood Wedding*.

With *Corporal Jan*, ApIvor had gone way out with his music and was using very unusual instruments, all in serial form or in equally inaccessible styles. I regretted my choice, it was utterly wrong. Nobody could identify a recognisable beat in the music and no piano score was available. Eventually when we managed to get a recording with reduced scoring made, it did not sound at all like the full orchestral score. Nobody could derive any inspiration from such music even though we had Norman del Mar conducting. A nightmare! I created the choreography from counts and had the music superimposed after the filming had been made. Bob Lockyer helped me enormously as I really was still very green. This was before he became a floor manager as he started to progress upwards within the BBC hierarchy, but he could already give me good advice on when to cut and which camera to use to avoid such things as jump cuts. Unfortunately ApIvor wanted to use his own ideas about mythology and witchcraft and virtually pushed Bob off the programme. I suppose it was good experience but I had taken on too much as producer, director and choreographer. I had no say in the choice of designer, which was an aspect I did not enjoy. You had to be well established before being allowed to choose your own designer and I found this very frustrating. The make-up artist was a trial too. 'I know all about ballet,' she said, itching to stick false eyelashes on all the women and get busy with her mascara brush. You just had to accept what you were given.

There was one scene in *Corporal Jan*, however, that I did love. It was set in an orchard in winter, covered in snow. It had to be filmed separately and demanded a completely different technique of shooting. We found a wonderful real orchard somewhere in Kent, just right, and sprayed it with artificial snow and covered quite a vast area of ground with white sheets. It had a very eerie look as a band of medieval soldiers tramped through. The scene could have been a fantastic piece if Bob and I had had some comprehensible music to work to and I had a bit more experience. Altogether I guess it has to go under the heading of one of my wrongs.

Humphrey Burton was always very supportive, even when I got things wrong, something I appreciated as I was only a guest producer. At departmental meetings he was honest about people's programmes. I had edited a programme about Maya Plisetskaya, the Russian ballerina, for length. In my attempt to include what I thought was a lot of interesting material I had included ten filmed extracts where probably five would have been better. 'Pretty disastrous,' Humphrey told me. I did not mind the fact that he criticised me as he helped me see that my finished programme was bitty. I was pleased to be told straight. I always felt secure when Humphrey was around. He was in the control room when we were doing *The Tribute*, for example. Humphrey made some amazing opera broadcasts and New Year concerts from Vienna. He is a very good friend still.

It was not long after this that television had to disappear from my activities when I staged *Giselle* and *The Sleeping Beauty* for the Royal Ballet companies, as well as undertaking productions overseas. There was simply not the time. I gave up television also because of my partial colour blindness. I have great difficulty in distinguishing between red and green and this was just when colour TV was coming in. This was a huge disadvantage. Otherwise television came naturally enough to me. I think I would have got on quite well if I just wanted a secure job but I was looking for more than that. During the 1960s there was a tremendous impetus among those working in television to explore the medium's possibilities, in part to justify its existence, particularly when it came to putting works created for the stage onto the small screen. Working with the people I did, this did not mean filming a stage performance in a theatre, which is the case nowadays on the rare occasions that ballet finds its way to television; rather it was much more of finding ways to reimagine existing works so that they would have comparable impact when seen on television. Today ballet on television means the occasional broadcast of a big production from a big company, usually lost in a non-peak viewing slot. Akram Khan's segment of the opening ceremony of the London 2012 Olympics was impressive in the stadium and on television too but it has not prompted a new exploration of dance filmed in the studio especially for television. The BBC broadcasts the Young Dancer of the Year competition, but it seems that it is the competition aspect that is more important for its producers than the actual dance content. David Attenborough, who was in charge of BBC2 during the 1960s when I was working at the corporation, did not like dance himself but regarded it as a public duty for the BBC to broadcast it. That led to many dance-related broadcasts. Unfortunately nowadays this ethos has largely disappeared. The BBC no longer has a dedicated dance producer and putting dance on screen is not a priority. The huge popularising potential of television for dance has been lost. Dance and film do co-exist, in TV, cinema and web relays but it is usually well proven titles that have selling power that are screened. What is new or experimental is largely ignored.

All of which said, television has never been my ideal way of watching dance, for there is a tension between what looks good on screen and in the theatre. With classical ballet, however, it is very difficult to get the filming angles right. What looks best for a choreographer and for the camera are frequently opposed to each other. Maggie and I invented a filming technique where the camera moved closer to the dancer as they travelled forwards in a diagonal sequence of steps which gave the viewer the correct feeling of movement. Angles are critical, particularly as classical ballet is designed to be seen from the front, not the side where cameras are mostly positioned in a broadcast of a theatre performance. Sequences designed to impress on the stage, such as Odile's 32 fouettés in *Swan Lake* are difficult to film with the same degree of excitement because the repetition of the consecutive turns is precisely that, too repetitive for the camera to remain interested. For the dancer that sequence is a hard and wonderful feat but it is just wrong for the camera and its impact is invariably lost. Another difficulty occurs when a choreographer has designed a moving pattern. That is immensely satisfying on the eye in the theatre but it is easy to lose the shape of patterns on film. It all comes down to how well the cuts between shots are made. I do not think that putting ballets designed for the theatre onto a screen or a DVD can ever be totally solved. It is never ideal. Still, I admire the way in which a good director can cut to something that is happening away from the main action in a flash to give a sense of the overall stage picture. Done sensitively, and benefiting from the quality of technology available now, when filming big ballets that sort of treatment helps convey the storyline more clearly and does not detract from the flow of the ballet overall.

I have been lucky to work several times with the director, Ross MacGibbon, on several BBC recordings of my productions of the classics and *Swan Lake* for Royal Swedish Ballet. As a former dancer, Ross understands exactly how a classical ballet is constructed and what for a viewer on a TV or cinema screen is important to see. He knows intuitively which way the choreography is going to move, to the extent that he can reduce the number of camera rehearsals when filming productions from Covent Garden, especially if he has filmed them before. Ross flatters me when he says the narrative in my productions is always clear which makes the filming easy for him. He knows my productions inside out, and having worked so closely with him the rapport we have built up means that I can happily trust him to interpret them on film knowing that he is making choices that I will be happy with. Which said, we do still have a few tussles over when to cut from one shot to another. Ross was also responsible for the live film which was screened concurrently with the actual action of Birmingham Royal Ballet's performances of *The Nutcracker*, staged at the O2 centre in 2011. The film was projected over the stage on a huge screen, as in such a cavernous venue the audience is seated a long way from the action. The simultaneous film was designed to act as an embellishment to the happenings onstage, acting as a prompt for the audience of key narrative details. Ross and I talked at length about what we wanted to emphasise. I did not want to alienate those who simply wanted to watch the stage. In essence the film showed what the audience should be watching and so cut from shot to shot less frequently than if this had been a conventional TV broadcast. The idea was to allow the audience at the O2 to concentrate on the stage but be able to look at the screen at key moments to involve them more with the story. That was the ambition, but I have to say I am not convinced we achieved that. I could never decide what was the more dominant presence, the live action or the film above it.

The same distraction occurs when choreographers deliberately choose to incorporate film into their works. I find that even with established choreographers, film frequently upstages their choreography, dominating it to such an extent that what the choreographer is trying to express in movement, their response to the music, gets lost. The results are only magnified when filmed or broadcast. But I do like big screen live relays in cinemas. They are marvellous for seeing the detail of a performance, and some people do tell me that it is now their preferred way of watching ballet. I hope cinema broadcasts bring in new audiences to ballet. I understand that screenings are often full but equally they are frequently ill-attended too on other occasions. What market research exists is not conclusive. According to the Royal Ballet, when my Covent Garden *Giselle* was screened during the 2013–14 season, a worldwide audience of 57,000 people saw it in cinemas, a similar figure to the 56,000 people internationally who saw *The Nutcracker* broadcast that season. I am faithfully assured that these attendance figures are higher than for earlier broadcasts, but given that these broadcasts go to over 1,500 cinemas in more than 35 countries, these audience numbers are not huge. I cannot help but think that some data is lacking. Also lacking is any market research about how many people are drawn to attend a live ballet performance in the theatre after having experienced a cinema broadcast. Cinema is a great populariser of course and I hope broadcasts do make stage performances accessible to people more generally. In turn, I hope this tempts more people to attend the theatre to watch ballet and dance, but currently it strikes me that audiences for live and screened performances seem to exist in isolation from each other.

Working in television influenced how I worked subsequently in the theatre. Doing something different helps you review your own specialism. What is essential is how to make an impact. On screen, the camera selects what you look at, but what is important in the theatre is that the choreographer or producer guides the audience so that they concentrate on what is most important and do not get distracted. It was certainly a useful ability to have acquired when I came to undertake the many productions of big classical ballets that occupied such a large part of my later career.

CHAPTER 4

John Cranko – Germany calling

J OHN CRANKO HAD a great influence on my life. I cannot over-
estimate his importance to the development of my career. It was John
who gave me confidence and encouraged me to try my hand at choreography. John was best man at my wedding in August 1954. Although we
were good friends, ours was ultimately a professional relationship. John
was really only interested in the present. Once a new work was finished
he tended to neglect previous collaborators but he did love it when past
colleagues turned up to performances. However, he always demanded
that his dancers gave 100 percent to him and his ballets. If there was
even the slightest disinterest shown by a dancer, John had no hesitation
in soon replacing them.

We first came across each other at St James's Ballet in 1948 where John
had been invited by Alan Carter to create a ballet for this newly formed
company, not long after John had arrived in London from South Africa
in 1946. Right from this very first meeting with Peggy van Praagh, ballet
mistress at Sadler's Wells Theatre Ballet, he had announced his intention
of becoming a choreographer. John was never a very good dancer, rather
awkward in fact, but at Covent Garden he was a courtier in the original
cast of Frederick Ashton's *Cinderella*, the first full-length English ballet to
be created just before Christmas 1948. John also gained stage experience
dancing small roles in *Giselle*, *Checkmate*, *Job*, as well as in *La Boutique
fantasque* and *Le Tricorne*. These last two ballets had a great influence on
John when Léonide Massine staged them. By then he had already started
to choreograph himself. From South Africa he brought with him his very

popular *Tritsch-Tratsch Polka*, a flirtation between two sailors and a saucy girl, originally made for University of Cape Town Ballet, today's Cape Town City Ballet. In London he choreographed *Children's Corner* first for the Royal Academy of Dance and later restaged it for Sadler's Wells Theatre Ballet. For St James's Ballet he made *School for Nightingales*, in which he gave me a lovely part. John and I got on well from the start.

Those were formative days. In the early 1950s several American ballet companies performed in London. I saw New York City Ballet's first season at Covent Garden which was considered by many to be something of a flop but it made a big impression on me. I saw George Balanchine's *Serenade*, *Symphony in C* and the humorous *Bourrée Fantasque* for the first time. I also saw a very different sort of Ashton ballet than I was used to, his *Illuminations*, created in New York, as well as Jerome Robbins' bluesy *Interplay*. In 1953 I saw American National Ballet Theatre, as it was then called, when they came to London. Their repertoire included Balanchine's *Theme and Variations* with Alicia Alonso, *Fall River Legend* by Agnes de Mille and *Pillar of Fire* by Antony Tudor. I was impressed by the power of communication that American dancers had. The way they registered over the footlights, the whole jazz thing, impressed me. The Americans had the confidence to do what we would have liked but never dared. They were not nearly as classical as British dancers of the day, in some ways they were quite crude, but they had more powerful techniques and above all, virtuosity. The way in which American dancers, male and female, performed was very sexy, lovely to watch and enjoy. The same was true too when later I saw Robbins' own company, Ballets: USA, in London. I was struck by how American choreographers, particularly Robbins, could take contemporary, everyday subjects as the basis for dance. That was a different way of looking at classical ballet and was very exciting, as the American musicals I saw in the post-war years had been too. All of this contributed to the sense of dissatisfaction I was feeling with my career with Sadler's Wells Theatre Ballet, so by 1951 I had decided to return to Kurt Jooss' company. Before my new contract with them started I had a two-month gap to fill. Three extraordinary things happened.

First, both John Cranko and Peter Darrell offered me work. Peter was a young choreographer starting to make his mark, but try as he might he could not get Ninette de Valois to trust him with a commission for

Sadler's Wells. Undeterred, during the early 1950s Peter made his first ballets at the Mercury theatre in Notting Hill. It was home of Ballet Rambert and housed too the Ballet Workshop, a club that gave many opportunities to young, and not so young, choreographers. It was run by one of Marie Rambert's daughters, Angela, who was married to David Ellis, a dancer in the company. From those days I can recall pieces by Michael Charnley who had danced with Ballets Jooss during the war when I was an apprentice there. The Mercury had a minute stage, about 15 feet square, which was very good for small dramatic works without too much dancing. I was cast as a mad murderer in Peter's version of Edgar Allan Poe's story *The Telltale Heart*. Peter got Kenneth MacMillan to design the costumes. This was before Kenneth had become established as a choreographer and was trying his hand at all parts of creating a ballet. He renamed himself Kenneth Aadams in a jokey attempt to get his name higher up the credits which were organised alphabetically.

The second piece of extraordinary luck I had was that John Cranko had been asked to put on a week of dance in Henley-on-Thames and he invited me to be one of the group. The artists John Piper and Osbert Lancaster both lived locally and wanted to raise money to save the town's Kenton theatre which was threatened with closure. John agreed to find some dancers and put a show together. Osbert had just designed John's ballet *Bonne-Bouche* at Covent Garden, for which he slyly juxtaposed the fashionable world of Kensington in 1910 with the perils of the African jungle. Piper too had designed a ballet for John the year before. This was *Harlequin in April* to a new score by Richard Arnell, a composer who had a considerable reputation at that period, having composed *The Great Detective* for Margaret Dale as well as another ballet for John, *The Angels*. Piper's designs for *Harlequin in April* were inspired by the horrendous fire that occurred in Hanley, Stoke-on-Trent, in 1949 when the theatre burned to the ground. The charred frame of the proscenium arch, just as much as Piper's experiences as a war artist, influenced him when he came to design John's ballet in 1951. That was the year that Piper acquired the lease for the theatre in Henley. It dated from 1805 and was the fourth oldest working theatre in the country but it was under threat of conversion into a warehouse. Subsequently, after our successful attempts at fundraising, Piper redesigned and improved its interior. The auditorium was papered in the same regency red strip as the Royal Opera House in London. A newly added green groom was decorated with bright green paper. Those weeks in summer 1952 turned out to be probably the most exciting of my life – for the third significant occurrence. It was there that I met Sonya, who, within a couple of years, was to become my wife.

I had already seen Sonya the summer before, onstage at the Mercury dancing with Peter Darrell in his first ballet, *Midsummer Watch*, a rustic pastorale. I had wanted to say hello to her then but those sessions were so short with barely enough time to get a piece lit and set onstage. However, it was not so long before we met properly when rehearsals started for John's Henley season. He had come across Sonya earlier that year when – as what the cast list called the première danseuse – she had danced his choreography for *Aida* at Covent Garden. She was in fact the only dancer and John's exhausting dances nearly killed her. Although I did not realise it, I had seen Sonya onstage during my earliest days of watching ballet in 1943. She had been a member of Lydia Kyasht's company, the Russian Ballet de la Jeunesse Anglaise. Sonya had danced in *Les Sylphides* and did duty as various court ladies in *Sylvia*, *Caisse-Noisette* and a *Cinderella* set to the music of Giuseppe Verdi in versions by Kyasht's daughter, another Lydia. In those days Sonya shared digs with Anne Woolliams who was known to throw her toast across the room if it was soggy and did not come up to scratch.

John, of course, I knew already. I enjoyed dancing in his ballets at Sadler's Wells, where he was resident choreographer. Some of my favourite roles were in his new generation of contemporary works. They appealed for their sense of theatricality. I was one of the dotty sailors and later Captain Belaye in *Pineapple Poll*. In the tragic *Sea Change* I was first one of the doomed sailors and subsequently the captain. I appeared in John's version of *Beauty and the Beast* many times partnering various beauties – Svetlana Beriosova, Patricia Miller, Annette Page and Maryon Lane among them. Later I created Captain Adoncino and was second cast for the clown Moondog, a role created by Kenneth MacMillan, in John's ballet *The Lady and the Fool*.

Kenneth was another of the six dancers that John recruited for the Henley season that July. He was then dancing as a soloist at Covent Garden and was very much regarded as a dancer to look out for. He seemed to excel in featured roles rather than supporting ones when he appeared to feed off the extra audience attention that he was receiving. However fluent Kenneth's dancing was – and the expectation was that he would become a principal – the truth was that he was suffering badly from performance nerves. John thought that this season away from the limelight would help him. Kenneth had already started to choreograph and John was very encouraging. He was marvellous at inspiring people to get the best out of them. It was really John, not Ninette de Valois who tends to receive all the credit, who paved the way for Kenneth to develop his extraordinary talent as a choreographer. It was John who gave Kenneth the idea for his ballet, *House of Birds*, based on the Grimm fairy tale, *Jorinda and Joringel*, although it was Madam who produced it in May 1955. John was going to do it himself but then decided it would be a good piece for Kenneth. How right he was, for it brought out the rather macabre and frightening aspect of Kenneth's work, about a witch who entraps young people and changes them into birds. It showed how masterly he was when tackling a narrative work. Steps, ideas and choreographic invention seemed to flow out of Kenneth, and within two years in the mid-1950s he had created six highly successful works.

The other dancers at Henley included Yvonne Cartier whom I knew from Sadler's Wells. She became a brilliant mime artist and teacher after repeated injuries to one of her feet that could not be operated on. Maggie Scott from Australia, where she returned as director of the Australian School of Ballet for which she receive the DBE, was there, as was Geoffrey Webb whom I knew from Metropolitan Ballet. He was terribly camp, outrageously funny. He became well known for his comedy roles, particularly in the pantomime *Aladdin* at the London Coliseum when as an understudy he replaced Bob Monkhouse in the lead and enjoyed much more success in the part. For our Henley season John Lanchbery arranged most of the music and Osbert Lancaster painted a smaller version of his backcloth for *Pineapple Poll*. Other décor was improvised from what could be found in a scrapyard behind the theatre, although Piper and his wife, Myfanwy, painted their design for one of Cranko's new works, simply called *Dancing*. The backcloth was predominantly grey and black, with shapes in yellow, purple, blue and red suggesting such objects as a wind-up gramophone, piano keyboard, pillar and ladder. Piper allowed me into his studio to watch him paint. This was a revelation. When Myfanwy queried whether he had intended to paint a particular tree-trunk pink I discovered that Piper had a form of red/green colour blindness. He had turned this to great advantage as it made his colour combinations unique. At that time I sometimes painted and told him I had the same difficulty. Piper admitted he often needed help sorting out his palette and relied on Myfanwy who would always point out a pink tree or the like. I adored them both. Piper was incredibly encouraging and tried to get me to continue painting, but I knew that I did not have any sort of real talent. Later I also discovered that he made pottery which was something that Sonya and I had been doing for some time too. He showed me how he mixed some of his glazes, which made a huge difference to our work. He went in for fairly crude shapes covered with strong primary colours, completely different from our more traditional and rather unoriginal shapes.

While we were at Henley, Myfanwy was working on the libretto for Benjamin Britten's next opera *The Turn of the Screw* and the composer was the Pipers' guest, but she still ensured we were all comfortable, cooking meals and arranging for us all to stay in an empty farmhouse on a nearby estate, Stonor Park, owned by a friend, Lord Camoys. I remember we shared the house with an abundance of moths and mosquitoes. I was the only one who knew how to manage the Aga cooker but I did become exasperated that nobody else was doing anything to help. I may have been chief cook but I was determined not to become bottle washer too. I told Kenneth and Geoffrey if they could at least take out the rubbish ready for collection by the bin wagon. 'Yes sir, yes sir,' they said as they trotted out with the refuse. They returned empty handed, telling me they had done what I had asked. When I opened the front door of the house I discovered that their rubbish was strewn all over the front step. Such is the life of a ballet master! But we were a good group together. True, Maggie and Sonya did not get on, not helped by the fact that I was interested in Sonya, not Maggie. Sonya was always on the phone early in the morning to her mother – and Sonya could boom. Maggie shouted down, 'Will that girl shut up! That voice is driving us all mad.' Maggie's husband, Dick Denton, was with her. He was keen on any girl that would have him – I'm not sure with what success. There were lots of parties, lots of goings-on. Geoffrey was very keen on Denholm Elliot, Sonya's boyfriend at the time. Kenneth was also mad about Denholm.

Altogether during that Henley season, although I was dancing 16 performances in practically every ballet with a broken toe sustained during rehearsals and coping with being company teacher and ballet master, I was in seventh heaven. The highlight was *Paso Doble* that John created for Sonya and me. Danced to traditional Spanish music, we were both dressed as boys, though Sonya was on pointe, all very tongue in cheek and erotic. We adored it and it brought us very close. Of John's other new works, *Dancing* turned out to be very beautiful. It was danced by Kenneth and Sonya plus two supporting couples, with music by George Shearing, the jazz pianist. It was successful enough to be screened on TV that September. John's other new ballet was *The Forgotten Room* which was danced to Schubert. Maggie was a woman engrossed in a book who becomes carried away by its events. I was the man in the story that she was reading. Fiction overtakes reality and the ballet ended with Maggie dead in her chair.

In comparison, *L'après midi d'Emily Wigginbotham* was a comedy tour de force for Maggie, as a very prim woman buttoned up in a sensible suit and shoes, at the mercy of her emotions as she confronted a statue of a decadent faun in an art gallery. *Umbrellas*, with music by Lanchbery, featured Geoffrey and Yvonne. She also danced John's *Beauty and the Beast* pas de deux with me. With Maggie as Blanche, Sonya as Mrs Dimple and Kenneth as Captain Belaye, the programme was completed by the pas de trois from *Pineapple Poll*. The season was so successful that it was extended for a further week. Publicity on the gossip pages of such newspapers as *The Daily Express*, for which Lancaster was the cartoonist, had evidently paid off. Of course Piper and Lancaster had a big following and people came down from London to see the show. After one performance Piper gave a party in his studio lit with candles, to which the London crowd all came and ate peaches soaked in brandy. Audiences also included the great and the good from Berkshire. The Henley locals came too. We did not care who came, so long as we had an audience and raised some money for the theatre. Our audiences may have been impressed but not so John's pet miniature dachshund Clytemnestra, or Clytie for short. She had beautiful eyes and pouting lips. One night mid-performance she wandered onstage, but having found nothing to interest her there, wandered off again. She settled herself in someone's lap in the auditorium. Clytemnestra's story was a tragic one. She was adorable but became a compulsive eater and got fatter and fatter. One day John went out having accidentally left the fridge door open. It was filled with sausages, butter and lots of other food. He came back to a terrible mess. Clytie had not been able to resist and devoured everything there was, causing her stomach to burst. She died as a result.

Enough money was made to save the theatre and it is still running some 60 years later. Britten asked Cranko that we repeat the programme at his festival at Aldeburgh the following summer. By then John had provided dances for another production at Henley, a staging of *Alice Through the Looking Glass* by Felicity Douglas designed by Kenneth Rowell. John's choreography was recognised as beautifully organised with minimum effort and maximum effect. It went on to transfer into the West End with Margaret Rutherford. Less happily, just before our season at the Jubilee hall in Aldeburgh, John had choreographed the dance scenes for Britten's coronation opera *Gloriana* at Covent Garden, unveiled in front of Elizabeth II and massed ranks of royalty and the establishment. The opera received a distinctly frosty reaction, which may have been the reason why Britten, and his partner Peter Pears, were distinctly cool towards us all during our time in Aldeburgh. Britten came nowhere near John although three dances from *Gloriana* filled a gap on the bill when a new piece by Kenneth did not materialise. He did dance the volta from *Gloriana* with Maggie Scott which they found to be one of the hardest things they had ever done. John's intricate footwork was absolutely exhausting. Otherwise the programme was largely the same as at Henley. George Shearing's Quintet played live for *Dancing*. Sonya and I reprised *Paso Doble*. I think it was the success of both these seasons that led John to ask me to become his ballet master in Stuttgart in 1961.

Just as I was about to sign a three-year contract to become a producer with the BBC I received a phone call from John. That John called was not in itself surprise. We had continued as friends and to work together. At the invitation of Kathleen Crofton of the London Ballet Circle he was asked to present an evening of new dance pieces at the Fortune theatre in September 1955. John made *Dances without Steps* with music by Alfredo Casella and *Corps, Cous, Coudes et Coeur* set to Stravinsky. Peter Darrell and Rupert Doone each made new pieces. The other work was a revival of a one-act ballet by Lev Ivanov, *The Magic Flute*, which Anna Pavlova had taken into her repertoire. I danced the principal male role of Luc.

I was pleased to be in it as I did not often get a leading role. John redid the ballet quickly. That is why I liked John. He got on with things. There was never a dull moment with him. I was always amazed at his facility. Sometimes the results were dreadful, sometimes wonderful. When in December that year John collaborated with the composer John Addison on his hugely popular revue, *Cranks*, he used to try out material for it on me to see whether it was good enough to include.

Addison also wrote the music for another show for which John wrote the book and lyrics. This was *Keep Your Hair On!* at the Apollo theatre in February 1958. It was definitely not John's finest hour. Set in a hairdressing salon, with costumes by Desmond Heeley, the set consisted of giant photographic blow-ups of society figures taken by Tony Armstrong Jones who later was married to Princess Margaret. I saw it at the dress rehearsal. It really was awful, with one of the cast, Erik Mørk, for some reason going round with a suitcase of butterflies. On the first night, the end of the show was drowned out by booing and an angry crowd gathered outside the stage door after the curtain came down. Some of the cast, which also included Rachel Roberts and Barbara Windsor, judged it safer to make their exit through the front of the theatre. Despite rewrites and changes the show survived for only 20 performances. Interviewed in the press soon after, John was resilient but unguardedly complained that the way ballet was produced in Britain was a hundred years behind the times.

When John called that evening in July 1961 he announced that he wanted me to go to Stuttgart to cast an eye over the company of which he had become director that January. It was very clear that he could not cope with everything and wanted me to become his ballet master. When I told him I was about to begin a career in television as a producer and director he shrugged it off, saying 'You belong in the theatre. Don't waste your time on television. At least come over for a few days and see what I am offering you.' John actually showed great insight into my character. I had learned already that the process of making television programmes had none of the excitement of live theatre. Half of it happens in the office where you worked out your filming script. So off to Stuttgart I went for three days but – as I felt needed, wanted and loved – I actually ended up staying for three weeks during the annual ballet festival. When I arrived, John announced he was short of dancers as he had just given Robert de Warren, an established dancer there, notice for undermining his authority. John had cast de Warren to appear as one of the four princes in *The Sleeping Beauty*. De Warren had refused. John told him that if he required de Warren to go on as a prince then he would do so. He had to, as stipulated by the terms of his contract. De Warren again refused, so John simply sacked him, telling him never to return to the company. It cost a lot of money to terminate his contract but it sent a strong signal to the rest of the company. John, however, was left short of numbers. He told me there was only one solution: I would have to help out and perform. By then I had not done class nor danced for about three years, and here I was, being expected to perform the pas de deux from MacMillan's *Solitaire*, the pas de six from John's *The Prince of the Pagodas* as well as a prince in the rose adagio in *The Sleeping Beauty*. I showed John how plump I had become. Unimpressed, he told me I had a week to get back into shape so I could climb into tights and a jockstrap – that ghastly thing that packs your bits together between your legs in an attempt to make them look tidy. Eventually I agreed to perform on this occasion but never again if I were to come to Stuttgart as ballet master. The great company friend Fritz Höver and his partner Uli who was a doctor all helped with some injections and something to give me some energy but they could not reduce my flab. Somehow I coped. I even did a performance with the company at the palace at Ludwigsburg, a smaller copy of Versailles with a beautiful baroque theatre. And of course when I did return to Stuttgart later I ended up doing character roles like Creon in John's *Antigone*, Friar Laurence in *Romeo and Juliet* and the king in *Sleeping Beauty*. John was very persuasive.

Nothing was hidden from me during my initial visit. I was seeing the company as it really was. I had in fact visited Stuttgart before, shortly after the war ended, with my sister, Joan. She was searching for a German school friend who had been forced to return home with her family when war broke out. I was en route to Italy to visit a friend I had met in Paris during a Ballets Jooss tour in 1946. My sister and I were shocked at the state Stuttgart was in, a mess of ruins and temporary buildings, as the city had been badly bombed during the final phases of the war. There was hardly any public transport so we had to walk for miles through the most awful wreckage. Luckily my sister could speak German well so we could get directions from passers-by. It took hours to find the street, or what remained of it, only to be informed at the local police station that the house had been totally destroyed, with no survivors. A few old parts of the city survived but it had largely been flattened during wartime. By 1960, when I responded to John's invitation, it had mostly been rebuilt if only in a very functional way, but I soon decided Stuttgart was where I wanted to be. The opera house was relatively new, built in the 20th century, and had survived the bombing. It is quite beautifully situated, in a park with an attractive lake and fountain.

There was a sense of life and vitality about Stuttgart. To go there was the right decision – it changed my life – but first I had to talk to Sonya. I knew she would not want to go. It would mean leaving her elderly mother and a large circle of friends in London. Sonya had worked hard to establish her career. After training with Audrey de Vos and performing with Lydia Kyasht's company during the war, Sonya started touring aged 14, with her mother sometimes acting as her chaperone. She appeared in a Christmas show in 1946 at the Royal Court theatre in Liverpool, *Goody Two Shoes*. A year later she was in a television film of Caryl Brahms' novel, *A Bullet at the Ballet*, which featured a young Donald Sinden in a leading role. In January 1948 Sonya performed a dance number with John Gregory in a television variety show, *New To You*, broadcast live from Alexandra Palace, which was also the occasion of Bob Monkhouse's television debut.

After John Cranko's seasons at Henley, Sonya joined Sadler's Wells Theatre Ballet briefly in February 1953 but it was not an environment that she particularly liked. Instead she found work in films. Sonya played Ah Mov in *The Planter's Wife* with Claudette Colbert and Jack Hawkins, set on a Malaysian rubber plantation. Television work for Sonya included episodes of the *Colonel March of Scotland Yard* series directed by Donald Ginsberg. Some of these were released as a compilation for the cinema. John Lanchbery did the music. Sonya's name was well down the cast list which was headed by Boris Karloff. What Sonya really loved was performing in the West End where she became well known in musicals.

By the time I was considering what to do about Stuttgart, Sonya was still dancing and really wanted to continue her career. Although she was frequently cast in exotic or oriental roles, this was something that Sonya did not mind. She loved performing and these parts did display her great beauty and charm. Sonya had enjoyed great success dancing the lead in Jerome Robbins' ballet sequences in *The King and I* at Drury Lane and a year later in 1954 she was a hit in the principal role as the geisha in *Tea*

House of the August Moon at Her Majesty's theatre when she took over from Tsai Chin.

On television in October 1957 Sonya played the title role of Cio Cio San in a BBC production of Giacomo Puccini's Japan-inspired opera *Madama Butterfly*. The cast consisted of performers who looked right physically for their roles, so although Sonya did not sing during the actual filming, she had spent months learning to mime the words. All the nuances of the role were seen, often in close-up. Both the performers and singers went out live from different studios. Nobody really knew how to film opera then but George Foa directed this production brilliantly. It was really beautiful and worked wonderfully even though Sonya and her singer double, Joyce Gartside, both twice made the same mistake at the same time but nobody noticed. Sonya's performance was acclaimed. By 1960, when Sonya next appeared in the West End in Rodgers and Hammerstein's *The Flower Drum Song* at the Palace theatre, she had become a mother following the birth of our children. In a dream sequence, a 15-minute ballet in the show, Sonya danced Mei li, a mail-order bride among immigrants in San Francisco's Chinatown. The Broadway production had been directed by Gene Kelly but in London it was replicated by Jerome Whyte. I was dance captain. The show had a record advance in ticket sales matched only by *My Fair Lady* two years earlier, but it was not Rodgers and Hammerstein's best. The critic Kenneth Tynan referred to it as a world of woozie song, punning on *The World of Suzie Wong*, another show of that era. Still, the production ran for nearly 500 performances, and eight shows a week is tough going but I consider it a very good training. You learn how to communicate with the audience and I have always tried to encourage choreographers to gain experience working in commercial theatre, as Cranko, Frederick Ashton and Ninette de Valois all did, and as Christopher Wheeldon is doing now. For me this was an important stage in my career as it was different from what I had experienced with ballet. But I knew the importance of what John was proposing in Stuttgart and I knew too that John adored Sonya. Having created the pas de deux for her at Henley, might not there be opportunities for Sonya in Germany too? Of course we had our children to consider too, but we need not worry just yet about their education as they were aged only two and four.

For me this was a wonderful opportunity: I was desperate to go. I felt I had not got anywhere in Britain. I was 30-something. I had not been happy with Sadler's Wells Theatre Ballet and left the company, again, in 1958. That September I was with the short-lived Edinburgh International Ballet, working as a dancer and assistant ballet master. Peggy van Praagh was its director and Charles Mackerras was music director. Supported by money from the Arts Council, the company had the lofty aim of presenting 12 new ballets at the Empire theatre during the three weeks of the 1958 festival, all with different choreographers, me included. I produced *The Great Peacock* about a moth of that name derived from the description by the entomologist Henri Fabre. I had heard some music by Humphrey Searle, his *Variations and Finale*, and I had asked him to expand it into a ballet. His music was dramatic but serial in form, dissonant and oddly phrased – and hence difficult for dancers, so he had to help them with counts. However, the ballet, choreographed on Claudia Algeranova and David Poole, was well received on the whole, although I was accused in *The Dancing Times* as lacking in imagination, having created a biology lesson rather than a ballet.

The others creating works for the festival were a roll-call of choreographers working at the time: Walter Gore created *Night and Silence*, a brilliant dance drama with music by Bach, for his wife Paula Hinton, who danced it with David Poole. It was the hit of the season. Andrée Howard did *La Belle dame sans merci* which was later adopted by the Royal Ballet, and John Cranko's *Secrets*, to Poulenc, was another ballet designed for him by John Piper. It had Henning Kronstam, the original Romeo in Ashton's version of the ballet, and Carla Fracci, John's Juliet in his first staging for La Scala, Milan, earlier that summer, as the husband and wife. John Taras did *Octet*, Dimitri Parlić made *Dreams*; George Skibine, *Fâcheuses rencontres*; Wendy Toye, *Concerto for Dancers* and Birgit Culberg, *Circle of Love*. Alan Carter's *Changements de pieds* shared a triple-bill with my ballet and Deryck Mendel made *Seventh Sacrament*. By some miracle all the ballets went on as advertised.

Noël Goodwin, writing in *Dance and Dancers* that October, considered me something of a twelfth man among this collection of choreographers, but praised *The Great Peacock* as vivid and poignant. My choreography was considered rough and immature but apparently it showed considerable development over *A Blue Rose* which I had made at Covent Garden the year before. Goodwin considered I had put some more senior choreographers to shame and was developing into a talent to be reckoned with. A London season was to follow our appearances in Edinburgh, but only four days before we were due to open at Sadler's Wells and with less than 5 percent of tickets sold, the season was pulled. Instead we set off on an international tour that took in Holland, Switzerland and Yugoslavia. Michael Frostick was our impresario but he behaved as if he was the artistic director, spending much of the company's money on grand dinners before we had opened. The reality was that he did not have any proper contacts for securing suitable bookings and venues. The cancelled season in London had taught him nothing. We were only an average success. The performances in Zurich were just about all right, but by the time we moved on to Yugoslavia, then under a communist regime, the money had run out, Frostick having wined and dined too many people. The venue where we were performing would not pay over our share of receipts and we were told we had to give extra performances at other venues. We refused, only to be told that we would be imprisoned if we did not perform. The company was effectively bankrupt. We got together and decided we would run away. Leaving our scenery and costumes behind early one morning, we ran across fields and were literally chased over the border into somewhere, I do not think any of us knew where we were, but somewhere somehow we managed to find a hotel and help from the British consulate. When we finally made it back to Britain, the orchestra had their instruments impounded by customs as collateral for creditors.

Western Theatre Ballet was another company with which I had tried to establish myself. It had been established in 1957 by Elizabeth West as managing director, with Peter Darrell as artistic director and principal choreographer. It was based in Bristol but it soon became evident that it needed to tour more widely than the south west to find enough of an audience. The critic Clive Barnes said the company's history was more chequered than a chess board and its progress had more downs than ups. Bravely the band of 12 dancers put on a repertoire exclusively of new works. Although Barnes complained that the repertoire consisted of ballets that regional audiences did not want to see – about a prison break set to Bartok or the H-bomb set to musique concrète – he recognised in West a director cut from the same cloth as de Valois and Marie Rambert. Sadly West's early, unexplained death means that assertion was never tested.

Western Ballet Theatre – which eventually became Scottish Ballet and inspired too the creation of Northern Ballet – was certainly the sort of company where novice choreographers such as me could try out their craft. I was certainly glad of the opportunity to choreograph for them in 1960 when I made *Musical Chairs*, using Sergei Prokofiev's *Musiques d'enfants* which is typically unpredictable with its shifting moods. The ballet was rehearsed at the Chiswick Empire during a tour of Charles Cuvillier's operetta *The Lilac Domino*. West used to hire out her dancers as a package to appear in musicals and pantos as a means of survival and to keep them together. There was no money for a rehearsal pianist nor indeed for a rehearsal room. I had to make do with a recording on a spool-to-spool wire recorder in the wings which was a nightmare to rewind to find the right section of the score when we went back over a certain section in rehearsal. Wire recorders made a magnetic sound recording on thin steel or stainless steel wire, all pre-digital of course. Nor was the luxury of rehearsing onstage terribly helpful as most of it was filled with the set for *The Lilac Domino* with its preponderance of stair-cases and mezzanine levels. Such were the jobs that you took on when trying to get established – it really was a case of just getting on with it.

Musical Chairs had its first performance at the Hanley theatre, Stoke, long rebuilt after the fire there some ten years before. It was considered one of Moss Empires' better venues for dance audiences at that time. My programme note suggested that *Musical Chairs* was about a group of young people in the Paris of the impressionist painters. Clive Barnes thought differently – more a case of eight people in a park without the first idea of the rules of musical chairs. He did like what he called the rather fauvist designs by Kenneth Rowell but thought my ballet was insubstantial, light-hearted and light-headed, sporadically interest-ing but choreographically too weak to stand up for itself. Well, he was wrong. It was well received, well danced and had a good life. Barnes was as dismissive as Darrell's *Bal de la victoire* on the same programme although by then he was a much more practised choreographer than me.

Peter was profligate in his ideas for ballets, often with contemporary subject matter, but as with his dancing his ideas were frequently more exciting than the choreography he produced. Later I choreographed another ballet for Western Theatre Ballet using a Haydn symphony and called it *A Ballet to this Music* – I could not think of a better title. The premiere was in Helsinki but when the ballet was later toured in Britain I was encouraged by some of the critical feedback at least. Barnes on this occasion was somewhat kinder. He thought *A Ballet to this Music* was a sound opening ballet, one that was worth its weight in sylphides by giving the dancers something technically challenging to do with choreography that demanded considerable ingenuity and charm. He flattered me by describing me, in many ways, as the most fluent of Britain's younger choreographers – and attributed that to the fact that I was an established teacher. As Peter Darrell's career and my own developed in different directions and we both became more established in our respective companies I did not see much of Peter's later works. I do recall once visiting him at his home in Glasgow where a highly promiscuous rabbit ran free and enjoyed humping people's feet, so long as the feet were male of course.

Otherwise in the late 1950s I was teaching and doing a certain amount of choreography for TV and musicals including *Gentlemen's Pastime* based on the Pygmalion story at the Players' theatre in March 1958. The stage there was tiny, even smaller than that at the Mercury. I also arranged the dances in *A Midsummer Night's Dream* at the Old Vic in December 1960, directed by Michael Langham who was not really right for the play. The cast loathed him. Barbara Leigh-Hunt, playing Helena, later said the rehearsals for *Dream* had been so bloody they were amazed they heard laughter on the first night. They had forgotten they were in a comedy. Nevertheless, Alec McCowen was a wonderful Oberon, and Tom Courtenay was Puck. The cast also included Judi Dench, early in her career. She generally got good reviews as Hermia but one critic said she would never have a career with the face she had. With comments like that it was fortunate nobody noticed my choreography. Thea Musgrave had composed music that was all rather contemporary and difficult. It floored me and my little dances for the fairies. Judi had just had enormous success as Juliet with John Stride as her Romeo in Franco Zeffirelli's production there – for which I did not arrange the dances. Those were done by Pirmin Trecu. He was a naughty boy, cheeky, known at Sadler's Wells for giving lip to Peggy van Praagh in front of the company, and in his private life too which is how he knew Zeffirelli. *The Tempest* was another play I did do at the Old Vic, but in the version reworked by John Dryden and William Davenant incorporating music by Henry Purcell. They added extra characters including a wife for Caliban, played by Joss

Ackland, which complicated things. I had a cast of about 14 dancers, including Yemaiel Oved from my ballet group at Sadler's Wells Opera, and six singers to animate as miscellaneous tritons, nereids, devils, spirits and winds. In the masque, while Charles West was standing centre stage as Neptune, his big toe wiggled up and down in time to the music, to the amusement of everybody else. While some critics thought that Dryden's version explained certain illogicalities in Shakespeare's original, the production was not that popular. One critic suggested that the Old Vic should cancel school groups from attending this *Tempest*, directed by Douglas Seale, as it was certain to put them off Shakespeare and Dryden in equal measure.

It was all experience, but fundamentally I knew I was young enough to try something new, which made me keen to move to Stuttgart. I still had the energy. From what I had seen, I liked Stuttgart. I was impressed by everybody there and really felt I could work there and handle the job having done some ballet mastering at Henley and for Sadler's Wells Opera. For me, being ballet master in a vibrant and exciting company was a wonderful alternative to working for the BBC, but I knew I was indulging myself having been so excited during my initial visit to see John. Taking the family to Stuttgart was really difficult. I came to feel guilty about asking Sonya to go and trying to convince my parents that I was doing the right thing by her and for our family. I think I managed to cover up my feelings of insecurity quite well, but actually I was very nervous. In those days there was all the carry-on and red tape about going to work abroad, especially Germany, involving endless queuing. It was enough to put anyone off – letting our house, visas, a work permit for me, insurance, banking arrangements, union issues. Finally we packed our Bedford van full of everything. We even took the fridge, I remember, I do not really know why. I had feelings of great insecurity about bringing Sonya to an unknown place with a strange language with no friends or relations to help her make a new life. We allowed three days to drive to Stuttgart, stopping at places in France and Germany en route. The Schwarzwald, the Black Forest area, was lovely, but Sonya could not appreciate it. The nearer to Stuttgart we got, the quieter she became. I could tell that she was thinking, 'With Peter working, and me alone, half-Japanese, what will I do?'

There were many problems to solve in Stuttgart which made everything challenging and raw. This was probably the most creative period of my life. I was ballet master, with John as my director, but I also had to teach. John was a pioneer so there was always a feeling of danger in the air. He was determined to prove the value of classical ballet. The previous ballet director, Nicholas Beriosov, had tried something similar, but despite some good productions, things had not worked out well. At the suggestion of Beriosov's daughter, Svetlana Beriosova, he had invited Cranko to stage his *Prince of the Pagodas* in Stuttgart in November 1960; Svetlana created the role of Belle Rose at its London premiere in 1957. This prompted Walter Erich Schäfer, director of the Stuttgart opera house, to appoint Cranko in place of Beriosov, mid-season. John was excited to have his own company, particularly after a year in London when he had not created any new ballets, but when I joined the company, every day there seemed to be a new problem and more tears. The dancers were mostly warm and welcoming, but I soon became aware of a certain undercurrent of hostility which was mainly due to the fact that John had given quite a few dancers notice. Some of the dancers he had inherited were good, some dreadful. One that nobody liked was the ballerina, Xenia Pally. She was French and liked to rule the roost. Xenia had got off to a bad start with John when she made it clear that she expected him to change the choreography for Belle Rose, the role she was dancing in *The Prince of the Pagodas*, to suit her. John, of course, did not comply. All the girls copied Xenia's bad habits. She had dreadful arms and was very mannered, not the true image of a classical ballerina. However, Xenia did have the best fouettés, those famous 32 consecutive turns in *Swan Lake*, I had ever seen. She could have had the best feet too but they had been spoiled by bad training and not working properly. Xenia's self-importance meant that she refused to accept any corrections. She never did class, essential for all ballerinas, nor did she wash her practice clothes that often. It was very difficult partnering her in the rose adagio from *The Sleeping Beauty*, the occasion when Robert de Warren had walked out and I was obliged to step in. She wore an elasticated belt with a large claw buckle. When it came to the section of fast pirouettes when she turns in her partner's hands, this buckle could have injured my fingers. I asked her to remove it. She refused. I declined to partner her. Reluctantly she took the belt off. After about six months John was able to get rid of her. She left and went back to Paris and apparently went to pieces.

When the company realised that John was serious about making changes they respected him for that but there were many dramas. It was not an easy time and John was always threatening to leave, mostly because of the unfair bias that favoured the opera company. I could sense that the whole company was waiting to see how I would treat them. I was quite appalled at the standard of some of the dancers but the union ruling was that notice could be given only during the first three months of the season and then only to dancers who had been employed for three years or less, so action had to be taken straight away. Really I was thrown in at the deep end. I was actually rather scared when I started, with so much to do at once, and I could not speak German. Ray Barra, one of the leading principals, was the real backbone of the company. He had been in Stuttgart for many years and did much to help John mould things in the way that he wanted. He was born in America to Spanish parents and had studied in San Francisco and New York but spoke fluent German. He knew all the ins and outs of the theatre, being popular among the opera singers too. Ray was passionate with quite a fiery temper but he was probably the most popular member of the company. He was a typically American extrovert with a wicked sense of humour and a repertoire of really filthy jokes which Kenneth MacMillan absolutely adored when he got to know Ray while working in Stuttgart. He created the principal male roles in *Song of the Earth* and *Las Hermanas* on Ray. For John, Ray was the first Romeo and *Onegin*. When Kenneth went to Berlin as director in 1966 he took Ray with him as ballet master and very much relied on him. Although all started well there, things got very difficult throughout the whole set-up. Ray decided to join John Neumeier in Hamburg in 1973 and worked there for several years before he branched out into a choreographic career himself and as a producer. He did this successfully for several companies including Washington Ballet among others. Ray helped everyone, especially John Cranko. Personally too, Sonya and I benefited from his help in every possible way and our children adored him. Ray now lives in Spain with his partner Maximo, where they have celebrated their 50th anniversary together. I visit them every year and they have become two of my greatest friends.

When John joined Stuttgart he had been given the title of ballet master and had been expected to teach, work with the principals and soloists, take all rehearsal calls and create at least three new programmes each year. Understandably he could not cope with this sort of workload. In any case he was not a good teacher although he was good at rehearsing. That is why he got me over although I was soon to discover there was no money in the budget for my salary. To my great relief a way was found to pay me through the theatre's supporters' organisation. And so it was me who had to teach, rehearse, occasionally choreograph and manage the schedules. In addition John asked me to take responsibility for teaching students too. There was no proper ballet school there then except for a handful of young children who were taught by the assistant ballet mistress, Anneliese Mörike. I got on with her quite well but I needed to. In those days you needed everybody's support. Anneliese was Birgit Keil's first teacher who remembers her warmly, but I could see that, though young, her pupils were already showing signs of bad training. I doubt it would have been possible to find any talent there, though you never can tell at that age. John begged me to take it over. I thought the job was really beyond me as I was already rehearsing the ballet company for three hours each morning and again for another three in the evening, so the prospect of another 90 minutes during the afternoon to teach children seemed too much. Nevertheless I agreed. I had not taught children before but was soon amazed at how much they can pick up quickly and then relearn the same thing in a different way.

This was the beginnings of the John Cranko Schule which Anne Woolliams, who had danced with Sonya in the days of the Russian Ballet de la Jeunesse Anglaise in the 1940s, was to establish later after I had left. As Anne de Mohan, she had danced in *School for Nightingales* which John had created for St James's Ballet and she became assistant ballet mistress there. Anne had a gift for comedy and was a good mimic. She used to visit Sonya in Stuttgart from Essen where she was in charge of the classical syllabus at the school run by Kurt Jooss. Working with him made a great difference to Anne's understanding of movement and influenced how she taught classical ballet. I have to say that I can remember horrible classes given by Anne. She expected her pupils, even company members, to arrive 30 minutes early to warm up thoroughly before they began her barre exercises. I have known her hit a student too. But I was an admirer. Anne was a good teacher. It was through our introduction that she took over the school in Stuttgart. To achieve that meant a big battle with the authorities that was finally won, and now the school is extremely successful.

I also inherited choreographic assignments that John did not want to undertake. I did a revue in London for him in February 1962, *Not to Worry* by Stanley Daniels. It was absolutely awful but the cast did include Prunella Scales who was terribly funny with a natural talent to amuse. I adored her. Years later she took part in a fundraising gala I organised at Sadler's Wells. John also gave me a couple of weeks off when I was asked to work on another musical in London, *Blitz*. It was written by Lionel Bart, then at the height of his fame because of *Oliver!* which was still enjoying its original run of over 2,000 performances. Expectations about *Blitz* were huge. Unfortunately Bart was directing too but he was no director. He seemed to believe in method acting and allowed the cast to develop their parts in whatever way they wanted. Lead singers were lost among the chorus even during their big numbers. There was no focus at all to the staging. I got called in to help by Donald Albery who was producing the show. The pre-London try-out was at the Odeon cinema in Edmonton. When I walked in I could see the cast groan. They had already seen three choreographers come and go. I whipped everything up and sorted it all out, putting the singers centre stage and chorus around the edges so everybody could at least be seen. Everything was being changed by the day. After every performance we all had to troop up to a room at the top of the building to learn about what was being changed next. Albery was very outspoken and he and Bart practically had fist-fights.

Somehow we opened at the Adelphi theatre in May with Princess Margaret in the audience. I only learned later on that once the show was up and running and I was back in Stuttgart the cast changed some of my choreography themselves. I was less than happy but the show actually managed a quite respectable run of about 500 performances. It was well designed to a certain extent by Sean Kenny. The opening was set during wartime in a Tube tunnel, complete with trains running, and in the last scene a bomb hits, bringing down the ceiling. The smoke effects for that had to be controlled, except on the first night the finale took place in a complete fog. You could not see anything. Noël Coward apparently said *Blitz* was twice as loud and twice as long as the real thing. Ian Albery, Donald's son, was stage manager for the show, which was a very difficult one to call, with people on walkie-talkies. Later Ian went to oversee the rebuilding of Sadler's Wells theatre. He received no public recognition for all he did, just a most awful, rather lopsidedly one-eyed portrait hung inside the stage door at the new theatre which gives the impression that he is leering at Ninette de Valois whose portrait is hung adjacent.

As it happened, I worked with Ian on my next show in London. Somehow, in October 1962 I found time to choreograph the musical *Fiorello*. It was by Jerry Bock and was based on the true story of Fiorello LaGuardia, the 1930s American congressman and mayor of New York. I quite enjoyed it. I was not really familiar with musical comedies at the time, so arranging the dances was a bit of a shock. I thought I would be able to rely on how the rehearsal pianist played, but Peter Greenwell, who was at the piano, was looking for a lead from me. The show was all very Jewish and Donald Albery insisted that the dances were authentic. I took myself off to the English Folk Dance and Song Society in Camden to do some research. I got lots of material for the dances and pretended they were all kosher. The try-out was at the Bristol Old Vic which I knew from my days with Sadler's Wells Theatre Ballet. It was a lovely theatre with traditional 18th-century staging effects such as a rolling cannonball along the wooden ceiling above the stalls, used to replicate the sound of thunder, which is still in use. The show was a hit. We loved doing it there, and there was a lovely feeling in the theatre. One number, 'A Little Tin Box', always got an encore. On the strength of the success in Bristol, Donald put the show into the Piccadilly theatre in London, much too big a venue. By now I was back in Stuttgart and did not know about the changes Donald was insisting on. Even the 'Tin Box' number was ruined with an extra verse and chorus. *Fiorello* ran for nearly 800 performances on Broadway. In London we managed only 56. For me personally it was unfortunate, as for the first time, based on the success of *Blitz*, with *Fiorello* I had been placed on a percentage of box office receipts, 0.75 percent to be exact. True, that is not a lot, but it all adds up after time. But not after 56 performances.

During our first two months in Stuttgart, Sonya and I had nowhere to stay so we lived in John's house which was on Botnanger Strasse, a hill outside the city. The company called it the Crystal Palace. All male dancers, whether straight or gay, were given girls' names. John's was Crystal, Ray's was Theda and mine was Renee. Sonya and I had two small rooms; we slept on the floor and could not unpack. It was very difficult, but Herta Zippel, who owned the house, did a lot to help. She was an extraordinary woman. She had lived through the wartime bombings, had suffered but survived those terrible times. She even gave birth to her daughter completely alone as she fled through the flames all around her during an air raid. Herta was more than a housekeeper – she looked after John wonderfully, which he did not always appreciate, failing to turn up for the evening meal that Herta had cooked. Almost invariably he would be out somewhere with somebody. At that same time John could be incredibly good to Herta and her partner, Puppo, a Sicilian. John managed to get him a special contract at the theatre as an apprentice. Puppo was very sensitive and inventive and actually created two remarkable pieces for the Noverre Geselschaft, the company's choreographic group. Sadly Puppo's lack of belief in his abilities, resulting from his early years of incredible poverty, got the better of him, and he took his own life.

Herta's daughter was called Dorothee. She was only 17 at the time, spoke English well, did ballet classes, and John looked after her; he helped her to blossom. He arranged for her to go to England to study painting and stained glass. Five years later Dorothee designed John's production of *Card Game*, designs still used today. One of John's many remarkable qualities was his honesty with dancers and the people around him, although in his excitement he would never overlook their shortcomings. This honesty with dancers could sometimes be hurtful. The main problem was that quite a few of them were unsackable because they had been there longer than three years and had been employed by Nicholas Beriosov. They were not at all to John's taste. Gradually he managed to find employment for them in other areas of the theatre. A case in point was Georgette Tsingurides whom John encouraged to study Benesh notation. It was soon discovered that she had a real gift for it. She successfully completed the course organised by the Benesh Institute in London and has since made a great career for herself as a notator. This was recognised in 2010 when Georgette received the Deutscher Tanzpreis for her great contribution to dance notation over many years and in an honorary membership of the Royal Academy of Dance in London.

Other dancers sought to exploit John. Several years before, in 1955, he had an operation to assist his breathing and to have his prominent nose reshaped. This was just before he went to France to create a new ballet based on Offenbach's comic opera *La Belle Hélène* for the Paris Opéra Ballet. When he returned, flushed with success, he confided in me that since the operation his life had changed. Suddenly he was the one being chased rather than him being the one, unsuccessfully, doing the chasing. From then on John became very promiscuous and he had no difficulty in attracting other men. This continued when he got to Stuttgart where he used to be out practically every night. Not that it affected his work, but there was at least one dancer who saw a way to take advantage of John. He was good looking, married but apparently available and willing to do anything if it might further his own career. He was not a good dancer and John had officially given him his notice, within the legal period, on grounds of his lack of ability. The dancer decided to contest that. In London, Wandsworth common had been one of John's haunts and the dancer had discovered the soliciting incident, sensationalised by the *Daily Express*, when John was arrested in Chelsea and was prosecuted. John was fined £10. At that time, being convicted in such a way meant the establishment turned its back on you. It was something at the Royal Opera House that de Valois was sensitive to which contributed to John's move to Stuttgart.

After we had eventually found our own place to live in the city, Sonya and I decided to host a party at our flat. It was hallowe'en. Most of the company came dressed as witches, ghouls, monsters and the like. The dancer hostile to John came with his beautiful South American wife. As the party developed, Edward Dutton, one of the American dancers, performed a brilliant send-up of a male stripper, ending up seemingly naked. Our young au pair was helping serve drinks. She saw this of course and thought it hilarious. A short while later somebody whispered in my ear that he had seen that dancer taking the au pair into the bathroom. Knowing that the lock was faulty I burst in to discover him trying to force himself on her. I told him the girl was under age and ordered him to leave. He countered, why then had I allowed her to watch an adult man performing a striptease? I told him Dutton was wearing all-over tights, which indeed he was. The next day he threatened to go to Walter Erich Schäfer, the theatre's intendant, to inform him of John's conviction in London and that I had given a party where a male stripper had performed in front of underage girls. He also threatened to go to the press unless he got his contract back. John was greatly upset but he was determined not to be intimidated. This did not deter the man. He upped his intimidation of John, threatening to go to the media the next day. In fact, Schäfer knew all about the incident in London although audiences and the press in Stuttgart did not. Somehow, that afternoon, Herr May, the finance director, discovered that the dancer's father-in-law was a convicted Nazi criminal, living happily in South America. Sensing that his bluff had been called, he left without going public. In my experience there were many underlying Nazi undercurrents at that time in Munich and Vienna as well as in Stuttgart. During this incident, as generally, Schäfer was wonderful. He was determined to have a first-rate classical ballet company at his opera house. He was very supportive of John even if some of the opera house's management team were hostile.

As I was to learn, it was a theatre where the prevailing attitude was resistant to change. Many employees and heads of department preferred to stick with what they had been doing for the past 30 years. Very complacent, very Mittel-European. The technical departments were particularly stubborn. When Peter Farmer worked with me in Stuttgart, he had great problems trying to get the wardrobe department to make bodices in the way that he wanted, different from how they had been done previously. With such a resistant approach, theatres soon lag behind the times. John fought that attitude with vigour. He utterly refused to adhere to the way the house had previously been run. He was in a constant battle to get time onstage away from the opera company in favour of the ballet. Unfortunately there were many times when things were not ready for us when we had stage calls. Usually this was caused by the previous night's show over-running, usually an opera, or because of a lack of efficiency or missing stage staff. There was great disparity in the allocation of stage time allocated to us, but even if we started late because of the opera we still had to stop, bang on the dot. There was, more fortunately, never any difficulty in getting money for new productions. Compared to London, where everything has to be costed in man-hours, Stuttgart was very generous, which was fortunate as we had to build up a new repertoire very quickly. There was a huge storeroom containing rolls of fabrics and materials and you could always find enough for a new production there without having to submit a budget for it. Thank goodness for John's creativity.

During my years in Stuttgart, John was typically creating four or more new ballets each year. During my first year, John reworked *The Lady and the Fool* and *Romeo and Juliet*, made initially for La Scala in Milan. They were both redesigned by Jürgen Rose, then a young designer whom John encouraged. John's *Romeo* had a very intense and passionate feel about it. It set the theatre alight even in rehearsal. The production converted a lot of people to ballet, including many technicians and stagehands. Although the actual choreography is somewhat repetitive and disjointed, I do find the passion and dramatic tragedy to be very strong. It certainly holds together the best, dramatically. Suddenly John was taken seriously. He was very hurt when he was not asked to restage the production for the Royal Ballet, but John never considered Kenneth MacMillan to have copied him when he came to do *Romeo and Juliet* in London himself in 1965. I love Kenneth's *Romeo* but the dramatic side of John's is stronger. It is hard to believe that both those versions of *Romeo and Juliet* are now over 50 years old and both are performed around the world still. For the 50th anniversary performance of John's, in 2012, many of the original cast returned to Stuttgart. Marcia Haydée, the first Juliet, was now her nurse. I was asked to be the duke but could not be there so they asked Ray Barra, the original Romeo, a much better choice. Egon Madsen, a former Paris, was Lorenzo, and the 84-year-old Georgette Tsingurides, a former gipsy, was still a gipsy. Birgit Keil and Vladimir Klos were the Capulets.

Among other ballets that John created was *Katalyse* or *The Catalyst* to music by Dmitri Shostakovich. Unfortunately John's alcohol consumption was on the increase. He used the canteen as his office, and frequent visits there before, during and after rehearsals led to more and more anxiety about his alcohol intake. Sometimes by the end of the evening rehearsal John would ask me to finish what he was doing as he would be past his limit. When John was creating ballets he would often disappear for another beer in the canteen or go out on his night-time adventures, leaving me in the studio. Parts of the end of the first scene of *Onegin* and *Romeo and Juliet*, in the crypt scene before Juliet kills herself, are instances where I created some of the choreography. More widely, John relied on me to do quite a lot of sorting out of his ballets. In *L'Estro armonico*, to music by Vivaldi, six couples weave in and out of each other, and John had the dancers doing a tap dance on pointe, not terribly pleasing for the girls as it not only hurt their toes but ruined their shoes too. One section was a complete muddle that I managed to unravel somehow. He knew what he wanted to happen but it took hours to sort out and became known as the Neckar Strasse section, just like the busy street next to the theatre with its eddying flows of cars coming and going, weaving in and out of each other. John was always grateful and I loved doing it. He would always go over anything I had done the next morning and put his approval on it or adjust as necessary.

The success of John's ballets stemmed in part from the impact that Ray Barra and Marcia Haydée created in them. Born in Brazil, Marcia had studied at the Royal Ballet School in London and arrived in Stuttgart from the Grand Ballet du Marquis de Cuevas in Monaco where John had seen her when he choreographed *Cat's Cradle* there. He adored working with Marcia, as did I. She was definitely not the audiences' typical image of a German woman, blonde, buxom and curvaceous. Marcia was very slim and was wonderfully expressive in the way she used her eyes and body. She could make herself look classical when she needed to. Initially the opera house staff called her the Wasser Leiche – the water corpse – but everybody soon realised Marcia was a star and the name was dropped. Strong and determined, Marcia soon acquired another nickname, however, being referred to as Hank. Marcia formed a remarkable onstage partnership with Ray. He was a very strong and sensitive partner with a very good stage presence, particularly in such roles as Romeo and Onegin which he created. All the ballerinas wanted to be partnered by him as he always knew when they were on balance when standing on one leg, especially at the end of a sequence of supported pirouettes where the ballerina's partner had to quickly step away, leaving her standing alone, perfectly balanced. Ray would spend hours helping Marcia fathom out some of the incredibly complicated lifts that John imagined but was unable to make work himself.

Marcia was also to develop a partnership with another dancer. When John heard reports about a talented product of the Royal Ballet School he sent me off to investigate. This was Richard Cragun. At his graduation performance in 1962 he danced alongside Kerrison Cooke and Vergie Derman in a new piece by MacMillan, *Dance Suite*. It was clear that Cragun was very promising, with a virtuoso technique and incredible power. As there was only a limited number of places in the Royal Ballet for overseas recruits which had already been filled and Ricky was American, I was able to offer him a contract in Stuttgart. Six months later, while still in the corps de ballet, he was Romeo opposite Marcia as Juliet. People were shocked but they were wonderful together. When

Alfonso Cata, Marcia's lover, left Stuttgart, she trained Ricky to be her partner, onstage and off. She and Ricky enjoyed a long and passionate association together. Ricky was very ambitious, incredibly hard working, a wonderful partner and extremely good looking. However, Marcia did not let Ricky partner her until John felt he had proved himself as a principal. Ricky had a phenomenal technique, strong as a horse.

In *The Taming of the Shrew*, which John created when Marcia and Ricky were lovers, John always allowed Marcia to get the upper hand over Ricky in the ballet. Their big pas de deux was a wonderful combination of comedy and virtuosity. It was beautifully worked out by John, but it was Marcia and Ricky's timing that used to bring the house down when they performed it. There was nobody more suited to the role of Petruchio than Ricky, with his virtuoso technique, masculinity, sexism. He dominated any scene he was playing and demanded your attention. This was his best role. He did not have to act the character, he *was* Petruchio, whereas in most of his other roles he looked as if he was trying to act. When I was choreographing *Namouna* in 1967 Ricky had an involved solo set to a complicated section of the score. I had worked out something in rough and he asked me to let him finesse it in private and he would then present the result to me. That was a wonderful collaboration. Ricky's subsequent career was not so happy. He became director of the ballet company at the Teatro Municipal in Rio de Janeiro, Brazil, where he made his new partner, Roberto de Oliveira, choreographer with disastrous results. Ricky's early death from Aids was mourned around the world.

In Stuttgart, there always seemed to be a group of dancers who were hostile to John, but I had not yet experienced a company before where dancers actually related to each other so closely. It was, however, difficult to find your way around. The rehearsal room was on the fifth floor, and the canteen where everyone tended to meet was under the stage, at the far end. John was resident there, usually with a beer. He used to say, 'Just come and ask me what you want. Everybody.' He could get terribly upset and cried a lot if he felt that people were not with him. When John got upset he drank too much. He was often drunk but it was not the alcohol that made him so overexcited. Once, pre-Stuttgart and pre-beer, while on tour with Sadler's Wells Theatre Ballet, after he learned that his stepmother had died of cancer, some of us went to a newsreel at a cinema, which happened to include a report about cancer. I sensed John was sobbing. He suddenly stood up and started screaming as he jumped across the tops of empty seats, shouting as he ran out of the cinema. John was very highly strung but had amazing hidden strength when he needed it. I remember when he had to give a talk to the Noverre Society, the supporters' organisation at the opera house. Jean-Georges Noverre was ballet master to Louis XVI in France and before that had a similar position for the Duke of Württemberg, the state in which Stuttgart is situated. John had been asked to demonstrate how he choreographed and created a new piece, working with Birgit Keil and her husband Vladimir Klos. I was still living at John's house at the time. Needless to say he had been out the night before, drinking. The talk was scheduled to begin at 10am. So that he would be ready in time I knocked on John's bedroom door at 8.30am. He was deep, deep asleep. He was absolutely out for the count. I had to shake him awake and remind him he was due to give the talk. 'I can't, I can't,' he said. 'You do it for me.' Somehow I managed to get him up and dressed. All the time he kept repeating, 'I don't know what I am going to say.' And of course the talk had to be in German which he had picked up very quickly, maybe because of his Afrikaans background. By then I had a Volkswagen Variant which I rather liked, except the clutch kept going. As I drove him to the theatre it was John who kept on going, 'Pete, Pete – what am I going to do?' Suddenly, as we were standing in the wings I felt him grow and take a few deep breaths and then on cue strode onstage to give the most brilliant talk. He then created a pas de deux in front of the audience and answered their questions extremely well. He was humorous and made people laugh. I could not believe it. As John came offstage he collapsed and literally had to be picked up and carried to a dressing-room. He was incapable of working the rest of that day, but for that hour he had been completely transformed and as full of vitality as anybody.

There were problems too worrying about Sonya. She felt trapped at the Crystal Palace. She could not face going on trams into town and was not able to drive in Germany as she did not have a licence. New flats were being constructed some way from the centre in a lovely area, but they were not due for completion for another six months. We managed to find another, very nice apartment on the ground floor with good neighbours upstairs, the Langners, on the first floor and 'Tante Astrid', the local kindergarten teacher, on the second. Sonya made some very good friends there, which helped her a lot. There was a large communal garden and a terrible hausmeister, or caretaker, a Herr Schmidt. He hated the English and children, especially our children. They enjoyed playing in a sandpit in the garden. Herr Schmidt had it removed after some sand spilled onto a footpath and was not swept up. Apparently this caused real anger among the other families who also used it. Herr Schmidt claimed he had been threatened with dismissal for the spillage of sand.

I loved Stuttgart but never felt comfortable in Germany with all its bureaucracy. It took us some time to settle in, although our children acclimatised very well at the kindergarten. Our daughter picked up German very quickly whereas I could only ever muddle through. She used to come shopping with me, my four-year-old translator. Living in our own space made a difference but it was still a problem for Sonya. She was lonely. She was not keen to work but John persuaded her to go to Munich, about a couple of hours away, to appear in some TV shows. She only went twice. The environment felt alien to her, without having any German and because of her Japanese background. She did not enjoy working with choreographers she did not know. Of course it was easier for me as I was working with a company that was developing fast, although it still had a long way to go before it was to become one of the great European companies, the famous Stuttgart Ballet.

Working at the pace he did meant that the quality of John's ballets could be variable, but his work was always very musical, particularly when working with a commissioned score without any overt story. John's ballets, however, were always intrinsically theatrical. Something of that quality is evident in David Bintley's works. Even John's apparently abstract works would be full of ideas relating to human emotions and feelings. He was good at communicating feelings – exhilaration, sadness, rage, passion – provided the music was right and getting the dancers to express feelings done not just facially but with their whole bodies while still using their classical technique. It was very important to John that dancers working with him were totally supportive and enthusiastic. He insisted that they gave themselves to him and became part of the creative process.

John had very clear ideas about how he wanted his ballets to be, but really it all happened with his dancers' involvement in the studio. He would take from their contributions just as much as they would take from his ideas. He was not great in rehearsal from a technical point of view but he was excellent in drawing out the dramatic interpretation of a dancer's performance. That is why Marcia developed into such a great interpreter of roles such as Tatiana in *Onegin*, Katherine in *The Taming of the Shrew*, and Juliet. John could make dancers see themselves as they really were, something they may not have been conscious of themselves. One thing that John simply could not stand was if a dancer altered a step to make it easier to execute or prettier to look at. Occasionally if he saw a step in another choreographer's work he would subconsciously copy it and was very reluctant to change it. John did a version of Igor Stravinsky's *Scènes de ballet* which was derivative of Frederick Ashton's ballet to the same score. One sequence of steps where the women are lifted side to side was identical to Fred's version. I begged John to change it but he refused, saying, 'It is so perfect to the music I simply cannot bear to alter it.' When creating, John became completely selfless and always got the feeling of the movement he wanted by demonstrating in his rather clumsy way, adjusting heads, arms, shoulders and feet as the dancers put the steps together. He was also quick to recognise that when a dancer performed a step differently by mistake he would keep changes if they looked better than his original. I particularly remember when he was working on *Romeo and Juliet* how very clear and precise he was about the mime scenes between Juliet and her family – every turn of the head, a hand being raised in protest and even when transferring the body weight from back to front or vice versa.

Among other works that John created during my years in Stuttgart, he produced his own productions of two famous Ballets Russes' creations, *The Firebird*, not nearly so good as the original but still very effective; *Daphnis and Chloë*, with Erik Bruhn and Georgina Parkinson, had some good moments such as Lykanion's amusement at her seduction of Daphnis, but overall it was nothing special. John did not give the story a contemporary setting as Ashton had except for putting some butch pirates in black leather, designed by Nicholas Georgiadis. John made three ballets to Glazunov's music, *The Seasons*, a *Raymonda pas deux* and a duet for Marcia and Ricky, *Hommage à Bolschoi*, very popular because of the Soviet-era lifts that John included: daring for the time, though they look less exceptional these days. John created to commissioned scores too, with *Wir Reisen nach Jerusalem*, the German name for the game of *Musical Chairs*, with music by Kurt-Heinz Stolze and *Variations* by Yngve Jan Trede, a display of various sports and athletics. John used Webern's music for *Opus 1*, a ballet I televised for a BBC programme, *Cranko's Castle*. The film was good, showing off the company quite well, but it left the impression of a one-man show whereas the great thing about John was how he always involved everyone, enlisting their support and ensuring credit was given where it was due.

The Prince of the Pagodas was revived. Alan Carter had produced another version of it in Munich, apparently without success, before John first brought the ballet to Stuttgart. It was the first full-length British ballet to have a commissioned score which John and Benjamin Britten had created together in 1957 in London. I saw the first performance and enjoyed the ballet if not the score particularly, although generally I do like Britten's music. The scenery by John Piper and costumes by Desmond Heeley were very colourful, full of fantasy. The designs in Stuttgart by Jürgen Rose were not as good. John conceived *The Prince of the Pagodas* as a fantastic fairytale, a mix of different stories, very different from the sexual awakening and psychological nightmare that Kenneth MacMillan adopted in 1989 in his version. I never thought John's original was a choreographic masterpiece. His talents were stretched too thinly across three acts. The scene where the moon crossed the skies was a lovely classical sequence but John succeeded best with theatrical elements. Belle Rose was first discovered centre stage imprisoned in a large cage before being allowed out. The reception in London was very mixed and certainly not the success that Britten expected. My sense is that the composer was never entirely committed to John's scenario and none of his attempts to revise the score did anything to improve the ballet. *Pagodas* was Britten's only score that was not published during his lifetime. John dropped plans for a subsequent reworking in Stuttgart when he felt he no longer had Britten's confidence. Peter Farmer was intended to design that cancelled reworking. He and John did not get on. When John inspected one of Peter's planned designs for a female dancer he said provocatively, 'Turn it upside down. It might look better that way.' Peter did not reply – he just suffered in silence. I doubt that John's original could ever come back now, but *Pagodas* is a ballet that I think succeeded best in its original form. It was the product of John's own imagination.

John also produced a new *Coppélia* in 1962. He introduced a new character, Swanilda's mother who was paired off with Coppélius at the close. John also staged a new *Swan Lake* the following year, a production he later staged in Munich. He made Siegfried into a joking playboy, disguised as a female fortune-teller when he first appeared. John's intention was to do anything that would destroy the perception of the prince as a soppy ballet dancer. The second act, by the lakeside, mostly used the original choreography by Lev Ivanov except for the waltz which John redid. Rothbart was the usual sort of bird but did not dance. In the third act he wore a big cloak which was made to billow dramatically upwards like wings by fans concealed in a trapdoor as Odile emerged through it unseen until he stepped aside. That was ghastly when the mechanics did not work. At the end there was a huge flood, made by billowing silk fabric across the stage, in which Siegfried was drowned. This was very effective, again when it worked. The designs were again by Jürgen Rose who was responsible for the décor in Munich. When I was asked to stage a production there in 1984 with the designer Philip Prowse, Rose was deeply insulted. Stuttgart's previous director, Nicholas Beriosov, had done a *Sleeping Beauty* which was not very good, but for John it was an important ballet to have in the repertoire. He changed it a lot and I helped him to make the choreography more authentic in style and execution. Beriosov was generally good at doing revivals of old ballets but his *Giselle* had been a disaster. That helped me later on, when, after John's *Swan Lake*, he said to me I must do *Giselle*. He believed it was important to have it in the repertoire.

John gave me opportunities to create my own ballets too. If I had stayed in Stuttgart I may have developed more as a choreographer, but I never felt it was something I had to do and get out of my system. In July 1962, I restaged *The Great Peacock*, created originally for Edinburgh International Ballet three years before. It was drawn from a piece of prose in an anthology about love by Walter de la Mare. I happened to lend it to Madam when she came to Stuttgart to see how John was getting on. I never got it back after she left the book in her hotel room. I did get from her what amounted to a compliment. She told me that while I was never the greatest dancer, as a teacher and organiser I was showing possibilities. The Great Peacock is a moth born with the sole ambition of finding a mate in order to procreate and then die. It had no stomach and hence no desire to indulge in sweet-smelling fruit and berries. It was a fierce fighter able to battle others of the same species. Once its mission was completed it would gradually lose its power and die. I drew the parallel with human beings, many of whom, when they have successfully achieved their ambition, may just as well die. Yolanda Sonnabend designed it in a very stark and powerful style. I reworked most of the leading roles for Marcia and Ray. The critic Horst Koegler hated Cranko at that time but I got on with him reasonably well. He considered that in its combination of music, design and choreography *The Great Peacock* was the most fully formed and complete ballet staged in the Stuttgart repertoire then. But he told me that was not meant as a compliment. What he really meant I never knew.

In April 1963, on a programme with John's *L'Estro armonico* and *Die Reise nach Jerusalem*, I created *The Mirror Walkers*, danced to Tchaikovsky's first orchestral suite, the pas de deux from which is still done at galas, including the one when I retired. A large dance studio mirror and ballet barre dominated the stage for *The Mirror Walkers*. While a girl is practising in front of the mirror, a man appears behind her, but when she turns to see who is behind her, he has vanished. She continues practising and the figure reappears, beckoning to her. They exchange places and the girl enters a strange world of reflections beyond. She moves among dancers frozen in time who gradually come to life. If this all sounds rather reminiscent of the mirror pas de deux in Cranko's *Onegin*, I should point out that *The Mirror Walkers* was made two years before. You might equally accuse me of copying Jerome Robbins' *Afternoon of a Faun* in *The Mirror Walkers*. It was, after all, made a decade before my ballet, but I had not seen it at that stage. But just to underline what great borrowers choreographers are, I borrowed from myself when I put parts of the pas de deux from *The Mirror Walkers* into both my different productions of *The Nutcracker*. After all, you have to get your ideas from somewhere. When *The Mirror Walkers* was acquired by National Ballet of Canada in 1970, the ballet gave Karen Kain her first featured role. She was then still in the corps de ballet but I knew she would be right for the lead. Celia Franca, founder director of the company whose dancing career had been limited by her rather awkward physique, was not keen on girls with perfect faces and long legs – and Karen was very beautiful. I insisted. She had a big success in this, her first big role. Shortly afterwards she was made a principal.

In Stuttgart too, thanks to John's encouragement, in May 1964 I made *Designs for Dancers*. It shared a programme with John's version of *The Firebird* and Kenneth MacMillan's *Diversions*. For my ballet I used Bartok's concerto for strings, percussion and celesta, a score that I have always loved. It was abstract and Egon Madsen dominated with his extraordinary understanding and feeling for the music. The amazing speed with which he executed a difficult solo which we created together was fantastic. Egon had joined the company at the age of 17 on the advice of Erik Bruhn, another Dane. Apparently, Egon had not been accepted into the company after his graduation exams in Copenhagen. This was a huge gain for Stuttgart as he developed into the most versatile and brilliant dancer. Not only did he have a very masculine, classical line and a light, high jump, but he could be both romantic, as Lensky in *Onegin*, and hilariously funny. As Gremio he sneezed his way through *The Taming of the Shrew* as though he really did have a bad cold. He had a dotty sense of humour, especially as the joker in *Card Game*.

We all had fun with a ballet that started out as *Quartet* which I intended for a ballerina and three men. I had chosen a quartet by Paul Hindemith. It was quirky but came together beautifully. I was really pleased with the result but nobody had remembered to secure the performance rights for the score. Three days before the first night in July 1963 I discovered we did not have the clearance. The music was only allowed to be performed as a concert piece. The dancers were upset but our four musicians involved undertook to find another score within 24 hours, which they did – some chamber music pieces by Jacques Ibert. We worked out how we could fit the existing choreography to the new music. With everybody helping, including John, we got it all together. In fact it all fitted perfectly with the exception of a couple of minor details. The result was far better, easier on the ear and – as *Quintet* – went well when unveiled alongside John's *Variations*, Kenneth's *House of Birds* and *Las Hermanas*. As *Quintet*, I restaged it for the Royal Ballet's touring company a year or so later in October 1964, where it seemed to find favour as a useful sort of ballet, quirky and amusing. *Quintet* had in fact been televised earlier, in May that year, by the infant BBC2, the prelude to a Sunday night discussion chaired by David Dimbleby as to whether Britain needed expensive overseas embassies, with a cast of Anthony Dowell, Georgina Parkinson, Christopher Gable, Bryan Lawrence and Laurence Ruffell. Whatever its success, I do not really consider the ballet to have been up to much.

Sonya and the children moved back to London a couple of years before I finally stopped working in Stuttgart in the summer of 1967. I had spent the previous two years commuting between the two, sometimes driving, sometimes by plane, teaching in both cities and doing some television work and musicals too. It all slotted together quite well, but it was tough going being split from the family. I was in London in September 1966 when I choreographed *Jorrocks*. This was a musical by David Heneker about the fox-hunting fraternity of Handley Cross Spa with such characters as Marmaduke Muleygrubs, Doctor Swizzle and Captain Misererrimus Doleful. Back in Stuttgart John was upset that I was not going to continue with him, although when I gave up our flat I did move back to John's house. On occasion I stayed too with Marcia and Ricky in their little house outside the city. John and I still had a good relationship but it dwindled when he knew I was leaving.

I got in a terrible state and needed pills to calm me down while I was making *Namouna*, the two-act ballet I created in June 1967, just before I finally left Stuttgart. It was a big production but I do not consider it to have been particularly good. It is about a slave girl in Corfu, and originally choreographed by Lucien Petipa. Peter Farmer did the most gorgeous designs for it. He really excelled. The music was by Édouard Lalo, extracts from which are more familiar from Sergei Lifar's *Suite en blanc* and more recently Alexei Ratmansky's *Namouna, A Grand Divertissement* for New York City Ballet. Musicologists claim to detect Wagnerian touches and suggestions of Ravel in the score; most of it is more akin to André Messager's music for *The Two Pigeons*. Some of it is fun, but equally some of it is awful. Kurt-Heinz Stolze, one of the resident conductors, knocked it into shape. Birgit Keil danced the title role and really was hilarious in a scene where she had to struggle to smoke a cigarette. She performed it brilliantly, to the great delight of audiences. John Neumeier was one of the dancers in the ensemble. John Cranko got wildly excited after the first night and described *Namouna* as 'our ballet for Stuttgart', one that I should not let other companies dance. But it only had a couple of performances before it was dropped. John never revived it after I was gone. I am unsure why, but suspect that it was probably because I was leaving the fold. John and I were never that close once I had left Stuttgart.

Kenneth MacMillan did a lot of work in Stuttgart too. He and John were not exactly great friends but they got on reasonably well. It was hard to read their relationship. At parties you would see them huddled together in a corner or on a settee intent on their conversation with each other. Early on during John's time in Stuttgart, Kenneth came to restage *Solitaire* and *House of Birds*, the ballet that John had suggested for Kenneth at Sadler's Wells in 1955. Kenneth also created *Las Hermanas* in Stuttgart in July 1963. Later, after opposition in London about Kenneth using the score of Gustav Mahler's *Song of the Earth* for a ballet, John invited him to create it in Stuttgart, with remarkable success.

There was a big bust-up between Kenneth and John during the making of *Miss Julie* in 1970. There was animosity among the Stuttgart dancers as Kenneth had insisted on importing Frank Frey from Berlin to partner Marcia Haydée in the title role, something to which John had acquiesced. Kenneth never liked anybody watching his rehearsals and John was determined to find a way in. That made Kenneth suspicious that people were trying to steal his ideas, a misunderstanding of the situation. Kenneth returned to London for a week and believed, on his return, that in his absence John had somehow interfered with the costume designs. There were problems with the scenery too. That provoked a major row that never should have happened. Kenneth never forgave John, a great shame as Kenneth loved working in Stuttgart and with Marcia. He only returned to Stuttgart after John's death with his tribute to him, *Requiem*. John did have a recognisably personal style, something that very few choreographers manage to achieve, but it was not as strong as Kenneth's. John once said to me, 'I am always so amazed that everything that Kenneth does has such a strong personal stamp on it.'

John's early death was a shock for everyone. Kenneth was terribly upset as, underneath, he and John had been close working colleagues. It is a shame that the Royal Ballet neglected John once he left for Stuttgart, but Frederick Ashton did not like his work although John did create *Brandenburg Nos. 2 and 4* at Covent Garden in 1966. In some ways it was an atypical work for John, neither humorous nor quirky. It was neo-classical and very musical in how it moved a large cast of dancers – a useful work for a company to have. Anthony Dowell was in the cast but he hardly knew John or his work. When John had originally intended to create *Onegin* for Covent Garden for Rudolf Nureyev and Margot Fonteyn, an idea that was vetoed by the board of directors as they objected to the idea of Tchaikovsky's opera music being adapted for a ballet, John had Anthony in mind as Lensky, with Antoinette Sibley intended as Olga. In fact Anthony was actually cast in the title role when the Royal Ballet attempted but failed to acquire the ballet in 1977.

As director, Anthony had enough difficulty finding space in the repertoire for the MacMillan and Ashton ballets, old and new. However, John's *Taming of the Shrew* was staged at Covent Garden after his death, a work ill-suited to the company. Now *Onegin* appears regularly and is very popular with audiences. I think it would still have been possible to import a few more of his ballets such as *Beauty and the Beast*, a small cameo. *Sea Change* was not at all bad even though its score, *En Saga* by Sibelius, was his 15th choice of music before Madam would let him do that early ballet. Birmingham Royal Ballet perform *Pineapple Poll* still, which survives because of its good sense of theatre; and the company has kept *The Lady and the Fool*, albeit with dreadful new décor. It is a sentimental piece but it has had a good life. Birmingham Royal Ballet has also performed *Brouillards* and *Card Game* but less frequently. *Initialen RBME* was inspired by John's closest muses, Ricky, Birgit, Marcia and Egon. *Initials*, to use the ballet's English title, is a large work set to Johannes Brahms' second piano concerto. It is one of John's most beautiful works and uses a corps de ballet who often copy the movements of the principals, so it is demanding for the whole company. It has a lot of complicated lifts typical of John's choreography. It is also typical of John's work in that it reveals the influence of Léonide Massine, in this case his symphonic ballets with big sweeping arcs of movement. But principally the ballet displays a sense of family or friendship that characterised so much of how John worked and ran the company in Stuttgart. John really pushed Kenneth to start choreography seriously, and he helped me greatly too. As a director, John was very strong, very emotional, almost violent, and would fight anyone without fear to champion his company. John was primarily a choreographer. He got through as a director as we did it together in the end. My career would not have been the same without it. Thanks to John I really felt able to face the future and the next phase of my life.

CHAPTER 5

Kenneth MacMillan –
pushing the boundaries

N OT LONG BEFORE his death in 1992, Kenneth MacMillan
joked about what a gala programme celebrating his career might
include. He suggested the rape scenes from *The Invitation* and *The Judas Tree*, the epileptic fit from *Playground*, the blowjob in *Manon*, the suicide pact in *Mayerling* and the concentration camp from *Valley of Shadows*. He could have as easily added death in the trenches in *Gloria*, the drowning in *Different Drummer* and death by strangulation in *Isadora*. Equally, from the earlier stages of Kenneth's career he could have selected the dead body in *Somnambulism*, the blinding in *Winter's Eve*, the hanging in *Las Hermanas*, the murder in *Cain and Abel* or the dance to death in *The Rite of Spring*. Kenneth also directed August Strindberg's bleak dissection of married life, *The Dance of Death*, for the Royal Exchange theatre company in Manchester in 1983. Yet for all the dark subjects that Kenneth's ballets and theatre work encompassed, his own deep-seated depressions, hypochondria and sensitivity to criticism, he was somebody with whom you could enjoy a laugh and a good joke, the dirtier the better. We confided in each other about our secrets and misdemeanours during our early years.

I do recall, however, the first time I saw Kenneth he was looking decidedly downcast. This was in September 1943. I had made an appointment to see Ninette de Valois, but before I could see her I had to be given the onceover by Ailne Phillips, Madam's personal assistant and a brilliant teacher. I checked in at the stage door of Sadler's Wells theatre which had been badly bombed. The auditorium was completely destroyed but the stage, rehearsal rooms and dressing-rooms were still being used by Sadler's Wells school. The grumpy stage-door man told me to go to a dressing-room on the second floor. I timidly knocked and entered. There were five boys in varying states of undress. Four of them were very tidy and getting into their school training clothes, black and white, with hair-nets to stop their hair flapping around. The fifth, very tall and slim, was wearing dark-blue woollen tights, no hairnet and looked rather sad. They all looked at me rather disdainfully except the tall one who smiled, somehow sensing how shy and nervous I was. He said I could change in the empty space in the corner. I duly got into my shorts and vest, very embarrassed as I did not have a jock-strap.

As boys do, I could tell they were all scrutinising my lower regions to see what sort of genitalia I had. Then they all vanished except the tall boy who said he would show me where the studio was. He was very helpful and explained that he had been offered a contract in the company but had to stay with the school until a vacancy occurred. That was why he did not have to wear the uniform any more. He told me his name was Kenneth MacMillan, which meant nothing to me when I met him for the first time that day. I said who I was and that this was my first proper ballet class. He suggested I stood next to him at the barre and he would try to help me understand the various exercises. At Bedales I had managed to watch the biology teacher's wife, Irene Spencer, a former member of Anna Pavlova's company, give a ballet class to some of the girls. I sometimes joined in, so had a bit of an idea of the exercises, but doing the class at Sadler's Wells that day made me appreciate quite how far I had to go. I do not think this mattered much as they were really just making sure I had the right number of legs, arms and feet and could move on the music. Seemingly I passed that test as I was told to book an appointment to see Miss de Valois at the New theatre, now the Noël Coward on St Martin's Lane, where the company was performing. At the time it was one of only eight of the West End's 30 theatres that remained open, the majority having closed because of the dangers of doodlebug bombs.

I did not see Kenneth again until July 1950, by which time he was in Sadler's Wells Ballet based at Covent Garden and I was a member of Sadler's Wells Theatre Ballet. We were just back from a visit to Cheltenham as part of the music festival there. Some of us had been to watch a dress rehearsal at the Royal Opera House of de Valois' *Don Quixote* in which Kenneth had created the role of Orlando Furioso. That was a ballet where Marot Fonteyn as Dulcinea waved her knickers at the Don of Robert Helpmann, I seem to recall. Very un-Margot, very un-Madam. Afterwards we went to the boys' dressing-room to see our friends who were in the Covent Garden company. There was Kenneth. He actually remembered me. I explained that although de Valois asked me to join the school I had instead been working as an apprentice with Ballets Jooss but was now with Sadler's Wells Theatre Ballet. Kenneth said he hoped to be coming to Sadler's Wells as he wanted to participate in the Sunday Choreographers, a group for aspiring young dance makers run by David Poole. I did not see the first piece he did, *Somnambulism*, in February 1953, but it caused quite a stir. It was about sleepwalking to music by Stan Kenton.

In May that year I did see Kenneth when he danced in Alfred Rodrigues' new work, *Blood Wedding*, based on Federico Garcia Lorca's famous play. Kenneth played the moon and Sheilah O'Reilly was death, two symbolic figures that seemed to draw two illicit lovers together. Kenneth made every step that Rodrigues created on him appear new and different. Around this time we were reviving Frederick Ashton's *Façade*. Previously the foxtrot had not been included as Ashton felt that the company was too young for this very sophisticated dance, but Peggy van Praagh, our ballet mistress, thought Kenneth, Margaret Hill, Hermione Harvey and I could do it. She asked Ashton's permission and he reluctantly agreed, with the caveat that we should not camp around too much but dance it straight. That way, Ashton said, it would have the right sort of humour rather than cheap laughs. Kenneth always felt exactly the same about his humorous ballets such as *Valse eccentrique*, a slow-motion pas de trois from 1956 where a girl is partnered by two suitors in Edwardian bathing suits and handlebar moustaches. Kenneth knew the *Façade* foxtrot very well, having danced it many times at Covent Garden, so Peggy got him to teach it to us. We were very funny in the right way and Ashton was very pleased. By the time Kenneth created his second work, *Laiderette*, for the Sunday choreographic workshop at Sadler's Wells in January 1954, I was cast among one of three couples. I was over the moon and became quite friendly with Kenneth. He had many female friends, though few male ones.

Knowing Kenneth, I began to understand what the word neurotic meant. He seemed to be in a constant state of worry, suffered from sleepless nights and mood swings, and was quite sure nothing would come off in his new ballets. Around this time he was living in a basement flat at Seymour Street off Edgware Road. While he was living in this flat, Kenneth's behaviour became increasingly peculiar. He never answered the phone. He became ill, drinking heavily. Really he turned into a dipsomaniac. On one occasion Peter Farmer, who was to live at the flat later, invited some friends round, one of whom was a spiritualist, which Peter had not appreciated. She told Kenneth to move at once. 'This house is dangerous. It has the smell of death,' she told Kenneth, which may have been insight from a higher plane or just an understanding of the local area. The building was not far from the site of Tyburn gallows, where public executions took place until 1783, and skulls and bones frequently turned up in the ground around there. Kenneth moved and his general state did improve.

While Kenneth was busy working on *Laiderette*, de Valois switched him from Covent Garden to Sadler's Wells. He was a beautiful dancer, the envy of us all as he had high legs and good insteps. His split jetés and penché arabesques were superior to all of ours, male and female. *Laiderette* was about a blind girl who was also bald, played by Maryon Lane. Kenneth had become obsessed with the music by Frank Martin and lived with the LP record day in, day out, counting every note. The record sleeve was literally covered with counts. Kenneth and Margaret Hill, his girlfriend at the time, would have big disagreements about the best way certain phrases should be counted, discovering hidden phrasing within the music and using its atmosphere to huge effect. What impressed me most was Kenneth's instinctive understanding but unorthodox use of music. It was a difficult score, and although Kenneth was unable to read music, I was amazed at how he took basic classical steps and made them look completely different, often asking us to try them backwards, turned in and with strange arms and body movements which now seem quite natural.

In rehearsals, Kenneth demonstrated most steps and movements himself and then made us develop them until they looked right. He was always demanding, his choreography was very complicated, much more so in those early days than in his later works. Needless to say, he suffered from appalling nerves throughout and was convinced that everyone thought it would be a flop. In fact, it was hailed by the critics as a work of near genius. We were all very surprised that *Laiderette* was not taken into the repertoire but the score required a harpsichord, making it difficult to tour. De Valois did not think it right for a new young choreographer to have money spent on them in that way. However, Marie Rambert snapped it up and it stayed in her company's repertoire for several years. De Valois did commission Kenneth to do a new work for her company. This was choreographed to Igor Stravinsky's *Danses concertantes* and went on at Sadler's Wells in January 1955. Kenneth's ballet is still performed by many companies. This was the real start of Kenneth's career.

Once Kenneth had proved himself as a choreographer he could not wait to give up dancing. His mood swings were fairly extreme; on some days he and Geoffrey Webb could behave recklessly, for example leaning backwards out of the rear dickey seat of a friend's Triumph Roadster while travelling at speed with their heads practically touching the road. Then on other days he would be full of despair and totally lacking in confidence. Shortly after John Cranko's Henley season in 1952, Kenneth was in a crash while travelling in John's car. It was a write-off after John lost control while taking a hump-backed bridge too fast. I think it was shortly after the car crash that he started to drink too much in order to overcome his nerves and feelings of insecurity. Over the years this reliance on alcohol was to take a hold of him. Kenneth's nervous condition worsened. He could never travel in a car faster than twenty miles per hour. The Underground was out of the question and he would not go near a plane, flying as seldom as possible. Later on, during his directorship of the Royal Ballet, there was an occasion when John Tooley found him asleep in the green room backstage at Covent Garden instead of being en route to America with everybody else. 'You're getting right on the next plane,' John told him.

De Valois wanted him to continue dancing, first because good male dancers were still in short supply and, second, there was no money for another choreographer's salary as Ashton and Cranko were both already under contract. Happily though for Kenneth, his success with *Danses concertantes* was so astounding that de Valois had no choice. Kenneth got his way. Even so, his insecurity and depression continued and he began to rely on alcohol more and more in order to get through long and exhausting days of nerve-racking rehearsals. Kenneth was, however, very quick-witted and fun to be with, provided he was surrounded by his few very close friends, a circle that besides Margaret – or Maggie as she was known – Hill included Georgina Parkinson who was mad about him, as well as Greta Hamby. Donald MacLeary, David Poole and Lynn Seymour were also part of that circle.

Kenneth had very strong likes and dislikes and was often accused of only using his friends in his ballets. He did, though, have a brilliant eye for recognising talent, often rescuing dancers from the ranks whose hidden talents were not always immediately apparent. Kenneth created *Solitaire* on Maggie Hill which embodied the solitary aspect of her nature. It was not unknown for her to go off and find some coal and proceed to eat it. Maggie was, though, a superb artist who had joined from Ballet Rambert. Although her style was rather different, she actually fitted in rather well and brought something very special to the many roles she performed. Maggie and Kenneth were close for a long time and helped each other a great deal as they both seemed to suffer from similar problems, feelings of loneliness and rejection, subjects that were to feature in many of Kenneth's ballets. Later I remember watching Lynn rehearsing *Romeo and Juliet* while Kenneth was in the process of creating the ballet on her. She would catch on instinctively to what Kenneth wanted and take it a step further in how it flowed into the next sequence. Kenneth would accept or decline her suggestions, but their feeling about movement was very much on the same plane, although of course they had their disagreements too. There were times when Lynn thought she was creating the choreography herself rather than following Kenneth's impetus. Later, some of Lynn's own choreography for her own ballets was individual and striking, and she did seem to be developing her own personal style.

I remember the time I saw Kenneth in Stuttgart when I was ballet master there. He had come to rehearse *Solitaire* and these were under way. I could sense some sort of change in Kenneth because his hair was now grey, white even, though he was still in his early thirties. But Kenneth told me how much he loved working in Stuttgart because he felt freer there and respected by the dancers, but apart from the leading principals he did not think much of the rest. I was very impressed with how he worked, much more confident than in his rehearsals in London. In July 1963, Kenneth was in Stuttgart again on Cranko's invitation and created *Las Hermanas*. He had not had a particularly good year in

London, with only one ballet that February, *Symphony*, danced to Dmitri Shostakovich's first symphony, which left critics underwhelmed compared to the enormous success of his previous ballet, *The Rite of Spring* a year before. Choreographers using symphonies as ballet scores had long been controversial. Léonide Massine had used the same Shostakovich symphony for his *Rouge et noir* as Kenneth now, but symphonic ballets were rare. With *Symphony* Kenneth was exploring an unfashionable genre. However, his use of the music, implying relationships between a shifting quartet of two couples, was typical of his work. The ballet ends with two men locked in a sort of combat, with a girl stretching out her arms as if looking for human contact. The other girl raises her arms in despair.

In Stuttgart, when Kenneth arrived, I sensed he was particularly nervous at the prospect of *Las Hermanas*. I was worried that things were not going to work out. Then Marcia Haydée and Ray Barra started working with him. As usual, he started with the main pas de deux and no one was allowed near. The rapport that emerged between them was wonderful; Kenneth became a changed man and he went on to create some of his most expressive and dramatic choreography. *Las Hermanas*, with music by Frank Martin, another score for harpsichord and designs by Nicholas Georgiadis, was based on Lorca's *The House of Bernarda Alba* and contained all the things that Kenneth could depict very well: sexual repression, violent lust, jealousy and dramatic intensity. It was, to my mind, the perfect combination of steps, ideas, music and good casting. I could not believe how much Kenneth had developed from someone without self-belief into a man with a purpose. It made me realise the necessity of making sure that choreographers have the right atmosphere and the right artists to work with. This visit to Stuttgart made a huge difference to his creative life. *Las Hermanas* was a triumph. His already individual style became even stronger. Cranko was actually very envious of the immediately recognisable look of his choreography and said that he knew no other choreographer with such a strong personal signature.

Kenneth adored working in Stuttgart and decided that somehow, somewhere, he must, like Cranko, have his own company, which in fact he did a few years later in Berlin. He went back to Stuttgart two years after that and created *Song of the Earth*, probably his greatest work. On one of Kenneth's visits he told me that he had been asked by the powers-that-be in London to keep his eyes open in case he saw something among the new works in Stuttgart that might be suitable for the Royal Ballet's touring company. By then I had already done *A Blue Rose* for them but no other commissions had been forthcoming. Kenneth watched me rehearsing *The Mirror Walkers* and said he liked it. Nothing came of that, but National Ballet of Canada and Norwegian Ballet both took it.

I decided to leave Stuttgart finally, reluctantly but mainly because of our children's education, when I was working on my full-length ballet *Namouna* during the spring of 1967. Kenneth was in Stuttgart at that time. He asked me if I would consider joining him in Berlin where he was about to become ballet director. Having made the difficult decision to return to England to make sense of my family life, I explained that it would be madness to switch to another venture which would be even more precarious, living in a city divided by a wall, virtually cut off from the rest of Europe and where I would be faced with even worse family problems. He begged and pleaded with me until I said I would go for a few days provided it was completely unofficial and nobody was to know why I was there. I said I was completely unknown in Berlin, or so I thought, and I also said to Kenneth that the only reason I was doing this was so that I could help him find the right person for the job, as by then I was experienced in German opera houses, their politics and working systems.

So off I set. News of my visit had got around. Although Kenneth was not yet director, he had indicated to the theatre that he hoped that I would be the new ballet master, if or when he took up office the following season. As a result I was greeted by a reception committee. I was shocked and surprised and tried to explain that this was just a private visit in order to get a feel for the city. I have to say they were delightful and told me they were so thrilled that I was thinking of joining them along with Kenneth, which I of course denied. Apparently everybody in Berlin knew of my reputation in Stuttgart as a teacher and also from the huge success of my production of *Giselle* in March 1966.

Gert Rheinholm, previously a big star in Berlin who was standing in as director until Kenneth officially took over, explained they had arranged a programme so that I could see every aspect of the theatre and meet various heads of department, as well as a tour of the city. It was sheer hell. I knew at once that I was right in my decision not to go. To bring up children there would be disastrous. One interesting aspect of the visit was meeting Tatjana, Victor Gsovsky's wife. He had been my teacher and ballet master in Metropolitan Ballet and she was now resident choreographer in Berlin. I had in fact already met her in Cologne at the annual summer school for dance where I was a guest teacher. Tatjana had said she was just visiting, but apparently she had been sent to watch my classes by the Berlin theatre direction, knowing they were going to need a new director fairly soon in Berlin. This was before they considered Kenneth and thought I might be a possibility. She came to every class I gave and applauded profusely at the end of each one. She was very complimentary, saying how she could see Victor's influence but loved the way I had integrated his methods with my own very individual style of classical teaching.

So, there Tatjana was in Berlin where she really was queen bee. She was standing in along with Gert Rheinholm until Kenneth arrived as director. It had been arranged that I would see rehearsals of her ballets which she supervised herself. She also gave one class. Each time I came into the studio she would stop the rehearsal and make all the dancers perform a reverence – a bow or curtsey – to me. I do not mind this in a school environment where learning respect, I believe, is rather important, but not in a company including all the principals. Very embarrassing. But I did like her ballets, very strong, passionate, inventive and communicative. When I got back to Stuttgart I immediately phoned Kenneth in London who was shocked at what I described. He swore that he had never mentioned to anyone that I was going to Berlin. However, he did admit that he had told a dancer in Stuttgart that he wanted me to go with him to Berlin. News travels very easily in ballet companies.

It was not long after this incident that the official announcement was made that Kenneth was going to be artistic director of the Berliner Ballet with Lynn Seymour as prima ballerina and Ray Barra as ballet master. Lynn had been Kenneth's muse for some time in London where she had famously been associated with his work. She was the perfect MacMillan dancer, with a body that could make all his amazingly inventive and offbeat choreography look natural, a superb classical line, feet that could almost speak, and wonderfully expressive eyes, strangely enough with a slight cast, that made her beauty even more appealing. She gave him inspiration, often anticipating his choreographic thought process, suggesting movements that fitted in perfectly with his ideas. They became a wonderful partnership and great friends, but their relationship was fairly tempestuous. They both had strong personalities with very definite ideas; but Lynn always managed to make his often extraordinarily difficult and inventive steps make sense and brought his characters to life. Who will ever forget the rape scene in *The Invitation*? Nobody has matched Lynn in that ballet, one that she really thought she had made, and it is the one that certainly made her famous. It is nowadays a period piece, perhaps the best after *Giselle*, and when *The Invitation* is revived in 2016 I will be curious to see how it has dated. But it is a ballet that must be revived while former cast members are still alive, and dancers love it because of the roles Kenneth provided.

I felt uneasy, however, about Kenneth's appointment in Berlin as it would be such a loss for the Royal Ballet, but I was delighted about Ray's appointment. He was a wonderful communicator and great disciplinarian. He had been unbelievably kind to Sonya and me in Stuttgart. I believe the transition in Berlin was a difficult one for Kenneth. I heard that he was drinking heavily; also that Lynn was having problems caused by a thrombosis in her arm. On the creative side, things started well for Kenneth, first with *Concerto*, to Shostakovich's second piano concerto and now performed by companies worldwide and still a revealing exposé of classical technique. Then came *Anastasia* in its original one-act form in June 1967. There was no money in the budget for it, so Kenneth improvised with bits of scenery and costumes from the theatre stores. It was a huge success thanks to Lynn's performance. Her silent screams in the psychiatric clinic were very powerful. I was mad about her performance. This was another example of how Kenneth and Lynn worked brilliantly together. It also showed how sometimes the less spent on a production, the stronger the choreography becomes. This is not an infallible rule, but as in George Balanchine's work with no décor, the choreography is much more visible.

I just wish I could have seen Kenneth's production of *The Sleeping Beauty* designed by Barry Kay in October 1967. At the time I was preparing for a new production for Cologne. Apparently Kenneth's staging was unbelievably sumptuous, incorporating all the grandeur and magic that any producer of the ballet longs to achieve. But even the Berlin opera house, with all its resources, could not cope with the lavishness of the production because it meant that the theatre had to be closed for several days every time it was scheduled in order to get the scenery in, built and lit. The production had only a few performances and sadly was never filmed or recorded. Another lost gem.

John Cranko succeeded as director in Stuttgart because of his inspirational qualities. He had too the support of the intendant of the opera house there. In Berlin Kenneth had neither. I went over to see him during his second year there and stayed in the flat where Lynn, Vergie Derman and Ray Barra all lived. Kenneth was not in a good state, sitting rather forlornly in a rocking chair with his crochet. Apart from going out for lunch once, he spent the whole time in the flat talking defensively about his many problems. He apologised to me that I had not seen the city but said he just could not bear to be outside the flat. He felt protected there. Berlin was fraught with intrigue.

Kenneth was never good at standing his corner in the battles within an opera house. When he was really angry about something I have known him to really go for somebody whom he believed to have acted wrongly. He was very tough with me on one occasion when he thought I had spoken to Mark Bonham Carter, one of the Royal Ballet governors, behind his back about the New Group's future direction. In fact it was Bonham Carter who asked to see me when I made it plain in answer to his questions that if the time came for the company to perform *Swan Lake* again, I would welcome it. Kenneth construed this as disloyal and was particularly sensitive about me speaking to a governor without having consulted him.

In Berlin, Kenneth had felt he could not rely on anybody and seemed to distrust even Ray. He really only trusted Vergie. Kenneth needed to work in private when he was creating. He always began with the dancers for the pas de deux along with only the notator and pianist. He did trust Monica Parker, who was extremely good at interpreting his intentions, but Kenneth was never in a happy mood when choreographing. While creating he was plagued by a lack of confidence. If people were watching, that made it worse. He felt he was always being judged.

Kenneth was very suspicious too that other choreographers would steal his ideas and steps, with good cause. This did happen frequently because Kenneth's strong personal signature made his choreography very distinctive and other people tended to be influenced by it. In *The Edge of Silence*, a ballet depicting a nether world somewhere between death and rebirth which Graham Lustig made for Sadler's Wells Royal Ballet in 1988, Graham used the same idea of a dancer jumping backwards to vanish below to conclude his ballet that Kenneth had used in *Gloria*. He was furious at what he saw as stealing and made Graham change the ending. I believe Kenneth too accused Wayne Eagling of using a lot of his ideas in a ballet he created for Dutch National Ballet and threatened a court case.

I had several similar experiences with him myself. He accused me of stealing a lift from *Manon* when I staged *The Nutcracker* in 1984 at Covent Garden, whereas in fact it was Kenneth who recycled my choreography as I reused the lift, in the pas de deux for Clara and the nephew, from my earlier ballet *The Mirror Walkers* which Kenneth had seen. Kenneth completely convinced himself that I had stolen from him, so I took the lift out. Similarly, when a poster design that included both our names seemed to suggest that I was the choreographer of his *Romeo and Juliet*, he told me I should get the poster redesigned. Kenneth's sensitivity to people attending his rehearsals was justified because it is easier to understand how the choreography is put together once you have seen it in process – hence why Kenneth was so suspicious of everybody. Even the ballet master or mistress, who is required to rehearse his work later, was not allowed in until Kenneth had finished. Whereas certain people thrive in difficult situations, and that was true with Kenneth to a certain degree, he did not have the right personality to thrive as a director, as was evident from his time in Berlin. I felt really sorry for him, but thought that he would be so much better off if he was just a choreographer.

It is hard to compare Kenneth's experiences in Berlin with those of John Cranko in Stuttgart. When John arrived in 1961 there was very little tradition. Nicholas Beriozov had introduced productions of the classics but had not managed to give the company the proper foundation of a full-time school on which to build a lasting future and develop talent from across Germany or overseas. John established a whole ballet tradition in Stuttgart which had, and still has, an international flavour. When Kenneth went to Berlin there was already a big tradition of neo-classical works mainly by Tatjana Gsovsky. The company was really a backing group for visiting star dancers. Talking to Kenneth when he was in Berlin as director, he did say he hoped to change the system. There was very little promotion from the corps de ballet to principal, for example. Cranko had enormous support from the wonderful intendant in Stuttgart, Walter Erich Schäfer, who was determined to prove that it was possible to make a classical ballet company in Germany. The opposition to that within the theatre, particularly from the opera company, was huge. Stuttgart, like many German cities, was completely opera, opera, opera, with the ballet company giving only occasional performances to give the opera a night off. John had to fight very hard, but he changed all that. In Berlin, by comparison, I was told, Kenneth largely absented himself from discussions about rehearsal time, resources for the ballet and production budgets. His unconventional domestic arrangements were used as a source of criticism as much as his plans for the company. Ultimately Kenneth did not have the strong support of Gustav Rudolf Sellner, the intendant in Berlin.

By the late 1960s, however, the Royal Opera House had invited Kenneth to take over as director of the Royal Ballet companies following Ashton's enforced retirement. Kenneth really thought this would be his salvation after his torrid time in Berlin. The directorship was a role that Kenneth wanted to fulfil, even though he was still recovering from a major stroke which occurred in Berlin, exacerbated by his alcoholism. His first work for the Royal Ballet since *Romeo and Juliet* five years before was *Checkpoint*, in November 1970 for the New Group. This was the start of Kenneth's campaign to get a better deal for the Royal Ballet and its productions. In the previous year, the Royal Opera had swallowed up over 80 percent of expenditure while the ballet companies' share, admittedly without any big new productions that year, had been less than 10 percent. There were 430 performances of ballet compared to a rival 135 of opera. Kenneth had seen in Stuttgart and Berlin how substantially the ballet companies in those opera houses were funded in comparison to London. Despite its heritage and international reputation the Royal Ballet was, comparatively, underfunded. Although Kenneth at that time had difficulty in speaking his mind, he certainly made himself clear with his actions. He surprised everyone with his hidden strength and determination.

Checkpoint was inspired by Kenneth's time in the divided city of Berlin and depicted a hostile totalitarian society in which all expression of human feeling was forbidden. Love could only be furtive. Coinciding with the start in Kenneth's directorship, the government reduced its Arts Council funding to the Royal Opera House. There the board's decision was to apply most of the cut to the touring company. Under John Field's leadership this had been built up to a strength of around 65 dancers with a large supporting staff and full orchestra performing big classics and present-day works. Under Field's direction standards were high and the company toured at home, including at Covent Garden when the resident company was elsewhere, as well as overseas. Under the new funding regime the touring company was reduced in numbers and the board had stipulated that new productions were meant to reflect the reduced circumstances. Kenneth was furious at this. In his perverse way he got Liz Dalton to design one of the biggest, heaviest, most complicated and expensive sets the company ever had to tour. Whether he did this consciously or not I do not know – but I can imagine him thinking, 'I'll bloody well show them!' Even on a good day it took 30 minutes to assemble the set, involving as it did scaffolding, back-projection and a huge electronic eye – and all this for a 20-minute ballet which essentially was an extended pas de deux. This was the complete opposite of the minimal sets designed for touring with which the New Group was expected to operate.

Kenneth cast Svetlana Beriosova and Donald MacLeary as a couple under observation by a surveillance camera at all times. Donald was a good partner for Svetlana, who usually appeared opposite her in princely roles at Covent Garden. He was tall and good looking. I first came across him at Sadler's Wells Theatre Ballet when I was helping with ballet mastering. I had to teach him to be a sailor in *Pineapple Poll*. He was a very quick learner. He also danced with Maureen Bruce in Alfred Rodrigues' *Saudades*. Donald was good in how he worked with choreographers, making suggestions about how things should go without pushing himself unduly, but in *Checkpoint* Svetlana and Donald had to climb the wall to which the surveillance camera was fixed, apparently unaided, though in fact they were supported by six men hidden behind elasticated plastic sheeting from which the wall was made. The lovers could express their love for each other only in the shadows, huddled in corners or in the camera's blind spot. At the end, the wall devoured the lovers. Only their hands were left visible as they tried vainly to reach each other.

Checkpoint was premiered at the opera house in Manchester. The first night in November 1970 was a disaster. Stage rehearsals had not been too bad, except the manager of the theatre announced that their insurance would not cover the cast, given the height of the wall and that they were not wearing a safety harness when they had to scale it. Svetlana and Donald agreed to appear only when they were sure that they were covered by the Royal Opera House's own policy. Just before the curtain was due to go up, the projector hanging from a bar in the flies and electronically connected with the cueing system crashed down onto the stage. The spool fell out and yards of film unwound. John Hall, our brilliant chief electrician, at once came to the rescue but said it would take some time to repair and reset everything. John Tooley, down from London for the premiere, came dashing backstage and insisted that an announcement be made – but declined to make it himself. The audience was already getting impatient, so it was left to David Rees, our company manager, to face the restive audience. He spoke quite brilliantly and assured them that it would be another five minutes before we would start. In fact it was at least another 20 minutes. This time it was the projector itself that jammed. Down it all had to come again, accompanied by the sound of a slow hand-clap and stamping feet. David Rees had to come in front of the curtain again to make another announcement. Finally everything was ready again and the ballet started after a wait of some 50 minutes amid ironic cheers from the public.

After such a delay it is not unreasonable to expect that what you had been waiting for was worth it. Sadly, this was not the case. All was well until the moment of the first filmed insert. It was completely out of sync with the recorded music, all the more galling as we still had to pay the orchestra for not playing live. For all its modernity of subject matter and design, Kenneth's ballet was considered immature. The music, which the composer Roberto Gerhard admitted was influenced by aircraft noise, was dismissed as excessively modern. What was missing, everybody pointed out, was any interesting choreography. After Manchester, *Checkpoint* was toured to Edinburgh and Glasgow but it only ever had 11 performances and was never seen in London.

For Covent Garden, Kenneth was fully occupied in planning his next full-length production, the expanded three-act version of *Anastasia*. In rehearsal it looked as though it was going to be a success. It was an ambitious depiction of Grand Duchess Anastasia's belief that she was the surviving heir to the Russian throne, what Lynn Seymour, the original *Anastasia*, described as an interweaving of Chekhovian nostalgia, violent Russian history and a climax in a mental hospital. True, Barry Kay was not an easy collaborator, but what he designed was a highly imaginative, if difficult to install, set. It consisted of a huge spiral vortex covered in gauze that was capable of indicating a glade of silver birch trees in the first act, an imperial ballroom in the second and Anastasia's deranged mind in the last. There was much excitement during the rehearsals, and morale at Covent Garden improved no end.

It was therefore a terrible shock to everyone when, despite the public's very positive response and the dancers' enjoyment of performing *Anastasia*, most of the critics damned it. They complained that Kenneth had not established from the start whether the ballet depicted actual events or were Anastasia's memories of them, so that it lacked a coherent storyline. Such a literal-minded complaint was not the sort of criticism to worry Kenneth as the construction of his ballets was often deliberately filmic, but he was deeply affected by the comments that dismissed *Anastasia* as filled with padding without weight or dramatic credibility. Some critics did praise the way Kenneth was able to indicate character through movement, particularly in a tender scene between the tsarina and the young Anastasia in the first act, but the shift from the music of Tchaikovsky's symphonies used in the first two acts to Bohuslav Martinů, coupled to electronic interpolations in the last act, was a problem for many viewers. It prompted walk-outs when *Anastasia* was toured to New York in 1972. Kenneth descended into despair. It is not an exaggeration to say he broke down completely and I became seriously worried about him. At the time there were whispers circulating that Rudolf Nureyev was being considered as an alternative director of the company, rumours that can only have originated with Nureyev himself or the Royal Opera House board.

Ballade was premiered in May 1972. Kenneth's overall state of health was still very fragile. The previous year he had been advised to stop smoking after his stroke in Germany in 1969. Otherwise, he was told he would have only a few weeks to live. With great strength of mind, Kenneth managed to quit, but he was vulnerable. Although he had been in psychoanalysis for many years, he seemed to have lost all confidence. However, by the miraculous arrival on the scene from Australia of Deborah Williams, then struggling to establish herself in London, Kenneth managed to sustain his resistance to drinking and smoking. He continued to create new ballets. *Ballade* was not one of his greatest but it was made to celebrate when Kenneth and Deborah were set up on a blind date by one of his closest friends, Jeffrey Solomons. Another friend, David Williams, came too to observe what happened. *Ballade* opened with four people watching a cinema screen, with their backs to the audience. The two on the outside – Kenneth and Deborah – evidently felt a strong attraction for each other when their eyes met. Their hands met too whenever the others, Solomons and Williams, happened to lean forward. This developed into a pas de deux expressing their feelings as the others continued to watch the film.

As in *Triad*, made five months earlier and included on the same pro-gramme, in which a girl disrupts the relationship between two brothers, in *Ballade* it was again a woman who alters the dynamic in the relation-ship of the men, as Deborah's presence in Kenneth's life was to do for real. She soon took charge. Deborah really saved Kenneth's life. He got back his confidence and health through her wonderful support. Deborah and Kenneth were married at the Chelsea register office in 1974. It was a very private occasion, with no big party. I was one of the witnesses, but as Sonya and I arrived after the ceremony had started, I was too late to witness anything. Then as now it was a nightmare to find a parking space and the wedding had to commence before we arrived. The other witness was Georgina Parkinson who was the original Rosaline in Kenneth's *Romeo and Juliet*. She adored him and his ballets and was always a very good friend to him, part of the dining club, the circle of intimate friends that Kenneth gathered around him. No doubt Georgina would have liked to have been more than that.

Georgina was for me a sort of catalyst of the Royal Ballet. She could sharpen the purity of Ashton's choreography with a slice of MacMillan's bitter passion. Vice versa, when tackling Kenneth's Juliet she would supply touches of Ashton's fluidity. She was the same in her daily life in the company with her extraordinary mix of vocabulary. About Violette Verdy she said, 'She's fucking beautiful but too sodding sweet for me.' I adored Georgina and her brilliant photographer husband, Roy Round. They were an amazing mix which worked incredibly well. She had one particular technical problem: pirouettes plagued her life. This was caused by her build, broad-shouldered and with narrow hips, which is not ideal when turning on pointe, although that build poses no problems for men turning on the ball of the foot. The best female turners are usually narrow shouldered with broadish hips. Rowena Jackson, with her small head, narrow shoulders, ample hips and calves, with not too much insteps, was an ideal turner. Nobody has come near her fouetté sequence in *Les Patineurs*.

When the time came for Georgina to stop dancing, she decided to go to New York, her favourite city, where she spent 30 years as a brilliant ballet mistress for American Ballet Theatre, also performing character parts in *Fall River Legend* and *Onegin*. Roy successfully re-established his photographic career there. I last saw Georgina as the queen mother in *Swan Lake* during American Ballet Theatre's season at the London Coliseum in spring 2009. She was looking far too thin but wonderful. At a dinner given by John and Anya Sainsbury afterwards, Georgina was on great form, but I never saw her again. At the end of that year she died of cancer in Manhattan. That was an awful shock. It is terrifying how someone so beautiful and vivacious, with so much still to give, can be cut down by this horrible disease. I still mourn her loss.

The premiere of *Ballade* was presented by the New Group, the name coined for the reduced touring company, in Lisbon in May 1972, a few days before the Covent Garden company was due to open its first season in New York under Kenneth's directorship and the first season since the retirement of Ashton, who was much loved by New York audiences. Due to Kenneth's fear of flying, he and Deborah travelled to America on the *QE2*, arriving only when the season was nearly finished. Sol Hurok, the company's longstanding promoter, was angry and it took Kenneth a long time to recover from the ill feeling that New York audiences felt by his late appearance. I think Kenneth purposefully avoided the opening night in New York as he was fearful of what the reaction might be. I met them at the docks and I could see that Kenneth was very nervous. He wanted to know everything that had happened in his absence.

The opening programme had been a gala, beginning with the shades' act from *La Bayadère*. The divertissements included my *Mirror Walkers* pas de deux with Merle Park and Desmond Kelly and Ashton's *Thais*, which went well. Kenneth's new pas de deux, *Side Show*, a comic circus act for Lynn Seymour and Rudolf Nureyev, fell flat, nor did *Triad* impress. Glen Tetley's *Field Figures* was coolly received as New York audiences had been familiar with Glen's sort of contemporary classicism for a decade. The last ballet was John Cranko's *Poème de l'extase* in which Margot Fonteyn, as an ageing beauty, was tossed acrobatically between her former lovers. John had created the ballet for his Stuttgart company who had already danced it in New York when it had not been a particularly successful showcase for Margot. Set against Klimt-inspired draperies, it traded on Margot's legend without adding to its lustre. I had to tell Kenneth that *Anastasia* had not gone well and Sol was not happy as he had wanted *The Sleeping Beauty* or *Swan Lake* in the repertoire.

I was in a fine state. This was my first American tour with the Royal Ballet. I was still new, and having to play director was uncomfortable. That season was sheer hell. I really was not ready for the big time, six weeks at the New York Met, but I had to learn pretty fast. For once Michael Somes gave me support, which was unusual. Always in America there is a lack of stage time. I wanted *La Bayadère* on the first night to really look as good as possible, to look marvellous. We had not really got it together in rehearsals and the placing was bad. We had to keep stopping the rehearsal as I was determined that it would go on up to standard, but *Bayadère* looked awful. I asked Michael if he thought we could overrun or whether that would create trouble with Hurok who was notoriously tight with the purse strings. Michael told me I should do what I thought was right and he would help. He went to Hurok and told him that we would be going into overtime as we were not ready and needed to get it right. For once Hurok was not angry, even though it meant more expense. It gave me a lot of confidence to have the support of Michael who was an old hand in such matters. On another tour Hurok insisted on having *The Sleeping Beauty* cut so it would not run into overtime. I refused, saying it would be presented complete – but I did go to the conductor and asked him to play fast, as I did not want another row with Hurok. He was pleased at the result and the performance did not suffer. For the 1972 season Kenneth had a rough time once he finally arrived, mainly from the fans who were vile towards him. There was an ante-room between backstage and front of house. As Kenneth walked through, fans would act out being sick accompanied by violent vomiting noises.

The Poltroon, unveiled in October 1972, was a peculiar and quite nasty version of the commedia dell'arte story of Columbine and Harlequin. Pierrot kills Columbine, which involved Brenda Last having to drop dead from a window, during a violently sexual pas de deux. Pierrot continued to dance with her lifeless body before killing the others. The ballet was considered nasty, sick even, and survived for only a couple of years. Some critics did question how Kenneth could produce new work of any lasting value when he had been the subject of hostile personal criticism on both sides of the Atlantic for the past two years.

With *Seven Deadly Sins* the following year, Kenneth was on more confident ground. It was a piece he had already choreographed for Western Theatre Ballet a decade or so before with Anya Linden and Cleo Laine. This time the performers were Jennifer Penney who was rather good and Georgia Brown who was wonderful. The designs were by Ian Spurling. True, the Royal Opera House was too big for the piece, it really needs more intimate venues, and it was too hard a piece to tour but the cast gave it some good performances.

Although Kenneth produced some new choreography for a new production of *The Sleeping Beauty* at Covent Garden in 1973, I had to interpret his intentions for the designer Peter Farmer without really knowing what they were. Kenneth was much more concerned with his next big ballet, *Manon*, which was unveiled in February 1974. He had a few false starts with it, particularly with the beginning, and the music is thin, but it all came together well and there was a positive sense among the dancers that the ballet would be a success. De Valois was still very active in the company and came to the stage rehearsals. She used to sit behind Kenneth in the orchestra stalls. 'You have got to get Madam away from me, she's making me nervous. I don't need her suggestions,' Kenneth hissed at me. The truth about Madam was that sometimes she could be right and sometimes wrong, so I could understand Kenneth's point of view. It is difficult for a choreographer to see what is required when a ballet first reaches the stage. It is something they need to see for themselves. I suggested to Madam she should swap seats to get a better a view. Of course she saw through the subterfuge but she did move further away. Not very much later she was gesturing me to go over to her. 'You've got to let Kenneth know he has got it wrong. He's using the wrong entrance for Manon. It would be much better on the other side.'

I assured Madam that although Kenneth was too caught up with the rehearsal just at present, I would find the right moment to mention it to him and was sure that he would bear her suggestion in mind. Well I did tell Kenneth what Madam had said, and he just said, 'Oh what rubbish!' She was back again the next morning and I expected her to query why her change had not been made. 'Oh no. I've changed my mind. I was completely wrong about that,' she said.

Kenneth was always able to get good performances out of people. Although he had a very definite sense of character and was particular about how he wanted his choreography performed, he would always ensure that dancers were comfortable with the feelings and situations that he was asking them to portray. The role of Manon was principally worked out on Jennifer Penney when Antoinette Sibley was injured, but it is a role that captured aspects of Antoinette's flirtatious personality. Kenneth's Manon has a hard edge; she has known poverty, having been brought up on the streets. That is somewhere she does not want to return to.

Manon is not a ballet that I want to see again and again, although I do prefer it to *Mayerling*. For all its historical veracity, with its scenario drawn from biographies and memoires, police and medical records, *Mayerling* has too much padding with all the business with the Hungarian officers and the group scenes. Ultimately some subjects are suitable for ballet and others are not. The narrative has to come over through the dance and the situation. In *Manon* the highlights are the pas de deux in the bedroom and at the end, but for a company ultimately it is not a challenging ballet as the big classics are. There is no real dancing for the corps de ballet, no big showcase numbers for them or enough opportunities for pas d'action or for the soloists. For Kenneth, crowd scenes were always something of a difficult duty. *Manon* falls down particularly in the port scene.

Of other ballets from that period, *Elite Syncopations* was Kenneth in relaxed mood. It was a piece where dancers tended to build up their roles. Choreographers do not like that. Kenneth wanted his choreography presented accurately. He was very concerned with timing and nuance, qualities which do make a difference to how a ballet looks. The following year, *The Four Seasons*, set to some of Giuseppe Verdi's ballet music from his operas, was a dance showcase, particularly for Monica Mason as summer, but it is not a work that will come back. A postponed revival of

Symphony did not establish itself when it finally returned, and it has not been seen subsequently.

Kenneth MacMillan was really the first person to recognise the great potential of Benesh notation. He asked Faith Worth, who was a great exponent of notation, to come and notate his new ballets unofficially. It sometimes happened that she never finished recording a ballet and incomplete scores accumulated under her bed. Other choreographers watched with interest and soon realised the great advantage that it would be when it came to reproducing their works. When the Benesh Institute was established, Kenneth became president and gradually many more companies supported it. Although it took some time for this form of notation to be accepted, Benesh has become a major contributor to recording classical ballet for most classical companies internationally. It was brilliantly invented by Rudolf and Joan Benesh. The notation stave is set out on the page along with the music stave running parallel, every musical note and dance sign can be read together. It has meant that the creators of ballets can register their works and acquire copyright, which is a huge step forward. In fact, it is true to say that Benesh notation is now indispensable and it is possible to have a permanent record lodged at the institute which can be used for reference. It is completely accurate and can also show dynamics and expressions. This must of course be agreed by the choreographer. It is an enormous aid to the creative process and makes the revival of anything from a solo to a scene with a cast of hundreds quick and efficient to set. It can also incorporate authorised changes that a choreographer or producer may make over the years but still retain the original. The hours and money and bad tempers that have been saved by this brilliant recording process are incalculable. The advantage over film, which is of course also very important, is that it does not show an artist's interpretation of a role, just the basic steps, musical timing and position and move of every part of the body. Benesh notation is also invaluable for analytical purposes by both medical and sports professionals. For me personally, Benesh notation has been indispensible. My productions of the classics, sometimes including sections of new choreography, do get mounted around the world. It is marvellous that a notator can set the whole ballet from the score.

Monica Parker is somebody who transformed the notation department at the Royal Opera House and staged Kenneth's ballets overseas.

Monica taught *Giselle* for me in Houston but she left early, before I arrived. She loathed the music, 'Those wilis are driving me mad!' she said. When I restaged *The Nutcracker* in 1999 I redid the snowflakes, keeping the patterns from the notation, but making them dance more. Grant Coyle was very helpful in that process. The one important thing to remember is that someone who knows the work should always go to the final rehearsals and bring it all to life. All theatre needs that. Luckily now there are several notators who do this beautifully.

In the case of MacMillan's ballets, thanks to his interest in notation, they are pretty accurately recorded choreographically. Notation alone, however, has not been enough to secure the survival of several of Kenneth's ballets, which are now owned by his widow Deborah. What is less fixed is the question of interpretation. Kenneth did not stipulate that. His ballets were an open script so long as the text was not interfered with, which is why I find the redesigns and new stagings of his ballets so questionable. Interfering should be against the law. *Romeo and Juliet*, *Manon*, *Solitaire* and *Danses concertantes* have all been variously redesigned. In Sarasota now *Concerto* has acquired panels depicting swaying trees and billowing clouds, thanks to Deborah. Some changes, such as for the crypt scene at the end of *Romeo and Juliet*, mean the tremendous sense of proportion and looming danger that the giant angel figures, originally designed by Nico Georgiadis, has been lost. Removing some of the tombs means that the choreography has to be altered too. Deborah believes that designs have to be altered over the years to maintain the freshness of a ballet. The difficulty comes in maintaining the feeling of the original. How do you adapt something created in the last century for audiences in this? A ballet should never become a museum piece. It must earn its place on the stage and sometimes that does mean a change of look. With *Anastasia* that ruined the ballet. I thought the way Kenneth had expanded his original one-act ballet into three resulted in *Anastasia* being a funny sort of work, but Deborah has messed it up good and proper in her subsequent restaging of it in 1996. Deborah's much more fundamental changes with *Isadora* and *The Prince of the Pagodas* were much more damaging. She changed them into how she wanted to see them. *Isadora* emerged as a multimedia talk or lecture demonstration and Deborah succeeded only in making *Pagodas* boring.

Kenneth adored Benjamin Britten's score for *The Prince of the Pagodas*. It sounds wonderful in the concert hall but theatre audiences have tended not to share his enthusiasm for the ballet. When Kenneth first choreographed it in 1989 his ballet succeeded better than in later revivals, but he really needed to have another go at it himself. Unfortunately the attitude of Britten's executors and Kenneth's untimely death meant that did not happen. When Deborah oversaw an overhaul of *Pagodas* in 2012 she failed to recognise that it is first and foremost a fairytale ballet with its set-piece ensembles. Deborah cut the classical ensembles until the audience was almost ready to go home. When I remonstrated with her about the changes, which I believe radically altered the nature of Kenneth's ballet, she told me that I did not understand anything about magic. Ah well. I will have to content myself with the good-luck card sent to me by one of the cast when I staged *The Sleeping Beauty* in Munich some 30-odd years before. It was addressed to me as 'the big fairy-tale magician'. It was interesting, however, the way in which the score for *Pagodas* was cut and reordered – it only served to highlight how episodic it is, without dramatic propulsion. There are too many numbers that conclude without any resolution, which was at odds with Deborah's aim of including only what was dramatically logical in her restaging. Her changes really did not help.

But who should stage a ballet after a choreographer's death is a difficult area. Could a different producer or choreographer be found? A new artist of whatever background working on another's territory is always problematic, as Peter Farmer's re-invention of Oliver Messel proved with the recreation of *The Sleeping Beauty* at Covent Garden. Deborah's decision to replace the creamy white floorcloth and wings that gave Nico Georgiadis' designs for *The Prince of the Pagodas* such a sense of a mystery and other-worldliness were made more prosaic with the black flooring and wings that Deborah imposed. Perhaps as an easel painter she does know something about choreography or staging or lighting and all the other elements that go to make up a production – but I really wonder.

During the last year of Kenneth's life I worked with him on two productions. Kenneth revisited his 1958 ballet *The Burrow* for Birmingham Royal Ballet in the autumn of 1991. *The Burrow* was created first for the Royal Opera House when Kenneth's ballet was intended to share a triple bill with two other new ballets by John Cranko and my own, *A Blue Rose*.

Kenneth did not want to unveil his new work alongside two other prem-ieres, so he claimed he could not be ready in time. In fact he was ready but managed to have his own first night separately a few evenings later. The tendency is for a ballet to fall flat without the original imagination at work that created it. I think that was true to a degree with the revival of *The Burrow*. It was a great hit when new. Returning to it, Kenneth reworked it considerably as the original notation and the archive film was fragmentary, but the ballet did not come over so well.

Since my days as Kenneth's associate our relationship had changed as I had become a director in my own right and separated myself from the Royal Ballet. I left him alone to work on the revival but I did think that Nico's new designs, suggesting a cardboard city in which the homeless scratch out an existence, very much an issue in the early 1990s, were overly complicated. He was notorious for always choosing the most expensive fabrics for his costumes until wardrobe departments got wise to him. They would swap the price tickets around on fabric swatches to curtail Nico's excesses. Many people have taken *The Burrow* to be a depic-tion of the wartime experiences of Anne Frank in occupied Amsterdam, but Kenneth was much less definitive. In his original programme note, and with the cast in Birmingham, he suggested a more universal drama about a group of people close to breaking point. Characters were types; an outcast, victims of intolerance who are themselves intolerant, a joker whose humour he uses to threaten, and a child without fear who inter-acts with a grand but hysterical woman, Anne Heaton originally. In Birmingham, Kenneth cast Marion Tait as the principal woman and made that role into more of an actress, too much of a change I thought.

Kenneth had adored Marion since he created *Playground* on her in 1979. This was a rather good but difficult ballet. It came about almost by accident. Kenneth had started work on another ballet but decided he did not like the music and cancelled it after two rehearsals. He redis-covered a score by Gordon Crosse that he had commissioned but never used and hoped an idea would emerge, which as *Playground*, it did. It was Kenneth's version of the Orpheus story but made before his own *Orpheus* in 1982. His fascination with that story stemmed from when he choreographed Gluck's opera at Covent Garden in 1961. *Playground* was set in an asylum. All the characters appeared to be mad, even the doctor. It was a work that demanded absolute conviction from the dancers.

It was very draining to perform, especially a Wednesday matinée to a half-empty house, but Kenneth was mad, in a positive sense, about Marion's performance. She was incredibly bold, a very good actress.

Kenneth also agreed that Birmingham Royal Ballet could dance his *Romeo and Juliet* which was staged in June 1992. I had decided against adding *Manon* to our repertoire as it was too heavy a production to tour easily. I had never really had the opportunity of producing a *Romeo and Juliet* myself. Some years earlier I had considered acquiring the version by Frederick Ashton, made originally for Royal Danish Ballet in Copenhagen in 1955. It was never a powerful staging but physically it was manageable. Fred was always worried about casting but liked the idea of Leanne Benjamin as Juliet, then in her early career with Sadler's Wells Royal Ballet. I thought we had an agreement when I went away with the company on a long international tour. Because of that I was not able to plan the production. On my return, I discovered that Peter Schaufuss was going to produce it for English National Ballet. 'I've got Leanne Benjamin for you,' he had told Fred, buttering him up, having lured Leanne to join his company, unbeknown to me. I think she needed to be sure of her new contract before telling me. In fact I believe it was when I first took Leanne and Roland Price to perform Balanchine's *Tchaikovsky pas de deux* at a festival in Japan that Schaufuss first saw Leanne dance. In retrospect, I recall them being frequently in cahoots there. Fred had always been dotty about Peter and so the ballet went on with his company. I was really sorry to lose Leanne but there was no stopping her.

As an alternative, I decided against commissioning David Bintley because I was worried about how he might tackle the elements of fate and doom in the story. Although upset that Fred had not even bothered to tell me about his decision in the event, it was a good choice to have Kenneth's version. I prefer his choreography for the principal characters, though what surrounds it is less good. Cranko's crowd scenes are better. I rarely go to see a performance of Kenneth's *Romeo* for the performance of Juliet, but when I approached him about Birmingham Royal Ballet performing it he was worried that there was nobody, in his view, within the company who could play Juliet from the dramatic point of view. This is the heart of the ballet. The ballerina does not have to worry about the role from a technical perspective as the steps are not that difficult, there

1. Sonya Hana, 1950s (Photo by © Roy Round)

(Above left) 2. Hans Zullig in *The Big City*, Ballets Jooss, 1940s

(Above right) 3. Kurt Jooss

(Right) 4. Ballets Jooss, *The Prodigal Son*

(Below) 5. James Bailey as the standard bearer, *The Green Table* by Kurt Jooss, Birmingham Royal Ballet, 1993, (© Leslie E Spatt)

(*Above left*) 6. In *Summer Interlude* by Michael Somes, Sadler's Wells Theatre Ballet, 1950; (*Above right*) 7. *Swan Lake*, Sadler's Wells Theatre Ballet, 1950s, left to right, Michael Hogan, Svetlana Beriosova, me (Baron); (*Below left*) 8. In *Selina* by Andrée Howard, Sadler's Wells Theatre Ballet 1949; (*Below right*) 9. In *The Telltale Heart* by Peter Darrell, designed by Kenneth MacMillan, Mercury Theatre 1952, (© Paul Wilson)

10. My modelling days, 1940s (© Rayment Kirby)

(Above) 11. With Pirmin Trecu, left, Colorado, 1951;
(Below) 12. Members of Sadler's Wells Theatre Ballet, with me back centre, Ottawa, 1951

(Above) 13. *Dancing* by John Cranko, with Kenneth MacMillan centre, designed by John and Myfanwy Piper, Henley, 1952 (© Paul Wilson)

(Left) 14. With Sonya Hana, *Paso Doble* by John Cranko, Henley, 1952, (© Paul Wilson)

(Left) 15. Portrait by
Clemence Dane, 1952

(Left) 16. Our wedding
day, 1954

(Opposite top) 17. Right, with David Gill, *Dido and Aeneas*, Sadler's Wells Opera, 1951;
(Opposite middle) 18. Sadler's Wells Opera, 1950s, with me centre, in *The Bartered Bride*;
(Opposite bottom) 19. Royal Opera, 1968, Monica Mason, lifted centre, in *Aida* (© Houston Rogers / Victoria and Albert Museum, London)

(Above) 20. With Yolanda Sonnabend discussing *A Blue Rose*, 1957; *(Below)* 21. Susan Alexander partnered by Edward Miller, *A Blue Rose*, 1957 (©Edward Miller / ArenaPAL)

(*Above*) 22. Claudia Algeranova and David Poole in *The Great Peacock*, Edinburgh International Ballet, 1958 (© Louis Klemantski); (*Below*) 23. Chesterina Sim Zecha with Nicholas Chagrin, William Marin and John McDonald in *The Trial*, Sunday Ballet Club, 1961 (Photo by © Roy Round)

(Above left) 24. Me potting (© Michael Murray); *(Above right)* 25. *Left to right*, Ray Barra, Marcia Haydée and Kenneth MacMillan, 1960s (Photo by © Roy Round); *(Below)* 26. *Left to right*, John Cranko, Kenneth MacMillan and me, Stuttgart, 1960s (© Werner Schloske)

(Above) 27. Me seated front right, BBC producers' course, 1960s;
(Below) 28. *Giselle*, filmed at Riverside studios, Hammersmith, 1959 (© Zoë Dominic)

(Above) 29. *Quintet*, Brenda Last lifted by Piers Beaumont, David Wall and Johaar Mosaval with Ronald Emblem, right, Royal Ballet Touring Company, 1964 (© Zoë Dominic); *(Below)* 30. *The Mirror Walkers*, Karen Kain, National Ballet of Canada, 1972 (© Leslie E Spatt)

(Top) 31. *The Sleeping Beauty*, Royal Ballet, the awakening, 1968 (© Houston Rogers / Victoria and Albert Museum, London); *(Above left)* 32. *The Sleeping Beauty*, Royal Ballet, Aurora's friends, designs by Lila de Nobili, 1968 (© Leslie E Spatt); *(Above right)* 33. *The Sleeping Beauty*, Royal Ballet, Antoinette Sibley as Aurora and Anthony Dowell as Florimund, 1968 (© Leslie E Spatt)

(*Above*) 34. The wilis rise from the ground, *Giselle*, Royal Ballet, 1971, designed by Peter Farmer (© Anthony Crickmay / Victoria and Albert Museum, London); (*Below left*) 35. David Wall and Doreen in Wells in *Giselle*, Royal Ballet Touring Company, 1968 (© Jennie Walton); (*Below right*) 36. Genesia Roastio, left with Lesley Collier in *Giselle*, Royal Ballet, 1985 (© Leslie E Spatt)

are no 32 fouettés that can ruin Odile for many ballerinas, but it is a role that demands passion and conviction. Kenneth thought it best if we could get Nina Ananiashvili, who memorably had brought fresh perspectives to Belle Rose in Kenneth's *The Prince of the Pagodas*, along with Alexei Fadeyechev from the Bolshoi to do the first few performances.

I had to oversee the production and accordingly set the wheels in motion. To my great joy I found that Nina and Alexei were free and would love to do it. Kenneth also wanted to use a new designer. Rightly he felt that the Georgiadis designs were too big for touring and a new look would make the Birmingham version different from that at Covent Garden. Typically for Kenneth he commissioned Paul Andrews, a young designer aged just 21, to redesign the ballet. Kenneth had seen his work at the students' graduation exhibition at Wimbledon College of Art. Romeo was Paul's first professional commission. Would this be too much for one so inexperienced to cope with?

There was considerable opposition from the board and the various heads of production departments at the Royal Opera House, where the sets and costumes were to be made. Kenneth insisted. Paul was an immensely gifted designer whose career was short. He died only five years later. He designed a set that incorporated ten large classical statues positioned on a colonnade. They all wore a helmet, sandals and little else, being differentiated only by the size of their genitalia. They became wickedly known as the cock ring, a joke that Kenneth enjoyed, but were immensely distracting. In the middle of one discussion about what could be done to make them less eye-catching, Deborah intervened with her suggestions. 'Oh do be quiet, you don't know anything about this!' Kenneth told his wife. He was always very single-minded about his work.

All was going well for this revival when it transpired that Ananiashvili was pregnant and suffering bad morning sickness but hoped she would still be ready for the first night. So we had to be prepared. Kenneth's next choice for Juliet alighted on Marion Tait. She was overjoyed. Nearing the end of her dancing career, then 41, Marion had wondered whether she might be cast as the nurse. She more than repaid Kenneth's faith in her. The more they worked together, the more they became good friends. Her Juliet was one of the best things that she ever did, earning her an Olivier award nomination and winning Dancer of the Year from *Dance and Dancers* and *The Evening Standard* ballet award. Marion captured the youthful quality of the role very well but also showed Juliet's drive and determination in the later scenes. You never thought that Marion was too old for Juliet. It was great for her that the chance of the role came along at a time when she was feeling a bit passé.

The night Kenneth died that October during the first night of a revival of *Mayerling* at Covent Garden, Birmingham Royal Ballet was performing *Romeo and Juliet* at the Hippodrome. Incredibly we did not hear about his death until I got home after the performance when Peter Brownlee, the Royal Ballet's manager, phoned me with the news. It was a dreadful shock. It was unfortunate that nobody at the Royal Opera House had thought to let us know earlier, as all of us in Birmingham would have wanted, for Kenneth's sake, to acknowledge him together in silence. As it was, I was there with Sonya at midnight alone with the news, knowing how upset the company would be when they learned the following morning what had happened but had not been able to com-miserate with each other. I did manage to speak to Deborah who had been sitting with Kenneth during the performance. He had begun to feel very restless and uncomfortable. He left the auditorium to walk around backstage where he collapsed and died alone in an empty dressing-room. Deborah was of course deeply upset but calm – as well as angry at the way Jeremy Isaacs, Covent Garden's general director, had announced the news to the audience before Deborah had informed their teenage daughter.

I gave the tribute to Kenneth at his memorial service. To be honest, I do not think he will go down in history as one of the Royal Ballet's greatest leaders: somehow he was too inward-looking, too sensitive. I knew shortly after Kenneth's first season as director in London started that it would not last. Although possessing a brilliant intellect and great artistic integrity and extraordinary inner strength, Kenneth found it extremely hard to combine his great talent as a choreographer with the huge responsibilities that he had to face as the director of a company of the magnitude of the Royal Ballet. That was why, in the end, he decided to give up the directorship and concentrate on choreography alone.

He will be remembered for enriching the companies' repertory with many new and different works. He added over 60 works to the repertory during the time he was director. Out of the 16 choreographers commis-sioned, 13 were working with the Royal Ballet for the first time. He was also very aware that the future did not just depend on new works and new approaches, but also on a respect for the past. The Royal Ballet organisation has a unique heritage created by many great artists, which he always insisted must never be overlooked as this is where the strength of its companies lay. He encouraged many talented young dancers and introduced great ones including Natalia Makarova, Mikhail Baryshnikov, Galina Samsova and many more guest artists to the companies. His casting of young or unexpected artists in major roles was well informed. He led major foreign tours to the United States, Brazil and Japan.

When he left in 1977, the company was in excellent shape. Tough as things were, it was a productive period and I feel privileged to have worked with such an extraordinarily creative man who has left such a rich heritage of great works; not just to the Royal Ballet, but to companies the world over. Kenneth and I had always worked well together but I do not regret that I declined his offer to become his assistant director in Berlin. The amazing thing about Kenneth is that although on the surface he sometimes appeared to be a very gentle person, fraught with nerves and ill health, underneath he had an inner strength that impelled him to do things his way, both as a choreographer and a director. This sometimes made him unpopular with the establishment, critics and his peers, but he always stuck to his guns. I think he was probably the most honest man with whom I have ever worked, and the one who suffered most in pursuance of his art. I have always felt a strong bond between us and a fascination for his extraordinary and unexplainable talent.

Somewhat enviously, John Cranko considered Kenneth's choreography to be more distinctive than his own, which is true, but I am not sure how individual Kenneth's choreography actually was. His language was largely traditionally classical but with changes to steps that tended towards the contemporary. When he created *Song of the Earth* in Stuttgart in 1965 I believe Kenneth was attempting to create something more contemporary but did not have the language at that stage to express his intentions. In most of his ballets, his choreography for the corps de ballet is mostly undistinguished. It is an area where I wished he really had put his mind to more, but the bourrées, a series of linking steps that he once choreographed for a group of girls at the Royal Academy of Dance, where they changed direction and formation, was simply done but beautifully so.

By the time that Kenneth created his version of *Hamlet*, *Sea of Troubles* in 1988 for Dance Advance, an ensemble of former Royal Ballet dancers organised by Susan Crow and Jennifer Jackson, Kenneth was working in a much freer, more contemporary vein. The ballet was made away from the pressures of the Royal Opera House. It premiered at the Gardiner centre in Brighton, and Kenneth created something expressionistic rather than literal. *Sea of Troubles* jumps from scene to scene, sometimes only seconds long, like a film, and has no linear logic. The cast of six switches between roles during the ballet. Kenneth's choreography was anti-balletic, stark and harrowing. In one moment Hamlet appears to hold Gertrude over her dead husband, seemingly supported by Hamlet holding only the back of her neck. In *Sea of Troubles* he created maximum impact with minimal resources and the resulting choreography was recognisably his own.

His works that survive best, however, and which are taking on a timeless quality, are such plotless ballets as *Concerto* and *Song of the Earth*. These should be sacrosanct. Yet even Kenneth's non-narrative ballets are more than pure dance. He once said at a choreographic competition that choreography is as much about ideas as steps. Kenneth was never short of ideas for ballets nor innovative ways of presenting them, frequently using new designers, commissioned scores or incorporating film or voice into his productions. Pushing the boundaries of what ballet could portray is what drove Kenneth forward. He was always anxious to get dancers to use their bodies to express feelings other than the balletic norms of love, sadness and joy.

His ballets were often about loneliness, fear, terror, lust, hate or sexual frustration. Consider his depiction of concentration camps in *Valley of Shadows*, dysfunctional family relationships in many of his ballets, mortality in *Gloria*, *Requiem* and others, and the nature of sanity, as in *Playground*. While his ballets were not always perfectly realised, construction and craftsmanship never being his strongest points, Kenneth pushed ballet in new directions. What was new and challenging then, however, frequently dates the fastest. Kenneth's most modern and provocative ballets are now the ones seen least. His big blockbuster ballets may be what attract dancers and companies for artistic and commercial reasons, but they and a handful of one-act works still seen only give a limited impression of Kenneth's range.

There was also a very witty and humorous side to Kenneth both on and off stage. When you spent time with him socially he really was amusingly good company. He was a good mimic thanks to being able to recognise dancers' strengths and weaknesses. He had quite a collection of dirty jokes hidden away. He used to ask Ray Barra to say something really filthy – and Ray would invariably oblige.

Onstage, Kenneth's *Elite Syncopations* is hugely popular with audiences. It is, I think, a bit too long but it has hilarious sections, particularly the Alaskan rag for the tall girl and short boy, created by Vergie Derman and Wayne Sleep, which is brilliantly funny, at least when played straight. This was Kenneth with his hair down, but when it was new in 1974, predictably critics found fault. They accused Kenneth of riding the popular wave of Scott Joplin's music that the film *The Sting* had prompted a year before. Kenneth's ballet followed Barry Moreland's *Prodigal Son – In Ragtime*, made for London Festival Ballet earlier that year also using Joplin's music, and Kenneth was seen to be following a trend, whereas he had been planning *Elite Syncopations* for some time.

As a performer, Kenneth was brilliant as the bossy sister in *Cinderella*, the role forever associated with Robert Helpmann. He appeared opposite Frederick Ashton as the timid sister in several revivals in the 1950s. His performance was captured on film in a studio recording made by NBC in New York during April 1957, which subsequently was released on DVD. In retrospect it is tempting to detect traces of Jack Lemmon's alter ego, Daphne, in *Some Like it Hot*, except of course that film was only released a couple of years later. Kenneth's performance is remarkably considered, recognisably feminine but still decidedly masculine in the best tradition of a pantomime dame, rather than camped up as a drag act as it is today. He was very funny.

Such was Kenneth's success he was offered the cross-dressing title role in Frank Loesser and George Abbott's musical *Where's Charley?*, based on the classic Brandon Thomas farce, *Charley's Aunt*, that was being staged by Billy Chappell in London in 1958. Kenneth turned it down, pleading choreographic commitments. This was actually some months before he created his version of *Agon*, and in reality Kenneth was too frightened to take it on. In the event Norman Wisdom played the role. Although Kenneth once said he hated Cranko's *The Lady and the Fool* for being too sentimental, he scored a huge success as the sad clown, Moondog, created by him in 1954.

Offstage, while travelling by ship to tour in South Africa that year, to pass the time Kenneth, along with David Gill who later became a highly successful film editor, created a silent movie using several members of the company. It was a parody of a detective thriller of the 1930s. Kenneth, as well as directing, played the leading investigator. He had of course played Sherlock Holmes in Margaret Dale's *The Great Detective* the year before. In the shipboard film Stanley Holden, who was to go on to create Widow Simone in *La Fille mal gardée*, was Kenneth's accomplice. I had a minuscule part as a confused, elderly gentleman obsessed with completing a ball game puzzle, oblivious to the frenzied activities going on around him. A private showing in a small cinema was arranged later for an invited audience consisting mainly of dancers, staff and technicians. It lasted only about 20 minutes, but throughout it was thanks to Kenneth that everybody fell about with hysterical laughter.

CHAPTER 6

Getting on with it

'JUST GET ON WITH IT' was the typically forthright maxim that Ninette de Valois shared with me when I was first put in charge of anything. During my long association with de Valois she gave me several words of advice. I particularly remember her telling me, 'Never waste time justifying your mistakes, just get on with the job in hand. We all make mistakes and nothing is to be gained by pretending they can be justified.' Both pieces of advice stood me in good stead during the years I worked alongside Kenneth MacMillan in the 1970s as his associate director and through the long period when I was director of Sadler's Wells Royal Ballet and Birmingham Royal Ballet.

When I finally finished commuting between Stuttgart and London in 1967 I needed to find what opportunities I could. I jumped at a chance to do some work in Israel for Jeanette Ordman who headed the Bat-Dor company which was just being established. International opportunities were rare in those days. I knew Jeannette from my days in television when she appeared in *The Sleeping Beauty* as one of Aurora's friends. Jeanette's ambitious goal was for the company to rival international standards, but she recognised in its formative stages she could not rely on Israeli choreographers. Besides me, she invited Antony Tudor and Rudi van Dantzig among many to work with the company. It was funded by Bethsabée de Rothschild who had moved to Israel a few years earlier following the failure of her marriage to Donald Bloomingdale, of the New York department store fame. Bethsabée had already founded the Batsheva Dance Company which was based on Martha Graham technique. Bethsabée was a patron of Graham and once during a tour by the company, clad in Dior and smoking Dunhill cigarettes, she acted as wardrobe mistress. The Bat-Dor was a vehicle for Jeannette who was artistic director, principal dancer and teacher at its school. She was also Bethsabée's partner and I quickly learned that Bethsabée liked to be bossed around. Jeanette exploited that. She was very possessive of her company but one thing it was not was a classical troupe. There was only one boy there who could do a pirouette. Altogether I staged four ballets there.

I decided to revive *The Great Peacock* which I had made first some years earlier. I also created *Concerto*, loosely based on classical ballet set to Handel and designed to display the young dancers. In the same mould I also made *Variations*, set to Vivaldi. I also restaged *Dance Macabre* for them. Putting the ballets on nearly killed the Bat-Dor dancers. Jeanette wanted to be the star of everything and had a good technique, but hers was a style of dancing that I did not like. The leading role in *The Great Peacock* was one she could do, but I had difficult times with her. I suggested to Bethsabée that somebody should really talk to Jeanette about how she was running the company. I was fed up as she was stealing all the rehearsal time for herself, despite having asked me to Israel to work with them.

Bethsabée invited me to her villa where we could talk in confidence so that she could learn more. It was palatial, full of art treasures and sculpture – and surrounded by security fences and barbed wire. This was not so long after the war in 1967 when Israel attacked Egypt, something that drew Syria and Jordan into a wider conflict. Shelling or mortar attacks were not uncommon and often we could not go out. We were sometimes two hours late arriving at a venue for a performance. It was all pretty unsafe with some nasty situations. And so it proved that day at Bethsabée's villa, if for different reasons. We sat down to talk by the swimming pool. I believed that if Bethsabée really wanted the Bat-Dor company to survive, she needed to be told some hard facts about Jeanette whom we assumed was somewhere in her own part of the house. Wrong! Jeanette was in fact sitting above where we were, listening to every word. She jumped down, screaming and shouting at Bethsabée. I could not think of anything better to do than to jump in the pool while the women fought it out. A huge row followed and Jeanette actually paid some heed to what I had told Bethsabée who, I am afraid, received a few rather nasty bruises.

What I did like about working in Israel was the strength of the Israelis, particularly the young men, who revealed an interior gentleness and friendliness despite displaying a strong or hostile exterior. This quality – sabra – apparently refers to a desert plant, the prickly pear, where a thick skin conceals a soft and sweet inside. Getting beyond that front was very satisfying. While I was in Tel-Aviv I gave a party for everybody at my flat. I got in a good store of alcohol and it was a great party. Everybody seemed to be getting suitably drunk but really hardly any drink had been touched, perhaps a quarter of a bottle of whisky and a couple of beers. I was told, 'We don't need alcohol to get excited, just water, fruit juice, music and good company.'

I remember vividly the day in the summer of 1969 when news came through from Berlin that Kenneth MacMillan had suffered a major stroke while attending the annual ballet week in Munich with John Cranko and Liz Dalton. I was at the Royal Opera House at the time and it all sounded very serious. Kenneth had suffered some paralysis on his left side and his speech slurred. His extreme stress, depression and alcohol and nicotine dependency that I had seen while visiting him in Berlin had evidently caused his body to send out a cry for help. The possibility that he might die seemed very real. At Covent Garden it was felt imperative that everything possible was done to get him back to London as quickly as possible, not only because of Kenneth's medical condition but because he was shortly to take over the directorship of the Royal Ballet.

To be absolutely honest, I never really knew why the board had chosen Kenneth to become director. I also found it hard to understand why Kenneth wanted the job. He had been miserable as artistic director in Berlin where, as in London, the ballet company shared a large opera house. The challenge of being responsible for the Royal Ballet with its two big companies, its smaller educational wing, Ballet for All, led by Peter Brinson, as well as taking an active role in the work of the senior school at Hammersmith, and its junior department at White Lodge at Richmond, was not well aligned with Kenneth's strengths, interests, personality or abilities.

I had declined Kenneth's offer to be his assistant director in Berlin in 1966. When he repeated the offer in London in 1970, an offer I accepted, neither of us was prepared for what followed. I thought I had a good enough idea of the areas where Kenneth would require support as director, but we were both wrong-footed by the politics, personalities and financial chess game in play at the time.

Kenneth's plans for his first season as director were extremely well thought out. In a nod to his predecessor, Kenneth's first season opened with Frederick Ashton's *Enigma Variations*, then only two years old, although Fred was later to complain to Kenneth that the ballet's subtlety was being spoiled by being performed too often. On opening night it was programmed with the first performance by the Royal Ballet of Jerome Robbins' *Dances at a Gathering*. At other performances during the run, other Ashton ballets, *The Creatures of Prometheus* or *The Dream*, were partnered with Robbins' ballet. Kenneth also programmed his *Romeo and Juliet*, still only in its fifth season. During the opening weeks of the season Kenneth paired the first Covent Garden performances of *Concerto*, which he had created in Berlin four years before, with Ashton's *The Two Pigeons*, then still relatively new.

Kenneth was keen too to broaden the dancers' approach to perfor-mance by introducing works by a wider range of choreographers. In a short space of time, thanks to Kenneth, Glen Tetley, Hans van Manen, Joe Layton, Christopher Bruce, John Neumeier and Jack Carter had created new works for the Royal Ballet companies. Several existing American works, but new to Royal Ballet dancers, were added to the repertoire. These included four other ballets by Robbins as well as five by George Balanchine and two from Herbert Ross. This was all very well considered by Kenneth. Adding a Balanchine triple-bill of *The Four Temperaments*, *Agon* and *Prodigal Son* to the repertoire were good acquisitions. Of course the company was criticised for not attempting the high-kicking New York style, but more seasoned critics realised that these were ballets that invigorated and exhilarated dancers and audiences alike. Style would be captured over time. Kenneth was also determined that such traditional jewels of the Covent Garden repertoire as Ashton's *Symphonic Variations* should go out on tour with the best casts. Unfortunately, with the excep-tion of a very few performances, this did not happen.

To function effectively, an organisation must be clear about the sort of director it wants. Unfortunately the Royal Opera House, not for the last time, got it wrong in its choice of director of the Royal Ballet. As far as I know, the position was not advertised and no selection com-mittee had been formed, so the decision was evidently taken at board level. They appeared to think it was more important to have Kenneth's enormous and searching creativity as a choreographer than someone with proven experience as a company director. The board also evidently appreciated that Kenneth had failed to grasp the administrative and managerial aspects of such a role in Berlin. Hence they appointed John Field in tandem with Kenneth. No stranger to the Royal Ballet hierarchy, John had run the touring company since 1955. He had taken up the challenge given to him then by de Valois of doing something about the classics. When he received the call from the Royal Opera House, John did not understand he was being offered a shared directorship. He was under the distinct impression that he would be responsible for the operational running of the company and future planning so that Kenneth could concentrate solely on his choreography. Unfortunately neither Kenneth nor John was given a job description. The truth was that Covent Garden did not want to lose John from the organisation, as they knew that London Festival Ballet, today's English National Ballet, was attempting to poach him as director. David Webster, shortly to retire as general director at Covent Garden, attempted to square the circle. He led both MacMillan and Field to believe, independently, that they would be sole director. For the rest of us left just to get on with it without insight into the board's true intentions, the situation was far from clear. The precise scope of Kenneth's and John's responsibilities was never explicitly agreed or communicated to them. Fault-lines were inherent from the start. The manner in which Webster had managed the departure of Frederick Ashton as director had already caused resentment within the ballet company, and what followed exacerbated the situation.

I was happy when Kenneth asked me to manage the touring company in place of John. This was a job I felt I had sufficient experience to undertake, and the job needed doing for the greater benefit of the company. Initially my title was assistant to the directors, later becoming Kenneth's associate director. For me, working with Kenneth and running the touring company was certainly a formative experience in learning how the Royal Opera House functioned – or malfunctioned – and in my understanding of what it takes to be a director. I could never have become director of Birmingham Royal Ballet, as the touring company became, without that experience. True, the impact on home life was very hard to cope with as

I was on tour a considerable amount, as well as having to be at Covent Garden as much as possible.

I deputised for Kenneth as a governor at the Royal Ballet School as he was not interested in its internal workings, only the talent it produced. Although he was never interested in teaching, he did have an instinctive recognition when he saw a good teacher. After all, he had been a brilliant dancer himself and certainly could always recognise quality teachers. Due to Kenneth's poor health at the time, he found it impossible to have any sort of public presence as director. He would only rarely take curtain calls after performances, engage with journalists or face dancers' meetings. To compensate for Kenneth I had to undertake a lot of these responsibilities, something that was not popular. He did not like telling dancers that he was taking them out of roles – I had to do a lot of that for him. Donald MacLeary made it clear that he was dissatisfied with the parts in which he was being cast. Kenneth asked me to explain why, a mistake I thought. He should have told Donald what I did, that you just have to accept that roles come up less often as you get older, particularly those requiring virtuosity. Donald accepted the logic but rightly felt that it should have been Kenneth who told him. But at least those who I talked to in such situations were glad they had somebody to talk to. I was able to more or less win them over.

At one early meeting, however, with around ten or so of the Covent Garden principals, when Kenneth and John Field were together attempting to explain their plans for the season, John threw his legs over the table and crossed his ankles and lay back in a semi-recumbent posture. 'There're going to be a lot of changes around here,' he said. Many of the dancers present had not met him before and were shocked. So was Kenneth. It was not a good beginning. Kenneth and John actually hardly ever met. About the only time they talked, John told Kenneth he was free just to get on with his ballets. Kenneth saw red but in some ways John's observation, however insensitively delivered, recognised that Kenneth's strengths were as a creator. He was not a good overall director, although he always imposed himself on the casting of principals where a director should. He did have a brilliant eye for recognising talent to be developed and discovering new designers as well as new choreographers. The organisational state and technical standards, however, were very mixed. The changes, demotions and salary negotiations that followed all made for a bad atmosphere.

When I had agreed to take over the touring company from John Field it was a company of around 65 dancers staging a wide repertoire including the classics. Its last performance in that form was in July 1970 dancing *Swan Lake* in Wimbledon, led by Doreen Wells and Desmond Kelly. In retrospect it was the end of an era. Practically before my signature was dry on the contract I learned that the Covent Garden and touring companies were to be merged because of a major cut in its Arts Council subsidy. The Royal Ballet was to become one fluid ensemble of 125 dancers. Touring would be undertaken by a group of 20 or so dancers including principals from Covent Garden, its composition dependent on the repertoire being performed. This was not the first time that such an approach had been attempted. In 1956, when the Bolshoi Ballet made its first appearances in London, one thing that struck de Valois, though probably nobody else at the time, was although the Bolshoi brought a large ensemble to London, the company still had enough dancers within its ranks to continue to perform in Moscow. As a consequence, Madam decided on uniting her companies and school as one organisation, a Royal Ballet, under one royal charter. Her intention had been to create a company of over a hundred dancers, some of whom would tour while the rest performed in London. She hoped that modern works created on tour would make their way to Covent Garden while London productions of the classics would be adapted for touring. Her vision of integrating the companies was never fully realised. There were some exchanges of dancers at corps de ballet and soloist levels. Some touring productions – *Solitaire*, *La Fête étrange*, *Danses concertantes*, *Pineapple Poll* and *Harlequin in April* – were restaged for the Royal Opera House stage where they tended to look lost. *The Sleeping Beauty* and other London productions in reduced circumstances went on the road. However much the talk was of integration, it was never achieved. The two companies, 'formerly the Sadler's Wells Ballet from Covent Garden' and 'formerly the Sadler's Wells Theatre Ballet from the Sadler's Wells Theatre' remained stubbornly unique, at least to themselves, even if the outside world of ticket buyers, here and abroad, was confused about which company they were buying tickets to see.

In reorganising everything in 1970 more notice should have been taken of this still recent history. However, in seeking to manage the reduction in government funding, the board decided to apply the cuts being forced on it in a distinctly uneven manner. This meant redundancies. Kenneth worked out his own list of those whom he wished to dispense with, word of which circulated around the building, but Equity allowed us to lose only dancers who had most recently joined rather than take a more considered decision about others who we may have preferred to shed. The focus of the touring company, now usually referred to as the New Group, would be on small-scale, more modern work. The press statement issued believed that the reorganisation would achieve greater flexibility than was possible by maintaining two distinct companies. Dancers would have more opportunities to perform a wider repertory and they would also benefit from speedier career development. That all sounds fine in theory or when such an idea is discussed around a boardroom table, but who actually knew whether this was possible? Who knew what it meant in human terms for the dancers, teachers and staff in practice? Dancers are not machines who can be automatically switched between venues, roles and choreographic styles at whim without proper care and preparation. Presumably all these considerations had been discussed with Kenneth and John, but it was a great missed opportunity that I was not included in those conversations. I had worked extensively with both companies as a guest teacher and by then had mounted new productions of *Giselle* and *The Sleeping Beauty*. I also had a strong connection with the school. But boards tend not to be much interested in the human dimension of their grand visions. Big ideas win official plaudits and personal recognition. That more human side of the reorganisation was terribly hard for the people who needed to make it happen. In reality, the new formula necessitated a lot of detailed reworking and rethinking. Much of that was down to me and I only got to know about it by the time it was a fait accompli.

Once the rehearsal period started in the autumn of 1970, huge problems arose with the co-ordination of the two groups. The concept of a flexible ensemble of dancers switching between two companies was admirable on paper but well-nigh impossible in practice. Jack Hart, who for a decade or more had made the schedules for class, rehearsals and performances, had resigned when Ashton left that summer. How Henry Legerton, who was now responsible for scheduling, managed to sort it all out, I will never know. He had been a brilliant character artist and excellent répetiteur for many years. He is an unsung hero if ever there was one. We were expected to present three programmes per week on tour which meant the necessity of having a minimum of three casts for each ballet. I had presumed that this had been sorted out by Kenneth and John before I started, which was just one week before rehearsals started. Not so. When I remonstrated with Kenneth he told me to stop worrying. Things would work themselves out he said, rather unconvincingly. I did not stop worrying, not at all. I did my best to work out some possible solutions. Throwing both companies together was disastrous for the corps de ballets. There were now 40, far too many, principals at Covent Garden without sufficient opportunities for them to get onstage to perform. Several dancers were moved over to the New Group. Some, including Vyvyan Lorrayne, who had been the first Isabel Fitton in Ashton's *Enigma Variations* just a couple of years before and had been the star of *Monotones*, came to me and begged to be part of the New Group. Joe Layton had seen her at a rehearsal and insisted on having her for *The Grand Tour*. She was delighted as she literally had no scheduled performances in the casting announced for the next season at Covent Garden. Patricia Ruanne moved to the New Group too but moved again to London Festival Ballet. Without any big works for her to perform, the New Group did not represent an interesting enough opportunity. At Festival Ballet, Ruanne went on to create Juliet in Rudolf Nureyev's production and was the first Tatiana when the company acquired John Cranko's *Onegin*.

I also faced criticisms from dancers who participated in Ballet for All. This was the brainchild of Peter Brinson, established in 1964, designed primarily as an educational initiative to take ballet to small towns and villages throughout the country. Supported by the Gulbenkian Foundation, it enabled the touring company to add an additional six dancers to its ranks who would for three months at a time go out on tour across the country with Ballet for All. The format of performances was something of a lecture demonstration, outlining aspects of ballet history and including danced extracts of major ballets. It proved popular with audiences, informative and easy to enjoy. It was well constructed by Peter and certainly made an impact. He sometimes drove me mad but he really loved the organisation. For young dancers Ballet for All was an early opportunity to get experience out of the spotlight dancing such things as the pas de deux from *Romeo and Juliet*. That was the source of the complaints that I was on the receiving end of. Some dancers really enjoyed being with Ballet for All. They got enormous satisfaction from dancing major roles, or at least parts of them, and being able to use their expressive powers rather than just being part of a supporting ensemble back on tour. Others thought the experience they got of leading roles with Ballet for All meant they had the automatic right to dance them with the company. Peter Brinson resigned in 1972 and Ballet for All deteriorated under its subsequent directors. After a funding cut in 1978 it was closed down.

Ashton's *Creatures of Prometheus* had been well received when premiered by the touring company in Bonn in June 1970. Transposed to Covent Garden in the autumn that year, something was lost in translation en route. Its lack of success did not help confidence. Jerome Robbins was working at Covent Garden for the first time with *Dances at a Gathering*. Hopefully it was the precursor to a new ballet from him. Concurrently Kenneth had invited Glen Tetley to create a new ballet for the New Group. Having both choreographers working with both companies at the same time caused major traumas from the very start. They knew each other from America but had never been friends. Jerry very much considered himself the senior. To describe relations between them as cordial would be an overstatement. Glen was working on *Field Figures* for the New Group. He was well established at Nederlands Dans Theater, and Ballet Rambert already performed his work, but commissioning him for the Royal Ballet was a new departure. Kenneth had deliberately chosen Glen because he wanted to break the barriers that were holding back our dancers from developing and extending themselves. He had done this himself with the Covent Garden company with *Song of the Earth* but wanted to push forward his approach with the involvement of others. Kenneth had given both Glen and Jerry a free hand in casting, but Jerry was withholding his choices, deliberately I think. He caused much anguish when he would sometimes make principals watch while he tried out members of the corps de ballet in roles that they thought they would be doing. This did not help morale at all. He was in any case perversely skilled at splitting up established partnerships of dancers so it was impossible to divine his intentions.

This continued and Glen still did not know who he could have for his ballet. He wanted to use Wayne Eagling and David Ashmole but Jerry had his eye on both of them. In the end he did not use either, having previously insisted that they both attend all of his, three-hour, rehearsals. David and Wayne had been at the Royal Ballet School together and worked together. They graduated together and were much in each other's shadow. It was better when they were apart when ultimately Wayne was based at Covent Garden and David stayed with what was to become Sadler's Wells Royal Ballet. In those days David would do class at Covent Garden and then go to rehearsals for the New Group at the Donmar theatre, hoping to get cast. Glen did manage to complete some sections of *Field Figures*, which was long, about 55 minutes, after he had been able to cast the few dancers that Jerry was not laying claim to. Ultimately I had to double-guess which other dancers I thought Jerry would be using, Antoinette Sibley and Anthony Dowell for sure along with Laura Connor and Michael Coleman, even though they were all also cast to be out on tour in *Symphonic Variations* that November. Somehow I had to help Glen with whom he could use. He had been demanding in his terms when Kenneth and I went to The Hague to negotiate. As Kenneth had a phobia about flying, we went by train and ferry, but as Dutch trains were on strike we had to detour through Belgium, a nightmare for Kenneth as he was not well.

Once there, it was good to watch Glen at work on a new piece about film, still in its early stages and so rather incomprehensible. We also saw some of Hans van Manen's work and this led to a very productive agreement for us to stage five of his ballets for the New Group. Glen too agreed he would create a new ballet for Covent Garden. He was extremely co-operative when he arrived in London, and when he saw Deanne – or Danny – Bergsma and Desmond Kelly doing class he was captivated by them. He insisted on having them as his first cast. Danny, both as a ballerina and a human being, was always so direct and open. She had a very astute eye and later became an excellent judge at competitions and a governor of the Royal Ballet after she retired from performing. I always valued her opinions and she was one of my favourite dancers. Tall and perfectly proportioned, she never looked lanky or gangly but was completely co-ordinated. When Glen first saw Danny and Desmond they smiled at him and he was hooked. They completely immersed themselves in his very contemporary style while using their classicism to great advantage. They inspired the whole cast, Jerry having given up his claim to them. I loved the collaboration with Glen. We became good friends. Kenneth was delighted too as it revealed a very contemporary way of using pointe work.

Field Figures had a successful opening in Nottingham in November 1970 and was cheered by the sort of audience who would not consider attending *Swan Lake*. I was encouraged to overhear audience comments appreciative of something different. I wrote something in the programme about the aims of the New Group, the first article I had penned. Mary Clarke, editor of *The Dancing Times*, contacted me afterwards saying I would be shot down in flames for what I said. Mary was always harsh on new choreographers and had a nasty streak in how she spoke about contemporary dance. I went to see her to explain more and found that we got on well. It was good to have contact with a critic as we rarely communicated and there were many misunderstandings. I found with Mary that I was able to discuss dancers and ballets, something I would certainly not consider doing with other critics. Mary had always been interested in Sadler's Wells Theatre Ballet and saw its young dancers as the future. She could still be awful in her reviews – I recall Madam once complaining that Mary had got too big for her boots and you would fre-quently hear others complain how Mary had been vile to them – but the way in which she spoke her mind was based on knowledge rather than an interest in personalities which other reviewers had. Some London critics who came to Nottingham for the New Group's first night were dismissive about what they patronised as a *Swan Lake* loving audience who attended, unjustly so. Nottingham was always regarded as a venue with keen audiences, well able to fill its Playhouse and Theatre Royal which were just next door to each other. As the local Nottingham paper pointed out, audiences there were already familiar with Tetley thanks to performances of his *Pierrot Lunaire* there by Ballet Rambert. Overall Tetley was seen to be pushing at the limits of classical technique in a way that Wayne McGregor's work for classical dancers is seen to be doing by some nowadays. But Tetley's *Field Figures* was some 45 years ago and it had already given a new dimension to classical ballet.

At Covent Garden, everybody who finally was cast responded mag-nificently to *Dances at a Gathering* even though rehearsals had been so agonising. It is a shame that more recent revivals there have fallen so flat. Apparently Susan Hendl and Ben Huys who revive the ballet nowadays follow Jerry's instructions for how it is danced by New York City Ballet. Dancers must not suggest any relationship at all in their interactions with each other. This is still followed, even after Jerry's death. The dancers in the most recent revival at Covent Garden were upset at this approach but had to comply. After that original run in 1970, before Jerry returned to New York, he left a detailed dossier of permitted cast changes if any of his approved casts were unable to appear. This did not necessarily involve a straight substitution of one dancer for another. The roles were designated only by the colour of the costume they wore but a certain colour did not necessarily perform the same dance at every performance. Dancers could be moved between roles, others introduced, colours dropped, combinations adjusted – but only with Jerry's express permission. The permutations were complex and seemed endless but there was one occasion when, in the event of an injury, none of the permissible alternatives was possible given the dancers we had available. I phoned Jerry in New York proposing our best option in the circumstances. Was it covered by his bible of possibilities, he demanded? It was not. As a result he refused permission for the ballet to be performed. We had to lose the whole performance. This was the first time in the history of the company that a ballet performance had to be replaced with an opera as this was the opening programme of the season and the next bill was not ready. It is still rare to lose a performance but in 2014 when there was no replacement for an injured Natalia Osipova in *Tetractys* it had to be pulled although the rest of the programme was given. Such situations cause a lot of bad feeling with the public.

The New Group tended to be remembered for its focus on contemporary work, but right from the start it was not only about that. Besides the premiere of *Field Figures*, the first programme it gave in Nottingham consisted of Ashton's *Symphonic Variations* and George Balanchine's *Apollo*. The second programme comprised such familiar works on tour as *Danses concertantes*, *The Rake's Progress* and Antony Tudor's *Lilac Garden*. I must admit to some ambivalence about this ballet. Marie Rambert ruined it for me when I once accompanied her to see her company perform it at the Jeannetta Cochrane theatre. She always went on about *Lilac Garden* as the greatest ballet ever. What work can withstand such a billing? Certainly not the *Lilac Garden* I saw that night thanks to the principal couple who were far too sentimental in how they portrayed their characters. Tudor only spent one day with us during rehearsals. The first thing he said was, 'This is not a sentimental ballet. Make it sentimental and it will not work.' He was so right. Tudor insisted the ballet is just about life and talked for a long time about each character in great detail, which was really helpful for the casts. They could understand that *Lilac Garden* is really about relationships, misunderstandings and human instincts going wrong. They all loved Tudor – and loved his ballet. Other ballets in the New Group's repertoire then included *Les Patineurs*, *Monotones II*, *Diversions*, *Las Hermanas* and *Beauty and the Beast*. Despite the expectation caused by the New Group label, audiences had the chance to see programmes that revealed the development of classical ballet in Britain, particularly on matinée days when eight different ballets were often performed across the two performances.

The reorganisation was supposed to mean that Covent Garden principals would sometimes be able to perform on tour. The intention was a good one but ballets with small casts do not necessarily look good on small stages. Ashton's *Symphonic Variations* was a case in point. It was only the second new ballet created for the Covent Garden stage in the post-war period in 1946. Fred's use of this large space was integral to its conception. Here it was on the distinctly small stage of the Nottingham Theatre Royal. The dancers looked out of proportion with the reduced sized set, a very number-three tour version complained one critic from London. More importantly the choreography looked cramped. There was a lovely cast from Covent Garden on the first night – Antoinette Sibley, Anthony Dowell, Jennifer Penney, Laura Connor, Robert Mead and Michael Coleman – but the ballet was not right. Opening night was Monday and the performance went well, but in truth the London cast could not extend themselves fully on the small stage. Nor were they in good spirits at being on tour and having to dance a schools' matinée and another evening performance in quick succession. Sibley and Dowell were particularly unhappy as they were due to dance *Romeo and Juliet* at Covent Garden that Saturday afternoon so their Wednesday matinée was distinctly under par. I let them know my feelings, which did not go down well, but audiences are very quick to spot anything less than wholehearted. We only managed to field that Covent Garden cast again in Edinburgh and Glasgow in subsequent weeks but not at other venues due to their rehearsal commitments in London. However, they had set a standard for other dancers to follow. Unfortunately for subsequent weeks in Leeds and Manchester, when the second cast took over, the difference was appreciable. Manchester audiences were always notoriously hard to please. In those days it was often a try-out venue for big shows before they reached the West End and we got a lot of complaints from audience members who could see the difference in quality and felt short-changed. Wayne Eagling was also upset to be sent out with the New Group. Kenneth liked the way he moved a lot but Wayne was a rebel from the start, not just later when he became Equity representative. The quality of dancing depended on the amount of rehearsal time available, but to paying audiences, rightly, we were still the Royal Ballet. When, during that tour, MacMillan's *Danses concertantes* was criticised for looking cute, and when some dancers omitted certain steps, it was obvious something was wrong. *Apollo*, with Svetlana Beriosova and Donald MacLeary, was not a huge hit. Another Balanchine ballet, his bravura *Allegro Brillante*, was found wanting more brilliance than the New Group provided.

The later addition of two ballets by Herbert Ross did not prove particularly successful. Ross had choreographed Marlene Dietrich's cabaret appearances whom Kenneth knew from his days in America in the 1950s. Ross' career began as a chorus boy on Broadway in the 1940s. A broken ankle soon ended his dancing days but while recuperating he visited a Goya exhibition. His darkly satirical etchings impressed Ross enough to make them into a ballet, *Caprichos*, It was part of American Ballet Theatre's visit to London in 1953 but I did not see it then. Set to a score by Bartok, a bored woman apparently invites two men to rape her in a stylised bullfight. Patricia Ruanne, Stephen Jefferies and David Morse were the cast for its revival in October 1971. It survived for only about a year. More durable was Ross' *The Maids*. It dated from 1957 when Kenneth saw it being made in New York. Like its source material, Jean Genet's play, the servant girls were played by two men. Nicholas Johnson and Kerrison Cooke were brilliant in the title roles, while Vyvyan Lorrayne was impressive as their controlling mistress. Their performances kept a place for the ballet over several seasons. It was rehearsed by Herbert's assistant, very convincingly. However, when he reported back to Ross in America, we were refused permission to continue to perform it. When I remonstrated, Ross told me, 'I don't care a fuck about the Royal Ballet. I only let the company do this ballet because of Kenneth.' I think Ross did not want to be associated with ballet any longer, feeling it detracted from his growing reputation as a film director. He made *The Turning Point*, the film that marked the screen debut of Mikhail Baryshnikov alongside Anne Bancroft and *Nijinsky* with George de la Pena and Alan Bates. It is true too that before Ross married Nora Kaye in 1959 she had enjoyed seducing an ambivalent but willing MacMillan while he was creating *Winter's Eve* for her. *The Maids* dated from when MacMillan was still involved with Kaye in New York.

The partnership between Kenneth and John worsened partly because John's office was at the Royal Opera House and Kenneth's was at Baron's Court. As associate to the directors I was somehow expected to keep the peace, but I struggled. I was constantly coming and going between both, trying to sort out casting problems and oversee rehearsals. Kenneth let it be known that if any dancer had complaints about dressing-rooms or the state of the loos they should see John. There was much dissatisfaction among the principals regarding Kenneth's casting. One ballerina drew up a chart showing her to have been unfairly neglected.

In December 1970 Kenneth threatened to resign, but when just before Christmas the Royal Opera House issued a statement it was to announce, with regret, the departure of John Field. Apparently he had resigned as the time was right for him to follow his career in other directions. The Opera House and John did not reveal what those directions might be but evidently the shared directorship with Kenneth proved untenable. To be honest, I do not think that anybody cared that much. John was known for how he looked after many women in the company but otherwise many at Covent Garden had hardly seen him. He was always in meetings or at lunch. I know that there had been certain clandestine conversations between John and some of the principals of the old touring company, so I found myself in a difficult position.

Prior to all this, John Field had been very good to me in persuading de Valois to commission me to create a ballet. This was *A Blue Rose* in 1957. I had spent time with the touring company as a guest teacher when John was in charge. While he was recovering from a heart attack I was asked to deputise for him on a tour to Italy and France. The press made much of what John's loss would mean. He had been with the organisation for 32 years appearing as a principal at Covent Garden and had spent the past decade building up the touring company. He was regarded as the person with widest experience of company management with broadest knowl-edge of dance outside London within the organisation. In comparison neither Kenneth nor I were judged to have sufficient experience and would have to learn the hard way, by getting on with it and presumably by getting it wrong. In particular, as the original announcement detailing Kenneth and John's appointment had included no reference to my own role, the news now, which stated that I would be responsible for admin-istration, was read to mean that I was assistant director to Kenneth. I was happy to work alongside Kenneth whatever title I had and he was certainly comfortable enough as director not to feel threatened by me as his associate. Part of the problem, however, stemmed from the fact that Kenneth and I had worked a lot together before and were good friends. Kenneth would consult me instead of John as a consequence but that was the wrong mix. The relationship between a director and assistant depends as much on the personalities involved as the division of responsibilities. Kenneth and John Field did not – could not – make that relationship work in the way Kenneth and I did then or subsequently in Birmingham when I was director and Desmond Kelly was my deputy. I have known others in comparable situations reject the notion of an associate director, preferring their number two to be credited solely as an assistant.

On John's departure I was made administrator, not actually assistant director. John Tooley, the new general director of the Royal Opera House, had persuaded me to accept a situation where I was still in charge of the New Group. That meant I still had to tour but was, in all but name, Kenneth's deputy overall. My duties, unwritten but expected by Kenneth, involved keeping Madam out of his stage rehearsals as he found her pres-ence unhelpfully intrusive. I had to speak for him at press conferences, I had to deputise for him on international tours when his fear of flying meant he was absent. I oversaw dancers' appearances across the two com-panies while being mindful of the schedule for the film of Ashton's *Tales of Beatrix Potter*, then in production. I had to work out casting for Fred's ballets with him as well as the overall planning of future programmes too. I had to manage the scheduling to accommodate guest appearances by Rudolf Nureyev and Margot Fonteyn, which always meant higher ticket prices. That meant lengthy negotiations with Rudi's agent, Sandor Gorlinsky. I did all this willingly for Kenneth but I was not really used to this sort of pressure. I was still trying to fathom out the way in which the

Royal Opera House worked. It had so many departments, and communication between them was appalling via internal memos, yellow perils
as they were called, and a ropey telephone system that did not allow for
external lines except for a few heads of department, directors and senior
stage management. There was no such thing as a typical day – so much
travel between companies, rehearsals, interviews, lunches and meetings.
On some days I could be backwards and forwards three times between
Baron's Court and Covent Garden. When we were on tour somewhere
close to London, such as Wimbledon or Golders Green, I could stay at
home in north London. I usually left about 8am and did not get back
until midnight. But I survived and part of me loved it and I did manage
to keep things going. I hardly saw my dear Sonya and family. She was
very calm and understanding but did not get too involved. Sonya did
not really like ballet that much although she was well known as a leading
dancer in West End shows.

The departure of John Field did not lead to any less volatile environment. There was still turmoil throughout the organisation. In February
1971, organised by their Equity representative, dancers voted in a
ballot. The result was unanimous in favour of Kenneth being removed
as director; otherwise they would go on strike. Even dancers who had
seen Kenneth's appointment as positive initially had now grown utterly
demoralised by what they saw as his remoteness. In the rehearsal studio
he would hide behind dark glasses, offering no words of encouragement or feedback. Dancers found they were drained by Kenneth's lack
of responsiveness literally pulling choreography out of them. The results
of the vote went to John Tooley who convened a company meeting. He
strode in and informed everybody that he was aware of the disquiet they
had expressed but told them to remember that their director had been
chosen by the board and the board was adamant that Kenneth would
remain as director. With that he strode out again.

Tooley's handling of the situation punctured its threat but a sense that
ballet was the poor relation within the organisation remained. Against
that background, in the spring of 1971 for the first time in nearly 15
years, the Covent Garden ballet company found itself out on the road
on a tour of the provinces, to use the terminology of the day. Included
were Southampton, Bristol, Leeds, Newcastle and Manchester which
replaced its then near annual sortie to America. That tour was, bar the

occasional week's excursion to some cities over the next 15 years, also the last. Other than Nureyev's one-act version of *Raymonda* paired with *Giselle* and his staging of *La Bayadère* performed with *The Two Pigeons*, the works toured – *Swan Lake* and *La Fille mal gardée* – were familiar from the days when the touring company was run by John Field. The 1971 tour came about because of pressure from the Arts Council. As audiences outside London were getting only a small, experimental group at the most once per year, they should also occasionally see the Covent Garden company. They were, it was argued, paying as much tax as Londoners. This was an argument used later by Jeremy Isaacs too when the arguments for relocating the touring company to Birmingham were being debated. For dancers, being out on tour was at least a way of getting more performances, which is what a dancer, a performer at heart, is mainly interested in.

Despite its unofficial name, the New Group was based on classical ballet training with pointe work, pas de deux, mime, virtuosity, batterie and where the corps de ballet plays an integral part in the choreography whether it is in old-style works or modern classical ballet. A company, therefore, needs at least 60 dancers to be able to present full ballets satisfactorily. There are some smaller classical ballets, but not enough to keep presenting well-trained dancers to their maximum standard technically and really dance in the right style. Unless the New Group was to be used purely as a graduate company for newly trained classical dancers performing small ballets on small stages to small audiences, something that it is not really satisfying or worth their years of training, it was inevitable that we had to grow to survive. If we were to last, and hopefully find a home of our own, I knew that all our dancers would have to be classically trained and the company needed to be an ensemble with principals, soloists and corps de ballet – which is what happened, eventually.

Box office results on tour for the New Group had not been good, and Kenneth and I decided action had to be taken. I had already had big battles with the management in order to secure a few more dancers so that the New Group could perform bigger ballets, but we still needed more. Dancers do not thrive on constantly rehearsing the same old ballets, nor can you develop audiences by forever recycling the same few titles – but touring was very difficult without the classics and recognised titles. Right from the first performances by the New Group in

Nottingham I knew that rather than looking after an experimental group and making it appeal to the public, my main focus had to be getting the company back to its proper size.

My chief concern was the word 'experimental' when applied to the New Group. One use of that word and you lose half your audience. The other worry was the label 'contemporary', which kept cropping up. Contemporary dance was in fact doing rather well at the time and I was sensitive to the impression that the New Group was attempting to poach audiences from Ballet Rambert, by now a contemporary company, and London Contemporary Dance. I kept thinking about Madam's words to me, 'Whatever you do, don't set yourselves up as a rival to the moderns', as she called them. 'They do it far better because of their training, and you will only take away some of their audiences, which is not fair.' In reality it was the other way round. We were losing our audiences to the country's other classical company, London Festival Ballet, now with Beryl Grey in charge before John Field succeeded her as director in 1979, as we could no longer include the big classics in our seasons through lack of numbers. Equally, I was very anxious to make audiences aware that classical ballet was not just tutus and sequins. I wanted people to understand that classical ballet had, and will, continue to develop and live on its own terms based on the seven forms of movement and five positions of the feet, rather than through switching to an imitation of the way in which contemporary dance was heading. Hence my battle before we had even started to get the New Group enlarged so that it could at least retain its sense of classical and demi-caractère identity where characters are created through the choreography.

In the wake of the reorganisation journalists were looking for the slightest excuse to criticise us. Critics complained of too much typecasting, too much use of choreographers' favourites, too little attention to individuals. Part of the changes involved amalgamating the two corps de ballets, which is one of the hardest things to achieve. A restaging of *Swan Lake*, which sought to combine the designs by Leslie Hurry used by the touring company and the choreographic text used at Covent Garden, was criticised by reviewers as a doubtful compromise and an analogy for combining the two companies themselves. The production was dismissed in the press as a right royal hotch-potch. A revival of MacMillan's *Symphony* was planned and cancelled and the premiere of his new full-length *Anastasia* was postponed when the Royal Opera needed more time to stage Michael Tippett's new opera *The Knot Garden*. Kenneth's *Concerto* had successfully made the transfer from the touring company to Covent Garden but there was still so much to worry about. I got a gastric ulcer. In those days, having such an ulcer meant a complete change of diet and special, fluid medication. That was very tiresome, particularly when touring. I also had very low blood pressure and my doctor was amazed that I could still manage to walk across the room. While travelling on the Underground across London, often several times in a day, I frequently fell asleep as soon as I sat down, but miraculously always woke up in time and never missed my stop.

In my desperation to find somebody to help me I approached Peter Clegg, valued then at the Royal Ballet School as a very good teacher. Doing so was one of my many wrongs. I was responsible for company class and all rehearsals. I wanted to recruit Peter to assist with all of that, but forgot to consult his bosses, the principal and director of the Royal Ballet School, before speaking to Clegg. This proved to be a huge mistake. I can only say I was blinded by overwork. Peter was pleased to have been asked but he urged me to talk to Michael Wood, his boss. I did and Michael promptly hit the roof, rightly so although I did not appreciate him complaining to the board about my behaviour.

Such occurrences meant that ultimately I told John Tooley that I could not work in this way and did not wish to continue at the Royal Opera House. I said I would like to devote all my energies to the New Group with the intention of gradually settling it back at Sadler's Wells with its own identity, possibly with the name Sadler's Wells Royal Ballet. This was agreed in principle. As a consequence, Jack Hart was persuaded to return from America to take charge of the administrative side of things. This of course would take time and did not happen for a few months. Meanwhile I had to continue coping with both companies but started to plan how the New Group could be enlarged and re-installed at Sadler's Wells. Hart, never my best friend, duly arrived but his stay was short as he evidently thought too much damage had been done by the amalgamation. Kenneth appreciated my problems and asked John Auld, well experienced as assistant director of London Festival Ballet, to become my assistant. John was also a superb character artist, a quality badly needed by the New Group. I was able to balance my time better, spending half on the road and the rest in London. This meant I was sometimes at home, which pleased Sonya, but for the company on tour it still felt that they had an absentee landlord as director. Dancers were sensitive to what appeared to be a lack of interest in them and our longer-term future was doubted, particularly as the touring group was running at a considerable loss.

By 1973 the New Group was sufficiently large and strong enough to premiere ten new ballets and to tour internationally again. The aim, I announced at a press conference with Kenneth, when he asked me to speak on his behalf, was the creation of new works including some by home-grown choreographers. That would give the New Group a distinctive presence performed alongside works important to the Royal Ballet's history that would probably disappear if not performed. We now had 40 dancers but relied on students from the Royal Ballet School to make up numbers in *Les Sylphides* for example. For bigger works, for walk-on roles anybody who could walk did so. *Raymonda*, which we had acquired in Nureyev's version of classical divertissements from the last act, was a stretch too but also another indication not only of technical depth but of how the repertoire was changing. Their inclusion of such had an immediate impact on box office, and audiences responded well. There was a real ensemble feel and sense of theatricality about performances even if they were not always rehearsed to the same degree they would be now.

The New Group was ahead of its time for the regions and short-lived in its original concept. At some venues such as Edinburgh and Glasgow audience numbers were dire. We were presenting quality programmes of new and recently created work but audiences were not ready for them. They expected tiaras and tutus particularly associated with the Royal Ballet's name. In comparison, at the same time, London Festival Ballet, today's English National Ballet, was touring such classic repertory as *The Sleeping Beauty*, *Giselle*, *Don Quixote*, *Coppélia*, *Les Sylphides*, *Études*, *Petrushka*, *Schéhérazade* and *Suite en blanc*, often to the same venues, thereby cashing in on the gap that the demise of the traditional Royal Ballet touring company had left.

Ballet Rambert under Norman Morrice was carving out its more modern identity where Glen Tetley was equally productive. London Contemporary Dance Theatre was presenting works by Martha Graham, Alvin Ailey, Robert Cohan and Paul Taylor. The choice of repertory available for audiences was more diverse than is toured nowadays by the major companies. There were more weeks of dance, more performances, more ballets. And that means bigger audiences all round. It is a fundamental of marketing: the greater the choice, the greater the market share for everybody.

Much new work is of course now produced by choreographers who run their own companies. Some manage to pull audiences to their work but others struggle. Was the New Group really too challenging in its concept? What would its impact have been if it had been allowed longer to get established? Who knows. Was it my fault that the New Group did not continue longer? Yes – in the sense that I was determined to bring the touring group back to full strength as a classical company in its own right. Perhaps the New Group could have continued longer if the repertoire had been right. There were some good ballets in the New Group's repertory but it had no resident choreographer and there were no budding choreographers at Covent Garden at the time. A company cannot keep on repeating the same works.

I introduced *Arpège* into the repertoire. I made it originally for the Royal Ballet School to stretch their technique while learning about the process of creating a ballet. It gave the advanced students the opportunity to work in a corps de ballet. I chose a harp concerto by François Boïeldieu, which from an orchestral perspective is bright, buoyant and eminently danceable, which surprisingly worked extremely well. As a result, Kenneth thought it would be a good idea to rework it on a more professional level for the New Group as there were so few small, classical ballets available. Brenda Last was the ballerina and I was able to really use her phenomenal technique. Frederick Ashton once said you always knew you could relax when Brenda – or Birdie as she is known – was dancing any difficult solo because she never failed to complete the usual two or three pirouettes bang on the beat with no wobbly hops at the end of a solo. In those days that was rare. I once saw Birdie take over a performance of *The Sleeping Beauty* at Covent Garden after the first act when the Aurora got injured. She happened to be in the audience, and although she had never danced Aurora and had certainly never rehearsed it, she is the sort of ballerina who would have a go and do anything to save the day. That sort of professionalism was instilled in Brenda during her formative years with Western Theatre Ballet in the 1950s, sometimes advertising that evening's performance by turning fouettés on damp pavements outside department stores. As for *Arpège*, it was a very useful piece and filled a gap. The problem was the passages of solo harp which, although lovely, were too lightweight even with amplification. They were not assertive enough and tended to subside into the background. I tried replacing the harp with a piano but the piece lost its charm and style.

The programme for my farewell season as director of Birmingham Royal Ballet at the Royal Opera House in May 1995 included an advertisement by Lanvin for its perfume, *Arpège*, as had the programme for my first tour to America in 1951. There was no especial significance in this, just a happy coincidence. When I was looking for a title, Lyn Wallis, then a ballet mistress at the Royal Ballet School, thought the ballet looked to be full of perfume and so it became *Arpège*. I always think, when in doubt ask Lyn: she knows just about everything, not just in dance but in all theatre, film and television. She is one of the most organised, kindest and helpful people I know – and very good company. I knew her first at the Royal Ballet touring company in the 1960s. She was a beautiful dancer with great breadth of movement. I have known her too as a director, at National Ballet of Canada, but have mainly worked with her as director of the Royal Academy of Dance. Her achievements there were enormous, travelling the world in its interests, and earned her the OBE. When cancer struck, twice, she was away from work for the minimum amount of time and nobody knew what she was suffering. She is as vivacious as ever, a really good friend for many years.

Another deliberately classical work I put into the repertoire in June 1976 was *Aurora's Wedding*. Essentially this was the last act of *The Sleeping Beauty* with the fairy solos from the prologue added, culminating in the grand pas de deux. Peter Farmer rustled up the set and some costumes from his short-lived production for Kenneth at Covent Garden, but the dance content came from my production there that had preceded Kenneth's. We performed it first on a tour to Switzerland and Italy. It looked particularly good on the stage of La Fenice in Venice. It was a useful work to have as it was a good finisher to an evening and was a chance for many young dancers to dance classical choreography. You only learn how to become a real professional by performing challenging choreography, the classics, onstage and not just in a rehearsal room. Every dancer wants to do a big pas de deux and classical roles stretch you to your maximum.

In other attempts to broaden our appeal in 1975 I staged *Coppélia* using the sets and costumes by Osbert Lancaster made for the Covent Garden production from 1954 by de Valois. Although I was influenced by her staging, I made changes to the mazurka and the scene with the dolls. Like Madam, I think Dr Coppélius can be played in a variety of ways. Robert Helpmann had always made the role a star vehicle whereas Frederick Ashton made it more sinister, which is an interpretation I liked. We performed *Coppélia* at the Royal Opera House that spring, along with my production of *Giselle*. Although a season at Covent Garden was welcome, a major issue remained our lack of a home with no administrative and rehearsal base, and so with John Tooley's blessing I started discussions with Sadler's Wells theatre about moving back there which would necessitate constructing a new studio. I was particularly anxious to make this happen as there was an impetus brewing in the mid-1970s to merge the New Group with Northern Dance Theatre, today's Northern Ballet, then still based at the University theatre in Manchester. I was not keen on that, although I did have exploratory meetings there. With the goal of giving the north of England its own ballet company for the first time, in 1969 Laverne Meyer had established a company with a repertoire that included such smaller works as Fokine's *Carnaval* and Jooss' *The Green Table*.

Meyer had gradually built a company of 18 dancers but artistic differences led to his departure. It was against this backdrop that I made a visit to Manchester. I remember only a very welcoming lady administrator, very organised but wearing a big picture hat – also a tatty office and a rather old bottle of sherry. The possibility of a merger was debated endlessly by the two Manchester councils, working groups and boards at countless meetings. Understandably the way it dragged on had a demoralising effect on our dancers. Eventually, in typical fashion, the councils, who were at complete loggerheads when it came to anything to do with the arts, failed to come up with the necessary funding to make the proposal a reality. The scheme was dropped. I was not sorry. To be honest, I was shocked that the Arts Council and the Royal Opera House had even considered this sort of merger as a possibility.

CHAPTER 7

Being a director

'ALWAYS REMEMBER THE board is there to work for you. You are not there to work for them.' I have always taken to heart that classic piece of advice from Ninette de Valois, very useful particularly when you have to deal with people with power around a boardroom table. They tend to think that you should follow them because they have the money or know a man who does.

I was made director of Sadler's Wells Royal Ballet in 1976 when I was 50. Actually for the first year the company was called The Royal Ballet on Tour. We did not get beyond our naming nightmares until 1977 when the new name was formally introduced. Frederick Ashton's *The Two Pigeons* and *La Fille mal gardée* returned to our repertory after their disappearance during the last days of the old touring company. I had never considered *The Two Pigeons* Fred's best ballet, but seeing it again in 2015 I saw much more in it choreographically. I was overjoyed when Fred came to Norwich in March 1976 for final rehearsals of *Fille*. This was a happy time. We made a fuss of him with caviar, champagne and more than a few vodka martinis – the vodka nearly filling the glass with just a dash of martini. He had just had enormous success with his first major ballet since he retired as director, *A Month in the Country*. He came to Norwich with Tony Dyson. Fred was never tied to anybody but he had a strong intellectual bond with Tony.

Also around at the time was Martin Thomas whose relationship with Fred was much more physical. Fred referred to him as his expensive friend. Tony had a lot to say after rehearsals, not in an interfering way, but he had a very good eye. He is now chairman of the Frederick Ashton Foundation and owns the performance rights to *Enigma Variations* and *Monotones*, a responsibility he treats more seriously than some trustees. He arranged for Margaret Barbieri, assistant director of Sarasota Ballet who has taken *Enigma* into their repertoire, to get together with Monica Mason, who knows the ballet well, so Maggie could benefit from Mon's experience. *Fille*, of course has lovely roles full of characterisation and humour. The work for the corps de ballet looks easy but is very demanding. Brenda Last, who had been coached in *Fille* before by Fred, produced her notebook of detailed instructions of what he had told her, how to manage all the ribbons for example. This immaculate attention to detail was invaluable for preserving the subtlety and nuance of the choreography. Brenda, though, has never been asked to formally coach the ballet since. Fred was very appreciative of how he was feted by the company and public alike during and after the revival. *Fille* was a good addition to the repertoire as a first-time ballet for new audiences.

That *Fille* and such classic works as *Les Rendezvous*, *Checkmate* and *Pineapple Poll* were back in the repertory revealed how far from its original intentions the New Group had shifted in the five years since its formation. Ashton's *The Dream* also returned to the touring repertoire with designs by Peter Farmer. Rudolf Nureyev guested as Oberon for a couple of performances with Marion Tait as Titania in Edinburgh. Rudi made a lot of the characterisation but had difficulty with the technique that is needed for Ashton's fluid and speedy choreography. Rudi loved doing batterie, where the feet beat together quickly, but only at a slow tempo, so where Oberon is required to undertake this at lightning speed in the scherzo it was pretty disastrous. But audiences did not mind and flocked to see him, such was the lure of Rudi's name. *The Dream* is a real test for the corps de ballet and Fred knew full well that I had been slaving away trying to make the girls' feet fit for his inspection when he came to rehearse them. 'Awful,' was all he said when he saw the production at Sadler's Wells. 'And as for that person doing Bottom. What was he up to?' That person was Ronald Emblem, a very good Bottom who had been coached in the role by Fred himself. Really Fred could be very difficult.

There was still considerable emphasis on the creation of original works, including those made by members of the company. David Morse did *Pandora* in January 1976 using the same score by Roberto Gerhard that Kurt Jooss had commissioned for his ballet to the same story. It was not that memorable except for the dances for Pandora herself, performed by Marion Tait, and she did have a hand in the choreography. All young choreographers suffered, as critics tended at the time, as they still do, to judge them as worthy or not, of becoming a successor to Ashton or Kenneth MacMillan. In truth not many of the new ballets we put on proved to have much popular appeal with audiences, in the same way they had resisted the more contemporary offerings from the New Group's early seasons. Looking back now, I am surprised how many ballets we found the time to introduce, but I was conscious of a huge wave pushing at classical ballet companies about the need for new works. Other than our association with Hans van Manen, which gave a different dimension to our programmes and were popular with dancers and at the box office, most of the works made for us during the last period of the New Group's existence and in our new form as Sadler's Wells Royal Ballet, were not suitable to go into the permanent repertoire. One ballet that did earn its place was *Gemini*, a ballet by Glen Tetley in May 1977. It was a killer physically for its cast of four but exciting because of its athleticism. Glen can be very inspiring and *Gemini* was a real tour de force, challenging for its dancers and popular with audiences.

In more classical vein I choreographed *Summertide* in October 1976 which did not stay long in the repertoire. I only revived it nearly 40 years later for Sarasota Ballet in November 2015 with new designs by Dick Bird, who designed the sets for David Bintley's *Aladdin* and who worked with him in Japan to produce a new, more three-dimensional realisation of Natalia Goncharova's famous designs for *The Firebird*. Originally *Summertide* was reviewed as an eager and busy ballet, musical if not particularly original, full of expectancy, rather akin to the company at the time, which I suppose it was. Barry Wordsworth suggested the music, Mendelssohn's second piano concerto, which was very danceable, but in retrospect the choreography was too non-stop. The finale was particularly hectic. I made it all originally in a flash, but for Sarasota I toned it down with the enormous assistance of Maggie Barbieri who had danced the lead in the ballet originally. In Sarasota it was sandwiched between MacMillan's *Concerto* and Ashton's *Marguerite and Armand*. I thought in advance this was rather unkind programming. Triple-bills work best with the dramatic ballet placed in the middle. Certainly that is where *Marguerite and Armand* or *A Month in the Country* make most impact. But thanks to the way Maggie rehearsed *Summertide* it turned out to be a better ballet than I remembered. I take my hat off to her and Iain Webb, her husband and the company's director. They both took a big step into the unknown when they took on the Sarasota company in 2007. Their intense hard work, and making Ashton's ballets the central attraction, has done wonders. I was privileged to be guest of honour at their Ashton festival in 2014 which attracted audiences and critics from London, New York and beyond. They also have my production of *Giselle* and other works by MacMillan, George Balanchine and Christopher Wheeldon in their repertoire, an impressive achievement. Sarasota Ballet is privately funded, and as a result of having developed a stronger financial foundation for the company, Iain's contract has been extended by a further ten years. There are not many directors who are in that fortunate situation.

Although new works are the lifeblood of a company it is so important to give another airing to successful ballets created during previous decades. That way they establish a performing tradition. For a director, the difficulty is that there is always so much to fit in, never forgetting that the balance of the programme is such an important aspect overall. That requires getting the mixture of periods right, as well as the balance of music and choreography. I was determined that Sadler's Wells Royal Ballet danced some of Balanchine's works and we acquired *The Four Temperaments* and *Concerto barocco*. They were a stretch, challenging ballets for dancers. You have to be brave with them, very extrovert. Pat Neary staged them very well for us and they seemed a good match for our dancers but they were not so popular with audiences.

The repertoire was also renewed with other classic revivals. Léonide Massine revived his *La Boutique fantasque*. This was a bumpy ride if ever there was one. Massine arrived with his three assistants comprising his wife, his official assistant Hannelore Holtwick, who may have been something more, and a notator who had recorded the ballet in Massine's own form of notation which they all had great difficulty in reading. They also came armed with three, differing films of the ballet. I had enlisted the support of dancers like Julia Farron and Pamela May who had danced roles in the ballet at Covent Garden to be on hand as necessary as they knew all the musical timings, steps and style. We also had the Benesh notation score of the old touring company version.

The first thing that Massine did was rudely to say no to everything. This was his ballet and he and his assistants were the only ones he would allow to rehearse it. Everybody else was not welcome, they must leave. Later it transpired that none of Massine's contingent actually knew the ballet properly and could only teach it from the films. I suggested it would help our dancers if they could watch those films. No. None of them was allowed to see any of the films which had been set up in another studio. Two days before the first stage-call when everything was to be ready the finale was hardly started. I had to go to Massine and threaten to cancel the first performances unless he stayed away for the next two days during which time I – with our staff – would put it together. I guaranteed that it would all be ready. He flew into a rage and refused. He finally left in a huff. In his absence we had very concentrated rehearsals and with no difficulty we got the whole finale together. Massine returned, as arranged – still in a huff. He took his seat next to me and just said, 'Show me.' The company was superb and went right through the long finale without a hitch. I watched Massine's face. It gradually changed from huge disap- proval to wide-eyed amazement. Thank goodness for our brilliant staff who had taught the principals and soloists.

I saw Sadler's Wells Royal Ballet as something very different from what the New Group had developed into. Besides important one-act ballets I wanted the company to be able to perform the big classics again. That was absolutely deliberate on my side. Ultimately too I wanted the company to have its own home in its own city as a major centre for clas- sical ballet away from London. Getting new work on while on tour, even once you have found suitable choreographers, is very difficult and very expensive. Most of our new productions were made by the Royal Opera House's departments so this involved sending wardrobe staff and the designer for several days at a time to wherever we were. That involved fares and expenses. Sets would be made at workshops in London then transported to where final rehearsals were occurring. A skeleton crew of carpenters would need to make any necessary alterations at the theatre as there was seldom a workshop available. Lighting rehearsals, including setting and making the plot, usually occupied a large part of the five days running up to the first night. That meant another big bill for three or five technicians. In recent years production facilities and rehearsal space have improved in theatres that produce their own shows, but receiving theatres, the majority of venues to which companies tour, rarely have rehearsal studios that are large enough for full-scale ballet or opera, essential when a new work is being prepared. Which said, the repertoire we managed to present was broad. In some cities, including Manchester, we were able to schedule visits of two weeks including two full-length ballets and three triple bills.

Although Big Top seasons were proposed by the Royal Opera House board they were put into action by Paul Findlay. They enabled us to tour to towns where there was no suitable venue large enough to house the company. These included Cambridge, Sheffield, Exeter, Scarborough, even Edinburgh and Plymouth which then did not have the theatres they do now. The Big Top was, as the name suggests, a circus tent, rented from Fossett's. It was a family business, run by Bob Fossett and his wife Kitty who had an act twirling a snake round her near naked body. In the regions, Big Top seasons brought very different audiences whom, I hope, went on to watch ballet again in more traditional settings. I liked the feel of the tent but it was not really the right environment for the big classics. On cold days we had to cancel some performances because of temperature problems. The company, rightly, refused to perform when it was too chilly.

Once, during a performance of *Card Game*, when a storm was raging outside, all the lights went out. The orchestra played on and the dancers kept going for three minutes in total darkness, an eternity. When the lights came on again everybody was amazingly together and in the right place. During one season in Cambridge when much of Jesus Green was under water the orchestra pit flooded and everybody got together during the interval to bail out the pit. At the start of the second act the leader of the orchestra very pointedly made his way to his chair, holding his violin high above his head, feeling for his footing. He sat down, feeling round for signs of dampness. He stood up again and minced out of the pit, again carrying his violin above his head. He refused to come back. No company spirit. He was a brilliant player but he was not much missed when his deputy took over.

The Big Top was never ideal but the company always coped – as did our audiences on some occasions. During one season when the mayor's wife took her seat at Lancaster the floor gave way beneath her. Consternation all round! During a performance in Battersea Park attended by Princess Margaret during very stormy weather the tent's roof split but everybody stuck it out. Sonya and I celebrated our 25th wedding anniversary with a big party in the Big Top during a season in Edinburgh in 1979. When the cake was wheeled in there was no knife to cut it. Extended pause while one was found. Sonya extemporised with a dirty joke, which she told rather well. That surprised a few people. Kenneth MacMillan absolutely roared with laughter. The champagne, for which I was expecting to pay, flowed, but nobody gave me the bill for it on the night. I had always got on well with Bob Fossett and thought that the champagne must be a present from him. Six months later the bill turned up – but I still liked Bob.

In 1977 Kenneth MacMillan resigned as director of the Royal Ballet in order to focus exclusively on choreography, dissatisfied with what he perceived was the board's attitude towards him and deeply unhappy at what being a director entailed. He had a somewhat masochistic relationship with John Tooley, Covent Garden's general director. Kenneth never discussed the fact that he was bisexual but I think at some level he was very attracted to Tooley. 'What a man,' he once said to me. John was a product of Repton and Cambridge, tall, straight-backed and handsome. Kenneth liked him a lot and was able to be honest and frank with him, but Kenneth's reactions altered when his contract and salary were being renegotiated, with lawyers involved on both sides. His ballet *Requiem* had been blocked by the board of the Royal Opera House as once again they objected to his choice of music, in this case liturgical. Kenneth too had been passed over in favour of the board's choice of Madam and Ashton to oversee yet another new production of *The Sleeping Beauty*, the previous staging by Kenneth having been particularly short lived.

Kenneth had discussed all of this with me before he resigned and I could not help but agree with his reasons. When he said that fundamentally it was not possible for the Royal Ballet to create an environment in which he could function as both a choreographer and director, I did say to him that whatever situation was created to help him, he still would not be able to cope. I told Kenneth that in all honesty the responsibility of leading the company was just too much for him. Surely it was much more important for him to continue as a choreographer, to which he just smiled and shrugged his shoulders. We went together to see Tooley. Kenneth was very clear when he said that he knew he was a much better choreographer than director. It was his wish that nothing should get in the way of that, especially with the huge responsibility of creating another three-acter, *Mayerling*, which he had already started.

Did I wonder whether I would be asked to take over from Kenneth as director? Not really, but I would have considered it very seriously if I had. What upset me then – and upsets me still – was that then, in June 1977, I was not even consulted. It seemed the board did not think it was worth questioning my abilities for the job after I had nearly bust a gut slaving away, trying to get both the Covent Garden and touring companies organised when Kenneth and John Field were not on speaking terms. I had to cope, or do my best to cope, with running both groups when they were on the verge of going on strike. I often wonder if the board had any idea of the part I had played during those awful times. They should at least have listened to my views. I had plenty to say.

When Kenneth formally resigned I had not applied for the job. I was, at the time, beginning to plan a return to Sadler's Wells for the touring company, devoting my energies to that and removing myself from Covent Garden. Paul Findlay canvassed my appointment with the board, who apparently did consider me very seriously. Paul told me I was in fact top of the list until Colette Clark, a member of the ballet committee, spoke. Colette was also a good friend of Margot Fonteyn and she had known Vera Volkova well too. I got on well with Colette, as long as we did not talk about ballet. Colette was also good friends with John Sainsbury, chairman of the Royal Opera House, and his wife, the former ballerina Anya Linden, both enormously generous contributors to Covent Garden financially and to the arts more widely. Additionally, Colette had been a member of Ballet Rambert's executive committee for many years. Kenneth had never particularly cared for her until he went on a holiday with the Sainsburys on Corfu where Colette was also a guest. In fact they suddenly got on extremely well and would go off on long walks together.

In discussing who should succeed Kenneth, to find a way forward the board looked at what Ballet Rambert had done about a decade before. This was when it radically reinvented itself as a contemporary troupe. Despite the still problematic move towards the more experimental with the New Group, the board was now evidently looking for somebody who would take the Royal Ballet in a more progressive direction overall. To do that, what was needed was an outsider, they thought. Norman Morrice was the man they had in mind. He was considered to be a man of intellectual breadth, force and charm and was promising to continue to develop the company along the lines established by de Valois. Norman had danced with Ballet Rambert in its classical days but was hardly known for his love of classical ballet. It was Norman who had proposed to Marie Rambert, the company's founder, that it should rediscover its roots in new work, a suggestion which led to Norman becoming director of the Rambert company in 1966. The logic was that the Royal Ballet could achieve a similar renaissance. Enjoying the reflected glory that it would bring herself and to her company, Mim Rambert herself was all for the idea. She and de Valois were scarcely known for their unanimity, so what did Madam think of it? It is inconceivable that she was not involved and Colette claimed that she had Madam's backing. Essentially pragmatic, I can imagine Madam thinking that it would be wrong to take me away from the touring company and had strong views on why contemporary dance should not be performed by classically trained dancers. That is why I find it incongruous that she should have supported Norman's appointment. She was adamant that the Royal Ballet companies should not be seen to be taking work away from contemporary dancers.

She had not thought much of Norman's ballet *The Tribute* for the touring company. It depicted a group of tourists caught up in a Mediterranean rite that included the re-enactment of a primitive ritual where a king is symbolically killed by his successor to ensure the harvest and the prosperity of the tribe. 'You've had your chance,' she told him when he asked about another commission. Madam saw Norman as providing a good critique of the Royal Ballet, but as director? If the board had asked around they would have discovered that Norman had made heavy weather of directing the administrative side of the Rambert company although it had only 16 dancers. Managing internal politics was not his forte. After he resigned from Rambert he went off to choreograph with the Batsheva company in Israel and was considering working in Australia.

Whatever the discussions, the first I knew of what was going on was when I was out on tour. I was told there was a phone call for me at the stage door. It was John Tooley informing me of Norman's appointment. He apologised for not keeping me informed, 'We rather forgot to let you know.' Presumably the people at Covent Garden considered me to be inferior due to my background at Sadler's Wells, at Stuttgart and with Jooss. Neither did they rate *The Sleeping Beauty* and *Giselle* that I had made for Covent Garden or consider the productions I had successfully mounted in major international opera houses. I had to content myself with pointing out, not just from personal vanity, but as associate to the director of the Royal Ballet and director of the touring company, that if only as a courtesy I ought to have been considered. That is what I put into a letter of protest to Claus Moser, as chairman, with whom I always got on well. No doubt I was piqued too that dancers from Sadler's Wells Royal Ballet had not been included in the queen's silver jubilee gala that had just taken place at Covent Garden. Claus at least had the courtesy to reply.

Truly I do not know whether I would have accepted the directorship if it had been offered. I am glad I did not. What Sonya thought of it all I never knew. She never told me. Sonya very much let me work out the answers to such dilemmas myself. 'You must do what you want,' she once said to me when I asked for advice, but I was shocked at Norman's appointment. Once he took on the role I did my best to keep him involved and informed about the touring company, now Sadler's Wells Royal Ballet. Early on I gave a party for him at our home so Norman could meet our dancers and staff, but really we did not see much of him subsequently. Personally I found Norman to be a very nice man and we got on well, but it is always difficult when somebody from another stable is appointed. Strangers to the Royal Ballet organisation, such as Norman and later Ross Stretton, found this difficult. It is a role for which you must feel right. At the time I certainly did not have confidence in my own abilities to become that director. It was only during my time in charge of Sadler's Wells Royal Ballet that I found I flourished. One of the challenges of the job as director of the Royal Ballet at that time, as Norman was to discover, was that you had three former directors, all of them choreographers, de Valois, Ashton and MacMillan, who owned both the performing rights and casting decisions for their ballets, peering over your shoulder, watching your every decision.

I believe that becoming director of Sadler's Wells Royal Ballet and the subsequent creation of Birmingham Royal Ballet was what I was now ready to do. In retrospect I am so very pleased that is what I did. The collective achievements of those companies are what gave me a sense of having got somewhere at last. Being director of what used to be frequently called the 'second company' does not do much for your ego but you never let anyone know you feel that way. 'Sister company' was a much better term. When I learned I had been passed over at Covent Garden Sadler's Wells Royal Ballet had a completely nomadic existence but I had great scope to develop dancers' careers and the company overall in the way in which I believed. The addition of new rehearsal rooms, office and wardrobe facilities at Sadler's Wells gave us a proper base. Previously we had very limited spaces in the wardrobe at the Royal Opera House and scenery was stored all over London and then only when we were actually performing there. We had 45 dancers, which grew slowly, incrementally, sometimes adding two new dancers in the corps when a principal left, to 50. I foresaw that if we did not increase numbers the company would not have a future.

Marketing departments were not as all-powerful as now, so programming was essentially at my discretion. This does not mean everything was straightforward. We were still part of the Royal Opera House organisation and I still had to present our plans for board approval. I wanted to expand the repertoire with *La Sylphide*, which they thought was a misprint for *Les Sylphides* on their board papers, but they advised that we should let Peter Schaufuss proceed with his production for London Festival Ballet in 1979 as their need for such a ballet was greater than ours. I believe though that we would have done it rather well.

These were rarely happy times, however. There were endless things to contend with, not least the particular problem of not being able to confirm dancers from the Royal Ballet School until after the Covent Garden company had taken first pick. The situation improved later on after Anthony Dowell became director. He was more understanding. I only got Darcey Bussell because Anthony did not feel he would be able to use her enough. He thought there would be more opportunities for her with us. The Covent Garden company already had too many girls with beautiful legs and feet. Kenneth MacMillan was upset when Darcey came to Sadler's Wells Royal Ballet. He had seen her at the school and I could tell from his facial expression that he was cultivating ways to bring her to Covent Garden, which he did to impressive effect in *The Prince of the Pagodas* in December 1989. I was sorry to lose Darcey so soon after losing Leanne Benjamin to London Festival Ballet when Schaufuss tempted her with the title role in Frederick Ashton's *Romeo and Juliet*. Leanne had been outstanding at the school and it was evident she would go far.

Often nowadays companies separate the artistic and administrative aspects of a director's role. When I became director I felt I wanted to have sight of both aspects, to know what was happening on all fronts. This was very much something I had learned from Madam. She was always clear that everybody had to shoulder all the responsibilities that went with their position. During wartime she enlisted the support of Donald Albery, who became a highly successful theatre impresario, owner and producer, to help her run the business side of company management. In later years he told me in fact that Madam had a remarkably sharp sense of the financial aspects of business and what to do when box office receipts were not good, how to budget and plan. Albery thought that all of that was second nature to Madam. At Sadler's Wells Royal Ballet I was supported by my general manager, Christopher Nourse. Together we took the decision to reduce the number of performances partly to reduce the injury rate among dancers but mainly because of the need to reduce costs. The Royal Opera House's finances were under scrutiny by the Arts Council and the touring company had always been seen as a drain on resources. In the days when I first toured with Ballets Jooss and Sadler's Wells Theatre Ballet in the 1940s and 1950s we did eight shows per week, with Sunday as a travel day. It is very difficult to maintain standards like that. By the end of the 1970s, because of union agreements, a dancer's working week was 33 hours with a performance counting as three hours. We were still giving eight performances, which left only nine hours each week to rehearse the repertory, create new works, rehearse covers, teach and coach roles. Overtime was inevitable.

As a result of the many audits to which the Royal Opera House organisation was subject, we had to reduce the number of productions that we toured. A week's engagement on tour now opened on Tuesday rather than Monday and we danced only two programmes, usually a full-length ballet and one triple-bill, seven performances in total. Compared to nowadays however, when for most touring companies only one production is toured and the first night is usually Wednesday, sometimes even

Thursday, we were still presenting a healthy repertoire and number of performances. Fewer performances means that productions are better rehearsed. Dancers can be better prepared as theatres nowadays are better equipped with rehearsal and technical facilities.

A director must take decisions that are made not only just on cost but which also take account of previous repertoire toured and attendances. That is always a balancing act for a director but it is essential if you were including a triple-bill, for the programme to appeal it must include a well-known work like *Petrushka* or *The Firebird*. These days, however, there are fewer venues on the touring circuits, fewer performances during a week in any one city and less variety in the ballets performed. This is not good for building regular audiences willing to give ballet a go. Nowadays touring companies have arrived at a situation where although they would prefer to tour more, it is actually cheaper for them just to rehearse. It costs companies such as Birmingham Royal Ballet around £150,000 per week to be out on the road.

Although audiences outside London may have less exposure to dance than in the capital, it in no way means that they are less appreciative of good ballet music, theatre, or indeed any of the arts. Contrast is vital. As I worked to develop the range and standard of Sadler's Wells Royal Ballet, alongside new works by David Bintley, Hans Van Manen and Glen Tetley, I programmed revivals of others by Cranko, MacMillan, Balanchine, Tudor, Ashton and de Valois. To expand our repertoire of full-length ballets I went to see Ronald Hynd's new ballet, *Papillon* for Houston Ballet. It was not his best but it enjoyed a huge success there. Ronnie had created a parody of romantic ballet, full of jokes that appealed to an American sense of humour. In Houston it brought the house down. His cast was very strong. *Papillon* was loosely based on the original by Marie Taglioni to an infectious score by Jacques Offenbach. It featured a comically evil shah and a jealous witch who transforms the heroine into the butterfly of the title in some attractive, mock-classical scenes. It did not really cross the Atlantic that well. The first night in Leeds was fantastic and people really laughed but we never recaptured that. The press were sniffy about it and we had a lot of injuries on tour to contend with. Flu can run straight through a company when everybody is on top of each other all the time. The mistake that Hynd had made, however, as Ashton pointed out, was that it is dangerous to mock the styles of previous generations. Recreations should always be done affectionately so that the public does not just laugh at the artistes but with them. In *Papillon* there was a pas de cinq which audiences never knew whether it was intended to be serious or was a deliberate parody. But *Papillon* paid its way and served its purpose.

I still wanted to expand the number of full-length ballets we had, as dancers always need three-act roles to challenge them; hence why we took over Cranko's *The Taming of the Shrew* from the Covent Garden company. Kenneth MacMillan had wanted to stage John's *Onegin* there in 1977 and plans were proceeding until Jürgen Rose, the designer, had refused to have his very delicate scenery and hangings proofed to meet the fire regulations. Somehow this had not been a problem when Stuttgart Ballet performed *Onegin* at the Royal Opera House in a memorial season in 1974, a year after John's death. Rose was adamant, however, and the production had to be abandoned only three weeks before the first night. *The Taming of the Shrew* was substituted. Although Marcia Haydée, John's original Kate, came for many of the rehearsals and danced a couple of performances, the ballet did not catch fire. Merle Park, scheduled to be Tatiana in *Onegin*, was miscast as the shrew. The company really felt at odds with John's choreography which in this ballet is rather rough and purposely brash. When I took it into the touring repertoire in autumn 1980 it worked much better. Out on the road, where audiences were not as sophisticated as at Covent Garden, they responded much better to the slapstick humour of the piece. Marion Tait was a brilliant Kate opposite the swaggering Petruchio of Stephen Jefferies, but it was a hard ballet for the company on tour. It moves so quickly and demands a lot of attack.

For other full-length ballets, I redid *Coppélia* in 1979. Peter Snow designed, almost as a child's picture book in style. Marion Tait was the first, deliciously naughty Swanilda in that production. John Auld was Coppélius. Nobody has ever bettered his performance, but David Bintley was memorable too, having first performed the role convincingly in his graduation performance when he was only 18. When I recruited him to the company in 1976 it was as a demi-caractère dancer. When Mikhail Fokine's ballet *Petrushka* was brought to life for us in 1984, David's performance in the title role was fantastic. He literally hurled himself around the stage when thrown into his cell, a possessed puppet, full of despair, terror and passion. He had to stop appearing in the role because he hurt himself with serious bruising all over his body. The production, staged for us by John Auld, was acclaimed, not just for Bintley's performance but particularly for John's attention to detail in the crowd scenes. Sergei Diaghilev stressed how important it is when reviving great works to realise that audiences remember performances to have been much better on first viewing than they actually they were, especially the colour and the action. John recognised this exactly and knew *Petrushka* from his days with the Borovansky Ballet in Australia. What a pity that an opportunity of collaboration between the companies was missed when John was not asked to revive the ballet at Covent Garden later. That revival, featuring Irek Mukhamedov, died a death through being mounted very accurately but lifelessly by the staff from notation. Indeed it is a pity that when Birmingham Royal Ballet's production has been loaned to other companies, for example to English National Ballet in 2013, that John was not involved to really energise the ballet. He was then still full of vigour and knew exactly how to make such a ballet live.

During the course of my career there has been an enormous growth of activity in the arts, including dance, not just in this country but around the world. That has not meant a comparable rise in the numbers of directors adept at managing it. Being a director is an insoluble job. Too often it feels like a case of just keeping going rather than being able to realise your grand vision for the future. So many elements seem out of your control or left to chance, but you must know how to harness them. A director needs to know the whole company, to make every member feel important and valued, and not just to concentrate on a handful of principals. But a director does need to know how to choose a principal. I have seen dancers promoted for the wrong reasons, when a ballerina is the wife of an existing principal for example. A director needs to know how to withstand that pressure. I lost David Ashmole as a principal from Sadler's Wells Royal Ballet when I failed to promote his wife Petal Miller. Her ultimatum to me was for her to move up from soloist to principal. That was a step too far. They both left the company as a consequence. Petal is a lovely Australian, an all-rounder who always finds a place for herself wherever she goes, be it in a company or school. She speaks her mind, writes rather good poetry and fairy stories and has produced some well-structured and beautifully rehearsed choreography. We had good times together and bad ones, but have always been friends. David was a very nice dancer who could do everything a top classical dancer could with a lovely clean technique. He became a truck driver in Australia and absolutely adored it. After returning to Britain as a very good teacher, David was stricken with a particularly nasty form of cancer which killed him. It nearly killed Petal too as she absolutely adored David. Her love for him is still incredibly strong. Like many of us old pros Petal is hopeless when she is not busy so she got herself back into working with the Royal Ballet School and other companies, here and overseas. It may have been hard to refuse Petal's request for promotion, but a director must on occasion be able to cope with decisions that are seen as unfair.

A director's choices must be based on talent and excellence. The ability to recognise a true, classical ballerina is a prerequisite but is an ability not shared by all directors. Ideally a director should try to make a plan for each ballerina to develop. I tried to do that at Sadler's Wells Royal Ballet, but when a dancer with great talent considers they are in the ballerina bracket they tend to want to dance everything. That is something that as director of the Royal Ballet, Frederick Ashton sought to resist. He firmly believed that suitability in one role did not automatically qualify a ballerina for another. That is not a way of thinking that dancers tend to subscribe to. They want to do everything and certainly as much as others, but some roles are just not right for some dancers. In this respect I had to be plain with Maina Gielgud. She first came to my notice through a ghastly solo by Maurice Béjart called *Squeaky Door*. She balanced on one foot for the entire piece, putting her other leg into various other positions. This ugly demonstration of body control helped make her famous. Years later Madam suggested I invite Maina to give some guest performances as the black queen in *Checkmate*. This was very good casting. Maina had a big success in the role, very powerful, strong and dominating. She was also very good as Myrtha in *Giselle* and the third movement of *Concerto* which is tough for the dancer as the section was originally conceived as a pas de deux. Maina certainly did not look as though she was dancing without the support of a partner. Without these roles there would have been very little for Maina to dance. When she wanted to do *Giselle* I had to refuse her, she was really too strong for the role who from the outset should look as if too much dancing might kill her, likewise any emotional shock. She accepted this. Maina made a great career for herself, dancing with many companies and becoming artistic director of

Australian Ballet, during which time we arranged exchanges of dancers between our companies. Her knowledge of the dance scene worldwide is fantastic and she has been most generous in advising me about how the opera house in Budapest is run. Maina is half-Hungarian and has worked there a lot. This was enormously helpful when I mounted *The Sleeping Beauty* there in 2016.

It is very difficult to make a plan for dancers as the repertoire changes so frequently. It may be three seasons or even longer before a ballet is repeated so a ballerina making a debut performance in one season may wait another two seasons before the ballet comes back. That makes it hard for a ballerina to reach her potential in a role. With the number of dancers capable of performing a role now, due to the improvements in technical standards, there are just not enough performance opportunities. Dancers do not develop in a rehearsal room. You only do that in performance, which is why ballerinas like to guest elsewhere.

Maintaining morale, so that when you ask somebody to do the impossible they feel it is possible, is another vital skill for a director. When you have a spate of injuries or a flu epidemic you can find yourself shuffling casting, asking dancers to take on a role they may not have rehearsed or phoning around the world for a replacement. Then there is the permanent balancing act of creating a repertoire that appeals to audiences, never mind what you think is beneficial to develop the company's technical and performing abilities. Finding new choreographers – and finding enough time for them to be able to create new work as well as enough performance slots for it to be performed – is yet another constant challenge. Those are all mostly artistic considerations, but I have never been employed as artistic director, always as director which, of course, involves making artistic decisions in conjunction with the administrators, choreographers and teaching staff – as well as keeping pace with the activities of other companies.

Being a director is more than a full-time occupation. Writing reports for the board. Dealing with unions. Worrying about new buildings and facilities. Figuring out how best to manage funding. Cultivating arts' ministers and sponsors, an ever-revolving door, to ensure the company has the best resources possible – always. When in charge of Sadler's Wells Royal Ballet I learned early to delegate, not to avoid facing difficult situations alone but because there are so many responsibilities that come your way, particularly casting. I had learned, working as Kenneth MacMillan's associate, when having mapped out the principal casting for the next three months, I would pass it to him and he would alter it as necessary, hand it back to me and then I would do the soloist and corps de ballet casting which would often involve many Royal Ballet School students. This took hours. When Desmond Kelly retired from dancing and became a ballet master I soon made him my assistant director and at once gave him the job of planning casting. He quickly assumed just the right amount of authority as assistant director and never overstepped the mark. I rarely made any changes in his proposals.

As director, I also discovered that it is sometimes good for dancers not to have everything perfect. Once they have it just right, the zip goes out of their work, and there is nothing worse than a complacent dancer. However much it is necessary for the director to be present in rehearsals and honest in their feedback that they give dancers after performances, a successful director cannot become too close to dancers. Difficult conversations about career development, technical ability and artistic expression sometimes need to occur and these form part of the director's responsibility.

Arnold Spohr was a wonderful director of Royal Winnipeg Ballet, a company he led for 30 years. When I saw him at work with his company in 1983 he was very strict with his dancers. He could scream and shout and interrupt all the time. I actually do not mind that. You need somebody who is capable of getting the performance on, but Arnold was very human as a director. He loved his dancers and excelled at pinpointing exactly the things that needed to be corrected. It is perhaps some measure of what the Winnipeg company thought of Arnold when on his retirement he was presented with a full-length fur coat and a Mercedes. When I was subsequently in Winnipeg reviving *Giselle*, Arnold appeared unexpectedly at a rehearsal. The company all applauded him and he bowed to me. He asked if he might be allowed to watch the rehearsal. I told him I would be delighted if he did. We had not got very far before Arnold interrupted proceedings, 'You girls are just as bad as you used to be. You don't watch each other!' he exclaimed – but he said it with great affection.

Tamás Solymosi, director of Hungarian National Ballet, is somebody else to impress me. The company's repertoire is classically based and varied. Tamás is positive with a strong personality. He communicates very well and inspires his dancers. He has got fight in him, which is necessary as the company shares an opera house. He still has much that needs to be put right – the lighting equipment is very old, the costume department is a nightmare and the whole theatre is bogged down with bureaucracy – but Tamás knows what he wants to achieve and has good people on his staff.

While at Sadler's Wells Royal Ballet I introduced annual reviews to the company. They are time consuming and exhausting but well worth it as it meant that dancers could see me not just when they had an axe to grind but we could talk about their work generally – and most of the time positively. Anthony Dowell followed, with good results he told me. When Anthony retired after 15 years as director of the Royal Ballet in 2001 he was the second-longest serving director after de Valois in the company's history. He talked at the time about the role being part of a bloodline, yet neither he nor I were consulted about who to appoint, or how, when he was about to retire. Though not having done a job is scarcely a recommendation for advising others, I, of all people, through my involvement with the Royal Ballet School and both its companies for over 50 years at that time, knew what the job entailed. I was informed by Michael Kaiser, at that time chief executive of the Royal Opera House, that I would be invited to talk to the selection panel which included Beryl Grey and Lord Eatwell, president of Queens' college, Cambridge and a former economic adviser to Labour leader Neil Kinnock. I heard nothing further until I was at the Royal Opera House to make an official complaint after trouble during a performance of *The Nutcracker* caused by the snow machine in the fly tower shedding its contents in a huge dense lump onto the dancers struggling onstage below. I mentioned to Kaiser that I was surprised not to have heard anything. He reassured me I would be involved. Two weeks later I saw in the papers that the appointment had been made. Kevin McKenzie, artistic director of American Ballet Theatre, was Kaiser's preferred choice but he was not available. So enter – and exit – Ross Stretton in quick succession, somebody who had not even applied for the job originally but who, like McKenzie, was known to Kaiser from his time as executive director of American Ballet Theatre. Such ways of carrying on give the impression to the outside world that ballet companies – as depicted in such films as *The Red Shoes*, so silly and unrealistic, and *Black Swan*, dreadful – are actually the norm.

Not so. Really such portrayals have nothing to do with real companies, although I do note that Benjamin Millepied, who choreographed *Black Swan*, became, however briefly, director of Paris Opéra Ballet. But such perceptions are damaging.

When, a decade later, Monica Mason was approaching the end of her directorship of the Royal Ballet, nobody initially included on the selection committee understood the detail of what being a director entailed. I know this caused Monica and her assistant director Jeanetta Laurence considerable concern, particularly as they could see the consequences of appointing an unsuitable, internal candidate. A bad decision, which Monica and Jeanetta could foresee, would lead to trouble in the nest, particularly among the ballerinas. The recruitment panel did include knowledgeable people. Some of them even knew about ballet, but not how a company actually functions. Their chair was Simon Robey, a senior executive from Morgan Stanley who heads the trustees of the Royal Opera House. They realised for themselves that they did not have the necessary insight to make informed decisions. I was invited to join the panel and I was delighted to be able to contribute. I did not say it at the time, as it was something that I did not see then, but in retrospect I believe it would have been better for a woman to have been chosen to advise the recruitment panel. Ballet is, in many ways, much more a woman's profession and the size and importance of the female corps de ballet means that a director is often taken up with decisions about it. In the wake of past errors, the board was particularly concerned that somebody competent should be appointed. This was a pertinent concern as most of the applicants were former or current dancers. The qualities required in a director extend beyond those just of a former dancer. Anthony Dowell's directorship, for example, could be defined as that of a dancer of a particular period although the experience of working with American Ballet Theatre for a couple of years certainly benefitted him.

The desirability – or not – of whether a director continues to perform or choreograph is also something that causes much debate. In 2012, candidates invited to interview were asked to present their choice of programming for their first three seasons and to defend their rationale. It was clear that some candidates had put a lot of thought into their proposals, some of which were impractical or not suitable for the company, but the interviewing panel was looking for new ideas, not necessarily a presentation of how things should be organised. I would have expected more enthusiasm from certain candidates, some of whom appeared to believe that a decision had already been made, which was not the case. A shortlist was called back two or three times. It was evident from how one candidate presented their plans and from their conduct overall that they would soon make an excellent director, which is how it turned out. I was impressed, as were the rest of the panel, but I was not convinced that Tamara Rojo was the right person to lead the Royal Ballet.

However much it is a director's job to shake things up, being the head of that company, part of a vast opera house with a big history, demands an appreciation of its founding principles. It is not necessary to appoint from within, but somebody who understands the tradition without being bogged down by it is a prerequisite. What a director thinks about schooling, how to balance a company's heritage with more commercial considerations, whether a director continues to perform or not, were all considerations that I scrutinised at the interviews. The candidate who had every answer for these requirements was Kevin O'Hare. It transpired that he nearly had not applied as he was happy in his current role as administrative director, and his friends twice had to encourage him to see what happened if he did apply. When his appointment was announced to the company they applauded solidly for several minutes, suggesting that he – and the appointment panel – had got something right.

As for myself, I have been described as the best director that the Royal Ballet never had. Such comments are always a boost for the ego but I do not take them too seriously. Although Kevin O'Hare is doing well as director of the company, it is too early to judge. He does seem to have established a very good relationship with the dancers and staff. Finding the right person is hard. There is no formula. You can only hope that your choice works out. Frederick Ashton liked the status of being director but saw the role primarily in choreographic terms, as a vehicle for his own work and as an opportunity to extend the repertoire with revivals of other choreographers' major works. Fred felt he was owed as much recognition as de Valois had enjoyed, but rarely did he lift a finger as director of the company. He only succeeded in the role because of his three assistant directors, his henchmen, none of whom actually liked each other.

I was able to help Kenneth MacMillan as director but he did have a very clear choreographic and artistic path of what he wanted to achieve.

Unfortunately only Kenneth could really see it, which meant he could be enormously popular or unpopular. He suffered terribly before he realised he was not a very good director. Kenneth's was a very passive strength. He could get across his point by hardly saying anything at a board meeting, yet when somebody allowed casting for future programmes to be published without seeking Kenneth's approval, he was on the phone immediately shouting his disapproval. 'How dare you give out information about my company and my ballets before I have cleared it?' he vented. In fact to have withheld the information would have been very serious for the box office. The details were unchanged since Kenneth had seen the proof, so understandably it was released as Kenneth was not available.

With the exception of Monica Mason, the Royal Ballet has not had a good director since Ninette de Valois. Mon's scale of achievement was different from that of Madam, yet she was a brilliant organiser although she sometimes nearly killed her dancers when she pushed them too hard. Monica was anxious to show what the company could achieve to the extent that she overworked everybody. This was evident in Kevin O'Hare's approach too but very quickly he learned that the health and spirit of the company must come first. The director of a ballet company is the dancers' champion, but he – or she – should not always think like a dancer. Monica can never be accused of relying on past successes to prove her worth. She was brave in her planning and I am sure her choices of new works from commissioned choreographers, welcomed by the company, will continue to have a positive effect on the future.

A wide-ranging vision is a necessity for a company director who must be able to see the bigger future. An artistic eye is essential, not just a dancer's perspective or that of a financial accountant. Maintaining a vision is not the same as wishful thinking. Planning a repertoire is as much about casting and about what roles dancers need to do as the choice of what ballets to programme to appeal to the public. Spotting what is not quite right at any given moment is a skill, as is knowing what to do when plans fly out the window because of all the flux and change on a daily basis. Getting the show on then is the priority. Having clear ideas about how the future will develop thanks to an understanding of how schooling, training and the development of creative talent including choreographers will support that.

A director requires a strong personality, bravery and the ability to talk convincingly to each and everybody, whether they are corps de ballet, funding bodies or sponsors, the media or unions. A director has to be a skilled politician and know, as Madam had warned me, how to get the board to work for you. The directors who get their way are frightened of nothing, as was Madam. She would challenge anybody, international stars, members of the board, anybody. She knew her mind and was articulate, always able and willing to fight for the ballet company that she had created – even if she did change her mind a lot. John Cranko said she was as variable as the wind and so her opinions were not worth considering. She certainly managed to confuse us all. I do wonder what Madam would have made of the task today, the vast organisation that is the Royal Ballet set amid an even vaster organisation, the Royal Opera House. The complexities and demands of the job, encompassing not only what appears on the stage but the manifold requirements for access and social inclusiveness that public funding carries with it nowadays, make the role extremely hard. Not that Madam would have shirked the challenge, and she was highly skilled at selecting the right people to fulfil key roles, another essential ingredient for a director to master. By then I had learned that being a director does not demand your permanent presence. Importantly too, the mark of a successful director is not the quality of their own work but also of those who surround you. What I did learn myself during the illness that caused me to step down as director of Birmingham Royal Ballet in 1995 was that, with Desmond Kelly and Derek Purnell temporarily at the helm, the company got on perfectly well without me. However, the future is another matter.

Being director of Birmingham Royal Ballet changed me a lot. Initially I was slow to see the potential of Birmingham – particularly as I was practically the last person to know about it. During the 1980s productions at Sadler's Wells Royal Ballet got bigger, as did the company's reputation. We opened *Papillon* in Leeds, *Swan Lake* in Manchester and *The Sleeping Beauty* and *The Snow Queen* in Birmingham. Sadler's Wells theatre itself was aware it was being outgrown. There were several attempts at planning an enlarged stage but they never really took off. There were many galas over the years designed to help raise funds. I was pleased when one I put together was described as the best gala ever. It featured many international ballet stars and famous personalities but managed to raise only

£500 profit, hardly a life-changing amount. Not that the new Sadler's Wells, which opened in 1998, is perfect nowadays, but front of house before the rebuild was pretty ghastly. Clement Crisp used to joke that when he dreamed of going to hell he would discover he was in the foyer of Sadler's Wells. Somebody else likened the glum décor to a municipal crematorium. Many people complained of cramped leg-room and terrible sightlines.

Backstage things were no better, horrible in fact. The fly tower was inadequate for large-scale productions and performers were hampered by the lack of space on both sides of the stage. One attempt at expansion meant dancers were apt to collide with a masonry column as they came offstage. On one side of the wings you were practically out in the street when you made your exit. Some of the dressing-rooms were on the top floor among the offices. The orchestra pit was reasonably large, but overall it was not a well-designed theatre. It required great feats of ingenuity to get anything on. It was fine for smaller ballets and we just about managed to do *Giselle* there, but the second act looked awfully cramped. Sadler's Wells lacked atmosphere. It was not a good theatre to show off the company. True, it was home, and much of our history – including an initiation rite when new male dancers had to undertake an army-style assault course that involved walking along a parapet on the roof of the building and jumping across a fairly wide gap to the neighbouring building to prove their masculinity – was rooted in the building. All the many schemes to improve Sadler's Wells over many years had been patch-up jobs. It did provide us, and several other dance companies, with a London showcase, at least for our smaller works. Very occasionally our larger productions could be seen at the Royal Opera House, the Lyceum or the Coliseum.

By the mid-1980s minds in London were starting to think that Sadler's Wells was not the future. In Birmingham, minds were further advanced. The city council there had seen how Simon Rattle's leadership had galvanised the City of Birmingham Symphony Orchestra into becoming a world standard band, one that had its home in the city to which audiences were willing to travel just to hear top class music making. The transformation of the CBSO was helping to redefine notions about the city itself. In Liverpool, a rival city for investment and regeneration, there was recognition that its Philharmonic orchestra had missed an opportunity in failing to hold on to Rattle, a Liverpudlian and previously the Phil's assistant conductor, when he left to join the CBSO. Birmingham was at the time branding itself as the heart of England, true in a geographical sense but a rather exaggerated claim otherwise. The council did have many civic grand designs in progress to help regenerate the city. In a rare and enlightened way, Birmingham saw that the arts had a role to play too. Birmingham was fully behind its own opera company, City of Birmingham Opera, run by Graham Vick, and the city was, less successfully as it transpired, in the process of providing a home for the newly reformed D'Oyly Carte company at the Alexandra theatre. There were plans afoot to develop the Bull Ring and the area of Hurst Street opposite the Hippodrome. There always were, but after the success of the National Exhibition Centre, the National Indoor Arena, then intended to be the home for the CBSO, was expected to open in 1992.

But I knew none of these plans for a new dawn in Birmingham. That I did become aware, I have to thank Jane Nicholas. She had been a member of Sadler's Wells Theatre Ballet and, in her subsequent career, had gone on to the British Council and was later the first director of the dance department at the Arts Council. Jane tipped me the wink. Her sister had attended Bedales and Jane herself had been my first girlfriend at Sadler's Wells Theatre Ballet. I find it always pays to part on good terms with your former girlfriends. Seriously, in the late 1950s when I was choreographing a musical at the Players' theatre in London, Jane contacted me, looking for a job as a dancer. Through a disastrous marriage she had lost confidence in herself and was struggling to get back on her feet. Of course I helped her, and she has never forgotten that. Jane's hobbies are pruning, weeding and collecting cracked porcelain. She has a shelf running around her dining-room full of teapots. She is heavily too into local politics. Hence all those shared interests and experiences are why we have always got on.

Jane alerted me to serious discussions afoot concerning Birmingham. It was being talked of as the home for Sadler's Wells Royal Ballet. This was not the first plan to find a more substantial home for the company away from London, but I had not heard a single word that the idea had come to life again. Jane revealed that members of the Royal Opera House were having conversations in Birmingham, but not even Anthony Dowell, director of the Royal Ballet nor Anthony Russell Roberts, the company's administrative director, were involved. This was typical of the way the Royal Opera House operated. For me, this was like the secrecy over the appointment of Kenneth MacMillan's successor all over again. Less personally, the Royal Ballet only heard confirmation of a definite decision to redevelop the Royal Opera House in the 1990s, long after the Royal Opera and orchestra were already establishing their requirements and competing for space within the refurbished building.

As it happened, Birmingham was one of our next tour dates. The city had been part of my theatrical baptism from my days with Ballets Jooss and Metropolitan Ballet. More recently Birmingham had always been a major venue for the Royal Ballet touring company and the occasional destination in the 1980s for the Covent Garden company when they stepped outside London. The city had a fine musical reputation and audiences were always good, but the Hippodrome – although it had been refurbished and extended to the tune of £2.2 million in 1981 when the stage had been refloored and its rake removed, a stage lift installed, the sound and lighting systems upgraded, the proscenium widened and a new fly tower constructed – was still not the best of theatres. Traditionally it had been a variety theatre with a large though shallow stage. Once I had to tell Princess Margaret to hold her breath as I escorted her backstage after a performance as a malodorous whiff from the gents' loo pervaded the entire length of a corridor. One corner was particularly uriniferous.

So during our autumn visit in 1987, when we were to unveil new ballets by Graham Lustig, Susan Crow and Derek Deane, the theatre's director, Richard Johnston, put his head around the door saying he would like to have a chat. He did indeed confirm there were plans afoot to establish the company in Birmingham. Thanks to the advance alert I had received, I was not too surprised, but our general manager, Christopher Nourse, was speechless. I was far from enthusiastic at the confirmation and did not like being ignored. Sadler's Wells Royal Ballet was still a Royal Opera House company. I was particularly sensitive to the company's place in the organisation because during the many audits of the financial workings of the Royal Opera House that the government had instigated during the 1980s, two things were always apparent. There was no essential financial mismanagement but the Royal Opera House's deficit could be eliminated if Sadler's Wells Royal Ballet was abolished. Never mind that we were regarded as having the most economical working procedures and systems.

Back in London I went to see John Tooley. He was very gung ho about the proposal. He could afford to be, as he would not be around to live with the consequences. He was in his last year as general director of the Royal Opera House before his retirement. Tooley's previous attempts to get the Royal Opera and Royal Ballet out of London and into regional theatres such as the Palace in Manchester, recently refurbished to house Covent Garden productions, had soon evaporated thanks to a lack of commitment to touring on the Royal Opera House's part. Manchester audiences too had been resistant to the productions toured, the prices charged and were less than impressed by the star names who came – or not – to the city. Clearly this scheme was another attempt to bolster the Royal Opera House's presence outside London, or so it seemed to me.

I was upset and rightly so. 'We were going to tell you,' Tooley told me. Now from whom had I heard that before? Claus Moser, then chairman, tried to pacify me too. He was always very supportive. Claus was a wonderful amateur pianist, a gentle man and a gentleman, unlike some people who sit on boards and who tend to love the sound of their own opinions. However, I was anything but pacified when they told me not to worry. Everything was all in hand, I was told. There have been many times when I have had disagreements at the Royal Opera House, but this was not one of those. I simply said that, as director of the company, I had a duty to my dancers. I would go to Birmingham to have conversations with people at the theatre and in the city to uncover their intentions. After all, I knew the people involved. I fully expected to discover that in order to become what we now call a global city, Birmingham – then aggressively seeking outside investment to regenerate the city as the alternative to London, preferable to Manchester or Glasgow – wanted to buy a ballet company as the backing ensemble for a collection of international star dancers, in a similar way to how football clubs now operate. I was particularly fearful that the council would want to have its say in our artistic planning, the tours and programmes that we would undertake. Really I thought that the company was being pushed out of the way, and nothing that could be said would convince me otherwise. But I was wrong.

When I went to Birmingham next and talked to Richard Johnston at the Hippodrome and people from the city council direct, I discovered that at this point they really only wanted to know what it would take to establish a top-class ballet company in the city by providing us with a proper home to allow us to develop. They had no wish to have any say in the actual running of the company. But they were anxious to start a feasibility study as soon as they could. I came away feeling very relieved, particularly as I was told the council really did not have a shopping trolley waiting to be filled by whatever company they could find off the shelf somewhere. They were excited at the prestige of attracting a gold-standard ballet company to Birmingham, in the words of Anthony Sargent, who went on to become the founder director of the Sage, Gateshead. Anthony at the time was head of arts for the council in Birmingham. He had developed an influential strategy document about the city's cultural development. Discussions were very much in exploratory stages, I was told by Anthony and others.

While nobody among the decision-makers in Birmingham was hostile to the idea, there was still some scepticism among councillors to be overcome in many meetings and conversations. It was only many years after the event that I learned that Anthony considered me – once convinced about Birmingham – to be an eloquent champion, apparently supremely practical, on the benefits of providing a home for ballet in the city. Anthony considered that, along with Graham Vick and Simon Rattle as part of a powerful triumvirate, I radiated confidence about the benefits to the city that enlightened investment in culture would bring. I was flattered to learn that Anthony thought that I had the diplomatic skills that could convince anybody from any background that classical ballet is exciting. I certainly felt that the council's intentions were genuine, and that the whole venture would be preceded by the feasibility study to establish what each and every member of the company thought about the impact of such a move. They would all be interviewed individually and in confidence by an external consultant. This would be followed by a year in which to undertake any necessary rebuilding work. The onus was on us to tell them what was needed to provide a proper home. All departments, the council made clear, including stage management, administration, wardrobe, and most importantly rehearsal facilities, would need to be comprehended and accommodated in a fully integrated preparation, production and performance facility.

I also pointed out that the company's relationship with the Royal Ballet School must be considered. Although the school's junior associates were based in the Midlands, additional costs for travel, accommodation and subsistence during rehearsal weeks needed to be factored into any financial equation. This was recognised. Importantly, too, it was always acknowledged that the planning and operational running of the company would remain with the Royal Opera House, in collaboration with the company itself. Financial separation was not considered at that stage. Increased financing for the company would come from Birmingham City Council and the Arts Council, but Birmingham would not push us to act as ambassador for the city on overseas tours in any more commercial a way than we did already on our international visits, then under the aegis of the British Council.

As a result of everything I heard, I again went back to John Tooley in London feeling confident that Birmingham's intentions were well worth considering. As a result it was decided to go ahead with the internal consultation and include everybody – dancers, orchestra, stage management, crew and lighting technicians, wardrobe staff and musicians, everybody – in the company. Christopher Nourse and I discussed the implications wherever we could while we were on tour, in this country and while abroad. There was, at the same time, still a company to manage, new ballets to rehearse, young choreographers to encourage, tours to undertake.

As a result, David Allen, a consultant who had experience of working with the Royal Opera House when its finances were under review by the government some years before, was brought in to carry out the first stage of an internal consultation. Christopher with his associates Derek Purnell and Richard Wright were instrumental in the way it was undertaken, really quite brilliant. Every single member of the company was given the opportunity to outline their concerns and make suggestions. I still do not know to this day who said precisely what as confidentiality was respected, but as I expected, the survey revealed lots of reservations about moving. The majority of principals did not want to move. They were distinctly unhappy at the prospect and did not see it as a career step. Many dancers asked about what redundancy packages would be available, no doubt aware that the Royal Opera House had approved the principle of paying twice the statutory minimum, although this had not been formalised in employee contracts.

The rationale for the move did strike a chord, but many were concerned about the loss of the company's historical links. There were issues too around changing the name of the company, although this was something that was not under consideration at the time. More were concerned about the upheaval of the move. Nearly 30 percent of the company said, unprompted, they were undecided, and over 15 percent said, again without being asked the question direct, that they would not go. All this against the background of the recent summer tour where audience numbers had been disappointing. In Birmingham we played *Giselle* to 86 percent capacity but a triple bill of *Flowers of the Forest*, *Bastet* and *Elite Syncopations* attracted only 64 percent. The autumn tour that followed did no better as audiences were resistant to a 15 percent increase in seat prices and less familiar repertoire on offer. This was just as the bottom had dropped out of the property market and interest rates had peaked at 15 percent, so company members who moved to Birmingham would be faced with selling their London properties at a loss. People worried too about the cost of moving back south if they decided Birmingham was not for them after all.

Personally, there was Sonya to consider too. She quite liked the idea of living in Birmingham and already had friends there. She was furious, however, when a newspaper article quoted her as saying, 'How could Peter possibly expect me to live in Birmingham?' If we must go, she was determined that she wanted a small, easy to run house in the city centre. In the end she was very happy to make do with a very nice house in the botanical gardens in Edgbaston with white peacocks for neighbours – even when they were less than well behaved when they got into the house.

As the company acclimatised to the idea, it became apparent that they were warming to the prospect of the move, but people still needed a lot of explanation and encouragement. There were many company and individual meetings to convince everybody of the merits. A committee of dancers and staff was formed that together with the orchestra compiled a long list of questions and concerns that needed answers. Overall, however, after David Allen undertook the second phase of the internal consultation which addressed everybody's specific concerns, the outcome was very good and he helped us create a viable business plan. People recognised that although it would be a struggle, it was the only option. Other alternatives had come to nothing. In Manchester the councils were at loggerheads over funding and it was unrealistic to believe that anything further could be achieved there. We were not keen on reawakening the notion of a merger with Northern Ballet Theatre, then run by Robert de Warren, and in the longer term that company left Manchester to make its base in Leeds. Newcastle came up as a possibility, though not a serious one as the Theatre Royal was hedged in by neighbouring streets and could not be extended.

As a result of everything it was clear that everybody wanted it to happen. In the event, everybody except one dancer went. Christopher too decided not to go but that was for purely personal reasons. Birmingham Royal Ballet owes him an enormous debt of gratitude, not just for his support during the relocation but for all the years he spent with the company that preceded it, through the thick and thin of the New Group and its evolution into Sadler's Wells Royal Ballet. Christopher has been equally successful in his subsequent career, as Jeremy Isaacs' assistant at the Royal Opera House, managing director of English National Ballet, executive director of Rambert and now director of the Frederick Ashton Foundation. He has also orchestrated many charity galas, award ceremonies and the Dance Proms wonderfully well.

We had a commitment from Birmingham City Council and the Hippodrome to provide everything that we had asked for – and we had not been shy about asking. Compared to Sadler's Wells, the Hippodrome's capacity was about 300 seats more, the stage was nearly four metres wider, two metres taller, and the grid was hung a good seven metres higher. What we asked for was an increased number of performances, greater funding, offices, studios, the company's own dressing-rooms separate from the theatre's own, green room, everything connected with the stage to make it comparable, wider though not as deep, to the Royal Opera House, the pit redone, video room, wardrobe storage, front of house refurbished, the auditorium reseated, as well as a properly equipped gym and physio department established. We were insistent that we needed 60 percent more changing space than we had at Sadler's Wells, twice as much office space, five times more physio facilities. These must all be purpose built and integral to the theatre. We were keen that rehearsal rooms had good floors for dance, the music store, changing facilities, green room and physio unit were all in close proximity to each other. We wanted particularly to improve onsite storage compared to what we struggled with at Sadler's Wells, but we had to accept that we would not be able to house all the scenery for our productions.

While facilities and money do not create success in themselves, the lack of them can certainly stifle it. Dancers go where they can get fulfilment. Besides the roles they dance, that includes the right leadership, facilities and level of funding. This was a once-only opportunity, and if we got what we wanted it would be wonderful. Our list of demands was what in an ideal world we needed without being profligate. I made it clear that I personally would not relocate to Birmingham without these facilities. The move must demonstrably advance the development of the company. That was my precondition. It had taken me 12 years to raise Sadler's Wells Royal Ballet to its current standard and size, and I was not prepared to jeopardise that. I had built up the New Group from 25 dancers in 1970 to Sadler's Wells Royal Ballet with 45 in 1976 – and after years of struggling to get an extra five dancers we were now at a strength of 57. I was concerned about anything being done that would cause the company to go backwards or harm its standing. Audiences had shrunk as a result of a reduced number of touring weeks being presented around the country – which were the essential purpose of what we did.

During the 1987–88 season the Royal Ballet performed 89 times at Covent Garden and had a further 16 performances in the UK and played to a total audience of 190,000 people. We toured for 14 weeks in Britain and performed six weeks in London to a total audience of 165,000 across 133 performances. In comparison, London Festival Ballet had nine weeks on the road and eight weeks in London, with 131 performances and an audience of 227,000 people. Their costs were lower too as London Festival Ballet toured only two full-length ballets, *The Nutcracker* and *Romeo and Juliet* that season, compared to the four full-lengths and four triple-bills we took around the country. These are the sorts of numbers that concentrated the big minds of the Royal Opera House. Comparisons with Festival Ballet were particularly worrying. If we were seen as their rival then the view at the Arts Council was that our funding – and existence – could no longer be justified. There were a limited number of cities that had suitable venues, but when you stop visiting a place, audiences go away. When all this was under review, the redevelopment of the Royal Opera House was yet to happen; it still felt like a pipe-dream. The meetings entailed seemed endless. The whole issue was discussed exhaustively within the hierarchy at Covent Garden. This led to discussions about the company's purpose and comparisons with other touring companies.

Here Jeremy Isaacs focused minds wonderfully. He and I had not got off to a good start. It had been arranged for us to meet at the Waldorf hotel in London in March 1988 when he was general director designate. Neither of us realised there were two entrances to the building. We both waited at the wrong door assuming the other was late. When we did find each other that day, Jeremy quizzed me about what I thought were the strengths of Sadler's Wells Royal Ballet – and what I wanted it to become. He made it clear he liked its whole-hearted approach that registered well with audiences, but equally Jeremy believed we fell short of international standards. He asked whether Sadler's Wells Royal Ballet was a training ground for the Royal Ballet or an independent company with its own repertoire. He intimated he thought it should be the latter despite its historical links. Jeremy recognised how our current leading dancers being required to switch between principal, soloist and featured corps de ballet work during the course of a week of eight performances was contributing to an unsustainable level of injuries. Jeremy made it clear to me and in subsequent more formal meetings that marketing would need to be improved, particularly in London, which is still the case. Sponsorship for new productions was a weak area, he considered, at a time when big productions were costing £300,000. A full-length *Raymonda* produced by Galina Samsova had been cancelled because we could not find a sponsor. More emphasis needed to be put on educational outreach, Jeremy considered, something that was to come to fruition in Ballet Hoo!, an initiative led by Desmond Kelly that involved a diverse mix of teenagers with dependency problems who used drink or drugs as a means of dealing with neglect, physical, sexual and emotional abuse or learning disabilities, dyslexia, autism or anger management. Thanks to Jeremy's prompt, Ballet Hoo! channelled these teenagers' energies towards appearing in performances of *Romeo and Juliet*. I did turn a deaf ear to another of Jeremy's suggestions, namely subtitles for ballet. More seriously he did also point to a growing apart of the two companies and urged me when we met at the Waldorf to find ways of greater collaboration, such as dancer exchanges, while being realistic enough to know this was hard to achieve in practice. He also saw that we needed to tour Britain more and go overseas less.

That would make becoming identified with Birmingham a challenge even though it would be our base. Fundamentally Jeremy believed that Sadler's Wells Royal Ballet was not seen enough across the country and could not be seen to best advantage at Sadler's Wells.

In board meetings Jeremy made it plain that the company was not a junior or feeder company for the Royal Ballet, nor was it a touring version of it. Under my direction, Jeremy said, Sadler's Wells Royal Ballet had become a breeding ground for new choreographers and needed to be strong enough to sustain that role. Most new productions now originated in Birmingham. The only theatre we experienced problems fitting them into was Sadler's Wells. Being based in Birmingham and performing extra weeks there could only bolster the company's role of taking international standard ballet to the regions. In all of these discussions it became clear that only two of the main board had ever seen the company perform on tour. There was much discussion about Sadler's Wells being our history and about turning our backs on our heritage.

While Sadler's Wells itself shilly-shallied about its planned redevelopment and ideas for the Lyceum theatre being used as a dance house came and went, Birmingham City Council doubled its grant to us for the forthcoming year. They were clearly serious. However, we knew too that a council cannot commit to longer-term funding levels. It took Ninette de Valois to cut straight to the heart of the matter. Sadler's Wells was the past, Birmingham is the future. Birmingham must be seen as a positive move and it was absolutely essential that the company should move, Madam insisted. Everybody fell into line behind her, 'Yes Madam.' Unanimously. I was very surprised as I fully expected to have to do a rethink, particularly as the cost of the relocation was not small. Privately Madam took me aside and told me, 'Peter, you have to stop all these endless meetings and just get on with it. You will never get this lot to agree, and what is on offer is far better than what you've got now!' I did manage to point out that, much as I was grateful for her support, the company was not run along the same lines as when she was director. Equity scarcely existed then and there was hardly anywhere else for dancers to go. Festival Ballet in those days was considered a particularly poor option.

To signal our intentions two press conferences were organised on the same day in January 1989, one at Covent Garden, the other at the Birmingham Hippodrome. This meant that Jeremy Isaacs, who was very supportive throughout, a boss who let you get on with your own job, together with several others of us had to dash to Birmingham by train after the announcement in London. Jeremy had spoken very well at that event and I spoke too. He outlined that Birmingham City Council would provide £1 million for three years which would be matched by the Arts Council. There would be a further £1 million towards relocation costs from the Birmingham Hippodrome Theatre Trust and a £4.1 million expansion of the Hippodrome itself. In 1990 this was a lot of money. Many people have criticised Jeremy for his very bold manner but he was incredibly helpful. The creation of Birmingham Royal Ballet would not have happened without his support.

As we travelled to the city that day, Jeremy insisted on cracking open several bottles of champagne on the train. This had made him distinctly garrulous at the Hippodrome announcement and left me with very little time to say anything. However, I did manage to say that Birmingham for us represented a greater opportunity and greater security. In no way did we feel we had been bought, but being resident there meant that we would be able to increase our seasons to five weeks each year and that I had the full support of the company. I said Birmingham was the place of the future, a wonderful challenge to which personally I had committed myself in the next five years. Jeremy chimed in again, saying Birmingham provided the complete diet for the company and audiences alike, then rushed back to London for another meeting. Apparently he slept for the 90-minute train ride and was completely back to normal and very much on the ball for his next meeting.

I stayed on in Birmingham after the press conference to speak to several dance critics and other journalists. I found them all to be apprehensive about the whole venture. I did hear from one journalist who had obviously enjoyed the hospitality too much, loudly proclaiming, 'This will be another of the Opera House's bloody cock-ups.' He vanished before anybody could challenge him. As if to prove him wrong, the following month a Covent Garden audience gave David Bintley's *Hobson's Choice* a standing ovation when it was unveiled. In planning for the future it was good to know that somebody with as much creativity as David was working with the company.

Although members of the royal family do not put money into projects personally, they can, and do, give their blessing and support. Princess

Margaret held receptions at Kensington Palace, including showing the plans and architectural model in her sitting-room, to encourage people and organisations to support the project. She had a genuine love for ballet and could critique a performance with real insight. She never liked Sadler's Wells theatre but still gave us tremendous support at all our seasons there. Her place has now been taken by her daughter Lady Chatto, who is equally supportive. She was a pupil at Francis Holland school in Sloane Square, Chelsea. It is a really good and friendly girls' school with an especially good dance department run by Val Hitchen, a former professional classical dancer. Each year it runs a rather good ballet competition to which I am invited as guest of honour. I present the various awards and it is just about my favourite occasion of the year.

The work at the Hippodrome went relatively smoothly despite some minor hitches. Derek Purnell acted as the co-ordinating force between the company and the theatre. Having been a soloist and then manager, he knew better than anyone what the real needs were. He did a huge amount of work behind the scenes to ensure that the dancers and staff were looked after properly, especially specifying the dance floorings and rest areas. Derek also oversaw the technical areas, scenery store and work-shops, all those essential aspects that architects tend to forget such as props' stores and access for scenery to rehearsal rooms. Derek is now enjoying great success as director of public engagement at the Wallace Collection in London where he has learned the history of practically every painting in the gallery. He is extremely knowledgeable about the whole building. A remarkable man.

Inevitably, despite the attention to detail displayed by Derek, there were, of course, several setbacks. One of these was quite amusing despite being a very serious and potential block on the whole project. Midway through construction, while the new studios, offices, changing-rooms, wardrobe store and scenery docks were being built, it was discovered that nobody had applied for the necessary planning permission for the building even to commence. I do not know how it was resolved and I chose not to enquire too closely. Everything went ahead smoothly. At least there were hidden advantages of being a client of the city council.

CHAPTER 8

Birmingham – forward

What's in a name? Sadler's Wells Opera Ballet, Sadler's Wells Theatre Ballet, the Royal Ballet (Touring Section), The New Group, The Second Company, The Splinter Group, The Other Company, The Royal Ballet on Tour and Sadler's Wells Royal Ballet. Those are just some of the official and unofficial names of the company that in 1990 became Birmingham Royal Ballet, the company with which I am most associated. Despite the plethora of names, the company was never, as some observers suggested, ever called Royal Ballet II in an echo of NDT2 or Ailey II that successfully delineate those companies' links to their parent organisations. One journalist once suggested The National Ballet of the Provinces would be a more fitting label, which even in the 1950s sounded less than politically correct. The naming by committee that has afflicted the Royal Ballet's 'sister' company finally came to an end when Birmingham Royal Ballet was established. In fact I wanted to retain Sadler's Wells in the title; it had great pull outside London, particularly in America. After all, Aston Villa football club proved that you do not need to have Birmingham in its title to be associated with the city. But the city wanted Birmingham Royal Ballet, which was logical enough. The name continued to cause difficulties in certain quarters, however. For some, the Royal was more significant than the Birmingham which they tended to drop. Overall the change was more than a new badge. Establishing a permanent home in Birmingham laid deeper foundations for 'the touring company' than it had ever known. It was the culmination of my career. For the following five years I was at last my own master and no longer answerable to the director of the Royal Ballet, only my own board.

The company moved in at the Birmingham Hippodrome during August 1990 to give us eight weeks before our opening performance at the end of October and to continue preparations for the new production of *The Nutcracker* which was to be unveiled just after Christmas and which we had already started to rehearse in London. There was plenty of time to acclimatise to the new facilities. Overall it was a good move. We were excited to be resident. Members of the council were very much in evidence on the first day. They had a very positive attitude and were delighted to have us in the city. They wanted it all to work. The canteen was not wonderful but the only wrong note was struck when one of the boys in the corps de ballet came to my office to complain that there was no window in their changing-room. Such are the joys of being a director!

For the company's first performance, on 30 October when Princess Margaret and Ninette de Valois led the audience, I decided to open with a triple-bill that featured three major choreographers of the 20th century, a programme that heralded the future. It was a moment of wry satisfaction for Madam. Decades before, in the 1920s when she was first attempting to establish a ballet company in Britain, she had approached Barry Jackson who ran the repertory theatre in Birmingham. In a setback rare for Madam he turned her down. Jackson claimed he was losing quite enough money staging plays without losing more on ballet. If he were to change his mind he would not consider de Valois, somebody of no proven experience. He would ask Bronislava Nijinska. For our opening night I travelled from London with Madam by train, the locomotive of which was newly named Birmingham Royal Ballet. She told me that what we were achieving in Birmingham set an example to other cities. She hoped for the creation of Leeds Royal Ballet and similar companies in Manchester, Bristol and Edinburgh. Birmingham is still the only one although Leeds has welcomed Northern Ballet as its own. There had been much debate about what our first performance should be. There was a considerable level of opinion that we should do *The Sleeping Beauty*, a production that had been unveiled in the city some six years before. I thought it was too familiar and too much associated with the history of the Royal Ballet. Birmingham was meant to celebrate a new direction for us, so our opening night consisted of George Balanchine's *Theme and*

Variations, Frederick Ashton's *Jazz Calendar* and the premiere of David Bintley's *Brahms Handel Variations*. Many people were surprised at my choice of *Jazz Calendar* with its designs by Derek Jarman, considering it a piece of leftover kitsch from 1960s' Carnaby Street or Kings Road, Chelsea, but it is more universal than that. There is genuine comedy in it and Michael Somes staged it brilliantly for us. Many too consider that British dancers cannot dance Balanchine, but I always place great store by what Balanchine himself said: 'I don't come to see it danced as an American would, but come to see it with an English accent. It's different.' Pat Neary always got the company up to standard when she staged any of Balanchine's ballets. I also wanted to include a new work in the opening programme. My brief to David was simple. I asked him to create something special that really used the big stage. As it turned out, and although I kept it in the repertoire for some time, *Brahms Handel Variations* was not one of David's more memorable ballets, something of a damp squib in fact, but you cannot always produce masterpieces to order – and David's success rate is pretty high. *The Sleeping Beauty* was performed during the second week and Philip Prowse's settings always look magnificent on the Hippodrome stage. Also that season we acquired Balanchine's *Symphony in Three Movements* and Kenneth MacMillan's *La Fin du jour*.

Having extra weeks of performances in Birmingham meant we needed extra ballets and it was impossible to fill the need with newly created works. In choosing what ballets to introduce, I, in part, selected works from the Covent Garden repertoire such as MacMillan's *Romeo and Juliet*, Ashton's *Symphonic Variations* and Bintley's *Galanteries*, works which had only rarely, if ever, been seen outside London. These ballets could now be seen to advantage thanks to the investment in the stage facilities at the Hippodrome. There had always been a sense of critics playing down Sadler's Wells Royal Ballet as second best. Sometimes that was true as it was hard to get the best dancers from the Royal Ballet School. We were still the same company of course and I wanted the approval of audiences and critics but only on our terms. I certainly noticed a marked improvement in the company's confidence and stature during the first six months. You could somehow tell that this was now their home. Dancers live for the present and love anything new. Their careers are fairly short, so if they feel that they are not achieving or getting noticed, they are pretty quick to move to other pastures. The fact that very few left during my five years in Birmingham as director meant that the company as a whole was staying together longer, which seemed to bring with it a feeling of maturity without sacrificing their youthfulness. Previously they had never been able to show themselves to their best advantage at Sadler's Wells. They were too compressed there. I could see dancers growing in class thanks to having decent studios. They had not been able to stretch fully before. There was a psychological impact too about performing on the Hippodrome stage, as large as that of the Royal Opera House. That all made them grow as performers. Not everybody can be a virtuoso, but they had become more focused and positive with a greater sense of pride and maturity, which is something that I have always admired in the Rambert company's dancers.

The new production of *The Nutcracker* that winter was certainly a stretch for everybody involved. I dedicated it to the city to show our appreciation for all they had done for us – a gift to the city. Anthony Sargent, former head of arts with the council in Birmingham, told me only recently that this gesture was not fully understood in Birmingham at the time. It only became apparent in subsequent years, when *The Nutcracker* was revived at the Hippodrome every Christmas, how special the production was to Birmingham. Because of the complexity of the staging *The Nutcracker* has only rarely been seen in other venues – you need to come to Birmingham to see it. I chose John Macfarlane as designer because I knew he would create something completely different from my *Nutcracker* at the Royal Opera House, six years previously. I had worked with John before when he designed *Giselle* for me at Covent Garden in 1985, but we did not get off to the best of starts with *The Nutcracker*. Of all the Tchaikovsky ballets, John told me, it was the one he least wanted to do. He also said he was not a fan of my production for the Royal Ballet which was firmly set by Julia Trevelyan Oman in the Beidermeier period of the early 1800s, the period in which the original *Nutcracker* story by E. T. A. Hoffmann is set. While John agreed he would do the new production, he made certain stipulations. He would set the first act, party scene, in the late-1800s, with strong, dark colours, reds and blacks, for the set and costumes. John also had very strong and imaginative ideas about the transformation after the party. He wanted his rats that appear from the fireplace to be very mean, starved and scary. When he saw the production, John Prescott, the former deputy prime minister, likened them to Old Labour emerging from the woodwork. John Macfarlane was also clear that we must find a way of integrating Clara into the action in the second act. His kingdom of sweets is not overly pretty but is a wonderful slightly impressionist fantasy world with which children can easily identify.

However extensive the new technical facilities at the Hippodrome were, they did not provide the stage lifts and trapdoors that enable complicated transformation scenes I had used at Covent Garden. I hoped too that the production might be seen in such venues as the London Coliseum where backstage equipment was much more limited than at the Hippodrome. I was conscious too that however much the Hippodrome was now our home theatre and that it played host to other dance companies and to Welsh National Opera for example, it was not an opera house. Most weeks in the year the Hippodrome was the venue for long runs of big musicals. Family pantomimes were big business from Christmas well into the new year. However good Birmingham had been as a tour date, our established audience was only a certain size. To survive five weeks of performances every year we would have to enlarge our audience base. *The Nutcracker* was one way to do that. For many people I hoped it would be their introduction to the world of ballet. I hoped too it would tempt them to try other productions. While over the past 25 years *The Nutcracker* has succeeded in attracting capacity audiences, playing to nearly 800,000 people at 500 performances, it has not had the same success in pulling newcomers to try other ballets. *Nutcracker* audiences are still distinct from those that attend the rest of the company's shows, but all of that was still in the future. While the production was taking shape I was in quite a state, a good state, which reflected the company's mood at the time. All of that was apparent too in the rehearsals. If a company is bored, then productions become boring. I set about not really to create a production that was fresh and new, but one that was full of life. All ballets, including *The Nutcracker*, have to live. I spent a lot of time getting the best out of the original story by Hoffmann and will never turn down any existing original choreography, but 90 percent of the Birmingham *Nutcracker* is actually mine as there is so little of the original left. Of all the productions I have staged of the classics, this is the only one I would describe as my own.

Although I was trying to be different, particularly with the story, compared to my production at Covent Garden, the storytelling is more fluent and has more impetus in Birmingham. Its accent there has always been on Clara's awakening to love. I have never had any deep psychological intent but wanted to depict a young girl who is affected by what happens at the Christmas party. Clara, for example, becomes a ballet student, while her mother is a former ballerina, and the fantasy sequences are all Clara's dream, not Drosselmeyer's fantastic tale as it is in London. The ballet is also about the power of magic, most definitely. In Birmingham, although Drosselmeyer becomes a magician instead of a councillor as in London, and despite all the showmanship of Drosselmeyer's party entertainments, they are magical happenings, not tricks. I was conscious, however, that *The Nutcracker* is seen by a non-regular audience probably more than by aficionados and I wanted to ensure that it is easy to understand. It has to work for everybody. And of course it is the magic of the music which is so inspiring. Everything is touched by this glorious, wonderful score. Some of Tchaikovsky's music in *The Nutcracker* is simply the best there is. It is in such moments as when the nutcracker doll is transformed into a handsome young man that you can really believe there is such a wondrous creative force as God. What else could inspire somebody to write such glorious music?

All the big Tchaikovsky ballets have a pivot around which the ballet turns. In *The Nutcracker* it is the transformation when the Christmas tree grows to giant proportions and the family sitting-room is skewed into a nightmare world as the orchestra plays full tilt and rats emerge from the fireplace. Done correctly, it shows the magic of theatre, particularly for first-time audiences. For the first act, John Macfarlane really was not keen on a Christmas tree that only got wider and taller as it grew, as at Covent Garden. We managed to find a way of suggesting that as the tree's branches got bigger and bigger they were pushing through the windows and walls of the house, which is what Hoffmann describes in his story. John was also very articulate about the sense of disorientation that Clara experiences in that scene. As the tree grows, everything else in the room is turning or moving. The audience should sense how frightening it is for Clara. All of this is extremely demanding not only for the designer but for the stage manager too, Diana Childs in Birmingham. The cueing, both lighting and scenic, is fiendishly complicated. I have to say it is the stage manager who sets up and co-ordinates all the cues at the rehearsals. Diana was amazing. She made a huge contribution to this production and joins my list of unsung heroes. In rehearsals we kept tripping over things that would not work. To make the transformation work involved a lot of people. Some manipulate the fireplace so it revolves and you have others invisibly pushing other pieces of scenery. Yet more are flying in and out different scenery and lighting equipment. We only saw whether it was possible technically at the final dress rehearsal onstage. To make it work very nearly killed us. I am not sure that John or any of the technical crew really knew whether it would be feasible. I remember John prowling about the back of the stalls and hiding from view when the scene began. If there were any mistakes in how the first pieces of scenery are moved or if the big elements like the fireplace are revolved wrongly, then literally they could be smashed. However, my favourite moment in the production is this transformation scene – especially when it nearly goes wrong. It is best when the timing is really on a knife-edge.

In Birmingham, in October 1992, we acquired Ashton's *Symphonic Variations*. Until then it had been the preserve of the Royal Ballet at Covent Garden. Michael Somes staged the ballet for us and proceeded to ruin it by making the dancers attack everything too hard, an approach that Wendy Ellis-Somes also took when she inherited the custodianship of the ballet. Somes would build people up only to knock them down. I asked him to soften it all a bit and let them express the music, by César Franck, and have lighter faces. All he did was to insist that the cast should smile all the time. As by then he had caused quite a few tears with his harsh criticisms, all they could do was grin in a very set way. It was a terrible shame. In such situations the role of the ballet master is crucial and there have been occasions when Desmond Kelly felt obliged to remove Jean-Pierre Gasquet, who now owns the performance rights for another Ashton ballet, *La Fille mal gardée*, from rehearsals because of his unhelpful approach. All credit to Desmond in that situation. Later on, after the first run of *Symphonic Variations*, Birmingham Royal Ballet went on to give some really beautiful performances of this great masterpiece.

Two years later, when Michael staged Ashton's *Enigma Variations*, he was a changed man, no doubt affected by the knowledge that he had a brain tumour which usually means having to face death – which in Michael's case occurred not long after this revival. Michael worked incredibly hard, made the company really characterise their roles and boosted their egos – so very different from when he had worked with us before. I think *Enigma Variations* is one of Ashton's greatest works – a loving depiction of Elgar's friends and intimates around the time he composed his great score. Although I was not present at rehearsals when Fred created this ballet in the autumn of 1968 it is evident that the strong sense of friendship and family that the ballet portrays were important to Ashton at the time. He had just been told that his contract as director of the Royal Ballet was not to be renewed and he was facing the prospect of retirement. Ashton was the company's founder choreographer, and now it seemed it no longer had need of him.

Enigma Variations can often appear to be a gallery of eccentrics. Indeed, it gives demi-caractère dancers plenty of scope for characterisation. More than that, the heart of *Enigma Variations* conveys deep and significant emotions which call for great maturity, artistry and interpretative abilities from the dancers, as well as technique. That to me is the essence of what a classical ballet is, and I think *Enigma Variations* demonstrates that wonderfully in how it gives opportunities to a company. Michael helped them achieve that wonderfully, even if there were some tussles along the way. Initially the sense of restraint and suggestion inherent in the piece was difficult for the company to understand and to perform naturally. At one rehearsal Michael made Kevin O'Hare, who was cast as Arthur Troyte Griffith, perform his incredibly fast and demanding solo three times in quick succession. Michael had never performed the role himself so he had no sympathies for Kevin about how physically challenging the solo is.

We had, too, the inevitable confusions that arise when dancers who have performed certain roles come in to help the new casts when they draw on what they did in performance, which is not necessarily what the choreographer intended. One scene, near the end of the ballet when Lady Elgar sees – or appears to see – the mysterious figure of Lady Mary Lygon arrive through the garden amid billowing clouds, caused particular debate. We decided ultimately that this was a scene that could not be taken too literally. Lady Mary is, after all, the enigma of the title – is she real or something from Elgar's imagination? There are many enigmas in the ballet in fact, which makes repeated viewings so interesting. Dorabella performs a flirtatiously innocent solo for Elgar, which perfectly suited the personality of Antoinette Sibley who created the role. The degree of flirtatiousness is ambiguous and requires to be carefully judged in performance. I had wanted to add *Enigma Variations* to our repertoire as I believed we had dancers within the company of the calibre to perform the ballet properly. Desmond Kelly was not so sure. The original cast, with Derek Rencher as Elgar, had left such an indelible shadow. However, my hunch about casting dancers who exhibited the characteristics of the real-life characters portrayed in the ballet, rather than the dancers who first portrayed them, proved to be the right one. Desmond, to his surprise, found his own way to portray Elgar convincingly, but the whole revival was a wonderful company achievement.

The Green Table was another ballet I wanted to add to the repertoire in Birmingham. It marked the start of my career in dance when I joined the Kurt Jooss company in Wolverhampton in 1943. It was a closing ballet in those days, and even when houses were only about a quarter full, a not unusual occurrence, audiences were always thunderous in their applause. It was still as powerful when Birmingham Royal Ballet revived it in 1992, and it stayed in the repertoire during my time as director. It has not been seen since. David Bintley much prefers another piece expressive of war, Frederick Ashton's *Dante Sonata*, which I also love but do not find so deep as Jooss' ballet which is much closer to its subject matter than other war-related ballets. *The Green Table* is not conventionally balletic. It is a dance drama where some characters do not dance. The opening scene depicts a group of masked diplomats engaged in a very polite and stylised display of disagreement around the green table of the title. As their disputes grow, they line up in two menacing rows brandishing pistols. They fire, and in the blackout that follows the menacing figure of death appears in place of the table. A standard bearer with a huge flag rounds up young men to become soldiers. What follows are images common to any war. A young girl says goodbye to her boyfriend. We see him killed in a battle and a profiteer steals a ring from his finger. The soldier's girlfriend is forced to work in a brothel by the profiteer. We see groups of women refugees, lost in fear and abandonment. Throughout the ballet, the figure of death insinuates itself into the action. There is a beautiful moment when death takes an old woman in his arms in a very gentle and loving manner. At the end an old soldier appears with a tattered flag which death takes from him and waves across the cast as they fall to the ground one by one. Death forces the profiteer to dance in agony before being cast into hell. Another shot is fired. Death disappears and the green table reappears. The diplomats are seen repeating their arguments, not making a sound, as the audience realises wars will go on – and on. The ballet uses lighting to dramatic effect to punctuate key moments and *The Green Table* is incredibly moving.

At Birmingham the ballet was staged by Anna Markard, Jooss' daughter, who had inherited the performing rights of his ballets. She had never trained properly as a dancer but had dabbled and now took responsibility for staging her father's ballets, often getting things wrong. She insisted on new masks for the diplomats, less grotesque and menacing than the originals, designed by her husband Hermann. The company had real difficulties with her. It is very hard for somebody who is not trained to teach and demonstrate to professional dancers. They do not like it. Marion Tait was cast as the old woman and I remembered I had a film of Pina Bausch in the role which I thought would be useful. Anna insisted, 'No way can you show that film of how things were done. This is my production!' When it went on finally, the company performed the ballet well but it did not have the weight and dynamism of the original, particularly in terms of how Jooss dancers used their body weight. Joseph Cipolla played the role of death. He was a very good performer, a good addition to the company, but he did not have the same heavy, lumpen weight as Kurt Jooss had in the role.

The Green Table was seen during Towards the Millennium, a programming initiative that took place during the 1990s. The CBSO showcased the music of the 20th century in its concerts, decade by decade. Of course there were complaints by the music critics that the CBSO's choice of repertory was not properly representative of the century, but associating ourselves with such a retrospective was a useful way of reviving some ballet masterpieces not normally seen.

Besides *The Green Table* we introduced to Birmingham audiences *Fall River Legend* by Agnes de Mille and *Pillar of Fire* by Antony Tudor, both from the 1940s. Rediscovering 20th-century masterpieces was a way of defining our repertoire and acquiring strong, narrative works. I wanted to get as much variation of ballets as possible without falling back on works from Covent Garden. Both the de Mille and the Tudor ballets had very good, dramatic roles for Marion Tait, and the company performed *Fall River Legend*, about Lizzie Borden the axe murderer, as strongly as my memories of seeing the original cast with Nora Kaye in America. Nora attended *Pillar of Fire* when we danced it in London and was very complimentary. I liked the ballet, it had a certain style, and again Marion excelled herself as the emotionally repressed Hagar. Like Carabosse in *The Sleeping Beauty*, it is a role that almost needs to be overacted, and Marion knew exactly how to pitch it.

Other important revivals during that time were Léonide Massine's *Choreartium* and *Le Tricorne*. By the 1990s Massine had become something of a rarity to British audiences. His toyshop ballet *La Boutique fantasque* had been a regular fixture in the repertoire of the former touring company and the Royal Ballet had restaged *Mam'zelle Angot* in 1980 without much success. Massine's gallery of humorously eccentric characters seemed out of fashion with audiences. In the 1930s, however, Massine had been a noted maker of symphonic ballets, like vast murals set in motion. The word *Choreartium* is apparently Massine's own invention, a combination of 'chorea', an ancient Greek ceremonial dance, and 'artium', a Latin word for art. The resulting ballet, a magnificent example of ensemble choreography for a cast of 34 dancers, is a visual depiction of the shifting moods of Johannes Brahms' fourth symphony. It was made for Colonel de Basil's company where Massine also created *Les Presages*, set to Tchaikovsky's fifth symphony. Tatiana Leskova, the fabulous prima ballerina and a former member of the de Basil company, staged *Choreartium* for us. I knew her through many visits to Brazil to stage *Giselle* for the company in Rio where she was director. We have remained goods friends ever since. She was very inspiring and a great personality who I loved working with. In Birmingham the company was crazy about her which helped ensure a big success with *Choreartium*. Tatiana was assisted by Nelly Laport, another de Basil dancer, who would whisper corrections whenever Tatiana could not remember something, 'I think it was the other leg, dear.' The company, once they had got into the style of the choreography, gave it their all, with Samira Saidi in particular dancing beautifully in the slow movement.

The ballet came up wonderfully well in its excellent new designs by Nadine Baylis, but it is another that has dropped out of the repertoire since my time as director. Despite the experience of working with Massine, I thought *Le Tricorne* would be another of his ballets that the company could bring something to. Unfortunately that turned out not to be the case. Lorca, Massine's son was now responsible for his ballets, but could not be with the company until the last three days of rehearsals. They did not progress smoothly. We had spent a long time unravelling the different versions of the ballet, but when Lorca finally arrived he had his own particular ideas. There was great confusion and we ended up not having nearly enough time to bring the ballet to life. Lorca was distinctly unhelpful. At that late stage, all somebody can do is help build the dancers' performances and confidence. Lorca was destructive. Everything was wrong for him. He did not approve of the characterisations. Actually he really did not know what was right. It was all very unfortunate. Balletomanes, who knew the ballet of old when the Royal Ballet performed it in the 1940s when it had been staged by Léonide Massine, himself complained about the style of this revival. Actually their criticisms were justified. A proper sense of style was something that we thought Lorca would be helping us with. As a ballet, I think *Le Tricorne* is not that well constructed, but the designs by Pablo Picasso are interesting, and when I had seen Massine himself dance the ballet he had really made it work. He was a wonderful character dancer. We really would have benefited from his input, had he still been alive – or somebody like Harold Turner who had danced the ballet in those days. Massine had encouraged Harold's early career when he appeared in his ballets *La Boutique fantasque* and *Clock Symphony* at Covent Garden as well as in *Tricorne*. Harold died backstage at Covent Garden in 1962 on his way to a rehearsal of *Les Femmes de bonne humeur*, another of Massine's which he was reviving. The key to Harold's performances – indeed the key to performing Massine's choreography well – is that he really threw himself into that sort of character role. The same too when Margot Fonteyn danced the miller's wife in *Tricorne*, which in her case was an example of casting against type. She always gave it more, and that made her performance register. For our Birmingham revival, Joseph Cipolla ought to have been natural casting as the miller but he did not feel comfortable at all in the role and ended up being rather dull. Vera Volkova once said to me that a man must always dance as if he is a caged tiger so that it always looks as if there is more strength within him behind the bars. Sadly that was unusually lacking in Joe's dancing on this occasion, but it was unfair to expect him to build up the role with nobody as an example. The same too with Monica Zamora who was normally very dramatic. The Spanish flavour of the wife's choreography does require a certain exuberance and exaggeration, but somehow Monica, being Spanish, was trying to make it too authentic. Interpretations got better during the run of performances but the revival seemed too clean and rather lacking in passion overall.

In 1993 I decided to revive Ninette de Valois' ballet *Job* which, other than for occasional performances of Satan's solo, had not been performed complete for over 20 years. I introduced the solo when it was danced by Irek Mukhamedov at the Barbican theatre in June 1998 as part of the celebration of Madam's 100th birthday. Julia Farron, who danced in the ballet many times, was vocal. 'That's not Madam. What's he doing that for?' De Valois created *Job* in 1931 for the Camargo Society, the forerunner of her Vic-Wells Ballet, She did not participate in the revival in Birmingham, which was supervised by Joy Newton and Jean Bedells, and she was in fact rather dubious about me wanting to revive *Job* at all. When I broached the subject with Madam she said, 'Oh not that old thing! Are you sure?', then before I could respond she announced, 'Now, about the casting. I want those O'Hare boys as Elihu and Satan. And I don't want . . .' She had it all worked out. Mary Clarke, editor of *Dancing Times* and the oldest of her generation of critics, was one of the few people who were pleased to see *Job* again. I had the sense that she liked how the company was developing under my directorship, and it was good to have her support.

The score for *Job* is by Ralph Vaughan Williams and was first designed by Gwen Raverat but is more familiar in the redesign by John Piper whose backdrops glow with dark intensity. I had seen it in the old, old days when I had just joined Sadler's Wells Theatre Ballet and did not like it as there was no real dancing. At the time of its creation de Valois' choreography looked unconventional, with most characters being barefoot and others in sandals. Nobody wears pointe shoes. *Job* is not a classical ballet at all. It was inspired by the biblical story of Job as well as William Blake's illustrations for it. The choreography is expressive but restrained. The ballet begins by showing Job's family living quietly and happily, depicted in deliberately simple steps. The scene shifts to reveal God sitting on a throne at the top of a flight of steps upstage centre. This was the scene that caused a young Kenneth MacMillan great embarrassment many years earlier. While still a student he had already been cast in some performances at Covent Garden. Madam chose him to play God because of his height. In rehearsal, when the moment came, there was a throne but no God. The rehearsal had to be stopped while God was found. Imagine the whole company having to stop a stage rehearsal for a missing student. When Kenneth finally appeared, he was sobbing in embarrassment. 'Who does she think she is, crying up there!' demanded Robert Helpmann who was playing Satan. The role suited his dramatic style, and his all-over body make-up was always terribly well done, but Helpmann was never a terrifying Satan.

The ballet continues when, challenged by Satan, God agrees to test Job's faith. Grotesque dancers portraying pestilences, messengers full of bad news and hypocritical comforters, all taunt Job in his misfortunes. Madam's treatment of the story, which resembles a Greek tragedy where disasters are reported rather than depicted, is similarly restrained. There are two violent moments. Job's household suddenly falls to the ground after Satan curses them, and later, as Satan tries to climb the flight of steps to reach heaven, a gesture by God causes him to tumble and fall down the steps back to hell. The company took to *Job* quite well, but really in those days Birmingham Royal Ballet were awful rehearsers. They only come to life onstage. So it proved with *Job* in performance. When we danced the ballet at the Royal Opera House that July in honour of Madam's 95th birthday, she hardly saw any of it. She was propped up on pillows in her box – really she was propped up on me – and fell asleep as soon as it started. At the end there was resounding applause and a spotlight singled out Madam in the box. Suddenly wide awake, she got to her feet to acknowledge the reception. With the spotlight turned off she sat back down again and promptly fell asleep again.

We performed *Job* too in Coventry cathedral that November to celebrate the 950th anniversary of the first church to be built on the site. Transferring a work designed for the stage into such venues is never ideal, but performed in front of the vast glass screen designed by John Hutton depicting angels and saints which is the transition point between the old and reconstructed parts of the cathedral proved an apt and atmospheric setting. The performance was given in the presence of Sarah, Duchess of York, whom I thought might be something of a trial. A gala performance at the London Coliseum a few years before had started without the duchess when she was late arriving. In the event at Coventry she could not have been more charming and thoughtful, presenting her flowers to Madam in whose honour the performance was given. The company generated a great feeling of intensity that evening. The fact that we had performed in the cathedral spread much goodwill for the company locally too.

In terms of the balance of the repertoire over the first five years in Birmingham, productions of established ballets but new to the company and audiences in the city amounted to nearly 30 percent of the repertoire. Of these, 17 percent were titles that had been previously in the Royal Ballet's repertoire at Covent Garden, but I also wanted to include works from other choreographic traditions – such works as Paul Taylor's *Airs*. Revivals of existing productions – including *Hobson's Choice, Paquita, Elite Syncopations, Les Rendezvous, Flowers of the Forest, Card Game, Five Tangos* and *Petrushka*, as well as the full-length classics – amounted to 45 percent of productions, so I was more than pleased to stage new productions of the established repertoire. These made up nearly 10 percent of the repertoire. The company did not have a resident choreographer in those years. That was David Bintley's position at Covent Garden until 1993 when he went off on a two-year sabbatical to gain international exposure and experience. Nevertheless David's ballets, including a revival of *The Snow Queen*, one of his early full-length works, and his first attempt at *Sylvia*, made up over 10 percent of those we performed. Madam was very interested when David did *Sylvia* in the autumn of 1993. At the time Frederick Ashton's much altered and adapted production had not been reconstructed at Covent Garden and there was little prospect of it being revived at the time, so Léo Delibes' great score was on the missing list. Madam applauded David for his musicality but she hoped that with *Sylvia* he would not have an attack of eccentricity or try to be funny. In that I think she was rather disappointed. Premieres of new ballets by a range of aspiring choreographers – Vincent Redmon, Matthew Hart, Oliver Hindle, Graham Lustig and Will Tuckett – represented another 15 percent of the overall repertoire, over 50 works by 20 choreographers.

On 4 May 1994 I was diagnosed with myasthenia gravis, a debilitating neuromuscular illness that attacks the body's auto-immune system so that antibodies that normally fight infections go wrong and start to attack the communication system between the brain and the muscles that control your movements. I was in hospital for four months but the effects of the condition persisted for five years and forced me to step down as director of Birmingham Royal Ballet in 1995. It felt as if I had to give up before I had really got going. I could understand the Royal

Opera House's board members' reluctance to keep me on. I was very seriously ill and seen to be past my sell-by date. But I was most certainly not ready to give up.

Before I understood there was a problem I had been with the company in Southampton, taking a rehearsal and coaching *Swan Lake* as well as catching up with Peter Farmer in Littlehampton. I became aware of a whistling noise in my teeth. I did not think much about it but it got worse and I found I could not speak properly. No matter, I carried on. On my way back to London, from where I was scheduled to fly to Brazil to revive *Giselle*, Sonya and I called on John and Anya Sainsbury in Hampshire for lunch. Anya had joined Sadler's Wells Theatre Ballet at the same time as me. She was very beautiful onstage and became a good coach and was always a good friend, very kind. She could see I was evidently not well when I could not swallow anything. They thought I should see a doctor. It was a Sunday but in any case I demurred. Anya insisted, and a doctor arrived but was unable to diagnose what was wrong but thought I might have experienced a mild stroke. Undeterred, we carried on to Heathrow and took off to Rio de Janeiro. During the flight I found I could not speak. I had double vision. Anything I tried to drink I vomited back. I have never kept a diary other than in a most rudimentary form, recording appointments and performances to be aware of. There are no entries for that week in Rio. Our schedule meant that as soon as we arrived there I had to go straight to rehearsals at the theatre. I survived somehow but went to our hotel as soon as I could, feeling dreadful. A doctor was found. He too was not able to diagnose what was wrong but recommended that we return home as quickly as we could. The following Saturday I was admitted to hospital in London. Four days of tests followed – including blood tests, an electromyography to assess my muscle activity and a chest CT scan to assess my thymus gland, and a brain scan. The diagnosis was myasthenia gravis. It was horrible. A tube was put into my nose to feed me. Medication started, every three hours, seven times throughout the day and night. I still had double vision but I could swallow better and my speech was slightly improved. Looking back at my diary now, I see I noted such entries as, 'Not such a good day. Eyes bad.' Frequently I only noted that I had experienced a good night followed by a bad morning. On another occasion when a new feeding pipe was fitted I just wrote, 'Ugh!'

I was on steroids and a drug that boosts the messages from the brain to the muscles. As in all medical situations, it was a case of trying different approaches to see what had the best effect. The medical staff were excellent, really looking after me despite being so busy. Sonya was absolutely fantastic. The phone at home never stopped ringing with people wanting to know the latest, which is very tiring in itself. Sonya dreaded the phone going. Fifteen years before, most people with the disorder died from it. The doctors discovered too much pressure behind my eyes and I had laser surgery. My diet was changed as there was concern about my potassium levels, but then I had to endure the feeding tube again. Eventually I was allowed out of hospital feeling pretty miserable and weak, but the effect of being at home made me feel nice and relaxed for the first time in a long while. We went to a service of healing in Coventry cathedral which was a very good day, a great experience and very moving. The following day I went to the Hippodrome to watch a rehearsal of *Paquita*. It was so good to see everyone again. But the next day was not so good. I was back in hospital, really demoralised. The nurses gave me a lot of comfort but I really felt I would never get better. A plasmic exchange was considered.

And so it went on: some good days, some decidedly not. Thank heaven for friends. Madam visited. I was so touched as she travelled from Barnes to the hospital in Holborn while confined to her wheelchair. Her visit meant so much to me and made me determined to get over the ghastly disease. There were flowers from Princess Margaret. Flowers from everybody, I could not believe it. Desmond kept me updated on progress with rehearsals for *Giselle* in Rio. Pamela May and her daughter Caroline helped me so much when I was unable to swallow. Just when I was giving up hope of ever eating properly again, she encouraged me to try some half-melted mango sorbet. Amazingly this worked. It slithered down. From then on my ability to swallow improved considerably. I told the National Hospital for Nervous Diseases about this success and the physiotherapy department there has since adopted this with patients recovering from these dreaded diseases. By the autumn I was back at work, but judging from my diary entries during *The Nutcracker* season I was far from well. The last entry for 1994 reads, 'Shaky and nauseous.' The end pages in my diary for that year list many unanswered questions I still had about the condition. Now I feel incredibly fortunate to be able to say that it took seven years for me to be completely clear of myasthenia gravis. The condition causes fatigue and the root cause has not yet been identified. Medication does help and I have a special lens in my glasses to correct the double vision. Without the onset of myasthenia gravis I would have stayed as director of Birmingham Royal Ballet longer. I had so many plans for the company.

I do regret having to leave. My last production for the company was a new *Coppélia*, unveiled at the Hippodrome in March 1995 and still in the repertoire today. I managed to start working on the production early in the new year but somehow Peter Farmer had by then managed to get the decisions he needed about the sets and costumes out of me while I was still in hospital. *Coppélia* is not a ballet that offers huge scope for reinvention but I did think there was scope to try a new ending. Over the years the one big change I made was to the conclusion, which was not in Hoffman's story. It always seemed a shame that the traditional finale almost forgets Dr Coppélius whose dream had always been to bring his favourite doll to life. At the end of the big celebration, when everybody happily returns home, Dr Coppélius is discovered seemingly fast asleep with the broken doll by his side. He awakens and to his utter amazement sees that the doll, his life's work, is coming to life. Happily they danced off together. Has *Coppélia* really come to life? Or has Coppélius fallen into an eternal sleep and is on his way to heaven? I left the audience to decide, but I knew it was the latter. To accommodate this ending I had to have Delibes' score rearranged by the company's rehearsal pianist and theatrically it all seemed to work rather well, but I am afraid this was another of my wrongs. It was just not right with Delibes' brilliant score. David Bintley was delighted how I had changed the ending and was really upset when at the next revival I reluctantly changed it back. But I did manage to incorporate Coppélius accompanying Swanilda and Franz as they left in the carriage with the new bell to celebrate. I do think Delibes' score is a great master work, one of the greatest ballet scores. I am glad I set it right.

During my last season as director in Birmingham I organised an exchange visit with the Stuttgart Ballet, the company where I had been ballet master for five years and with whom I had a very good relationship. They brought a double bill of Kenneth MacMillan's *Requiem* and *Song of the Earth* to Birmingham. I made a curtain speech before the first-night performance outlining John Cranko's importance to Stuttgart and to me. The Birmingham dancers were very much aware that the performance they were about to see would be special, but for some unfortunate reason the second cast performed that night and they did not look at all well rehearsed. The second performance went better when Marcia Haydée appeared in the Pie Jesu from *Requiem*, a section that was inspired by Charlotte, Kenneth's young daughter playing with Marcia in the rehearsal room when he created the ballet in Stuttgart in 1976. Overall it was not the most successful of visits. Nor can I say that our return visit to Stuttgart in May was a wild success either. We performed *Choreartium*, Ashton's *Enigma Variations* and *Pillar of Fire*. The dancers were well received but *Enigma* was a bit too English, too reserved, for German audiences. It was Tudor's more obviously dramatic study of repressed emotions in *Pillar of Fire* that was liked best. But still I have always been welcomed warmly when I go back to Stuttgart, but these days there is only Reid Anderson, the director, and notator Georgette Tsingurides who knows who I am.

International touring was something that the company did less of once it was installed in Birmingham. Although we worked proactively with the economic development office of the city council to co-ordinate the commercial benefit of overseas visits, we simply had fewer weeks available to tour overseas because of our now longer seasons at the Hippodrome. Such few international visits that we did make – to Hong Kong and Bangkok in the spring of 1993 when we performed *Romeo and Juliet* and *The Sleeping Beauty* and a short week in Turin in January 1994 when Irek Mukhamedov joined us for *La Fille mal gardée* – were recognised as occasions of mutual pride for ourselves and Birmingham itself, rather than the company being sent by the city council to fly the flag in commercially important countries.

It was enormously beneficial for the company to have Irek with us, they loved him – as did Kenneth MacMillan who really was instrumental in Irek joining the Royal Ballet. Besides Colas in *Fille* he also partnered Miyako Yoshida in *The Nutcracker* which was another good example for younger dancers. Although Russians tend to do things their own way and Irek got the backs up of rehearsal staff at Covent Garden, I think that the Royal Ballet has missed an opportunity in allowing Irek to go to English National Ballet as a rehearsal coach.

Outside Birmingham the majority of our touring pattern across Britain remained unchanged in the early 1990s. Some venues close to

Birmingham were discontinued, logically so. In London we performed at both Sadler's Wells and the Royal Opera House. We had a regular presence in Manchester, Glasgow, Edinburgh, Plymouth, Sunderland, Southampton and Cardiff. That regularity is so important for building healthy audiences who look forward to your next visit. That helps box office too. We were still touring to venues such as Bradford, Leeds, Liverpool, Eastbourne, Oxford and Norwich, traditional ports of call on the old touring company's circuits. The majority of these venues have dropped from the schedules through a combination of reductions in Arts Council funding and the way it manages which companies serve which venues, choices that were often seen to be driven by politics rather than what is best for generating strong audiences for ballet. Thanks to a reallocation of funding, Southampton and Bristol are now back on the company's itinerary, which is positive.

My last season in Birmingham in June 1995 included some of my most enduring productions for the company – the new *Coppélia* as well as *The Sleeping Beauty* and *Swan Lake*, which continue still – as well as some important additions including *Choreartium*, *Enigma Variations* and *Las Hermanas*. My last night was celebrated in a gala, an amazing night even if it did go on rather a lot – but then again I suppose my career had done the same. Princess Margaret, the company's patron, phoned from San Francisco to say she was changing her plans and would attend, which added some sense of occasion to proceedings. I had asked for one of my favourite ballets, Balanchine's *Serenade*, to be performed, and my wish was granted. On the night I thought it was wonderful, but in the cold light of day I suspect it was not that well danced – but the feeling and energy the company displayed were wonderful. The rest of the programme was meant to be a surprise, but actually I guessed what was going on during the week before when I heard so much familiar music emerging from the rehearsal studios. The whole evening was a mix of familiar faces and bits and pieces from some of the ballets that had been part of my career.

Students from the Royal Ballet School appeared, including Nao Sakuma and Chi Cao, who went on to become much admired principals with the company, and who that evening danced Balanchine's *Valse fantaisie*. There was a scene from Madam's *Job*, Miyako Yoshida returned to the company to be partnered by Sergiu Pobereznic in my *Mirror Walkers* pas de deux, while Marion Tait and Joseph Cipolla performed the balcony scene from Kenneth's *Romeo and Juliet*. Karen Donovan, Michael O'Hare and Stephen Wicks performed the Lily of Laguna scene from *Hobson's Choice* and Sherilyn Kennedy and Kevin O'Hare were the leading couple in *Theme and Variations*, performed complete.

After the second interval came *Façade*. Among the large cast, Miyako Yoshida shed her skirt and performed in her bloomers to the manner born in the polka, Galina Samsova was the milkmaid, with David Bintley, Alain Dubreuil and Desmond Kelly her mountaineering milkmen who morph into a human cow, their fingers forming the udder. The foxtrot was a walk down memory lane of names from the days of the old Royal Ballet touring company with Margaret Barbieri and Merle Park partnered by Stephen Jefferies and David Wall. Derek Deane and Wayne Eagling, always competitive rivals, were a perfectly deadpan duo in their boaters and blazers in the popular song. To the great delight of the audience, in the tango, Anthony Dowell oiled his way around the floor before upending Antoinette Sibley as the debutante. All in all it was a most wonderful tribute and I am thankful to John Auld, Desmond Kelly, Christopher Nourse and the whole company for organising it. I was determined to say the things I wanted in my farewell speech, something that Jeremy Isaacs was worried about as the evening was already quite long. He was a good friend but he was always quick to interrupt me when he thought I was talking too much at meetings. Talk about pot and kettle. Jeremy had warned me that Princess Margaret needed to leave promptly after the performance. This I knew was not true. Mid-speech I felt Jeremy tap me on the shoulder. 'Remember what I said,' he told me. I ignored him. I think after all those years I knew how to leave the stage. I was happy too to make the evening a charity gala to support the Myasthenia Gravis Association which had done so much to support me during my struggles with that wretched disease.

I was determined that, despite my illness, my retirement would not be the end of everything. After the farewell in Birmingham and the summer holidays I was soon back in Munich, reviving *The Sleeping Beauty* there that September. And so it continued over the next 20 years, reviving my productions in Japan, Europe, South America and Canada. When I was 70 I decided to learn the violin, which I had always wanted to study at Bedales but which my parents had refused in favour of the piano. A near neighbour of ours in Chiswick at the time, Patricia Lousada, a former dancer during the formative days of New York City Ballet and whose wide experience of the dance world had made her exactly the right sort of person to have served on the board of the Royal Ballet companies, warned me against starting to learn the violin at so advanced an age as mine. 'But you could learn the cello,' she suggested. I knew that her partner John was an American lawyer professionally but also a brilliant amateur cellist. He very kindly gave me lessons and invited me to use his second-best cello. I loved learning the instrument. It gave me another dimension to my life which I needed. I took the cello with me wherever I was working, at home or abroad. I only had an adequate ear but I felt I was getting on really well. However, it got harder to make progress. Sonya was less than impressed with the results. She really much preferred wind instruments and jazz music in any case. When Sonya became ill with Alzheimer's I stopped, but really I had lost interest in everything then, with the exception of Sonya herself.

In my retirement I have found it hard, being based in London again, to be as involved as I would like with the company in Birmingham. I say that not out of a sense of interference but I want the company to be the best it can possibly be. Birmingham has been an important part of my career. After all, I had laid the foundations and will always be interested in how it continues to grow. Practically I became director of the company that was to become Birmingham Royal Ballet some 20 years before we actually moved there, when in 1970 I was made responsible for the New Group, that small, experimental ensemble that dared to venture into the world of modern dance with Glen Tetley and Hans van Manen. When I handed on the baton to David Bintley in 1995 the company was in essence already 25 years old. I cannot tell you what a relief it was to discover that this extraordinarily creative dancer and choreographer wanted to take over the company.

As the company celebrated its 25th anniversary in Birmingham in June 2015 I was able to congratulate David on his directorship. He inherited a company with a balanced repertoire of old and new works, including many of his own ballets as well as those from international choreographers. I have to say that although the company was in good shape then, there was still plenty of scope for improvement, especially with the men, which is something that has been achieved under David's leadership. The company has lacked a true ballerina after Miyako Yoshida moved on to Covent Garden. She is much missed. There are several contenders, however. Since 1995, importantly too, David has created over 20 works for Birmingham Royal Ballet and introduced ten original full-length ballets choreographed by him to the repertoire. But there have been times when the company has been regarded as second best. Indeed there were times when the company felt second best when David was absent in Tokyo where concurrently he was director of National Ballet of Japan. I know this was a matter that prompted serious concern at senior levels within both companies, but at the same time I am delighted that, under David, both companies are ready for anything. Birmingham Royal Ballet has become recognised in its own right. It is particularly popular in America now. That is a fantastic achievement.

I go back to Birmingham fairly often these days, both to oversee my productions and because I am invited by good friends in the company. Paul Grist, the company manager, is brilliant. He anticipates what I need and nothing is too much trouble for him. He is very good at his job but kind with it. I always find it a joy to work with the dancers. While I still feel able to make a contribution, I realise more and more how important it is not to let a familiar staging become dreary. I still go to all the premieres, important revivals and choreographic evenings when I can. To mark how far the company had progressed under David's leadership, the 20th anniversary in 2010 was an occasion attended by Prince Charles, the company's president, and the Duchess of Cornwall. Charles, who had formally knighted me, the queen being overseas, was very interested when he talked to me very knowledgeably. I was quite relieved to be included and the performance contained my filmed memories about various aspects of the company's history projected onstage.

The repertoire danced that evening acknowledged the past too, with extracts from MacMillan's *Concerto* and *Romeo and Juliet*, Ashton's *The Two Pigeons*, Balanchine's *Theme and Variations* and *Slaughter on Tenth Avenue* as well as the grand pas de deux from *The Nutcracker*. Numbers from David's full-length ballets, *Sylvia*, *Hobson's Choice*, *Beauty and the Beast* and *Aladdin*, celebrated the present and David's interest in producing original works. Scenes from his *Carmina burana* and *Orpheus Suite* represented the sort of theatrical, one-act work with which David has sought to popularise ballet and give a distinctive identity to the company. The rest of the programme heralded the future with *Printer Jam* by Kit

Holder, one of the company's dancers given opportunities to choreo-graph by David, and a beautiful waltz choreographed by Samira Saidi and performed by the Elmhurst School for Dance. It all slotted together rather well, which is not always the case with galas.

Five years later, the 25th anniversary in June 2015, was a Bintley dou-ble-bill. I did not mind that at all. The company put over *Carmina burana* very well alongside David's new ballet, *The King Dances*. It displayed David's fascination with the world of Louis XIV and the court ballets of Versailles. The new score by Stephen Montague sounded modern but used 17th-century dance measures. David too used a period vocabulary of movements, petit batterie, small jumps, formal patterns, but in a modern way. It was an interesting idea, well presented but overlong although danced well. At the end, the audience at the Birmingham Hippodrome roared its approval at having their own company. The applause was almost deafening as they saluted David. I think Birmingham was telling David that they knew how lucky they are to have him as director. To occupy such a role, with any company, for so long in today's environment is certainly an achievement. Michael Clarke, the company's chairman, and a former principal dancer, Robert Parker, now director of the Elmhurst School of Dance in Birmingham, both made moving speeches that also acknowledged how I had led the move to Birmingham.

It is good to be remembered. I felt really appreciated, and at a recep-tion after the performance David spoke well about how much I had helped him over many years and said it was thanks to me that he had the job. This was strictly not true. While I was in hospital with myasthenia gravis everybody in the company was in a panic that I would not be able to finish my last season. There was no succession plan in place. Jeremy Isaacs did not seek my opinion but that was not something I would have expected of him. A member of Covent Garden's ballet committee, Tessa Blackstone, at the time also head of Birkbeck college, did come to see me in hospital and talked to me about various names, but I was not in a state to have any influence. For me it is a source of pride that it is a company that audiences follow so loyally now. Yet at the Royal Opera House nowadays there are only a few dancers and staff there who under-stand the hard-earned history of the Royal Ballet's touring company and really know what Birmingham Royal Ballet represents. I can fully appre-ciate that Royal Ballet dancers do not have many opportunities to see performances by their counterparts. They work so hard and the last thing they want to see when they are not dancing is another company. Which said, very few Covent Garden dancers come to watch Birmingham Royal Ballet, although some, such as Natasha Oughtred, have made the switch to join the company to further their careers. You have got to see a company perform really to know it. I am pleased that there is a much greater awareness among students at the Royal Ballet School about Birmingham, both in terms of coming to see performances and as a positive career choice for them.

I feel – and this is believed by the city council too – that Birmingham Royal Ballet has brought a different cultural energy to the city. The company is a great contributor to the cultural education of people who might not normally attend arts events. Having a resident ballet company has added to the city's cultural credentials, making them, along with the Ikon gallery and the CBSO, really first class. I know that Anthony Sargent considers that ballet, and culture in general, became a powerful plank in the self-confidence of the city. Of course that does not mean that ballet touched everybody. On one occasion I got talking to a taxi driver as he ferried me across the city. He made some observation about ballet not being for him, although his wife went. 'Had he been to see it?' I asked him, continuing 'I could get you tickets.' As chance would have it, I had the same taxi driver some time later and our conversation followed similar lines. I repeated my offer to provide him with tickets, but to my knowledge he has still not been. I get the same reaction in London.

Still, for me personally, Birmingham earned me my knighthood – although I nearly did not get that. I was in the studio one day rehearsing the company when my secretary Jayne Leeke rushed in to tell me Downing Street was on the phone, insisting on speaking to me in person. It will be about funding again I thought as I went to take the call. It was always about the money. In fact, the voice from Downing Street wanted to know why I had not acknowledged the invitation to become a KBE. I assured them I had received no such invitation and quickly made it clear that I most certainly would like to become Sir Peter. As I was about to put the receiver down, it occurred to me to check what address Downing Street had written to. They mentioned an address in Finchley that I had not occupied for about 20 years – and provided to them by the Royal Opera House.

CHAPTER 9

Making a reputation – *Giselle*

I T IS ONLY THANKS to the fact of having done so many other things – modern dance, commercial theatre, choreography, performing, teaching – that I felt remotely qualified to stage new productions of full-length classical ballets. To be recognised as such was certainly not my life's ambition. I never thought my career would be defined by *Giselle* nor wanted to be known just for *The Nutcracker*. I came to the classics quite late as a producer, when I was nearly 40. Earlier on during my days at Sadler's Wells I was told one day that Sonia Arova, whom I had known while with Metropolitan Ballet, was rehearsing the pas de deux from *Caisse*. 'What's *Caisse?*' I asked. The nearest I had got to *The Nutcracker* was during wartime when Sadler's Wells Ballet brought the second act of *Caisse-Noisette* to Cambridge in February 1944 with Margot Fonteyn and Robert Helpmann. When I was first with Ballets Jooss, although I enjoyed the company of the other dancers, I socialised frequently with students of the university. I used to proclaim to them, 'You have to forget all that classical stuff. Put it out of your mind and come and see Ballets Jooss. Modern dance makes you suffer and feel.'

Over time in the late-1940s when I first saw *The Sleeping Beauty* and *Swan Lake* as well as the last act of *The Nutcracker*, they were all so artificial. The way mime was performed was so very exact with the emphasis on stance and the placement of the elbow, arm or fingers. The storyline did not seem to matter and audiences did not understand the mime at all. When I first saw *Giselle* I certainly did not bother to understand the mime. I saw a variety of casts perform it before I was so captivated by the Bolshoi with Galina Ulanova in 1956 at the Royal Opera House and I made a point of learning the mime so that later when I came to stage the ballet I could ensure that I was able to get the dancers to do it in a meaningful way, with expression and body language which made all the difference. Even on that occasion with the Bolshoi, although the corps de ballet danced beautifully, they appeared as lovely spirits rather than evil wilis determined to get their revenge by forcing any passing men to dance to their deaths. I was not moved except for Ulanova who really made me cry.

I have always thought the story of *La Bayadère* to be pretty silly. That is a ballet I would never attempt even if I was desperate for work. I have never understood how anybody can accept the plot. The characters are not credible although I do like the beautiful dancing in the shades' scene, particularly in Rudolf Nureyev's staging which uses a corps 32-strong. Rudi was always a big champion of the full-length *Raymonda*, an enthusiasm I never shared. The plot defies logic. But *Raymonda* is very exposing in terms of fundamental classical technique. Artistically, the classical divertissements in *Raymonda*, as in *Paquita*, demand a high level of style and finesse. I like the Bournonville style from Denmark in *La Sylphide*, but that is a ballet that has never appealed to me except for the leading sylph herself. I have never been near it as a producer. The production by Peter Schaufuss, seen most recently in London in 2015 with Queensland Ballet, is so wonderful that I think it should always be done that way. Ballets like *Swan Lake* often offer wonderful work for the women of the corps de ballet but there is not much for the men to do except rather a lot of lifting.

It was *Coppélia* that prompted my conversion to classical ballet and mime, when I saw Peggy van Praagh dance Swanilda at the Prince's theatre in London in 1944. She and the rest of the cast made me realise that classical ballet could be about real people and not just fairy stories. *Coppélia* became a much more human way to appreciate classical ballet. With its recognisable characters and toyshop setting it is a good ballet for children too, but I have found they tend to get bored easily during the last act, which is really just a series of divertissements. By then the story has been resolved. Later I saw Peggy's own staging in Australia. I very seldom like other people's productions but hers was good, if somewhat overblown. I never thought I would end up trying to make those big five ballets – the three by Tchaikovsky, plus *Giselle* and *Coppélia* – acceptable and believable fantasies for present-day audiences, at the same time remaining faithful to their creators in terms of how the story, music and choreography are presented. This has, in part at least, occupied 50 years of my career as it turned out and I consider it a great advantage that I came to the classics late, as I have never taken them for granted. I love them in varying degrees and for various reasons. I am really happiest when the story is strong and dramatic and when the music is powerful. Then I can pursue the central theme of the story in how I produce the ballet in question and ensure that any subsidiary episodes support the main action. To sustain an entire evening solely through dance and mime calls for a huge amount of activity – and imagination – to ensure the viewer remains entertained. Much of what happens in a ballet may have nothing to do with the actual story – the cygnets in *Swan Lake* for example. In creating a full evening's entertainment, should any part of a ballet turn out to be boring or out of keeping with the action overall, then my guiding approach has been to cut it. I would love to cut the cygnets as they just break the mood of the lakeside with their brilliant pizzicato, but there would be an outcry from audiences.

At the same time it is important to make sure that all the choreography that still exists is used but performed in a way that is attuned to present-day standards. We have a lot of the original choreography for *Swan Lake*, more for *The Sleeping Beauty*, even more for *Giselle*, and with *Coppélia* most of it still exists. But *The Nutcracker*, probably now the most popular ballet of all because it celebrates Christmas and has the most beautiful music, has very little surviving. We must make sure that what choreography we have is given its proper due. After all, just as audiences go to the opera primarily to hear the singing, they go to ballet to see the dancing. That can be helped by a good story which improves the emotional pleasure in a ballet such as *Swan Lake* yet these days it seems some audiences go just to enjoy the dancing, choreography and virtuosity of the dancers and to hell with any stories. But it is still the big full-length ballets with stories that sell out. The important thing in these productions is to keep the story clear and credible with the characters strongly drawn. I wonder at the wisdom of engaging three, of five originally planned, different choreographers to work on a new *Nutcracker*, as is the case with the most recent production by Paris Opéra Ballet.

I think one reason why I managed to put on my own productions as successfully as I have was that, apart from that first Bolshoi *Giselle* and *Romeo and Juliet* I saw, with all the other stagings the stories did not make sense or the narrative aspects were kept separate from the dancing. Other than the dances for the star roles these productions were all pretty dreary, lacking in continuity and imagination. When I was ballet master in Stuttgart, John Cranko decided it was very important for the company to do all the accepted classics – more if they could be found. As he had already staged his own versions of *Coppélia* and *Swan Lake* he said *Giselle* would be next – and I had to do it. He knew my rather ambivalent feelings and convinced me that there was an opportunity to make *Giselle* good theatre. Consequently I started by asking myself, what works about the ballet? What parts of *Giselle* are boring? Is the action logical? I did not get too bogged down in matters of authenticity. You need to exercise some poetic licence in making ballets from other periods work for modern audiences. That means these ballets are more than a display of technical ability. 'We saw them get their legs right up, so now we understand how classical ballet should look,' was how my neighbours in London greeted me years later after a performance of *Giselle* by a certain French ballerina they had just seen. They were most perplexed when I told them that high extensions in classical ballet are a recent acquisition, and although marvellous in modern classical ballets, they completely distort the classical line in such ballets as *Giselle*. Classics require stagecraft from dancers and demand a beautiful line – not contortions. Dancers learn exactitude when they perform the classics. They raise the stature of a company. Classics transform its reputation. Audiences believe that if companies do not perform the classics then they are not actually capable of doing so. Their estimation of you drops as a consequence. My intention is to make classics work for modern-day audiences – without destroying them – through enhancing their emotional and passionate qualities found in the combination of wonderful music and expressive movement. It is a myth that the steps all have a particular meaning. No. It is the way they are done that gives them their meaning.

What we consider today as classics did not really exist in Britain until the 1930s when Ninette de Valois, working with Nikolai Sergeyev, gradually introduced carefully considered productions into the repertoire.

She was a disciple of Sergei Diaghilev, with the desire to create new works where dance, music and design were equal partners, but she recognised early on that the classics were an essential cornerstone of the standard repertoire for any serious classical company. They were challenging to stage but they appealed to audiences because of the narratives they told with wonderful music and provided a showcase not only for ballerinas but the company as a whole. They are demanding for the corps de ballet and help set a standard and prove a company's worth. I do not believe that Madam ever wanted the classics to dominate as they sometimes do. Rather, for a dancer, learning to perform a classic teaches you how to dance well in other things. That is something that you can learn only in the classics – even as a swan or a wili – when each individual dancer moves exactly together with their neighbours. To be a good corps de ballet dancer requires great skill and can be very rewarding. As a director I used to wish there were more ballets that I could call on beyond the big five plus the shades from *Bayadère*, George Balanchine's *Serenade* and *Symphony in C*. Directors often programme Balanchine ballets if they do not have any traditional classics in their repertoire at the time. They provide a demanding workout, technically and artistically, and audiences mostly welcome them.

I particularly wish that choreographers working today would create new ballets that do more to incorporate the corps de ballet in a bigger way. There are very few, although I do like the way Christopher Wheeldon uses the ensemble in his ballets. I have quoted many times the words attributed to Madam about respecting the past, concentrating on the present and heralding the future. Getting the balance right within that mantra is crucial, particularly when it comes to staging the classics. Kevin O'Hare, director of the Royal Ballet, has discounted productions of such titles as *Paquita* and *Raymonda* in their full-length form, ballets that have been resuscitated at Paris Opéra Ballet by Pierre Lacotte and Rudolf Nureyev as showcases for Parisian schooling and technical prowess. O'Hare considers *Paquita* and *Raymonda* the sort of ballets that are not well aligned to the dramatic performing tradition of the Royal Ballet and I rather agree. Wayne McGregor was invited to stage *The Sleeping Beauty* in Paris, though at that point he had never seen the ballet. He subsequently saw it at Covent Garden – and decided it was not for him to produce a version himself. Yet the classics do still appeal to contemporary choreographers.

Mats Ek, a former theatre director and once assistant to Ingmar Bergman, saw Giselle herself as already insane. That being the case meant there was no need for a mad scene. Ek set the second act in a psychiatric ward of a hospital, suggesting that the patients, the wilis, were confined there as the result of being social outcasts. At the end, Albrecht is left naked, with Hilarion covering him with a blanket. What happens to him next is left for the audience to decide. Ek deliberately worked against the ballet's traditional text and imagery: Hilarion danced Giselle's first act solo; Albrecht and Wilfred first appeared in contrasting white and black tail suits. It was Hilarion who appeared to Albrecht's music carrying a blue flower to Giselle's grave. Critics observed that Ek's production worked best at those moments when it was furthest away from the original conception. I did not like Ek's approach because setting the action in an asylum, with a Giselle who had already lost her mind, completely reversed the dynamics of the story. It was a complete distortion. Now Akram Khan is producing a new *Giselle* for English National Ballet. Khan's respect for his native Bengali kathak traditions is evident in his work. When he choreographed *Dust* for English National Ballet in 2014 he appreciated the expressive power of classically trained dancers and their musicality, so Khan is an interesting choice. When Sadler's Wells Royal Ballet performed *Giselle* in India in 1985 we discovered just how different cultural traditions can be. In particular the notion of an afterlife there was alien to the one depicted during the European romantic era in *Giselle*, and we found we needed to explain the concept of ghosts in pre-performance, introductory talks.

When I staged *Giselle* in Stuttgart in March 1966 I had already assisted Margaret Dale with her one-hour version for BBC television in 1958 with Nadia Nerina and Nikolai Fadeyechev. That led to *The Sleeping Beauty*, televised the following year. There was also a *Coppélia* and *The Nutcracker* in this series of black-and-white films. I cannot say that the experience of filming ballet for television was a help to me when I came to mount these ballets for the stage. I was more concerned for making them work in theatrical terms for modern-day audiences. These days audiences tend not look at such ballets in the same way as their predecessors. How could they, given the way in which tastes and fashions have developed over the intervening years as audiences have experienced so much more? When Cranko asked me to stage *Giselle* I told him that I did not know the ballet well, I had never been in it and I had never really liked it, except for the performances by Ulanova and Fadeyechev with the Bolshoi. They genuinely did make an impression, even if the ballet had not. John insisted and gave me six weeks' leave to go and find out about *Giselle*.

Back in London I did a lot of research. I studied Cyril Beaumont's book *The Ballet Called Giselle* and got hold of Paul Czinner's film of the Bolshoi production which used 12 cameras. I discovered much about the many versions of the ballet there had been. I studied Faith Worth's notation for the Royal Ballet and spent considerable time understanding the motivation of each character. Right from the start I learned that the main things to concentrate on were the music, how the story – or at least what there is of it – could be properly understood and, importantly, the style. By that I mean that how every step that is danced is uniform and the corps de ballet align their arms and legs exactly together. In more practical terms, having ensured all of that, the corps should not be covered in patchy blobs of unsympathetic light. Weeks of concentrated work coaxing perfect alignment out of a corps can so easily be destroyed by the whim of some lighting designer eager for attention. I decided to use Peter Farmer as designer and had preliminary discussions with him. When I came back to Stuttgart I was full of ideas and keen to get on with it. John, meanwhile, was at work with *Concerto for Flute and Harp*, using music by Mozart. This gave the men in the company something to do while the women were involved with *Giselle*. John's new ballet was for two leading couples, Ana Cardus with Richard Cragun, Ilse Wiedman and Bernd Berg but, in a counterpoint to the ensembles in *Giselle*, it had a male corps de ballet. John's ballet was full of linear formations and patterns, a male ballet blanc, ideal as a curtain raiser.

Giselle in Stuttgart in 1966 caused something of a sensation, simply because it took the story seriously and was very moving. In Germany *Giselle* was regarded until then as something of a joke, bathed in unlikely blue moonlight. I have never seen blue moonlight, have you? That graveyard scene should really be cold and quite macabre. Given carte blanche by John in Stuttgart I found a more realistic way of presenting the characters. Albrecht was carefree, desperately in search of some love before he has to enter an arranged marriage. As portrayed by Egon Madsen, then only 23 years old, Albrecht was full of life, a randy young man from the castle out for a good time, not some kind of effete, lovesick stage prince. Of course we were not the first to conceive Albrecht in this way. This had very much been the approach taken by Rudolf Nureyev earlier in the 1960s after his defection. But Egon did this more successfully than any other Albrecht I have worked with. In comparison, in the second act, as he mourned *Giselle*'s death, Egon's characterisation was full of despair and remorse as the wilis try to dance him to his death.

In comparison, nearly 30 years later, when I worked with Carlos Acosta as Albrecht for the first time, although a wonderful artist, he was not the greatest actor-dancer. He was not too happy with some sequences he was required to perform. There seems to be a worldwide tradition of male dancers being allowed to bring their own steps. Not in my productions, unless somebody is incapable of performing a certain step – when of course he should not be doing the role. Carlos did not like the long, grieving walk around the stage that Albrecht performs as he approaches Giselle's grave, particularly when he had to walk upstage with his back to the audience. He did not like revealing his bum. I do not know why, it certainly has sex appeal. Zoltan Solymosi was the same. Carlos did agree to do what I insisted on, but he was not happy, especially as I would not let him wear his own costume. That is another no-no in my book. But Carlos performed as rehearsed and is a good partner. In Yuri Grigorovich's *Spartacus* at the London Coliseum in 2007 he was stronger even than the Bolshoi's own men and acted far better.

With *Giselle* I wanted to be true to what the ballet's creators had intended. The characters' relationships with each other were expressed through the feelings indicated by the mime – although in that production we did not use the mother's mime scene, where she warns Giselle, 'Over there in the depths of the forest there are the graves of young girls whose spirits have become wilis. They will rise up at midnight with their queen and force every man who crosses their path to dance until they die.' I had never seen it convincingly done and it just held up the action and did not work musically very well either. That mime in Stuttgart was based on how the Royal Ballet performed it at that period, but they did not have the complete sequence. At the time I thought it was unnecessary. Later I did reinstate the passage, but only when I had managed to find the authentic version which greatly added to the build-up of the drama as it is important to convey the mother's sense of unease about

Albrecht. Now I include the mime in its entirety in all my stagings – and *Giselle* has taken me to Cologne, Frankfurt, Munich, Amsterdam, Rio de Janeiro, Toronto, Winnipeg, Ottawa, Houston, Sarasota and Tokyo, besides Stuttgart and London.

Marcia Haydée was my first Giselle. We worked a lot on the role and she was very malleable. We had one adventure after the dress rehearsal. There was a real sense that the production had come together well, with a lot of excitement in the theatre. However, a ballet master that Marcia had known from elsewhere took her off to a rehearsal studio unbeknown to me, insisting that the ending of Giselle's first act solo was wrong. I was using Ashton's choreography and this ballet master made Marcia learn the version performed by Ulanova, which is actually easier technically. Marcia was in a terrible state of indecision as she knew I would not approve. I was furious when I found out. Marcia performed what we had rehearsed. She had rave reviews. Nobody had ever seen a Giselle like hers anywhere in Germany before. She tackled the character rather well and practically was helpful to Peter Farmer about the cut of her bodice and waistband. Peter's first act costume for Giselle was yellow, as in the first production, and Marcia made no objection to wearing the colour, unlike some ballerinas who refuse to wear it. As Giselle, Marcia was completely new. Birgit Keil was the first Myrtha but subsequently she was also a very moving Giselle. Hilarion had traditionally been presented as a cardboard character, an unfortunate pantomime villain, with a red beard, old and nasty. I never saw Hilarion that way but somebody who is sincere although not that bright. For realism's sake the hunting party included some falcons, which I discovered in Hermann Göring's old falconry in a ruined castle near Stuttgart, and some lovely red setters. When later Peter and I wanted to do something similar at the Royal Opera House and turned to Bill Bundy, the stage director who organised that sort of thing, he found us some setters that barked constantly and cocked their legs over the scenery, as well as some uncontrollable, squawking falcons. They had to go.

Working in Stuttgart I had not yet read Ivor Guest's important book about romantic ballet in England, which gives an account of *Giselle* as danced by Carlotta Grisi, the first ballerina to perform it. In a description of that first performance, Giselle takes Albrecht's sword and deliberately plunges it into her heart and dies. In Stuttgart we left it for the audience to decide. Did Giselle stab herself or did Hilarion manage to get the sword away from her in time? It was only when I was working on the ballet again a couple of years later, in May 1968 with the Royal Ballet's touring company, that I made the scene more explicit. Doreen – Dor – Wells and David Wall were the first Giselle and Albrecht, a popular pairing, but David did not enjoy partnering Dor in this particular ballet. He was a very good actor whereas she excelled in flowing, beautiful movements where nothing is ugly. In *Giselle* David found it hard to get a response from her. Dor never came out of herself. It was as if she was performing with a curtain drawn. Hers was a pretty Giselle but she could not throw herself into the mad scene. David also performed Albrecht opposite Elizabeth – Betch – Anderton who really was a great exponent of *Giselle*. It was Betch who told me about Guest's book and that really there was no doubt about Giselle being a suicide. It is the reason why Giselle is buried in unhallowed ground as she has committed a mortal sin and is prey to the evil wilis. If she had died of natural causes she would be protected in the confines of the church. Why else would Giselle seize the sword unless she was not intent on killing herself? She always holds it towards herself.

The meaning of the sequence where Giselle traces a circle with the sword on the ground is open to interrogation too. Is Giselle marking out the confines of a safe area for herself in a way that is counterpointed in the second act when Myrtha indicates her circle of power? In the rest of the scene Giselle, I think, believes that the sword is chasing her and she tries to escape it. She is frightened by what she sees as a symbol, half-death and half-phallic, which has power over her. Most Giselles follow my logic for the sequence of the scene, which is based mostly on how I saw Ulanova perform it in London in 1956. This is what I have always adhered to, but I still face opposition from some ballerinas, even normally intelligent ones, who struggle with Giselle's suicide. Galina Samsova found it hard to kill herself, for instance. Sylvie Guillem was such a pain. Her Covent Garden debut was in the role when Nureyev, still as Albrecht, first introduced her to London in 1988 during his extended round of farewell appearances. I liked her in those days and she performed the role as we rehearsed it. But later, when she again appeared with the company, she had become very much the star. She had changed so much. She would not listen in rehearsals, 'I do not kill myself. I do it this way.'

By then Guillem had staged the ballet herself, for Finnish National Ballet in 1998. At the time she said she was drawn to *Giselle* as it was a ballet for a woman, not a dancer. She claimed that the ballet made no sense dramatically. Guillem was concerned particularly to make the choreography a logical expression of the dramatic situation, not an end in itself. She did in the event alter many steps and situations. Her approach was not as radical as Mats Ek's and was concerned particularly in making the action more naturalistic – not, I suppose, so removed from my own approach though many of the details were different. For example, at the start Guillem had Albrecht disguising himself as Loys in his cottage. The warning mime normally performed by Berthe was assigned to several villagers and Giselle performed her first act solo to music usually allocated to the peasant pas de deux. In the mad scene there was the conventional business with the sword, the taunting and the running about. Giselle's embrace of her mother and Albrecht was left ambiguous for the audience to decide how she died. Perhaps illogically in the second act her tombstone was replaced by the garland used to crown her during the harvest celebrations. All I know, whenever subsequently Guillem appeared in my Covent Garden production I could not convince her to stab herself. Yet the idea for Giselle to commit suicide extends all the way back to the original production of 1841. It was scarcely a new idea.

I believe our role as producers and performers is to respect a ballet's originators but to make their creations work for modern audiences. We must think back to how it would have been in those days. The world of *Giselle* was full of superstition and myths that people believed. Suicides were a logical consequence of that. And, to be realistic, whoever died of a broken heart? It would probably take three months at least. And, if she did not intend to stab herself, why did she snatch the sword and rush around the stage brandishing it? In Russia too they do not like the idea of suicide at all. I once had an exploratory meeting about me doing a production of *Swan Lake* for the Bolshoi Ballet. All seemed well until I was asked about the ending. I told them that Odette throws herself into the lake to kill herself, to be followed closely by Siegfried who dies in the same way. They immediately lost interest. One of the Bolshoi's dancers present was horrified and said to me, 'You cannot have suicide. You finish with hope and happiness for the audience.' A happy ending was a requirement of Soviet ballets, showing the triumph of the beneficent power of the state.

After my first go at *Giselle* I staged it again in Cologne in 1967. This was a terrible let-down after the extraordinary success in Stuttgart. The reason? It was simply because the Cologne dancers were not really good enough. The first act, although it had very simple choreography in the main, is very difficult to sustain. But it was the second act that really seemed to fall apart. It was not for lack of trying, but the long relentless dances led by Myrtha as the wilis force Albrecht to dance to death were too exposing. Peter Farmer designed again. The Cologne staging led to being commissioned to mount *Giselle* for the Royal Ballet. I was concerned primarily to restore its dramatic validity. That was – and still is – an important concern for me. A few months earlier, in January 1968, I had arranged the dances in a new production of Giuseppe Verdi's *Aida* for the Royal Opera which was luxuriantly designed by Nicholas Georgiadis. This was the first complete opera televised live and in colour direct from Covent Garden. It had Gwyneth Jones, Grace Bumbry and Jon Vickers as the protagonists. Peter Potter was the director. I had first met him when we were both in the army hospital after I had injured my back during primary training. Peter had a terrible leg wound that would not heal. He was an officer and in a different part of the hospital, but as there was nobody ever to talk to, he sent me a message to say he wanted to chat.

In Civvy Street Peter was a theatre director and he knew of my involvement with Ballets Jooss. Later we did a musical together. I was staging all the numbers and Peter did not like to tell the cast which of these he was cutting when they did not work. I had to do that for him. Rehearsals for that *Aida* had their moments too, but compared to staging new ballet productions, the opera company had far more stage time to prepare. We used to rehearse at the Opera Centre in Mile End Road. I remember some battles there with the conductor, Edward Downes. The ballet music in *Aida* is already very fast and Ted, at the piano, proceeded to ruin it by playing it far too quickly for the dancers to keep up. Romayne Grigorova, ballet mistress for the Royal Opera, was very good at getting conductors to co-operate, but even she could not get Ted to slow down. 'I am the music director,' he insisted. He really was very stubborn. In any case, that ballet in the middle of the triumph scene is always a headache for directors and choreographers alike. I knew it from before. I danced in the previous production by Margherita Wallman. I had to enter walking across a rostrum and down some steps while carrying

Gillian Lynne above my head in a two-handed bum lift. I got on with Gillian. When the production went out on tour we did what I always hate when dancers do it to me – we changed Wallman's choreography to suit ourselves. So when I came to stage this scene myself, instead of the usual dance depicting ceremonial pomp, I decided on something that appeared more spontaneous. Some of the crowd, David Drew and Ken Mason who were cheering the Egyptian victory, broke out from the rest and started to dance out of sheer joy at the triumphant end of war. They were joined by a young woman – Monica Mason – who joined in their frenzy, followed by more of the crowd. It was the first time I had worked with a principal dancer from Covent Garden, and Mon was marvellous. She really caught on to the music and would do anything. I still like the concept and it worked to an extent, but not well enough. It is very hard to make dancing look spontaneous and I was too new to choreography to do that successfully. It was all too obvious that Monica was really a rather special dancer, not just a member of the common throng.

So working with the touring company on *Giselle* the same year, I was determined to reconsider how the characters interacted with each other. I wanted the mimed passages, as well as the mad scene which can drag, to be much more dramatic. Mime is one area that is often cut in other productions, particularly Russian ones, but I am convinced that the use of mime can be a great aid to the story telling – provided it is done with conviction and clarity. So often where mime is still taught in ballet schools it is in a very dry, academically correct way. Contrast is one of the most important parts of choreography and contributes so much to holding the viewers' attention between a seemingly endless sets of dances. If mime is performed with passion – making the arms, hands, eyes, express the meaning as well as the correct gestures literally – then it can be beautiful. While the presentation of classical ballet has improved enormously in Britain over the past twenty years, I regret that mime seems to be on the way out. As long as the full-length classics are performed they will always benefit from the inclusion of mime. Unfortunately it is no longer taught in the curriculum of most schools. If you do not learn it there, you will only ever get an approximation of it when you have to perform it with a company.

Frederick Ashton considered the prologue of *The Sleeping Beauty* to be a masterpiece of construction partly through how mime is used as counterpoint to the many processions and danced sequences. He was never able to accept the idea of a Carabosse being danced and always insisted on Petipa's conception of this role as a mime figure. This is what gives stature to the character and this is integral to the structure of the ballet overall. In a similar way, I consider that it was a mistake by Gillian Lynne in her reconstruction of *Miracle in the Gorbals* in 2014 to have Christ dance, which did not occur in Robert Helpmann's original. The lack of contrast that resulted diminished the stature of the Christ-like figure and somehow reduced his powerful and dominating presence.

I restored the mime in *Giselle* so that it was evident that Berthe wanted her daughter to marry Hilarion rather than the unknown young suitor, Loys, the disguised Albrecht. In one small but dramatically telling moment in that 1968 production I had Giselle stand posed between Berthe and the supposed Loys, visually torn between the two. I was encouraged that reviewers noted that the dance scenes grew naturally out of the mimed passages, like an aria growing out of recitative in opera, and that the mime was seen to be a wholly plausible means of communication. It was flattering to read that this *Giselle* was considered the pointer for how future productions of the classics should be done. Not everybody was impressed, however. I happened to bump into Marie Rambert at the BBC one day. 'I hate you. You have done *Giselle* better than me,' she grumbled to me in her heavily accented English. 'Thank you for the compliment,' I replied, to which she just growled but with a twinkle in her eye. I should admit that I had first come across the work of Peter Farmer when I saw the *Giselle* he had designed for Ballet Rambert, so perhaps Mim had cause to be aggrieved.

My staging for the touring company was adopted at Covent Garden in 1971, which is when I took the opportunity to make use of the hydraulic lifts there. As Myrtha summoned the wilis from their graves at the start of the second act, they appeared to rise from the ground, gradually becoming visible as the stage lifts brought them into view. This was the occasion when my father was present at a performance. He appeared to be quite impressed. He had never shown much emotion but he did seem moved on this occasion. At least that is what he wrote to me in a letter afterwards. It was a beautiful letter, but as he could not easily express his feelings, it was signed only 'Bernard Wright'. A shame really, as I felt he needed to cry. My mother had recently died.

With *Giselle* there are also many considerations of casting that make all the difference. Generally I prefer the three characters, Giselle, Albrecht and Hilarion, to be young and passionate. There have been, of course, many more established Giselles who have made the role work, particularly in the second act where they miraculously transform themselves from a peasant girl into a spirit. Ulanova particularly stands out in this regard. I was completely smitten by her interpretation. In the first act she had both passion and humour. She made the audience laugh with her as she stared slack-jawed at Bathilde's finery. In the mad scene she was completely caught up in the tragedy and did not need to let her hair down to appear deranged. When it came to the second act, she was completely transformed as Giselle's spirit. She brought tears to my eyes.

More recently, I liked Lesley Collier who was the first to dance my 1985 Covent Garden production. She chose to mark her retirement a decade later in the role when she was generously partnered by Irek Mukhamedov. I owe Lesley a huge debt of gratitude for the way she rehearses *Giselle* and *The Nutcracker* for me, first for her innate musicality which she imparts, and her insistence on it. Then there is her attention to detail and her understanding of Petipa-style. There are so many versions of these great pas de deux and solos. Lesley has danced them all herself and knows the best way to cope with their idiosyncrasies. She will never alter anything unless she discusses it with me first and is at pains to provide beautifully worked out suggestions. I value her friendship and honesty. Already outstanding in the corps de ballet, Lesley proved to be a brilliant interpreter of so many classical roles. I loved the way she danced that deliciously fast first solo in *La Bayadère*, and she was remarkably moving and passionate in the dual role of Odette/Odile in *Swan Lake*.

Giselle is the ballet that probably makes the greatest demands on the ballerina both technically and interpretavely. I have rehearsed many dancers in this role but I particularly like working with Marianela Núñez, the celebrated ballerina from Argentina now with the Royal Ballet, especially as she also dances the role of the evil queen of the wilis at other performances. This requires a completely different approach than that for Giselle. This is not because I think she is better than the others; it is because she has the right attitude and uses her phenomenal technique to enhance her characterisation in order to really become the tragic Giselle and, most importantly, to forget 'self'. Margot Fonteyn and the great

Vera Volkova both said it is only when you achieve that do you become a true ballerina. I always feel that when Marianela is rehearsing it is the role that comes first and making sure that every gesture, every glance, every change of expression projects to the whole audience, and that is no mean task in that huge auditorium at the Royal Opera House. Alina Cojocaru was a great Giselle when she first did it with me in 2001. We worked well together and she won rave reviews, but later when she went off onto the guest artist ciruit she never recaptured the original impact of her early performances. She did everything on feeling. Her performance became more introverted, which did not project.

To my eyes the Giselle to move me most is Natalia Osipova. When I first saw her I could not believe the lightness of how she jumped and moved. She absolutely bowled me over. She was special because she gave the impression of completely immersing herself in the role. She has the most incredible classical technique but makes it speak. She looks like a peasant girl dancing. Osipova has her own ideas, which I really do like in a dancer, but these were never a problem to reconcile with my own approach. I had thought she would be difficult to handle because she is so strong, but she was very polite. In fact she was quite nervous about working with me but we had a very good rapport though we had a tussle about Giselle killing herself. She missed doing that in her first performance. When we worked together in January 2014 she had already performed the role in London with the Mikhailovsky company the year before, a very old-fashioned staging, a relic of another age. Natalia told me how much she preferred my production for its dynamism. I adored how she could jump in the second act seemingly without any plié or preparation. I am used to Giselles looking rather spiritual but loved how Natalia still looked human.

In her graduation performance in 1983, at the age of 19, Leanne Benjamin impressed many people for what they saw as a remarkably mature performance. Some youngsters are able to slip into a classical role easily without achieving that perfect sense of style. Leanne had very expressive eyes and, coached by Lyn Wallis, understood the contrasts between the acts well. She had a natural dance quality. For somebody at the start of her career, Leanne's was not a perfect but a very good sketch. To really do *Giselle* a ballerina must study the role – a great deal – to find a way to interpret the steps and situations. A young dancer needs to be able to see what others do with the role and not learn it solely from one teacher. That way they can develop their own interpretation after seeing others.

Lynn Seymour was cast as Giselle very early in her career by Madam but she took quite some time to understand the role. She could not reconcile Giselle's motivation or behaviour. She felt the key to Giselle's collapse in the mad scene was some form of mental breakdown. I worked with Lynn and Egon Madsen at National Ballet of Canada in Toronto in 1970, a production that is still in the repertoire there after 46 years, most recently revived in June 2016. The designs were by Desmond Heeley, and although somewhat changed over the years they are always rich in colour. Working with Lynn it became evident that she was struggling with her interpretation. We discussed it and I was not so adamant about the idea of suicide in those days. I convinced Lynn to kill herself though her preferred reading elsewhere was as a remote and highly strung young woman whose world is smashed when Albrecht deceives her. In Lynn's mind that is what prompted Giselle to stab herself. *Giselle* certainly provides a ballerina with something real to express other than just steps, but the interpretation must abide by the producer's concept.

Musically there is much to consider too. In Toronto I worked with Ashley Lawrence to reorder sections of the score, particularly at the start of the second act, to make the ballet more logical dramatically. Ashley was the best music director I have ever worked with. His arrangements never sounded as though the music had been cut or reordered. There was a new orchestration in Toronto too from the company's own conductor, which I had naively agreed to. I did not like it, as the music drew attention to itself. For the sequence where the wilis hop across the stage in arabesque the arranger had added his own clever bits – clank, clank, clank.

The orchestration used at Covent Garden has been changed more latterly. It is now by Joseph Horowitz which I prefer. The score is still not great but that does not stop *Giselle* from being a classic. I find it perfect for this tragic story seen through gothic eyes. I have, depending on the size of the company, changed the order of the music. In Stuttgart I first reworked the peasant pas de deux into a pas de six. Although it was in the first production, set to music similar in style to Adolphe Adam's own, though actually by Friedrich Burgmüller, I thought a dance for two virtuosos at this point seemed to break the dramatic line of Giselle and Albrecht's story. Spreading the dance over six dancers made a huge difference. Depending on the size of the company, the pas de six can be rearranged for four or even revert to two dancers.

Changes need to be made for the right reasons. When the Stuttgart Ballet was presented in New York in the summer of 1969 by Sol Hurok he insisted on including the pas de deux as a vehicle for Richard Cragun who otherwise was not cast in the performance. This sort of display piece was exactly what I did not want when I rearranged it. A further recurring question is the placing of Giselle's solo in the first act. Does she perform it for the duke and Bathilde or during the crowning festival with her friends, which is where the score locates it? When it follows the peasant pas de deux it looks wrong, but when this sequence is performed as a pas de six the solo looks better. If the decision is to retain the pas de deux then it is better to save the solo until Bathilde asks Giselle whether she has ever loved. But there is still a problem. When I staged the ballet in 1985 at Covent Garden I wanted Giselle to have two solos, one with the peasants, the second performed for Bathilde. I had discovered another number in the original score entitled Giselle's solo. Frederick Ashton had choreographed this for Antoinette Sibley as the second solo in the peasant pas de deux when he produced the ballet in 1960. Antoinette was amazing in it, although some other dancers found it very difficult. But there was another problem. The music for that solo is actually by Giacomo Meyerbeer and does not really fit sound-wise with the rest of Adam's score. When I removed it, Michael Somes bullied me to rein-state it. 'It's our heritage,' he insisted. I lost that battle as Somes shouted me down, needless to say. One day I will get Fred's beautiful solo for Giselle back in where it belongs. She needs another solo in the first act as there is a long section when she hardly dances at all and her character demands that she is always dancing. However, I have never been able to get Giselles to cope with even more jumping.

It is always very sad when a company decides not to continue with a production, as happened with mine in Stuttgart and Birmingham. Both had a good innings but after John Cranko's death, when Marcia Haydée became director, she did her own version of the ballet in which she changed the story. Unofficially the company called it *Hilarion*, danced by Ricky Cragun, as the ballet became so much more about him. Although

I thought I was going to do a new staging for Birmingham after mine was retired, I did not think that a new *Giselle* was really necessary there. In London, my first attempt was the one made for the touring company before it was adopted at Covent Garden and where it stayed in the repertoire for much of the 1970s until Norman Morrice, then director, was anxious to do his own *Giselle* to help him get to know everybody, which was perfectly understandable. I had a lot of respect for Norman and worked with him when I was in television and directed two of his ballets for the small screen. I liked him a lot and there was certainly no animosity between us when this happened. The sets used by Norman in 1980 were the old ones by James Bailey recycled from Ashton's 1960 production. Bailey's involvement with the ballet at Covent Garden in fact went back to 1946 and his designs reflected that. Actually his sets did not need that much work to bring them up to scratch. Unfortunately, as Norman had not really worked on a large production before, he found it very hard to project the action across that notoriously difficult gap of the orchestra pit between the stage and the auditorium at the Royal Opera House, especially as Norman did not use the conventional mime sequences. His staging was retired after only a very few performances.

Norman realised it had been a mistake. He had failed where I had succeeded elsewhere, so he subsequently asked me to put on a completely new production in 1985, to be designed by John Macfarlane whose work we both admired and who had designed some of Norman's work at Ballet Rambert. Much of John's early career was spent working with Jiří Kylián at Nederlands Dans Theater, Jochen Ulrich's Tanz Forum in Cologne and on many of Glen Tetley's ballets in America and Europe. Thanks to the introduction from Norman, I now had the opportunity to work with John myself – which was quite a shock. He is a highly accomplished artist, not solely a traditional stage designer – although his *Giselle* has become more traditional over the years as we have made changes to it. You have to be strong with John but he has a wonderful sense of theatre and of the stage. He is a lovely man and a huge talent. I only wish he did not spend so much time working in opera.

Now over 30 years old, the production has been through certain modifications over the years, and after the most recent refurbishment is looking really beautiful. Clement Crisp, *The Financial Times* critic, however, has repeatedly claimed that the proliferation of trees designed by John means that nothing of the action is actually visible. In designing the ballet as he did, John deliberately sought to distance *Giselle* from the overly prettified Ruritanian world depicted by James Bailey. He wanted to create an impenetrable wood that traps people within it. The ensuing sense of claustrophobia and of no escape caused the characters to behave in the irrational ways they do, which I think is a convincing framework for the supernatural events that the ballet portrays. This was particularly apposite in the autumn of 1987 when the production was performed after the hurricane that felled many trees in southern England. Yet Arlene Croce, for 25 years the critic of *The New Yorker* and never a fan of mine, considered John's forest setting to have been trampled by a charge of elephants. Still, it was this staging that Alicia Markova asked to see on the occasion of her 90th birthday in 2000. She adored it, but Clement, who adored Markova, said in a later review after her death, that my production would make her turn in her grave. At the next revival, after John and I had made some alterations in both acts, Clement told me as we bumped into each other in the foyer that he really loved the changes we had made. 'Super!' he said. Yet a couple of years later at a subsequent revival, which included the same improvements as before, he again decreed there were far too many trees. When I staged *Giselle* in Houston for Ben Stevenson in 1986, Clive Barnes was invited to review it for *The New York Times*. He arrived looking a mess, in a dirty tee-shirt that only came halfway down his huge belly. His tummy button protruded, his trousers were filthy. But the company spoiled him enormously, inviting him to a lunch with the rich and influential folk of Houston where we ate from a gold-plated dinner service. He gave us a rave notice. Really, that was the equivalent of buying good notices.

I first worked in Munich in 1974 thanks to Claudia Algeranova – Claudie – whom by then I had known for over 30 years. Notionally Claudie ran the office but the Bavarian State Ballet in Munich was one of those companies where the director never seems to last for more than three years. Victor Gsovsky had been in charge for a couple of years during the 1950s, as too had Pia and Pino Mlakar. Alan Carter and his wife Joan Harris survived somewhat longer. They were followed by Heinz Rosen, versed in the traditions of Rudolf Laban, who recruited Konstanze Vernon as his ballerina. John Cranko combined Munich with his Stuttgart directorship during the late 1960s but found the working conditions and prevailing attitudes there far from conducive. He was followed by Ronald and Annette Hynd. Munich was certainly an unhappy venue for Lynn Seymour when she was director in the 1970s, but she was only one of a number of short-term directors during that period, including Edmund Gleede and Stefan Erler. They all suffered from the ballet company's prevailing sense of its secondary importance to the opera. Claudie practically ran the place and she encouraged the then director, Dieter Gackstetter, to get me over to stage *Giselle*. The ballet had a long history in Munich, having been first danced there in 1845 only four years after its premiere in Paris. The theatre in Munich is lovely, with a big stage and a good atmosphere. In those days I had no notator or assistant so I had to do everything. There were a few wrongs along the way but rehearsals for *Giselle* went well although the second studio was tiny. Konstanze Vernon, by then the company's leading ballerina and who subsequently became director, already exerted considerable power and I was forced to make her first cast. She was all right but not great. Claudie appeared as Berthe, Giselle's mother. She had a good instinct about things and candidly told me before the first night that the production was going to be a disaster as it had been over-rehearsed, but in the event it was a success, a sell-out in fact, with people offering any money for seats. That *Giselle* is still in the repertoire, alongside the version by Mats Ek, most recently programmed in September 2016. Having both stagings in the Munich repertoire means that it is possible to see two different versions of the ballet when they are staged together on matinée days.

However reluctant I was when I first staged *Giselle*, I have never got bored with the ballet in the five decades since my first production. Lighting is of the utmost importance and John Macfarlane has stipulated that David Finn oversees Jennifer Tipton's original lighting at each revival at Covent Garden. Elsewhere I now have Peter Teigen light my shows whenever I can. After so many productions of the ballet I still love *Giselle*, but now find it better to ask Desmond Kelly to oversee the various revivals as I have become too close to them. Desmond was a superb Albrecht and always brings great attention to every aspect of revivals. There are still questions that intrigue me, I find. Some aspects you can never totally resolve. The important thing is to try.

Giselle the ballet is very familiar, but Giselle the girl is somewhat a mystery. She is probably illegitimate. We meet her mother, but who is her father? Could she have some blue blood that marks her out as different in some way? Had Giselle's mother suffered from another duke's droit de seigneur when he would have had the right to take her to his bed on the eve of her marriage? Might Albrecht simply be a case of history repeating itself? I rather have the feeling that all the way through the ballet Giselle herself is actually pregnant.

I once accidentally tripped across a more radical rereading. I recall one schools' matinee of *Giselle* when, as a curtain raiser to the performance, we presented a behind-the-scenes look at the world of ballet. As I was outlining the plot I heard myself revealing to the assembled audience of young children and their teachers, 'Of course Hilarion is really in love with Albrecht.' I heard a guffaw from the wings and John Hall, the chief electrician, comment, 'We're in for a right fairy story today!'

I did manage to right that wrong, but mistakes like that do tend to come back to haunt you. As do some productions. When I was in Stockholm in 2000 preparing for my production of *Swan Lake* there the following year, I happened to coincide with Natalia Makarova – Natasha – who was in the final stages of mounting her new *Giselle* for Royal Swedish Ballet. Except that her production was not really new at all, as I discovered when I watched a rehearsal. Although the production and choreography were credited to Natasha, as I watched the first act unfold I realised that many of the staging details – such as when Hilarion finds Albrecht's sword in the cottage and compares its crest with the hunting horn hung on Giselle's cottage or when Wilfred retrieves Albrecht's cloak from his cottage as the hunting party is approaching – were identical to my first staging in Stuttgart in 1966 and in subsequent iterations. These were innovations original to me and not found earlier. I realised that Natasha was in a very difficult situation as she was in the final stages of getting it all together. She explained she had no knowledge that these details were anything but original, common to every *Giselle*. In any case, she explained to me, she had based her entire staging on the film made for television by Rudolf Nureyev in 1979, and produced by Stanley Dorfman for ATV with a cast that also included Lynn Seymour and Monica Mason. This added a whole different dimension of complexity and problems. Although filmed in Britain, Rudi had imported the company from Munich, where I had staged the ballet in 1974, to provide the supporting ensemble for his film. He had also imported – without my permission – all of the mime, all of the peasant dances and all the second act from my Munich production. All uncredited.

The first I knew about what I considered to be this theft was when I saw the broadcast on television. I was not able to talk to Rudi about it. His schedule meant he was never in one place long enough to find him. In any case, this was not the sort of issue about which he would much concern himself. Instead I contacted my solicitor. If they were working for you they were wonderful and I had already had experience of them on another legal case surrounding *Giselle*. When National Ballet of Canada performed my production for them on tour in Tokyo, they informed me three days before it was due to be broadcast that my fee would be £50. As I held the performance rights I told them they could not go ahead without agreeing a more suitable fee and named a deliberately large sum. That knocked them sideways. They went ahead with the broadcast – and what followed was a marathon of litigation. My solicitors were known for never losing a case and they went at it with a will. To manage the time differences between Toronto and Tokyo they employed their own teams of lawyers in both cities to negotiate an acceptable fee for me, somewhere in the region of £10,000 I believe. But as the negotiations went on – and on, for nearly two years – in Canada and Japan, there was little hope of me coming away with a decent amount as most of it was going on endless legal fees. I called the whole thing off, much to the fury of my lawyer. In fact I ended up with something like £200 after all the costs had been paid. The situation had got completely out of hand.

This was very much on my mind when I contacted the solicitors again about Nureyev's TV film. There was some recognition from Rudi that he should not have appropriated my production in the way he had, but no admission of liability. My lawyer was sure that we would win if we went to court – but I agreed to settle without ever going there. That, I am afraid, was another of my wrongs. I wish now we had our day in court. I am sure the lawyers were right and that we would have secured substantial damages. That film is still available to buy on DVD and I have never made a penny out of it. So you can imagine my feelings when I saw what Natasha thought to be her own work unfolding before my eyes in Stockholm. I asked her to do all that she possibly could to make those elements that were at issue more her own before the first night, then still two weeks away. Failing that, would she restudy these scenes for future revivals? I was pleased that Natasha agreed to change the scene with Albrecht and Wilfred, but otherwise she referred me to her agent, Jane Hermann in New York, whose list of clients is a veritable who's who of the dance world. I made the same points to Ms Hermann – and, in reply, was informed that I was guilty of making veiled threats about litigation against Natasha's actions. The claims I was alleging were without substance, I was told. Rather than face another protracted legal wrangle I chose the higher ground and had to content myself with pointing out that if Natasha did not wish to make further modifications I would let the matter drop. After all, neither she nor I owned the ballet but we shared the same desire for it to continue to live for audiences today. I am, however, comforted by the fact that Natasha's production only had a few performances before it was dropped, but I have an awful feeling that if we let ballerinas have their way, *Giselle* is one of those ballets that will become full of awful, unclassical contortions. That is the way things are going. As my neighbours revealed when they saw *Giselle*, the public will clap at anything so long as ballerinas get their legs up and it all happens in the dark. Not that I am mentioning anybody in particular.

CHAPTER 10

Frederick Ashton –
awakening *The Sleeping Beauty*

I WAS INTERESTED TO SEE that for his production of *The Sleeping Beauty* in 2015, Alexei Ratmansky turned to the notation and drawings that Vladimir Stepanov made in 1903 of Marius Petipa's original choreography from 1890. They are held at Harvard University in Massachusetts, an archive I consulted when I staged *The Nutcracker* for the Royal Ballet in 1984. As captured by Stepanov, *The Sleeping Beauty* was a broad form of entertainment, full of character dances, pantomime and children as well as classical dancing. Over the next hundred years or so the ballet evolved in the Soviet Union in different ways from the west. Along the way, *The Sleeping Beauty* lost much of its multi-faceted variety.

My own feelings about *The Sleeping Beauty* have always been mixed. I have been watching productions for the past 70 years or so and been very much involved in several over the past 50, but apart from some magical performances in certain roles, I have never yet found this so-called pinnacle of classical ballet to be particularly satisfying. *The Sleeping Beauty* is a difficult ballet. At its heart is a battle between good and evil, but one without much drama. It is too easy for the prince to find his princess. Guided effortlessly by the Lilac fairy, in most productions he does not even break sweat. I was appalled at some of the boring dances that seemed to get in the way. You spend a lot of time waiting for the title character, Aurora, to appear. She does not make an appearance until halfway through the first act – actually the second because the ballet begins with a prologue. Then there are long gaps when Aurora is absent. As we do not meet her prince until the next act, I had always considered the story weak but with great possibilities. Critics in 1890 summarised it as they dance, they fall asleep, they wake up, they dance some more.

Matthew Bourne has attempted to strengthen the narrative by incorporating new characters into his rather gothic version, a gamekeeper and Carabosse's son, who both have a rather unhealthy fascination with Aurora. The result is a good show but one where I am critical of Bourne's choreography. Dramatically, the transformation scenes in *The Sleeping Beauty*, so important, to me have always seemed scarcely to exist. The graph of excitement of how the ballet should build is compromised by its structure, and overall it is far too long. To me, the acts have always felt like four different ballets strung together. For a producer, the placing of the intervals is always a problem as each act is complete in itself and ideally they should all be followed by an interval, but this would involve an enormous amount of overtime for a lot of stage staff, musicians, front of house and performers.

In my production for Birmingham Royal Ballet, the intervals are placed between the prologue and the first act, and after the second. I made cuts elsewhere to ensure that there is time to include an awakening pas de deux, which I feel strongly should be the focal point of the prince's journey. Pruning the hunting scene is a pity but, unless it is done with the same level of grandeur as the rest, it is not worth doing. Tchaikovsky's music for those hunt dances, however, is not his best. I have always tried to tighten the structure to make it dramatically more interesting, something which is difficult to do. I do not know whether I really achieved that. I was keen to make Carabosse a continuing menace during the journey through the forest. That voyage is wonderful musically and it is always a shame to reduce it, but overtime is always an issue. There is a problem too with the divertissements in the last act. For contrast's sake – and it is important to recognise that the whole ballet is built on contrasts, good and evil, classical and demi-caractère dancing, mime and dance – you cannot run all the classical numbers together. To put the pas de quatre next to the bluebirds followed by the grand pas de deux is not a good balance. For the sake of variety you have to keep the cats, always popular, although the number is quite classical, as well as Red Riding Hood and the wolf. That number is always a favourite, particularly with matinées full of children. The bluebird pas de deux is, strictly speaking, a demi-caractère number although many dancers do not understand that. She is a princess under the spell of a magical bird, which is all in the choreography if you look at it, but the nuance needs to be pointed in performance. It is often done, at both Covent Garden and Birmingham Royal Ballet, too classically, just two birds twittering together.

Another major consideration is not to mix the fairies and humans. They represent different worlds and the staging should respect that. The fairies' solos in the prologue are simple from an academic point of view so that each fairy can embellish them with the characteristics of the gift that they bring. They have to be done perfectly from a technical perspective, but at the same time they must be projected strongly, really performed, to reveal the fairies' expressive qualities. It is up to each dancer to do something with the solos – otherwise they become boring. The actual steps do not mean a thing, but performed with passion they become something different. If a dancer concentrates only on producing a perfect arabesque then they cannot concentrate on how to give character to the step. I first saw Pauline Clayden as the breadcrumb fairy. She talked all the way through her solo, 'I'm scattering breadcrumbs here, I'm scattering breadcrumbs up there, down here and everywhere.' As she did so she was audible onstage but her constant chatter helped her really perform the solo. It became exciting. Choreography cannot be too difficult to perform otherwise it just becomes dull.

I was first invited to produce *The Sleeping Beauty* in Cologne in 1968, on the strength of my production of *Giselle* there the year before. The girls had such bad legs they could not possibly be dressed in tutus, so I asked Peter Farmer to put them in shift-like dresses. Frederick Ashton, then director of the Royal Ballet and about to stage a new *Beauty* himself in London that December, came to see the production. It was incredibly beautiful to look at, designed in the most ravishing colours, with deep blues and purples, Farmer at his best. Peter is one of theatre's true painter-designers. In his studio, pictures prop against the walls, with easels and drawing-boards everywhere. Jars of brushes and pots of paint jostle for space. Peter's costumes were always beautifully evocative and made the performers look good. His set designs used the grand tradition of 19th-century scenic illusion to its fullest and appeared completely natural. He unfashionably but unashamedly worked on flat cloths and never used the modern method of ceiling-mounted projectors to transfer designs onto the scenic canvas that has been adopted by many set painters. Peter also worked on the recreation of Ashton's *Sylvia* at Covent Garden when it was restaged after a 30-year absence in 2004. Peter was asked to fill the gaps for missing scenery designs by Robin and Christopher Ironside, as well as designing a new set in the spirit of Claude Lorrain, the 17th-century landscape painter who was the Ironsides' inspiration.

Peter has probably designed *The Sleeping Beauty* more often than any other designer, ten productions at least. In Cologne his shifts looked magical, much better than stiff tutus and they did help obscure the defects of the dancers' legs. The German critic, Horst Koegler, did not agree. He complained about the many layers of veils, tulle, chiffon and silk. Three of the four acts took place behind gauzes which were used for projections during the transformations. He did also say – when you were able to get an occasional glimpse of the choreography – it was possible to discern many differences compared to the production by Kenneth MacMillan in Berlin the year before. Choreographically, the prologue and first act kept close to what Kenneth knew from the Royal Ballet. He did make new dances for the hunting party; for Aurora and her nymphs in the second act. He restored the jewel fairies in the last act, expanded to a pas de sept but the divertissements were restricted. In particular, Kenneth created a most wonderful mazurka for 30 dancers, drawing on many steps and patterns that Tatjana Gsovsky gave him from what she remembered from her time in Russia.

Apparently the changes I had made with more modest resources were not all for the worse. Huge dark-blue beating wings accompanied Florimund and the Lilac fairy during the panorama and the curtain fell on a shower of meteors after the awakening. Koegler preferred my garland dance during which the princes arrived over Kenneth's and he liked the courtly formality of Cologne, but I have never felt that Koegler was somebody whose compliments I could trust. The actual performances were excellent apart from the Carabosse of Gise Furtwängler who played the role like an army captain with the odd 'Sieg Heil' thrown in. Ana Cardus, from Stuttgart, was technically fine as Aurora, although she danced without much excitement.

When Ashton saw me afterwards he was very complimentary though tactfully never mentioned the dancers. Subsequently I was invited to have lunch with him in London. I had grand visions of eating at the Savoy. Instead I was met at the stage door of the Royal Opera House by Michael Somes, and my delusions of grandeur were quickly deflated. He directed me to the staff canteen for fish and chips with Fred, for which I ended up having to pay for us both. Fred really could be mean. After he retired as director I still had to visit him at his house in Chelsea to agree casting for his ballets. I was never offered a cup of tea, nothing. Only once, when I arrived in a terrible state of shock as I had just witnessed a child run over in a motor accident, did Fred behave any more generously. He offered me some sherry – half a glass. A small glass. Over our battered cod Ashton asked me to work with him as producer of *The Sleeping Beauty* as he just wanted to rechoreograph certain parts of it anew. At the time it seemed everybody was impatient for a new production. The existing one, by Ninette de Valois and designed by Oliver Messel, was nearly 25 years old, produced for the reopening of the Royal Opera House in 1946. It had achieved near mythical status, but having been performed all round the world it was looking very tired. During my time as ballet master in Stuttgart, in 1964 the Royal Ballet's touring company brought a cut-down version of this *Sleeping Beauty* to the city. The Stuttgart dancers, who at that stage did not have great belief in themselves as a great classical company, were not impressed, rightly so. The quality of the dancing and the production were much compromised in its circumstances reduced for touring. The ballet lacked logic on repeated viewings.

The Sleeping Beauty is a huge test of a designer's practical skill and imagination. I cannot pretend to have totally admired Messel's designs for it. Compared to the decidedly modest staging that de Valois undertook in 1939 at Sadler's Wells theatre, with its functional sets and muted costumes by Nadia Benois, coming six years after the privations of war, the Messel *Beauty* – as it came to be known since his name was printed in larger type on the poster than those of Petipa or Tchaikovsky – was the ultimate in luxurious spectacle. For an audience living still with rationing it was a fantastic display, the epitome of sophistication. Messel's trademark was clashing colours, claret and sage green, turquoise and yellow, pink and orange. For his sets, his sources included architectural perspectives by the Bibiena family and the delicate landscapes of Jean-Antoine Watteau. The vision scene in the second act always seemed to me to be from another ballet with its elongated, semi-abstract trees. The first act was always my favourite in terms of action as we at last got to see Aurora. I did think it was a bit much, however, that having already waited through the prologue and then a whole scene with those wretched knitting ladies – I do not include them any more as I got so fed up with them – and then the waltz, finally, when we got a glimpse of Aurora, in arabesque framed briefly in a rose arch high up in the centre of the back-cloth, she disappeared. True, she did reappear almost immediately at the top of a sequence of rostra, all eyes looking at her, but unfortunately, for technical reasons I believe, the rose arch was soon abandoned. That initial impression of Aurora was never nearly as effective afterwards. I knew in fact that it was Ashton who had arranged that entrance back in 1946 and he was very upset when the designers of our new produc-tion in 1968, Lila de Nobili and Henry Bardon, were unable to achieve the same effect. There is always a carry-on about Aurora's first entrance, which is such an important theatrical moment. Not Lila, or Peter Farmer nor subsequently Philip Prowse; nobody has ever got it right for me. As designed by Lila, Aurora was seen initially on a balcony on top of what some critics mistook for the palace stables. An unimpressive stable yard was no place for a royal birthday party, they complained.

Lila was commissioned as designer by Fred on the strength of her work for *Ondine* a decade before. That was a ballet which to me was not so great as people thought, except for Margot Fonteyn and with Alexander Grant whirling and twirling as Tirrenio. The score was the problem for me: I could not love it at all. I originally liked Lila's designs, but when they were revived in 1988 without her involvement they looked unfinished and too dark. Lila had her own strong ideas, some of them misjudged. This made things difficult for me as producer. Fred expressed no ideas of his own. The romanticised gothic style was Lila's choice, based on Gustave Doré's illustrations of Charles Perrault's fairytales. Fred just accepted it. When I queried with him how to get over the anomaly of the hunting scene, where the dances are all eighteenth-century country dances, Fred just said, 'It's a fairy story. Just do it.' I was not to worry about anachronistic medieval mazurkas. I was pleased and honoured to have been asked to collaborate with Fred, but it was evident that it was down to me to make it all work. I realised that although he, as director of the company required me to consult him on artistic matters, in fact he preferred me to work direct with Lila in Paris, where she was based.

Besides the costumes which are credited to her, Lila also designed the set for the prologue and the last act. For the rest, Henry Bardon, a very good scene painter and technical assistant who was her associate, carried out her wishes. He adored her and was absolutely under her spell. She said, 'I have got Henry because I can't cope with a big show,' although she had in fact designed many operas, particularly for Franco Zeffirelli.

Lila was incredibly kind and generous, with little money, little because she gave it away to beggars. Lila also gave many of her costume designs to members of the wardrobe staff. They subsequently turned up in New York galleries with astronomical price tags attached. I only discovered after the show went on that Lila had nothing left from her fee because she had been paying for her own travel costs between Paris and London. Apparently these, and her huge telephone bill connected with the production, had not been written into her contract and so she paid for them herself.

During preparations I went seven times to Paris to see Lila's work in progress. Where Lila lived in three rooms was positively Dickensian. She cared for her mother there. After Lila retired as a designer she became fascinated with plumbing. She hated extravagance. Usually when invited out to eat at top Parisian restaurants, Lila would order just a few potatoes. Fred never went over to Paris. The more I did, the lazier he got. He was a nightmare, but that summer Fred had been informed that he would not be continuing as director of the company. He would be retiring in two years' time. That autumn he unveiled *Enigma Variations*, suffused with nostalgia, but involved himself with *Beauty* as little as possible.

Fred wished to wait until he could see the sets fully lit on the stage, though he was keen to see the ballerinas' costumes once the final fittings had taken place. That meant storing up trouble, big trouble. The company was quite frankly very unhappy in their costumes. The court outfits were made on 1880s styled corsets from which the dancers soon managed to remove the boning to make them less constricting. For the fairies and their attendants, the girls complained not only of long skirts imposed by Lila to convey a sense of period, but bodices shaped by two pads of foam rubber. It had the effect of giving the dancers little tummies, something they loathed. Nor did they like the curved hip-pads which gave shape to their skirts. These were made up with five layered underskirts, in silk and different thicknesses of net. The skirts got shortened by the day.

I loved rehearsing with Deanne Bergsma as the Lilac fairy – but poor Danny. She had become famous for her rendering of the role, dressed in a short tutu in which it was possible to dance her solo in the prologue. However, I had the idea of making Carabosse and the Lilac fairy into symbolic figures representing evil and goodness. I had always wanted the Lilac fairy to be more of a mime role with a big dress as a counterpoint to Carabosse, as in the original. Lila created a knee-length costume with wings which did look more substantial and right for the character with layered underskirts of pink-grey stiff net under a skirt of crinkled silver fabric decorated with sequins, pearls, brilliants and flowers. It looked lovely but was wrong for all the difficult jumps and turns the character has to execute. I think Danny had quite a rough ride with it. Nevertheless, she was excellent at the end of the second act in the mime scene with the queen after the awakening. I cast Pamela May as the queen where her natural elegance was seen to great advantage. Ultimately, however, the fairies' skirts were changed back to tutus but they still attached to the longer bodices designed for the skirts so the compromise looked poorly proportioned. The cavaliers had blue face make-up which became a joke among the boys. Lila's designs were, however, full of many imaginative touches. One very clever idea was a bird's nest that had been built during the hundred years' sleep on top of Cattalabutte's ermine cap, worn by Stanley Holden. Such was Lila's attention to detail it was made from real twigs, raffia and feathers. The Songbird fairy, originally Ann Jenner, had a head-dress with jewelled birds that appeared to float above her head. However imaginative such details are, they cannot really be seen by the audience. For the awakening scene we decided against having the courtiers emerge from their slumbers in clothes that had somehow been magically preserved over the passage of time. Lila designed costumes that clearly showed signs of decay, dyed, sprayed and painted in tones of pale blue, turquoise and ochre to give a deliberately dusty quality.

Rostislav Doboujinsky, who went on to work on the film of *The Tales of Beatrix Potter*, designed the heraldry as well as the animal masks and costumes. The wolf that chases Red Riding Hood had a Robin Hood red felt hat cheekily perched between his ears. Besides the usual rats and mice, Carabosse's retinue also included grotesque toads, frogs and dwarves. One change I wanted to make was for Carabosse to be played by a woman. Previously the role was associated with Robert Helpmann and Ray Powell, but I saw Carabosse as a beautiful woman, no longer young but rather like Myrtha in *Giselle*, though embodying a different sort of evil. I cast Julia Farron. She always made her presence felt in solo roles which she considered her forte. She did them terribly well and was a great performer. Julia was a strong Carabosse, stronger even than Monica Mason in the part later, but she needed to be. How she suffered with what I put her through. Lila had a fixation about Carabosse having a lizard's tail. When I queried how this would be visible against her long skirt, Lila just said she would make it visible. I wanted Carabosse to make a flying exit at one point but her tail just drooped flaccidly as she did so. I cut the flying. Instead I had Carabosse disappear down a trapdoor, big skirt, big sleeves, tail and all. I kept that. How Julia shouted and screamed as she descended through the trapdoor. She had a voice that could be heard anywhere. Fred just said to me, 'Do tell Julia to shut her trap.'

The production turned out to be full of conflict. The lighting designer was Bill Bundy who had never got on with Lila. They had worked together on Zeffirelli's Covent Garden *Rigoletto* a few years previously, and Bill was always determined to exert his authority over Lila to the extent that he purposely seemed to make her requests impossible. After one meeting, Lila never came to another lighting rehearsal. So many people felt they had the right to voice their opinions when I changed anything. Michael Somes, Jack Hart, Ashton's adjutants, and the ballet mistress Jill Gregory, one of the few women in the company who had resisted Hart, were particularly discouraging about details I wanted to alter. Somes and Hart did not want to change a step from what Madam had done in 1946. There were terrible rows onstage. Poor Fred was verbally attacked by Somes while choreographing a new garland dance. Somes told Fred, 'That was rubbish! Start again.' Fred could see what was wrong but happy enough for other people to take over. Things really reached a bad state when, at the end of the first full stage rehearsal with the orchestra, we had to go into overtime as the growing trees at the end of the first act just would not grow. Somes and Hart never usually got on with each other, but on this occasion they ganged up and attacked me in front of the rest of the company. They accused me of going beyond my brief and ruining the ballet. Fred for once opened his mouth. He told Somes he had gone too far and ordered him to leave. I was by then convulsed with terrible nerves and rage and made my way to the office of the general director, John Tooley, across the other side of Floral Street. He tried to calm me down with the help of a glass of sherry as, shaking, I told him that unless those two monsters, the worst nightmare of my professional life, were kept out of my rehearsals I would withdraw my services. All praise to John who, realising that I was serious, took action and I never saw the pair again.

I did make certain changes after seeing the ballet in performance. In the first act, I had reallocated the music for Aurora's friends' second dance to a group of courtiers, while the rest of the court moved off as if to be served refreshments. This left the stage emptier for Aurora's coda when she discovers the old woman with the spindle. It also seemed to me to be more dramatic when the courtiers were called back to find Aurora prostrate on the floor, as if dead. Actually it was distracting, and confused audiences and critics alike. But for once, surprisingly, Somes approved. He thought this was a brilliant touch. More true to form, Michael did upset me very much when during the run I discovered he had persuaded Fred to cut a most moving section of mime I had introduced where the queen expressed her despair at the apparent death of Aurora. The superb music, not usually performed, fitted beautifully and paved the way for the transformation of the old woman into the triumphant Carabosse. I actually think it was one of the things I got right and have since included it in my productions in Amsterdam, Birmingham and now Budapest.

Although Fred's choreography has had a huge influence on me professionally, I was never close to him personally. During his wartime days as an intelligence officer in the RAF he came to Wimbledon to see a performance by Ballets Jooss, not that he liked his style of work. After the performance he came backstage and I was introduced to him. He smiled at me in that typically homosexual way. I was very embarrassed, particularly when he gave me a camp little wave of the hand as he left.

Many years later, my relationship with Fred during the rehearsal period for that *Sleeping Beauty* was difficult to define. Gradually he made it pretty clear that he wanted to restrict his contribution to new choreography. Besides the new waltz, which with its circling formations which recalled a maypole dance and provided a way to introduce the four princes, two individually and the remaining pair together, in a huff at discovering a rival, Fred choreographed a new fairy solo in the prologue, a solo for the prince in the second act to music interpolated from the last where Fred also contributed a new pas de trois. His most enduring addition was an awakening pas de deux to close the second act. That scene usually concludes when after the kiss everyone awakes and then runs forward into a tableau and makes a gesture of triumph as the curtain falls. It really is so unsatisfying. When the ballet was first presented in St Petersburg the story was not made much of. The dancers are what Petipa wished to show the audience. But when *The Sleeping Beauty* was first presented in the west by Diaghilev, and by de Valois at both Sadler's Wells and Covent Garden, the story and mime were made more of. There was more sense of theatre generally.

I had discovered a most wonderful, romantic section of the score, the entr'acte, part of the prince's journey, a musical sequence that was usually cut. Tchaikovsky, I believe, supplied too much music here and for the panorama, but not wanting to waste a good tune reused it for the theme where the Christmas tree grows in *The Nutcracker*. Usually, in productions of *The Sleeping Beauty* the climactic moment of the awakening of Aurora and how she falls in love with the prince is usually over and done with in about three minutes. Like countless others I am sure, I have always felt short-changed by this. I asked Fred, therefore, if he would consider creating an awakening pas de deux using the beautifully lyrical music I was suggesting. I went armed with a record and played it through with him. He loved it and asked to listen again. He then proceeded to enact Aurora opening her eyes, reacting to the prince, being nervous and shy. Then Fred said he had heard enough. He loved the idea and agreed to do it. There was always a good feeling in the house when the curtain came down after that pas de deux.

From Fred I did learn how to absorb music before starting to create dances. That is, dances that become the music, not which are created to it. I learned too about contrast. Even if the music is all one level, it is important to create a contrast to keep the audience involved. The contrast in classical ballets between mime scenes and pas d'action is very important for this reason. Never compete with the music. Never be averse to borrowing steps from others. Ashton used to say all the steps are to be found in Enrico Cecchetti's teaching methods, the great Italian dance virtuoso – the original Carabosse and bluebird in the first *Sleeping Beauty* – and later a teacher whose approach was formalised as the Cecchetti method, important to Ninette de Valois and Marie

Rambert alike. The trick, as Fred said, was just making this basic lexicon of steps your own by the way they were executed.

Another fundamental was never to exaggerate. Ashton had been bemused by the cool reaction to *The Two Pigeons*. It was criticised for not being contemporary. This was 1961, and the new wave of kitchen sink drama depicting rape, domestic violence and every previously taboo subject was finding its way into ballet too. Ashton believed, however, that ballet was not primarily about ideas or trends. Concepts or subjects did not necessarily make for good choreography. For him, ballet was primarily a matter of how choreography is crafted, which is what makes Ashton's ballets endure and ultimately achieve classic status. In the case of *Cinderella*, I loved Fred's ballet when it was new in 1948. I knew the story first as a panto when I saw it four years earlier at the Winter Garden in Drury Lane, site of today's New London theatre, with Hermione Baddeley as Minnie, one of the ugly sisters. Prudence Hyman was the fairy godmother, waving her wand. She was an established dancer who could do everything, or so I thought in those days. Over the years I found Fred's *Cinderella* a tiresome ballet. Perhaps I saw it too much – and the company danced it too often, though not as much as *The Sleeping Beauty* which used to play six-week seasons of seven shows per week. Fred's *Cinderella* is not, I think, a ballet that will come back again until it is completely redesigned.

The prologue for *The Sleeping Beauty* was imagined by Lila as the queen's levée and set it in her bedroom, recovering from the birth of her daughter Aurora. This proved very problematic. To fill all the processional music, Lila suggested a parade that included a goat which was symbolic of nourishment for the growth of the baby. It pooped on the stage of course and had to go. Lila had the idea too of the fairies arriving as if descending a moonbeam, which was impressive to watch for the audience. The intention was for them to glide down on an escalator which, when costed, proved to be much too expensive. In practice we had to make do with a semi-transparent piece of scenery lit to look like a moonbeam. The slope it hid was precarious for the dancers.

There were other times when I was not sure quite what Lila intended. She wanted a real fire in the hunt scene, but I remember telling David Ashmole, who was still a student and appearing as a page, that I could not really tell him exactly what to do as I did not know. David was very polite. 'Oh I can light a fire. Just tell me when and where and how to get off,' he said. We had problems too with the other animals that Lila wanted. One idea that did not get beyond the dress rehearsal was for Florimund to arrive on horseback for the hunt. Donald MacLeary in the first cast was a brilliant rider and could manage a horse beautifully. Most others cast in the role, Keith Rosson included, were terrified of the idea. The horse, an old cart nag that Bill Bundy had found somewhere, was certainly not the white Arabian stallion I was expecting. It clomped over the different levels of the set which were built of wood, looking and sounding awful. The horse went as well. The panorama when the Lilac fairy guides Florimund on his journey to Aurora did impress, at least when the boat consented to move, but by the time we reached that point, I confess I had gone too far. Behind a gauze you could see a magic light which revealed the Lilac fairy, actually Danny Bergsma with a lighted sparkler on the end of her wand. All very tiresome for poor Danny who struggled to control her hysterics while waving this wretched child's firework at the prince. The second stage call pulled me to my senses and I cut it.

At the final dress rehearsal we had four Auroras onstage, all rehearsing the rose adagio at the same time. It was the only chance they got in costume and with the orchestra. There were princes all over the place. We muddled through. At the end of the first act, as the court was put to sleep, bits of forest grew at the sides of the stage, but it never worked as I intended it should. It looked okay, no more than that. The staging was too complicated and involved for the mechanics of the stage at that time. The panorama sequence had underground grottoes which always needed more time than we had to get them set up, so they had to be simplified. I have had many disasters with that scene. In Munich some years later, Peter Farmer designed a magical bird that was to be worked by four boys but the production department refused to build it. In the end I had people running around with big feathers. Now I think this scene works best in my Birmingham staging if we could only get the lighting better. For the awakening, it was Lila's idea to position the sleeping Aurora at the top of the castle, the walls of which the prince has to scale. As he kissed her awake everything disappeared into nothingness, which was an amazing moment although difficult to achieve. Aurora and her prince appeared to be suspended wonderfully in space, alone.

As it turned out, many of Lila's ideas proved unpopular. Carabosse first appeared out of a huge fireplace in an explosion of dry ice. She was surrounded by real dwarves and midgets. They were a nightmare. I learned that you should never mix the two, they behave horribly towards each other. One dwarf confided in me saying, 'You know I have got a really big cock.' When Margot Fonteyn appeared in the production, she refused to perform alongside them. We had to use pupils from White Lodge instead. Nor did the critics like Lila's idea of a castle tower becoming transparent to reveal a gloating Carabosse casting spells amid flames after Aurora had pricked her finger. The hunt scene was not much liked either for appearing to take place in a quarry or what certain reviewers likened to Wookey Hole. For the last act, Lila set the wedding celebration in a russet-coloured marquee, arguing the court would not have had the time to rebuild the palace after the hundred years' sleep, which was a logical enough idea. Her costumes though were the same colour as the marquee and so the dancers tended to disappear.

This *Sleeping Beauty* had a bumpy ride in America the following year. It had a very mixed reception. The public loved it, especially when Fonteyn appeared with Rudolf Nureyev. Unfortunately, it had been my wish to restore the music used for the divertissement featuring the three Ivans to its original place in the score in the last act. That meant taking it away from the grand pas de deux where it had been previously used as the coda. New Yorkers appeared to accept this change until Fonteyn and Nureyev appeared. A large gang in the gallery planned a protest, so when the music started following Aurora's solo, they burst into a deafening, concerted shout of 'Margot, Rudi', on and on through 32 bars of music until their reappearance when they burst into applause with which the rest of the house joined. You can only learn from this sort of episode. Although I was being faithful to Tchaikovsky and Petipa, and the first complete staging by Sadler's Wells Ballet in 1939, Fred and I decided that on balance it was more important for the grand pas de deux to have a coda to give it a proper sense of completion. I made the change at the next revival, a change that I have also included in my various other productions over the years.

My considered view is that, much as I loved and admired Lila da Nobili, she was not the right choice for *The Sleeping Beauty*. Petipa and Tchaikovsky's original took place during the hundred or so years spanning the 1700s. This was not Lila's favourite period, so that is why she insisted on going back to the Middle Ages as seen through the eyes of nineteenth-century medievalism which she did love. For me, Petipa and tutus go together in the same way as the polonaise and court dances in the hunting scene. I was also to blame in some ways as I am a romantic at heart, but the Petipa *Sleeping Beauty* had not originally been conceived as a romantic ballet, rather as a showcase for the magnificent Mariinsky dancers and the wonders of the imperial theatre. Most of all, it revealed Petipa's beautiful and inventive choreography. *The Sleeping Beauty* was created, however, in the 19th century in Russia with a huge company in a vast state theatre. *The Sleeping Beauty* can never have worked in the 21st century as originally conceived when performed by a company half the size and on a much smaller stage. It is because of this I have found *Sleeping Beauty* to be far the most challenging of the classics that I have attempted.

I really suffered a lot mounting the production in 1968 and rather felt like the fool for stepping in where angels feared to tread. The production was performed only 66 times over the course of three revivals. Compare that to the longevity of the previous Messel production from 1946 – some 23 years. As I worked on the production with Fred, the expectation was that it would last as long. When the critics saw the finished result their response was gloom at the prospect of it lasting anywhere near as long. In the event, things came to an end much sooner than that, after Kenneth MacMillan became director in 1970. Dalal Achcar, a close friend of Margot Fonteyn, was underwriting a tour to South America and she stipulated that *The Sleeping Beauty* must be included as it was a ballet that was not much staged there. As it was not possible to take Lila's complex sets to any of the planned venues, Kenneth had to create a new production in a very short space of time. It was not something that he involved himself with very much. He was busy with another new production and in a bad way healthwise. The intended designs by Beni Montresor – red, white and blue with lots of silver, strange props and different levels to the set – simply did not work. Peter Farmer was brought in to produce alternatives. Kenneth simply gave the cast list to Peter, but that was all. Having already undertaken a modest production with me in Cologne, Peter knew it would be impossible to replicate any of the tremendous grandeur that Kenneth had conceived for his staging in Berlin, designed by Barry Kay, in such a short time. This was dropped after only a few performances due to its enormous complexity and size.

Peter had only about six weeks to design a production that would normally require at least a year to complete. Sadly it was all too rushed. Inevitably, the production was rather thrown on but it was able to tour to Brazil. This was during Peter's blue period and what he produced was not great but the way the curtains billowed in the awakening scene was beautiful, an effect he repeated for me in Munich some three years later. But the production by Kenneth was performed only 38 times.

Petipa created *The Sleeping Beauty* as a showpiece. Some of the guests at the christening scene were played by actual courtiers from St Petersburg, which is partly why there is so much processional music. Those scenes are beyond the resources of most companies. When I did it in Munich in November 1976 on the big stage of the vast national theatre there, Peter designed a whole sequence of characters, including a bishop and his retinue and a succession of ambassadors, who paid their respects to the royal family in an attempt to fill out the music.

There were other dramas in Munich too. The company's prima ballerina Konstanze Vernon – or Connie as she was known – was not in town but she made it clear that she expected to be first cast. I had different ideas as Konstanze's technique was not right for Aurora. In fact I would have loved to cast her as Carabosse. I decided on another dancer as Aurora, Gislinde Skrobin, who although a little on the plump side, had proved herself when I had previously staged *Giselle* there. She had the personality and feet for Aurora. I made it clear to her, however, that she must lose some weight. From afar Connie issued threats but Gislinde was working hard although it was evident that she was gaining rather than losing weight. She was in a nervous state and unfortunately part of her weight problem was alcohol related. When Connie reappeared she insisted on her ballerina's rights. I simply told her I could cast whomever I chose, at which Connie promptly injured her foot to explain her non-appearance in the role to 'her public'. I really do not think they were much concerned.

I had a lovely first night telegram from the Royal Ballet wishing me a Wright success but the production went only moderately well. One newspaper review was headlined 'Bombastisch wie Old-Hollywood' which with my still limited German was clear enough for me to understand.

Gislinde Skrobin managed to appear as Aurora but hers was not a good performance. Peter's designs, however attractive on paper, did not match his usual standards onstage. He had somehow chosen materials for the costumes that were too shiny. The effect was of cheap satin. Nevertheless, the production stayed in the repertoire for 26 years. It was due to be succeeded in 2003 with a new one by Anthony Dowell designed by David Roger, but that never reached the stage as the Munich opera house suffered a huge cut in funding. Peter's sets and costumes were pressed into service again when Ivan Liška and Irina Jacobson put on a very traditional, stop-gap staging.

With my own productions I could always rely on Claudia Algeranova, the company secretary in Munch, to fill me in on what state they were in. She really had a director's eye capable of assessing which dancers were not fully committed or feigning injuries, who was genuinely struggling with certain steps, who needed extra support – and importantly what audiences really thought. As a former ballerina, Claudie always thought that she was right about details of choreography that I had got wrong. 'No Claudie, I am Wright,' I would insist. 'No Peter, you are Wrong,' Claudie would counter. It still remains a joke between us all these years later.

I next produced *The Sleeping Beauty* for Dutch National Ballet in 1981. I admired the company, run then by Rudi van Dantzig, and they had a lot of good works in their repertoire. He was wonderfully supportive and excited to have a new *Sleeping Beauty*. I do love Amsterdam, having worked there previously in 1977 when I did *Giselle*. Han Ebbelaar and Alexandra Radius – Han and Lex – were the principals on both occasions, very different in the roles and genuinely classical in style. The production looked good in the relatively small stadsschouwburg theatre. There was a wonderful atmosphere there. I was relieved that Amsterdam did not have the same union overtime restrictions as in Britain. There is no cut-off time for the orchestra unlike here where, if you go over the three-hour limit, you automatically have to pay overtime to all staff, not just the orchestra but dancers and front-of-house too. Although I have always sought to prune *The Sleeping Beauty*, I did always want to include an awakening pas de deux as I had persuaded Fred to do at Covent Garden in 1968. That was something that he choreographed very beautifully. However, Dutch National was not a wealthy company and could not afford the royalties required to use Fred's choreography, so I ended up

choreographing a new pas de deux myself. Fred's was more formal and
courtly, similar to what the audience was yet to see in the last act, than
my more romantic attempt which has now become very popular. The
music was the entr'acte from the second act which provides a dramatic
and emotionally logical end to the act.

For Amsterdam I chose Philip Prowse as designer because of his very
good knowledge of period. Earlier in his career he did the costumes
for Rudolf Nureyev's stagings of *La Bayadère* and the pas de six from
Laurencia at Covent Garden, as well as *The Nutcracker* with its backdrop
of dangling Smarties for the kingdom of sweets at Peter Darrell's Scottish
Ballet. He also designed a *Swan Lake* produced by Geoffrey Cauley in
Zurich. Philip had a parallel career as a director, of the Glasgow Citizens
where he designed and directed many plays. He has the most wonderful
sense of theatre. He recognised, however, that he did not have any choreographic ability and so could never produce a ballet himself, otherwise he
would have put me out of a job. This is why he was still willing to design
ballets without assuming any of the producer's responsibilities. With
ballet he recognises that it is the designer's job to work in close collaboration with the choreographer's vision. In that respect he was marvellous
to work with and he contributed so much to *The Sleeping Beauty*, from
Carabosse's entrance to her frustrated final exit. Philip used to joke that
designing for dance was a holiday for him. His job was only to make everything look lovely, after which he would put his feet up in the stalls and
watch everybody else worrying about the technical problems. Totally
untrue of course, he never stopped slaving away, determined to get every
last detail of the sets and costumes absolutely perfect.

I first met Philip when he came to Stuttgart when Kenneth MacMillan
was staging *Diversions* there, with Philip's designs. The Stuttgart company
found the ballet very difficult technically which did not help the atmosphere, but John Cranko and Philip did not get on with each other. They
bitched the whole time but Philip did produce some designs for a gala in
Stuttgart. I had always found Philip's work to be very inspiring. When
we worked together in Amsterdam, however, I could not understand
his first designs at all. They were very abstract. After he had calmed
down his approach the final designs proved to be very grand and elabo-
rate, with wonderful period detail in both the scenery and costumes.
His sets glowed with a beautiful coppery gold sheen and established the

milieu of the court of Louis XIV, the sun king, in an instant. His courtiers were beautifully coiffured and clothed. Philip was amazing in what he managed to get onstage at the stadsschouwburg, which is relatively small. The production was probably too big for the theatre but it did look wonderful and it is still in the repertoire 35 years later. It had to be remade when it moved into Amsterdam's new muziektheater which is larger but has ghastly sightlines.

Philip designed long, sweeping dresses for the Lilac fairy and Carabosse, which worked well to establish their authority as representative figures of good and evil. Joanne Zimmermann was Carabosse. She absolutely terrified me. She had an icy, freezing stare that transfixed you. In fact she had this all the time, not just in performance, which was quite unintentional. In fact she had a lovely smile and was very friendly. She performed all the mime wonderfully. Mea Venema, who now assists Hans van Manen, was the Lilac fairy. She had the most beautiful and warm personality in the role, a complete contrast to Joanne. They both loved doing their roles. Our *Sleeping Beauty* knocked Amsterdam sideways. We were the talk of the town, well at least the theatre-going town. Hans was crazy about the classicism of the ballet. That was such a relief as the previous production of the ballet staged by Roland Casenave and designed by Norman McDowell, based on an earlier version by Bronislava Nijinska and Robert Helpmann for the Grand Ballet du Marquis de Cuevas, had not been successful. As a consequence, *The Sleeping Beauty* itself had a bad name in Amsterdam. So successful was our production that it was televised.

John Tooley came over from London to see it live and was horrified at the prospect of me adopting it back in Britain for Sadler's Wells Royal Ballet. 'You cannot tour that,' he said, but it was a staging that was made to tour although we had to slim down some of the costumes over the years. Initially when we did put the production on in Birmingham in 1984 Anita Landa was utterly swamped by all the swags and layers of the queen's voluminous robes. She is always the ultimate professional, totally dedicated to dance. Anita did so much for me and I admired her when she was a principal with London Festival Ballet. Her life has been spent on tour. Married to Michael Hogan for many years, Anita is loving and giving, totally Spanish. She laughs, she cries and expects the highest standards from everybody. She is always well turned out, standing in fourth position in her high heels giving company class. She was excellent as the queen in *Sleeping Beauty* and wonderful as the queen mother in *Swan Lake*. She knew exactly how to make an entrance and make an exit.

When *The Sleeping Beauty* was new in 1984 it cost £150,000. Tooley had never let us spend so much on a touring production before. Nowadays it would be at least seven times that, a figure which is beyond the resources of Birmingham Royal Ballet and indeed many other companies. But it always sells extremely well. Companies are still keen to have *The Sleeping Beauty* in their repertoires, and buying in an established and recognised production is one way of managing the risk and expense, which was the case when the Hungarian National Ballet acquired my production in Budapest in April 2016. Yes, I am still at it and just managed to get it on there thanks to Denis Bonner who knows my productions well and has assisted me enormously around the world. Miyako Yoshida, one of the best Auroras ever, coached the principals. Denis and Miyako worked for several weeks on their own and my role is to fine-tune the details ready for the stage rehearsals. I have to say that by the time I arrive, most of the work has already been done beautifully and accurately.

I had been to Budapest before, in the 1970s when Kenneth MacMillan was director of the Royal Ballet. We had quite a time getting there as Kenneth would not fly. We went to see *Spartacus* by László Seregi, that marvellous director, a production that is still in the repertoire. He had created his version of *Spartacus* in 1968, the same year as the more famous version by Yuri Grigorovich for the Bolshoi. Our intention was to see whether we could acquire the ballet for Covent Garden. Maina Gielgud was in it – she later staged it when she was director of Australian Ballet – and Seregi's ballet was very good, certainly much better than the Bolshoi's. It was, however, too big for the Royal Ballet. As compensation, in Budapest I do remember the lovely Bull's Blood wine from the Eger region of Hungary – delicious!

Of all the great ballerina roles, Aurora is the toughest. When I first saw Margot Fonteyn in the role I was in a state of near ecstasy, really knocked out by her detailed and magical performance. I had never seen a ballerina who could balance so well that it made you hold your breath. She really could portray a character and bring out the different aspects of the role. I had liked her since I had seen her as the flower seller, one of her first leading roles, in Ashton's *Nocturne* at the Prince's theatre during the war when, in a grey, threadbare bodice and white skirt, her simplicity, sadness and purity impressed me hugely. Like most films of her, the recordings of Fonteyn as Aurora do not really capture her special qualities. In fact it took her a long while to really conquer the part but she was to become the greatest Aurora ever. She developed the role, first seen as a young princess shyly making her public debut and being courted by the four princes in the first act, then in the dream sequence in the following act when she has the most moving spiritual quality before awakening to love and finally becoming a mature and beautiful woman as she is married in the last act. She portrayed a real sense of character, unlike many Auroras who, although they dance the role well, show no real development and remain flatly one-dimensional all the way through. Others approach it too much as a gymnastic display. Few Auroras really find all the variety and sense of development in the character. But then Margot did have the benefit of Frederick Ashton to rehearse her.

I quite liked Moira Shearer. She was stronger than Fonteyn and could do all the quick sections but her manner was more artificial. Alina Cojocaru was good and could have been very good, but she did it too much in her own way. Had she worked with her coach more closely she had the potential to be wonderful. She was too much Alina dancing Aurora rather than Aurora being danced by Alina. Miyako Yoshida was lovely and so musical but not over dramatic. It took her a long time to understand about showing her emotions and using facial expressions, which Japanese people find difficult. She thought it was enough just to dance. I recall once rehearsing her as Odile in Hong Kong. I kept pushing her to give more. She was exquisite but not alluring, and without any passion. She ran off the stage in tears saying, 'Peter Wright, he hate me.' I did not hate her at all. She is practically the most exquisite dancer I have ever known and she was to become one of the most expressive and technically perfect ballerinas that I have worked with. She had the stamina that you need for *Swan Lake* as indeed she had for Aurora, so that nothing looked forced. I had not realised how much effort she put into her performances to make them look effortless. There was never any strain. Everything looked easy and light. That takes a lot of concentration and hidden muscle control.

The Sleeping Beauty is challenging for soloists and is the most challenging classic to bring to the stage successfully. It can become boring if it is not performed with great style and energy. I have come to the conclusion that if you cannot give it the full justice it demands with its intrinsic lavishness and technical standards, then it is better not to attempt it. I wonder how much has been spent over the years in the attempt at trying to do justice to the ballet. After his productions in Berlin and London, Kenneth did go on to mount a much longer-lived staging for American Ballet Theatre with designs by Nicholas Georgiadis, a staging that has been adopted by English National Ballet using Nico's costumes but with new sets, again by Peter Farmer. When Madam first saw my *Sleeping Beauty* for Sadler's Wells Royal Ballet with its designs by Philip Prowse, she told me, 'This is the production we should have at Covent Garden', praise indeed as her considered staging of the ballet, designed by David Walker, was still in the repertoire there. That staging was abandoned by Anthony Dowell, when as director he did his own production with Maria Bjørnson in 1994. In turn this was replaced when Ross Stretton took over the direction, inviting Natalia Makarova to mount a production designed by Luisa Spinatelli. This failed miserably due to the fact that the British have their own tradition with the great Russian classics which we know in different versions that stem from the productions staged by Sergeyev and de Valois here in the 1930s.

British dance has changed so much over the decades, but essentially the British way with classic ballets is so much lighter than the Russian approach, which is what made Makarova's approach so ill-suited for the Royal Ballet. I was appalled when I saw it, it lacked passion. Just look too at how heavy Rudolf Nureyev's production at La Scala was. Over the years, Royal Ballet productions have changed in interpretation and have reflected different influences, but when Monica Mason and Chris Newton took up the challenge of *The Sleeping Beauty* in 2006 at the Royal Opera House, visually they went back to the old Messel production of 1946, as modified by Peter Farmer. This is something I would never have done. Designers have to live, which is why I am sure Peter accepted the commission, but he was no admirer of Messel's abilities. Many costumes, as well as the sets for the panorama and awakening, were reworked by Peter. The costumes have been remade again subsequently – more expense – to make them closer to Messel's colour schemes, but sadly the mix has not worked. Messel was right for the austerity years after 1945 but he was not a period designer. For me he never displayed that essential quality needed for this ballet where the contrast of periods is integral to the development of the story. I consider returning to a production designed 60 years after it was designed a terrible waste of an opportunity. I feel the same about Ratmansky's decision with American Ballet Theatre to return to the designs of Léon Bakst from the Ballets Russes' 1921 production. As reinterpreted for today's eyes, too many compromises are required.

However successful in its day, what worked in 1921 – or in 1946 – is not necessarily right for today. Going back to the past in this way is retrograde. I believe productions of the classics do not go out of fashion and remain fresh if they operate within the periods that the ballets depict. I could never present *Giselle* as a modern girl who goes mad in a contemporary setting. I rely on the work of my designers. Philip Prowse is no great scenic painter so his designs are built to show off the piece they are framing. He does that miraculously and his designs do not detract at all. You gain the whole feeling of the ballet in just a moment with Philip's work, unlike that of a lot of designers more interested in beautiful details and the quality of their painterly effects. That may be interesting for a while, but they are not something that you want to look at repeatedly. Philip understands the construction of period costumes too. The cut of a bodice, for example, influences how a performer stands and moves and is important for giving a sense of authenticity. Philip's designs, and those of John Macfarlane, achieve that convincingly and are built to last. They are not works of art to be looked at in their own right or something which performers have to fight against, but display the artists onstage to perfection. With the classics the producer has much to do to make these works appealing to modern audiences while still maintaining the tradition and respecting the choreographic style. Returning to historical sources, you always run the risk that what you are presenting will look old – or at least old-fashioned. Beautifully rehearsed and wonderfully danced in Petipa's shining choreography, because of the old sets and costumes, at Covent Garden *The Sleeping Beauty* struggles on.

CHAPTER 11

⇾⇾⧽ ⧽⧼⧼

More classics, *Coppélia*, *The Nutcracker* and *Swan Lake*

I MUST HAVE PERFORMED in or seen *Coppélia* over a thousand times during my career. The first time that I staged a classic, or rather a part of one, was *Coppélia*. This was in 1958 in Chester when I was running the opera-ballet at Sadler's Wells Opera and staging choreographic excerpts at the Royal Academy of Dance's regional centres. I knew *Coppélia* extremely well as it was performed constantly by Sadler's Wells Theatre Ballet in Britain and overseas during the 1950s. I was not thinking of doing my own production but rather carrying out my brief to stage the third act with two of our dancers playing the leads. The theatre in Chester helped by loaning bits of scenery and some props. I just loved doing it.

When I next staged *Coppélia* in 1975 for Sadler's Wells Royal Ballet I again did not have much in the way of resources. I managed to get it on without any budget thanks to Lili Sobieralska, head of wardrobe, who borrowed bits of money from the maintenance allowance for other ballets so we could spend it on refurbishing the old sets and costumes for *Coppélia* by Osbert Lancaster. These were first made for Ninette de Valois' Covent Garden production over 20 years before. It had countless performances on tour under John Field and it did again in my resuscitated staging. The principal roles in *Coppélia*, if the mime and action are observed, provide wonderful opportunities for dancers to invest the characters with their own personalities. Brenda Last and Marion Tait spring to mind particularly as Swanilda with Alain Dubreuil and later Roland Price as Franz.

Coppélia was useful to help extend the company's technical range, but that production was tired. The board needed no convincing that money would soon be needed to be spent on a new staging. Years before, Madam had established a very good relationship with the stage design department at the Slade art school and had formed a design advisory committee at the Royal Opera House. Kenneth MacMillan had discovered Nicholas Georgiadis at the Slade which led to a long association beginning with *Danses concertantes*. Peter Snow later took over from Georgiadis as director of the Slade's stage design course for 25 years. His students included Derek Jarman, Yolanda Sonnabend and Philip Prowse. Peter asked me to give an informal lecture to students at the Slade about the rights and wrongs of designing for ballet. I went along with a dancer to show what impact a costume can have on supported pirouettes, lifts and enhancing the dancer's line. The students lapped it up but it was not possible to formalise this into anything more permanent because of the constant lack of time, space and money. It was a result of this involvement that I invited Peter to design *Coppélia* in 1979. Earlier in his career he designed for Joan Littlewood's Theatre Workshop at Stratford East and the first British production of Samuel Beckett's *Waiting for Godot* in 1955 – the same year that he designed Ashton's *Variations on a Theme by Purcell* at Covent Garden. I liked Peter's rather primitive style and his very strong use of colour. Some of his designs for *Coppélia* had the qualities of a child's painting.

With this particular ballet, a producer should respect the story, which is very good, and respond to the wonderful music. The difficulty with *Coppélia* is that it is a very classical and often sophisticated ballet, although the story is about real people. I used to invite Pamela May to coach the Swanildas. The role was one of her best. She had personality and danced with great panache and style, qualities that are needed in *Coppélia*. When I heard that Pamela was due to be in Japan as an examiner for the Royal Academy of Dance, I asked her to coach the Swanildas there too when I was staging *Coppélia* for Star Dancers Ballet. She was just brilliant with them. In my view, Dr Coppélius is not a foolish old man but is something more mysterious, elderly and forgetful. John Auld was always the best to embody these qualities. Roland Petit was a disturbingly menacing Coppélius in his own production, waltzing with the naked body of the doll that he has created, but his more sinister and heartless reading was one I did not like at all, however much I love the ballet itself. When

Galina Samsova was director of Scottish Ballet I let her acquire my production designed by Peter Snow for the company. The way they had
matured under her leadership and gained a sense of style suited *Coppélia*.
It was a pleasure to work with them.

I regard *Coppélia* very much as a classic. It has all the main ingredients including 90 percent of the choreography which is now recorded in
Benesh notation. I consider myself lucky to have had more than one go
at it, but it was really only my third attempt, working with Peter Farmer
in 1995, that I felt we had got it right. We managed to give it a sense
of period. Somehow the mixture of the beautiful and charming score,
the story by E. T. A. Hoffmann and the mixture of peasant-style dances
combined with the proper épaulement of the classical choreography –
which so suits Swanilda and her friends, as well as the dance of the hours'
divertissement – all makes for a satisfying whole. Added to that, I think I
managed to integrate the various mime scenes, in particular the extended
one between Coppélius and Franz when he gains entry into the toyshop
in search of Coppélia. All the gestures are based on what we know of the
original commedia dell'arte sequences, but I do believe that, as classical
ballet has developed and has been released from its very strict rules which
allow dancers to express themselves more, so the same is happening to
mime. The tendency in most companies these days is, I am afraid, to
abandon mime and replace it with usually inferior dance sequences. Yet
contrast is so important in dance. When done with humour or sadness,
or terror or love, mime can only hold audiences' attention. *Coppélia* is
certainly a ballet that does that.

Turning to another ballet inspired by a Hoffmann story, *The
Nutcracker*, it is perhaps surprising that this ballet, which balances the
books for countless companies worldwide, was once not so ubiquitous.
When I staged it at the Royal Opera House in 1984 it was not such a
fixture as now. Rudolf Nureyev's child's nightmare vision in 1968 was
the first by the Royal Ballet at Covent Garden. Then *The Nutcracker* was
more the province of London Festival Ballet. They responded with a new
Sleeping Beauty, the Royal's signature work. Rudi's *Nutcracker* only lasted
until 1977. Ashton's *Cinderella* and *La Fille mal gardée* were popular
Christmas alternatives at the time.

The Nutcracker is a ballet that tends to divide audiences. For many, it
is a once-a-year family excursion, a seasonal treat for tiny tots dressed

up in tulle and tiaras. Then there are others who consider their tastes too sophisticated to overdose on sugared almonds and the other sweets depicted in the magical kingdom. *The Nutcracker* is the exception among the classic ballets in that it never had a satisfactory story from the outset. This provides the producer with considerable scope. The original scenario was based on Hoffmann's *Nutcracker and the Mouse King* which was constructed like two separate stories with scarcely any connection. In the ballet, the leading characters do virtually no dancing and the leading dancers have virtually no place in the story. A producer has to decide who motivates the story, Clara or Drosselmeyer. Is Clara a ten-year-old interested in toys – or 16-year-old adolescent interested in boys? To what degree does the producer reconcile the two acts? How far does he indulge every small girl's identification with Clara and her desire to become the Sugar Plum fairy? That is a role to which many dancers aspire, and while companies may be able to field a dozen or so Sugar Plums during the course of a long Christmas season, it is a role that demands a real ballerina. Very few dancers have that. I like my Sugar Plums to be like fragile porcelain. Natalia Osipova danced it nicely when she joined the Royal Ballet in 2013 but she was too real. I could tell from the start she would not be ideal. She had style but was insufficiently regal. Since then her style has hardened. Seeing Lauren Cuthbertson as the Sugar Plum fairy in 2015 was a wonderful example of what real determination, hard work and patience can do. After all the years of injury and illness that Lauren has experienced, she took her place as a prima ballerina. She danced it to perfection. Her presence, confidence, musicality, virtuosity, speed and expression were astounding. I never wondered whether she would survive this toughest of all pas de deux and killer of a solo. You could see at once that the stage was hers. The more setbacks Lauren had, the more determined she was to overcome everything. As the Sugar Plum fairy, everything was judged just right. No forcing or straining – she looked as if she could do it all over again, full of sparkle, lightness and precision, a real achievement.

Adding to the appeal to producers and choreographers of *The Nutcracker* is that most of the original choreography by Lev Ivanov was lost, apart from the grand pas de deux and his notes for the snowflakes. How all these questions are answered will determine what the choreography, storytelling and design will be like. When I was asked by John

Tooley to undertake *The Nutcracker* for the Royal Ballet I had already had some exposure to it, choreographing some of it for Margaret Dale's version for television. I was familiar with Rudi's version designed by Nicholas Georgiadis, which was very heavy and rather peculiar. It had some good moments, but Nureyev's choreography was out of feeling for the period. In the waltz he used couples, where the women went down into splits on the floor to be pulled up into arabesque by their partners. Rudi redid the grand pas de deux where he had the ballerina balance on his extended leg held in arabesque. Of course all the ballerinas wanted to perform with him, but it was a tough show.

When asked to produce a new *Nutcracker* for Covent Garden, I had no intention of producing something tasteful for an opera house audience. I wanted to honour the spirit of the original by having a sense of period and bring the story to life. Above all, I wanted a sense of magic. I was very ambitious in how I wanted to exploit the theatre's mechanics to effect the transformations that are integral to this ballet, too ambitious as it turned out. At that time, ballets had not made much use of the stage lifts, though I was outdone the following year when Wayne Eagling made *Frankenstein, the Modern Prometheus*.

With *The Nutcracker* I found I also got bogged down in trying to be too authentic to Ivanov's choreography from 1892. Clement Crisp introduced me to Roland John Wiley, a musicologist at the University of Michigan whose primary interests are Tchaikovsky and Marius Petipa. It was Crisp who suggested that Wiley was the 'must see' person if I was seriously interested in the original *Nutcracker*. My idea was to understand how it was first performed and base it on that. I did an enormous amount of research with Wiley, which did not impress everybody. Frederick Ashton quipped that to be historically accurate I would need to employ ballerinas with 38-inch busts, not today's generation of flat-chested amazons.

The classics last because of the music and choreography. That is why they continue to come back. But judgments are still required. Some of the original choreography is really not that special – or no longer exists. I could not find any notation for the snowflakes, a pivotal scene where the ballet moves from reality into fantasy. There were patterns but no steps, evidently intended for 61 dancers, presumably a queen and five groups of 12 snowflakes. As I did not want to include a snow queen, I redid the patterns and invented my own steps. The result was quite different and much better, I believe, than what we knew of what went before. The choreography for the angels, who pass a lighted candle from one to the next in a line across the stage, was my invention, although this was inspired by a German nativity play that Ballets Jooss used to appear in during my days working in Essen. It certainly was not the invention of the designer, Julia Trevelyan Oman, as her husband, Roy Strong, has suggested.

The first act was a combination of sources. The children's dances and the battle scene are mine. The adult dances are based on de Valois' sharpening up of Nikolai Sergeyev's staging for the Vic-Wells Ballet in 1934. Like George Balanchine, I gave Drosselmeyer a nephew, whom I called Hans-Peter, who turns out to be the nutcracker prince, an element that featured in Hoffmann's story. Unlike many productions, I included dancing dolls at the Christmas party bursting out of pies, as happened in 1892, as well as a Vivandière doll, again something seen originally. This solo, although based on traditional sources, is by Joy Newton, a dancer from the early days of British ballet with the Vic-Wells company who became a teacher at the Royal and Turkish national schools. The truth is that nobody knows whether these were created by Ivanov or Petipa. All the business with the sleigh that carries Clara away with Drosselmeyer's nephew was my invention.

The sleighs – there were in fact three of them – were a nightmare to co-ordinate. I intended that the sleigh first came up on a lift with Drosselmeyer and circled the stage more. That got simplified when the sleigh kept breaking down. I lost count of the number of times I asked the stage manager, 'Have you charged those batteries?!' The act closed when the sleigh flew across the backdrop, a magical moment. Not so when at one performance the sleigh swung back into view and dangled miserably on the end of its wire. That is why that was cut. Getting the sleigh on and off as it arrived at the top of steps of the magical kingdom was practically impossible.

In the second act I omitted Mother Gigogne and her little children who emerge from her skirts, as I did not like the music or the character. It does not fit with the style of everything else. The floor patterns for the waltz of the flowers and the grand pas de deux are based on Ivanov's originals. Early in her career Pamela May had danced Ivanov's choreography and she helped me a lot in creating something in the same style. During my research I had seen a photograph of the first Sugar Plum fairy being pulled along by the prince while standing on a length of chiffon during their grand pas de deux. It seemed a nice idea, and Anthony Dowell and Lesley Collier spent a lot of time on it, but it was something that was dropped at the first revival. It never looked right. As the prince manipulated the chiffon he managed to pull parts of the flooring inset into the stage too, often to the sound of a skidding noise.

I had wanted Peter Farmer as designer, but that was a suggestion that did not find favour within the Royal Opera House. Lots of people had many other ideas about whom I should use. I settled on Julia Trevelyan Oman, whose work I knew. At Covent Garden she had designed *Eugene Onegin*, *La bohème* and *Die Fledermaus*. I had always liked her designs for *A Month in the Country* because of their light and space. I was principally familiar with her work for television. She designed Jonathan Miller's *Alice in Wonderland* and, when filmed at the BBC's Ealing studios, her set for the courtroom was the largest constructed there at that time. I was going to do a TV ballet with Julia but somehow that was one of those projects that did not come to fruition.

I got on well with Julia and Roy outside the theatre when Sonya and I were their guests at their home in Herefordshire. However, I soon found her really quite difficult, but then the best designers generally are demanding to work with. We had big tussles and difficult times. I was not alone. She was on the receiving end of much stage crew banter too. She was difficult with the scene painters who were replicating her design for the wallpaper, pulling out actual pattern books of the period which they were expected to translate exactly. Julia was renowned for her great authenticity, right down to how to turn the hem of a skirt for a particular era. She was very much the professor with a huge knowledge of period style. All her costume designs were accompanied by a historical reference. She had endless drawers of buttons and passmanterie.

During our preparations, we went to Nürnberg, where Drosselmeyer lived in Hoffmann's story, to absorb the local colour and provide Julia with source material and references. There she developed a passion for gingerbread figures, which ended up decorating the Christmas tree. Her original idea was for the set in the second act, which replicates the cake seen during the first act party, to be painted a particular shade of gingerbread. This was an idea not terribly well realised as the scenery was painted a rather bland shade of peach. The cake was in any case made from white filigree sugar icing, so the association was lost on audiences. When the production was restaged in 1999 I managed to get the set repainted to resemble the cake more closely, with additional silver gilding to give it more sparkle. It was quite a feat to accomplish the change, as Julia was so single-minded. Working with her, I came to realise that although she was extremely good at recognising lovely effects and references in her research she had no real fantasy. Julia could not show me a whole design for a complete setting for each act. As she had worked a lot in television, where only a corner of a room appears in a shot, and where the designer must ensure that everything visible is authentic, Julia was very good at showing me lots of corners filled with details from our excursion to Nürnberg. I learned in retrospect that her approach was similar to her designs for Ashton's *Enigma Variations* which is full of odd corners and wonderful detail.

The first night in 1984 was a gala in aid of the NSPCC, the children's charity, which the queen and many members of the royal family attended. This was only some six weeks after the premiere of my new *Sleeping Beauty* for Sadler's Wells Royal Ballet. Clearly I believed in putting myself under pressure as I was already busy with a new *Giselle* for Covent Garden the following March. For *The Nutcracker* I was much influenced by Hoffmann's conception of Drosselmeyer. There is a sadness about him, a solitary figure, old and unattractive with an eye patch that scares children. His nephew has been transformed into a wooden nutcracker by the evil king rat. Drosselmeyer attends his god-daughter Clara's party in the hope that she will be able to break the spell on his nephew. As she does so, Drosselmeyer rewards her with a journey to a magical world. This is essentially how I saw it when the production was new. I was horrified to discover in the programme for the royal premiere that another synopsis had been printed that did not tally with the stage action at all.

Vivien Duffield was the chief fundraising force for the Royal Opera House in those years and her partner Jocelyn Stevens was close to Roy Strong, Julia's husband. Donors and patrons sometimes, in their desire to be associated with a particular event, feel that it is their own production. Stevens had taken it upon himself to oversee the souvenir programme. It was certainly elegantly produced with gold embossing on the cover, set designs highlighted in gold ink, beautiful endpapers and a red ribbon as bookmark. I had not been involved, even though I had overall responsibility for the production, hence the inclusion of the wrong scenario, written by Roy Strong. Worse than that, although there were pages and pages listing patrons and donors, nowhere was there a mention of any of the cast. Performers' biographies were not included as is customary with the Royal Opera House's nightly programmes. Needless to say, there was no mention of me anywhere, nor of Gennady Rozhdestvensky, the conductor. But neither was Tchaikovsky mentioned, so at least we were in good company. I begged John Tooley that the programme be reprinted. For once a wrong was righted. Tooley had it redone with the correct synopsis, a decision no doubt helped by the fact that the British Printing and Communication Corporation was one of the sponsors. Thank heavens for sponsors.

I loved working with Rozhdestvensky. He was a really nice man and had conducted a lot of ballet. He was, however, used to the regime in the Soviet Union where the conductor was supreme. Rozhdestvensky would not budge on the tempo for the dance of the mirlitons. I had choreographed it at normal performing speed for dancers, but Rozhdestvensky knew the music as a folk tune from his childhood and conducted it that way – much too slowly and agony for the dancers.

The first night cast should have included Alessandra Ferri as Clara. She had already made her mark in Kenneth MacMilan's *Valley of Shadows* and earlier that year had enjoyed enormous success in her debut as Juliet. In fact I never got as far as doing anything with Alessandra as she went off to Milan to do Odette in a film of *Swan Lake* directed by Franco Zeffirelli. Which ballerina would not? They all like to be able to do everything. In the event, Julie Rose was a very sweet and pretty Clara, really quite charming. The cast had Lesley Collier as the Sugar Plum fairy and Anthony Dowell as her prince, John Auld as Drosselmeyer and a young Jonathan Cope as the rat king. A year later I decided to have Clara played by a student from the Royal Ballet School rather than a company dancer. A 13-year-old Sarah Wildor, still in her early training, was the first to perform the role that way. I changed to students because I felt Clara should be naive and guileless. Initially Sarah was awfully careful, whereas what I was looking for was spontaneous naivety. I had to jolly her performance along. When I thought there were no more suitable Claras in the school I changed back to young dancers in the company. I do feel that wonderful music to which Clara dances really needs to be expressed. For that you need a more established performer. That way the ballet has more heart and is an opportunity for audiences to experience a lovely expression of young love. As long as the production lasts I will keep it that way.

For the gala, the Royal Opera House looked glorious. Harvey Nicholls had provided the Christmas decorations. There were candle-covered trees in the crush bar; the tiers of the auditorium were ornamented with branches decked with cinnamon sticks, pomanders and gingerbread characters. The grand tier was ablaze with the fire of real diamonds. That evening ticket prices ranged up to £250 which now is sadly commonplace at the Royal Opera House, but over 30 years ago that was exceptional. £2,800 was charged to sit in the grand tier adjacent to the royal party. The evening raised £660,000 but gala audiences are notoriously more interested in themselves than what is happening onstage. The reaction during the first act was slow. It felt like the audience was sitting on its hands. After free interval champagne provided by Moët & Chandon the audience was much more enthusiastic and applauded everything in sight. It had been such a bumpy ride getting that production on. Julia's set for the second act tapered inwards the further upstage it went, which reduced the area left clear for dancing. It was much too small for the waltz. Overall, the performance was rough and much of the stage mechanics was sticky. There had not been enough time allowed for stage rehearsals to get everything right. Sitting in the audience was sheer agony. As I squirmed in my seat at all the moments when things were not as they should be, Sonya said to me, 'Relax! There's nothing that you can do.' She was quite right. I was experienced enough by now to know that producing a classic will be agony however much you want it to succeed.

There had been some bad days during rehearsals. Even now after more than 30 years there are still troubles. This *Nutcracker* is one of the most complicated shows at the Royal Opera House to run. During this production's early days the old union agreements were still in place and the working practices in place were far from ideal. During the transformation scene, co-ordinating how the room grows, with the timing of the giant-sized toy fort and doll's house, was hardest. I had planned it to be more complicated than it is. The stage lifts that cause the tree to grow have to be matched to the music so that the tree reaching its full height coincides with the crescendo in the score. That sounds a simple thing, but if you have a conductor who goes too slowly, as Russian conductors tend to do – and this production has had many guest Russians – then you spoil the impact. On the old stage the tree was made like a concertina and tended to jerk erratically as it unfolded. The tree is only about 18 inches in depth, but when it is properly lit it looks three-dimensional. Different conductors, different casts, different stage crews can really make a big difference to the success or otherwise of a production. You really are in the hands of the stage managers and crew who work fiendishly hard to keep the standard of presentation so high.

Over the years I have made various revisions but the production has always been mellow and reflective. When *The Nutcracker* returned to the newly refurbished stage at Covent Garden in December 1999 I took the opportunity to revisit it. A lot of people were fond of the production, but in terms of design and some of the characterisation, I found it rather dull. I emphasised more the romantic interest between Clara and her nephew. One change I introduced was at the end when Clara returns to reality. Outside her family's house she catches sight of a young man who looks like the nutcracker from her magical journey. I wanted to create an ending that was suggestive of Clara at first believing that her adventures had been dreams but, after she sees Hans-Peter again in the real world, she understands that the events may have actually occurred. It is not exactly true to the letter of Hoffmann, but it is in the spirit of the story. I think I managed to give the production a new lease of life when I renewed it in 1999. I put a lot of my Birmingham staging into it. Overall, I would have liked it all to be a lot more colourful, but I had to be governed by Julia's knowledge of period.

In retrospect however, alternating three new opera and three ballet productions in the first six weeks of the newly refurbished Royal Opera House, was over-optimistic. Technically not everything was ready. New, supposedly sophisticated, computerised systems for moving scenery as well as orchestrating lighting and staging effects had not been tested sufficiently. *The Nutcracker* certainly suffered. A fire alarm, for no reason it transpired, meant that we lost an unbelievable amount of time during one of our stage rehearsals. Despite new working practices, the unions, particularly representing the electricians, were still very strong at Covent Garden. Despite huge efforts backstage, the stage machinery was not under control. Trapdoors took an eternity to close. The new, special lifts designed to make the angel appear out of the Christmas tree did not function. The tree itself only started to grow too late in the proceedings, way off the music. Pieces of scenery got stuck and loud hammering noises could be heard coming from backstage. The floor surface for the second act produced a striking number of very squeaky noises. Nowadays I feel in safe hands with Johanna Adams Farley, the stage manager, who is brilliant at how she copes with all the complicated ballets at Covent Garden. There was one occasion, however, soon after the reopening, when a cue was missed which meant the stage lift did not move. That meant in turn that the tree did not grow, so Johanna had no choice but to bring down the curtain. I have never really understood what causes the Christmas tree to stop growing mid-way, although that still happens on bad days.

Nevertheless, this production of *The Nutcracker* at Covent Garden has stood the test of time. This is due in enormous part to Christopher Carr who has had a long career with the company as a ballet master. He does exactly the same with my production of *Giselle*. Most of the classic ballets as well as those by Frederick Ashton are difficult to recreate as they require a very specific style. It is of course much easier if you have danced these ballets yourself and Christopher is able to draw on his years as a soloist with the companies. He never refers to notes or DVDs but through his extraordinary ability to store the complete choreographic patterns and steps in his brain, he manages to get *The Nutcracker* – with all its many different casts – on the stage without much difficulty. That is no small feat as time is always limited, and because of the number of works in preparation at any one time it is not unusual for dancers to arrive at a rehearsal not knowing which bit of what ballet they are about to rehearse. I just cannot believe that this production, over 30 years old, always looks like new when it is revived. That is thanks to Christopher's way with it that it always lives and breathes. His energy and enthusiasm are extraordinary.

When I came to stage *The Nutcracker* in Birmingham in 1990 I adopted a freer, more youthful and romantic telling which I think was more appropriate for that company. This was much more the Wright *Nutcracker*. The experience of making the Birmingham production showed me what needed tightening up in London. *The Nutcracker* is popular with children of all ages because it is a ballet that can be understood by everybody, but without its associations to Christmas and its Tchaikovsky score it would not have survived. The endless numbers of children in George Balanchine's production do the ballet no favours. For youngsters in the audience *The Nutcracker* holds their attention as it is relatively short and there are not so many fairies interrupting proceedings as in *The Sleeping Beauty*. I was conscious of how necessary it is to maintain children's interest in the audience. I have always thought that the second act is hard going for them as they tend to tire when they have only dancing to watch. That is what my grandchildren told me anyway. It is always good to have a different perspective on your work. John Varsarnyi is a friend whom I knew as Sonya met his wife Tania at evening classes, along with her good friend Dilys Ward. She had never been to a ballet until Tania took her. A dentist from a dental family, John is not so keen on ballet himself but I find his observations very discerning as he sees it all in a completely different light. Tania, Dilys and John are all knowledgeable. I have always enjoyed having friends from outside the world of ballet.

It is my Birmingham *Nutcracker* that has been staged in Tokyo and Australia. When Desmond Kelly mounted it in Melbourne for Australian Ballet in 2007 it was their fourth *Nutcracker*. Their most recent had been Graeme Murphy's *Nutcracker: The Story of Clara* which was set in the 1950s, Clara was an ageing ballerina who had somehow ended up in Australia, perhaps a relic from the days of those old Ballets Russes touring companies, the precursors of the Borovansky company that became Australian Ballet. The elderly Clara recalls her past life in flashback during her final days in a retirement home, before dying at the close. It is the sort of production that cannot be revived too often.

When David McAllister, the current director, wanted to have a more traditional staging I was happy to let him have my Birmingham version. In fact it was Desmond who did most of it. I went over only for the last three weeks and thought the Australians performed it superbly. It was their most labour-intensive production. There are, for example, over 10,000 hand-sewn beads on the Sugar Plum fairy's costume, making it the most lavish and expensive tutu in their repertoire, at a cost of the Australian equivalent of nearly £5,000. John Macfarlane actually describes that as his least favourite costume as a tutu gives the designer least scope for invention. The thing to remember about big productions is that it is not only what you see onstage that contributes to the cost. For the Sugar Plum fairy or her prince, probably four costumes need to be made to take into account the different dancers during a run. Nowadays there are untold casts for the principal roles. Some costumes are made to have a life of at least 20 years, which does not come cheap. That all has to be built into the initial budget and it is always a stretch for how many costumes it will cover.

The Birmingham *Nutcracker* was performed at the O2 centre in London during the festive season in 2011. That was the end of my Christmas that year. The technical and lighting rehearsal was Christmas Day itself, beginning at 8.30am. At 8.40am the electrics broke down and they did not start again until 5pm. Have you ever tried to find an electrician on Christmas Day? We lost a whole day of preparation which meant we had to open without an onstage run-through or dress rehearsal. I have to say I felt ignored as the problems mounted up. I was running around the place getting very out of breath. How we ever did open was a miracle. We all had to be very ingenious. It was only thanks to the ingenuity of Peter Teigen, the lighting designer, that we got the show on. He was absolutely amazing in how he coped. Peter now lights all my productions. We argue a bit, which is healthy. I like working with him because I know he will always get you out of difficulties.

For that O2 season we used the same sets as for our conventional performances at the Hippodrome, but with the wings opened out and set wide. I thought it looked marvellous. Unfortunately, the O2 had insisted on allocating the press seats on the first night themselves without involving our own public relations people. I had insisted that critics must have a full view of the stage, but in their wisdom the O2 sat them in seats where only half the action was visible. We managed to move them after the interval but most reviews concentrated more on the O2's sightlines than the show. The big innovation for us was performing on a large thrust stage that extended into the stalls. This meant adapting much of the choreography for entrances and exits so that they did not just fall off the stage.

Another feature that required careful attention was that the wires which work the magic tricks and the flying goose in the first act should remain invisible. To project in such a cavernous venue as the O2, the orchestra was wired to the centre's 600,000-watt sound system, and of course there was the issue of how the dancers would be seen. The great thing about a touring company such as Birmingham Royal Ballet is that the dancers are used to performing in all manner of venues, some vast, some ghastly, particularly on overseas tours, and they have learned to adapt very quickly. To aid them, in the O2 we had a gigantic screen over the stage onto which a simultaneous live film relay was projected. The screen footage was skilfully directed by Ross MacGibbon as a prompt for what of the live action the audience should be looking at. Ross understood about balance and the screen not overpowering the stage, except when we wanted it to, but I am not sure that we reconciled how film and live action are combined. Still, taking *The Nutcracker* to the O2 was an interesting experiment, though one not to be repeated. There had been some discussion with Lilian Hochauser, the promoter, about staging *Swan Lake* there. She and I met after the first night when the O2 was practically deserted after everybody had gone home. Lilian was upset by what she saw as a lack of appreciation shown by the O2 and towards her financial contribution to the season. It made a loss for her. Nobody had looked after her on the evening or more fundamentally expressed their gratitude. I was upset too as she had done so much for us and hoped it would not affect our relationship for the future. But Lilian was very hurt and determined that she would not underwrite another O2 season, so the idea of *Swan Lake* there foundered.

I can understand why some people complain that the old classics are performed so often in order to fill theatres. For a classical company, the more variety it can have among these great works from the past, the richer its heritage becomes. When the great Ukrainian prima ballerina Galina Samsova joined Sadler's Wells Royal Ballet in 1976 I thought she was just the person to mount a suite of dances from *Paquita* for us. It would be an ideal way to increase our range of short classical works. It is a ballet that demands a great sense of aristocratic style and also restraint. Wisely, Galina had kept all her notes from ballets she had danced in Kiev, not only principal roles but corps de ballet too. She was very enthusiastic about the idea but warned that it would need many hours of rehearsals. But not only could Galina demonstrate true ballerina quality in the title role but she could rehearse the many solos for the girls that were technically very challenging. There is plenty for the girls' corps de ballet but only one male role. Rehearsals were a joy, with Galina demonstrating every step and nuance beautifully. She demanded a certain restraint in the arms and no grinning. 'Do not exaggerate and always look as if you could give a bit more' were her hallmarks. It is very easy in this ballet to overdo everything and get carried away. Performed in that way it becomes a vulgar knees-up, something that I have often witnessed. Although the choreography is very clear, the actual floor patterning is very complex and needs constant attention to keep the movement full and passionate, especially the arms which must swirl together and stay aligned. The opening performances in 1980 were really good. Some reviewers noted that given the company's recent past as the New Group, this must be the first time some dancers had worn a tutu professionally onstage. I particularly wanted to add *Paquita* to the repertory because I was anxious too to get the company up to size and standard so that it would be possible to do *Swan Lake* again. It had been out of our touring repertoire for over a decade and although London has seen thousands of *Swan Lakes*, the regions then had not.

After *Paquita* I did not fear any comparisons and felt in October 1981 that the time was right for Sadler's Wells Royal Ballet to have its own distinctive *Swan Lake*. No serious classical company can be without one. It is a ballet that enables a company to acquire proper classical style, especially the corps de ballet. I can always watch the second act to see the corps perform actually quite basic choreography – but perfectly. The way the corps dances in *Swan Lake* is a completely different proposition from *The Nutcracker* and *The Sleeping Beauty* and makes a huge difference to the success of a performance. *Swan Lake* really demands a lot of effort from everybody to make it work. It should not, however, become the permanent diet for performers or audiences, but rightly or wrongly *Swan Lake* is many people's first sight of ballet. While audiences do not have to understand every moment, every gesture, particularly if they get carried along by the music – and I do not assume they read their programmes – the action onstage has to be strong and clear.

I certainly did not understand the mime the first few times I saw it. Mime should always relate to what is going to be danced and, in *Swan Lake* particularly, convey a sense of impending doom. Everybody should be able to understand that Siegfried, the prince, has fallen in love with the swan queen who is held in a spell by Von Rothbart which must be broken. For the pas de deux by the lakeside to be appreciated properly, it has to be performed superbly. Then it can bring tears to the eyes.

It would be an awful shame if choreographers could no longer create similar pas de deux, but I have not come across any in recent ballets. It is not just a love story but a lovely combination of music, movement and experience which makes *Swan Lake* a joy to behold. Although I love much of the choreography, for me it is the music that makes *Swan Lake* so wonderful.

I am pleased that together with designer Philip Prowse we decided to give the ballet more urgency. Philip more than me had always felt that *Swan Lake* was a gothic, romantic tragedy. As a producer, I began by asking myself questions about what we see when the ballet starts. We see Siegfried and his mother, the queen, but no king. Why? That gave me the idea of depicting the king's funeral procession in the opening tableau. The court is in mourning. Having established the idea of the king's death, Philip depicted a court in half-mourning, dressed half in black which was visually very striking. And black is Philip's favourite colour. Although the decision to stage the production had been taken at the beginning of 1981, we only had the financial go-ahead nine weeks before the opening night. That was an extremely tight timetable in which to get the sets and costumes made. When we got to the first dress rehearsal onstage in Manchester, there was literally no space to move in the ballroom scene because of the enormity of Philip's costumes. 'Oh Philip, what have you done to me? Nobody can dance a step,' I exclaimed as I tried to position characters in odd corners. Gradually everyone got used to the costumes and once the dancers had been placed it all looked wonderful.

When the ballet begins, Siegfried is not married, and so for dynastic reasons the dramatic impetus depicts his need to choose a bride, although personally he has no wish to. To establish Siegfried's situation I gave him a solo in the first act and then included him in what is normally a pas de trois for three unnamed characters. This dance occurs early in the ballet and attracts a lot of attention as it is the first solo dancing that the audience sees. But who are these people? Why are they here? To make this section contribute to the development of the ballet, I had it performed by Benno, Siegfried's equerry, who tries to entertain the prince on his birthday by interesting him in two courtesans who dance with him. With Benno's encouragement, Siegfried joins in with the dance. That is something that all Siegfrieds tend to like and is, I think, one of my better pieces of choreography. Incorporating Benno in the dance is also a way of having him as a more substantial figure in the ballet. In my early days with Sadler's Wells Theatre Ballet in the 1940s, Benno participated in Siegfried's pas de deux with Odette in the second act, quite why we never knew. All Benno had to do was support Odette as she fell back into his arms during the pas de deux. Presumably Pavel Gerdt, the original Siegfried, needed help with the partnering. In fact when I was not cast as Benno I was one of the huntsmen who had to stand at the side of the stage throughout that scene. Again, we never knew why or thought to ask. By strengthening the dramatic context of *Swan Lake* it becomes the prince's story but remains the swan queen's ballet.

Extremely important is the style for the scenes at the lakeside. I personally prefer the Russian style for *Swan Lake*, not because they get their legs higher and bend backwards further than most, but I find that as in a bird's wing, where the feathers are slotted into the bone structure, Russian dancers use every part of the arm with control and precision and do not just flap. On the other hand, although Russian backs seem more flexible, moving further backwards and forwards, thanks to Enrico Cecchetti's method, our training here allows a much greater range of movement. With Cecchetti port de bras, the body moves forwards and sweeps to the side, then to the back before continuing round to the starting point. This is something which is so important in Ashton's choreography. I remember that divine ballerina Lesley Collier used the top part of her back to great effect. To teach Russian style you need somebody who really understands its particular qualities. That person when this *Swan Lake* was new was Galina Samsova. She was still dancing ballerina roles and was a great exemplar to younger dancers in them. I asked her to work with me. Galina staged the choreography she knew from her days in Kiev by Alexander Gorsky, a former régisseur with the Bolshoi Ballet. In the second act, Galina particularly focused on the swans' use of their arms as well as the phrasing of the choreography, introducing a dance for the leading swans, taken from the Kiev production she knew. As the experience of performing the ballet was new to most of the company, everybody really benefited from having Galina involved. I loved what she did. She made such a difference in how the steps were performed, how pirouettes were finished, how people carried their arms and shoulders. Galina was there all the time, rehearsing people, being strict with them. It really made a difference. *Swan Lake* is a romantic ballet and that quality was what Galina managed to highlight. I liked that, being very much a romantic myself. Galina really showcased the corps.

Otherwise I choreographed a new waltz and substituted a polacca in place of the peasant dance. I cut down the number of princesses who compete for Siegfried's hand, usually and implausibly all wearing identical dresses, and removed the dance for the prospective fiancées. I had them introduced by ambassadors as part of their respective national dances and choreographed new solos for the Hungarian, Polish and Italian princesses. Galina redid the czardas and restaged the Spanish dance in the style of Gorsky. I made a new tarantella. Despite Galina's involvement, we did not get as far as replicating the deep back bends typical of Russian performances, where dancers' heads touch the floor – but we tried. These dances really have to be performed as showcase numbers but I was determined to make the action more dramatic throughout. In my experience, in the old days, nobody stayed to watch the final act, like nowadays there is often an exodus after the shades' scene in *La Bayadère*.

I based the last act in *Swan Lake* on the Konstantin Sergeyev version familiar in Britain but with new patterns and formations. We cut passages choreographed to music not in the original score. I made a new pas de deux for Odette and Siegfried, revised the second swans' dance, the storm scene and apotheosis. I was concerned always for Von Rothbart to be credible. I have never seen this embodiment of evil work when portrayed as an owl wearing ballet shoes, as he frequently is. I love the fact that Rothbart's cloak can turn into wings. He is a demon. There is probably another whole story waiting to be told about what happened to Rothbart. I like him to be strong and powerful, which adds to the force of the ending. In their fight, Siegfried pulls off Rothbart's helmet to reveal a skull of death. The swans drive Rothbart to hell. Previously a Siegfried, Desmond Kelly, my first Rothbart, loved doing the role and was extremely powerful in it. As Rothbart is vanquished, in the skies above, the spirits of Siegfried and Odette are reunited. Benno emerges from the lake carrying the drowned body of Siegfried. The spell is broken. That is how I see the ending.

Now when I look at the production, still in the repertoire after 35 years and magnificently danced by Birmingham Royal Ballet in autumn

2015, there are elements I would like to revisit. The czardas and mazurka could both be more exciting and I would add a Russian dance to that gorgeous music in the third act; I do not want to give away any surprises but I would still like to have another go at this great ballet.

I have seen and worked with many swan queens. I did not like Margot Fonteyn in the role when she first did it. She was as cold as ice, with stiff arms. It was amazing to see how she transformed her portrayal over the years. Moira Shearer was rather too spiky and her nature was somewhat artificial. Natalia Makarova was great if unmusical but somehow she got away with it. Sometimes it is good to be off the music. She used the music's flow with her very expressive arms, but oh so slowly. Although she came to the role late, when she was 35, Merle Park was excellent for her musicality as both Odette and Odile. She became the music. Marcia Haydée was good as Odette as her interpretation had a very expressive feel for the movement and she could be very emotional. Her Odette did not have the high legs that we see now, and the role is one where you can use the height of the legs to good effect, provided it does not look acrobatic. Marcia observed the differences of character between the acts. Hers was a remarkable and musical interpretation. Though physically not right, Lesley Collier had passion and feeling. When I staged the production with Galina Samsova she was dancing the role a little too late but she was one of the greats. Marion Tait was very expressive and made a character out of the part. Miyako Yoshida took a long while to get into the role and express its emotional side, but once she did she was superb. Celine Gittens I like very much, she is remarkable with the correct line. I am sure she will develop into one of the greats. Jenna Roberts is absolutely marvellous, a natural.

It was *Swan Lake* that won me the 1981 *Evening Standard* award for dance which was presented to me at Sadler's Wells by Madam the following March. The party afterwards was very jolly, with many friends and colleagues present. The programme that night included MacMillan's *Solitaire* and it was memorable too for how Kenneth slapped Lynn Seymour's face in front of everybody. He accused her of being drunk and failing to sufficiently appreciate the costumes designed by his wife, Deborah, for his work in progress, *Quartet*, an extract from which was previewed that evening. Lynn was furious not on her own behalf but that the incident had upstaged the award being made to me. In any case

I regarded it as a just recognition of what the company had achieved with *Swan Lake*.

I think it was George Balanchine who first said that it did not matter what ballets are programmed, so long as you had a swan in the title. It was a sleight of hand that did not really work with David Bintley's first full-length ballet, *The Swan of Tuonela*. Although *Swan Lake* is a ballet that everybody wants to see, it was a flop when it was new. That certainly underlines the fact that a ballet does not have to be perfect to be a classic, but I wonder why choreographers and producers active today lean so heavily on the classic titles. Why does Matthew Bourne not produce more original ballets? I have a lot of respect for him. I like *The Car Man* by him which is more original, very violent and very effective, a real shocker. If I had never seen *The Sleeping Beauty* and his version was the only one available, then I would probably like it, but would it be a seller without Tchaikovsky and the title? Would people rush to see it? His *Swan Lake* is amusing but it does not contain anything great choreographically. It uses an existing structure and score but it is not the real *Swan Lake*. It works as a novelty.

If you are going to make changes with already established successes there should be a reason to change, not just for its own sake. I learned from Ninette de Valois that when you are spending a lot of money you have to be ready and give reasons why you have done so. You really have to be ready. When John Cranko first pushed me into producing *Giselle* I was determined to make it as good as it could be, but I was nervous about making changes. To tackle a big classic you need experience of directing big scenes and making dramatic points rather than just producing choreography. Young choreographers or former dancers run the risk of still looking at a big ballet only from a dancer's perspective. I think this was at the root of why some previous productions at Covent Garden did not succeed fully. Of course you have to start somewhere, but you must first learn the rules before you can break them. However marvellous it is to have notation, and film, nobody really knows how the classic ballets looked originally. Nobody can possibly put on a staging that returns to how they first appeared with any certainty. I am conscious in making my own judgments I look at these ballets with modern eyes. These days, the fashion, manner and speed of how we look at something has changed. We used to do things in a slower way.

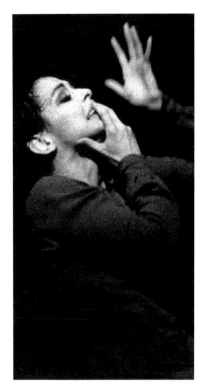

(Above left) 37. Lynn Seymour in *Anastasia* by Kenneth MacMillan, Royal Ballet, 1971 (© Anthony Crickmay / Victoria and Albert Museum, London); *(Above right)* 38. *Grosse Fugue* by Hans van Manen, New Group, 1972 (© Anthony Crickmay / Victoria and Albert Museum, London); *(Below)* 39. Desmond Kelly and Deanne Bergsma in *Field Figures*, New Group 1970 (© Zoë Dominic)

(Above left) 40. Brenda Last and Kenneth MacMillan in rehearsal for *The Poltroon*, 1972 (© Anthony Crickmay / Victoria and Albert Museum, London); *(Above right)* 41. Patricia Ruanne in *Twilight*, 1973 (© Anthony Crickmay / Victoria and Albert Museum, London); *(Below)* 42. Peter Clegg, left and Hans van Manen with the New Group rehearsing *Grosse Fugue*, 1972 (© Anthony Crickmay / Victoria and Albert Museum, London)

5031y mchn d
205tp London gb
zczc gtn8108 Lbt938
dpmc co gblb 015
LondonLb tf 15/26 1108   26 XI 76   12 45

                                          Y

peter wright bayerische staatsoper   4158
munichwestgermany

hope this is the most beautiful sleeping beauty
    Love kenneth

(Above) 43. Design by Peter Farmer for
The Sleeping Beauty, Bayerisches Staatsballett
Munich, 1976; *(Above, inset)* 44. Telegram
from Kenneth MacMillan, Munich 1976
'hope this is the most beautiful sleeping
beauty love kenneth'; *(Below)* 45. With
Princess Margaret and Sonya, Royal Opera
House, 1980 (© Donald Southern / Royal Opera
House / ArenaPAL)

(Above) 46. Working in Amsterdam with Het Nationale Ballet, 1970s (© Pieter Kooistra);
(Below) 47. Coaching Joanne Zimmermann as Carabosse, *The Sleeping Beauty*,
Het Nationale Ballet, Amsterdam, 1981 (© Jorge Fatauros)

(Above) 48. Design by Philip Prowse for *Swan Lake*, Sadler's Wells Royal Ballet, 1981; *(Below left)* 49. Galina Samsova (© Roy Jones); *(Below right)* 50. *Swan Lake*, Sadler's Wells Royal Ballet, 1981, Galina Samsova and David Ashmole (© Leslie E Spatt)

(Above left) 51. Samira Saidi as *The Snow Queen* by David Bintley, Sadler's Wells Royal Ballet, 1986 (© Clive Barda / ArenaPAL); *(Above right)* 52. Ravenna Tucker and John Auld in *Coppélia*, designed by Peter Farmer, Birmingham Royal Ballet, 1995 (© Bill Cooper / ArenaPAL); *(Below)* 53. *Paquita* produced by Galina Samsova for Sadler's Wells Royal Ballet, designed by Peter Farmer, 2007 revival (© Bill Cooper / ArenaPAL)

(Above) 54. *The Sleeping Beauty* designed by Philip Prowse for Sadler's Wells Royal Ballet, 1997 revival
(© Bill Cooper / ArenaPAL); *(Below)* 55. Margot Fonteyn, right, with Margaret Barbieri, Sherilyn Kennedy
and Derek Deane, *The Sleeping Beauty*, Miami, 1986 (© Allen Malschick)

(Above) 56. With Ninette de Valois, 1993;
(Below) 57. Accepting the 1981 Evening Standard award (© Donald Southern / Royal Opera House / ArenaPAL)

(Above) 58. Birmingham Royal Ballet and the staff of the Birmingham Hippodrome on the set of *Enigma Variations*, October 1994 (© Bill Cooper/ArenaPal); *(Below)* 59. Birmingham Royal Ballet, 1990

60. Karla Doorbar as Clara in *The Nutcracker*, designed by John Macfarlane,
Birmingham Royal Ballet, 2015 revival (© Roy Smiljanic)

(Above left) 61. Nao Sakuma as the Sugar Plum fairy, *The Nutcracker*, Birmingham Royal Ballet, 2004 revival, (© Bill Cooper / ArenaPAL); *(Above right)* 62. Marion Tait in *Romeo and Juliet* by Kenneth MacMillan, Birmingham Royal Ballet, 1992 (© Bill Cooper / ArenaPAL); *(Bottom left)* 63. Marion Tait as Carabosse in *The Sleeping Beauty*, Birmingham Royal Ballet (© Bill Cooper / ArenaPAL); *(Bottom right)* 64. Momoko Hirata in *Theme and Variations*, Birmingham Royal Ballet, 2010 revival (© Bill Cooper / ArenaPAL)

65. Miyako Yoshida and Petter Jacobsson in *Theme and Variations* by George Balanchine, Birmingham Royal Ballet, 1993 (© Leslie E Spatt)

(*Above*) 66. The finale of *Façade*, my retirement gala, Birmingham Hippodrome, 1995;
(*Below*) 67. Celebrating 25 years of *The Nutcracker*, with, left to right, Peter Todd, former director
Birmingham Hippodrome, Marion Tait and Kit Holder, 2015 (© Roy Smiljanic)

(Above left) 68. With Patricia Neary; *(Above right)* 69. With Miyako Yoshida;
(Below) 70. Third from left, with, *left to right*, Colin Nears, Tony Dyson, Peter Brownlee,
Denis Bonner and Peter Farmer, 2004 (© Leslie E Spatt)

(Above) 71. Seated centre with Darcey Bussell, with left to right, Jonathon Cope, Lesley Collier, Donald MacLeary, Edward Watson, Merle Park, Beryl Grey, Monica Mason, Jeanetta Laurence, David Wall, Julia Farron, Wayne Eagling and Alfreda Thorogood, 2000s
(© Johan Persson / ArenaPAL)

(Left) 72. Rehearsing Danielle Browne and Ricardo Rhodes in *Summertide*, Sarasota Ballet, 2015 (© Frank Atura)

(Above left) 73. Kevin O'Hare, left, with Robin Gladwin, winner of the Sir Peter Wright Scholarship, Yorkshire Ballet Summer School, 1998; *(Above right)* 74. James Barton, left, winner of the 2002 Sir Peter Wright Scholarship, Yorkshire Ballet Summer School, with Christopher Powney (© Andrew McMillan); *(Below)* 75. With pupils of the Francis Holland school Sloane Square, London, 2010s

Television has changed all that. Everything now is so quick, and that is a shame. That is what taste today demands as we all assimilate things far more quickly. This has had an impact on storytelling just as much in ballet as in plays in the theatre or on television. It has always informed my approach too in making classic ballets work for modern eyes. It is a shame, however, that we are no longer able to appreciate choreography and a style of production that were designed to unfold at a slower rate. Slow can be beautiful.

I have often been asked what classics have been created during my eight decades working in ballet. Can a classic be recognised as such in its own lifetime? I do not believe so. Classic status is only awarded after the creators are dead and gone. In that category, those that have stood the test of time in their entirety include Mikhail Fokine's ballets *The Firebird, Petrushka* and *Les Sylphides*, as well as *The Green Table* by Kurt Jooss. More recently, there are perhaps possible exceptions that prove their worth in their creators' lifetime, George Balanchine's *Apollo* and *Serenade* for example, but it is really too early to judge. With Ashton's *La Fille mal gardée* there is nothing to change. *Symphonic Variations* and *Scènes de ballet* have to be absolutely clean and perfect to work. The music of *Romeo and Juliet* always draws me in, but I do not see that anybody's version is a classic. The main issue is to get the balance right and usually there is too much street dancing. I was excited by Leonid Lavrovsky's production for the Bolshoi and when I first saw Cranko's in Stuttgart as well as MacMillan's in London I was very moved, but more modern updates just look awful. Some of *Onegin* is quite lovely but it has its weak moments. John's sense of theatre and communication in *Romeo* is stronger than Kenneth's, but his choreography is stronger. He had a gift for creating choreography that really caught hold of you. Apart from the pas de deux in *Manon* and *Mayerling*, however, those ballets are not interesting choreographically, particularly in how the corps de ballet is used. *Song of the Earth* is a top piece and I love *Requiem*, but time will tell. I was fascinated by *My Brother, My Sisters* and liked *Different Drummer* when it came back in 2008.

A classic ballet does not have to have great music. The music in many ballets, *Onegin, Manon, Mayerling*, is no worse than for *Giselle*. What you need is good theatre music. The deciding factors for a classic are form, communication and choreography. A work of art does not become a classic by putting all the right ingredients together. Something indefinable takes over. It is called talent and even then does not work to order. During my career, what classical ballet achieved went up an enormous amount. In the last two decades, however, it has diminished somewhat due to its willingness to be involved with contemporary dance. It may well go down before it comes up again, but I have no doubts about its return.

Ballet should always be entertaining, whether comic, tragic or abstract, and should always be a part of theatre and communicate with audiences. I find that many choreographers today are moving away from theatre, and that saddens me, particularly in the way that they are no longer writing great roles that compare to the great, classic examples. The productions of the classics that I present are not mine at all, they are my versions of the originals, and I always try to be faithful to them. Nowadays some choreographers produce versions which alter the story and with their own choreography. If it were not for the music and the title they could be anything. I believe it is really important to have narrative works and have ideas to communicate. Dancers are not just there to show off their technique and line – their potential to express themselves is enormous. Remember what Anna Pavlova said: 'Classical technique is a means to a beginning – not an end in itself.'

CHAPTER 12

New ballets – something borrowed, something blue

G REAT MUSIC, great paintings and indeed great choreography often come from mistakes. When you recognise such moments grab them for they are rare and valuable. Producing new ballets can sometimes be a painful process, so most choreographers prefer to work in private. The only choreographer I know who does not mind working publicly is David Bintley, but he too can have his bad days when he does not allow anybody near the studio. Many who attempt to choreograph really suffer, a kind of mental trauma. I once asked John Cranko why he choreographed. Was it for himself I wondered? 'I suppose so,' he replied, but after he had thought for a while longer John, who had no real religious feelings but did have instincts about faith and creativity, added, 'Not really. I think they are for God.'

As a director it is generally better if you do not interfere with the creation of a ballet until it is finished unless the choreographer asks you. I did once find a way to ask Lynn Seymour to revise the ending of one of her ballets. She had been exploring choreography in various workshops as well as making *Gladly, Sadly, Badly, Madly* for London Contemporary Dance Theatre. She made several works for Sadler's Wells Royal Ballet too. *Rashomon* was good. It had tension and invention but *Intimate Letters*, about a married woman and the men in her life, was really a disaster here, and again when it was presented in Munich in autumn 1978. The music was Leoš Janáček's second string quartet but I think Lynn was as much prompted by its subtitle, *Intimate Letters*. Recordings of Albert Finney, Sara Kestelman and Diana Quick were heard reading the composer's letters to his mistress. I never fathomed why she chose these artists as you could hardly hear them. For some reason David Bintley was a maid. Lynn's ballet *The Court of Love* lacked passion, while *Bastet* had too much of it. It was all about sex and depicted a girl and a boy who could not get it together. They invoked the Egyptian goddess, Bastet, who showed them how to achieve some sort of satisfaction. That may have been the case for them, but the ballet itself never had a proper climax. I thought it worth talking to Lynn. She agreed to have another go with a new ending. Just do not finish with another orgasm, I told her. Michael Berkeley wrote some more music – which Lynn proceeded to use for another big bang. Thank heavens for Andrew Logan and his wonderful designs, and June Highwood, clad in lamé and strutting like a stripper, as Bastet, the cat goddess, and seemingly, as far as Lynn was concerned, also goddess of sex.

Choreography cannot be taught but there is so much background to it that can be absorbed in the way one thinks. Requisite skills include how to plan and break down the music, design, the possibilities of various types of group movement such as alternating, symmetry, decreasing and changing circles, as well as how far you can push the human body, which is very important. All these can be taught – but not choreography itself although examples can be suggested. Ursula Moreton was one of Ninette de Valois' most faithful disciples whose name is remembered in a choreographic award made by the Royal Ballet School, where she was once director. She started a production club at the Royal Academy of Dance, a section of which was devoted to choreography. John Cranko was very supportive and created several studies of different choreographic possibilities. Each one contained certain types of movement and structure designed to help young choreographers form a base on which to base their own inventions. I used to teach these. I got a wonderful response from the students. However, this only occurred within in a school background and it needed to be developed a step further but the money ran out and it had to stop – the same old story.

When John Field was responsible for the Royal Ballet's touring company he suggested that I might like to make a ballet. I had done a couple of small pieces for the Sunday Choreographers, a group at Sadler's Wells which David Poole had started, which had gone well. I jumped at the invitation. Although I did not have any ideas at that point, I quickly rustled some together which I had to present to Madam. I knew of a wonderful piece of music, Samuel Barber's *Souvenirs*. I worked out a piece about a rose that gets passed between different lovers in a set of shifting relationships. My starting point was Arthur Schnitzler's play *La Ronde*, which I knew from the film. The rose eventually finds its way back to the person who started it all off. I thought this must be a very special rose so it became *A Blue Rose*, my first ballet in December 1957. Madam wanted to know all about it. She had already given me wise counsel about choosing music, warning me how important it was to be confident that I could actually compose steps to it when reduced to a piano score only. It is a long and laborious process, choreographing to recorded music. Madam had never heard of Barber, 'An American!', but I chose part of the score that I thought she would like, not too romantic but quite sharp and busy. She was always very clear that choreographers should not just choose music they love but rather something that has some rhythm and beat that inspires you to make steps. Otherwise, she said, it will just become background music. Anyway, she thought I had made a good choice, 'Just get on with it,' she decreed.

Yolanda Sonnabend designed *A Blue Rose* for me, her first ballet, indeed her first designs for the stage. I came across her as she was finishing the theatre design course at the Slade. Madam knew William Coldstream well, the artist and fine art professor there, and often sought his advice about new designers. He showed me the work of three students whom I met. Yolanda was the obvious choice. I loved her shapes and wonderful colours even though her work was a bit untidy. Yolanda went on to design several of Kenneth MacMillan's ballets, and later, Anthony Dowell's production of *Swan Lake*. On paper her costume designs looked very approximate. I thought this was unfortunate but she said very little attention was given to costume design on the course, certainly nothing about materials, making and practical problems such as how fabrics hang when a dancer is lifted.

Her designs for *A Blue Rose* led to a lot of problems. I remember a fitting for Susan Alexander, one of the soloists. The wardrobe director at Covent Garden, Olive Cranmer, could not tolerate designers who did not have the craft skills she thought essential to the job. Yolanda's designs had gradations in shading that were to become her hallmark, but because of background at the Slade she knew nothing about fabrics, cut, how to make a bodice, anything practical. Susan was standing on a raised dais in the wardrobe office as the costume was fitted to her. I could tell Miss Cranmer was making Yolanda suffer. She was attempting to tell an assistant how to pin a swathe of orangey-yellow material. Actually Yolanda was tough underneath but she was evidently hoping that somebody would do it for her. 'You've designed this, surely you know how you want it to look,' queried Miss Cranmer. 'Yes,' replied Yolanda, 'there is the design. Isn't the making of it your job?' Miss Cranmer thundered a resounding 'No' in response. I sensed there was going to be trouble and slipped away to find Madam who rather crossly dropped what she was doing and followed me back to the room. She demanded to know what the problem was. 'This new designer doesn't seem to know how she wants it to look,' said Miss Cranmer, in front of Yolanda. 'Well, presumably like this design indicates,' Madam said, kicking off her shoes as she got down on her knees and asked for some pins, 'Hold that. Pin that. Move that. This must be the underskirt. That falls to this level. So what's the problem?' she said as she quite brilliantly put the costume together. As Madam strode out, she turned around and said, 'I hope you have all learned a lesson. And for goodness sake, don't make the skirt too long. The poor girl has to dance in it!' Then with a nod to me and a glare to Miss Cranmer she was gone. Reviewers at the time recognised that Yolanda was primarily an artist, not a stage designer but her set, abstract shades of apricot with black lines, was praised as one of the most interesting seen at Covent Garden in years. The costumes, however, were criticised for lacking the strong hand of an artistic director. If they but knew.

A Blue Rose was planned to go on at Sadler's Wells so it was a terrible shock late in rehearsals to hear that it would be staged at the Royal Opera House, just after Christmas 1957. The company's contract with Sadler's Wells theatre was being terminated because of budget problems. I worried what would happen about the sets which were being made for the smaller stage. 'We'll fiddle them,' Madam told me, ever practical. *A Blue Rose* shared the bill with Cranko's new ballet *The Angels*. It was Madam's intention that another new work, *The Burrow* by Kenneth MacMillan, would complete the bill. He was not happy at the prospect. His first ballet for Covent Garden in 1956, *Noctambules*, had achieved considerable attention. Typical of Kenneth's work at the time, it was quirky and dark, with a brave choice of a commissioned score by Humphrey Searle. The theme was a vengeful hypnotist who exercises control over a soldier, a young couple and a faded beauty. It was a good piece but one not destined to have a long life. Kenneth, however, attracted a lot of attention thanks to it and he knew how to maintain that. He claimed that *The Burrow* would not be ready in time for the first night shared with John and me, and so won his own premiere a few days into the new year.

The Angels, Cranko's new piece, did not go well. Clover Roope, who danced in it, recalls hearing booing. I really suffered too with *A Blue Rose*, it was a very sensitive time. De Valois had established Sadler's Wells Theatre Ballet as a place where future leading dancers, designers and choreographers could try their wings before being exposed to the big stage, big audiences and big critics at Covent Garden. Following the recent funding crisis, however, here I was having to create my first ballet in the very conditions that Madam was trying to protect people like me from. I found the whole episode very dispiriting. The reviews were pretty vicious. Peter Williams, editor of *Dance and Dancers*, considered the Covent Garden stage the deepest of deep swimming pools and quite unsuited to novice swimmers. He thought Madam had in effect thrown me into the deep end of ballet to see whether I could swim. His judgment seemed to be that I neither sank nor swam but just about managed to stay afloat. Probably fair comment – but to have my choreography described as haphazard, spasmodic, derivative and repetitious hurt. Although *A Blue Rose* was not a great piece, it stayed in the repertoire for about three years. It worked well enough on a long, 34-week tour of Australia and New Zealand later that year, although that was one tour I was not part of as I was then freelancing in television and musicals. Whatever the success of *A Blue Rose*, Madam did not ask me to choreograph another ballet at Covent Garden. With her you had to impress her with the chances she gave you. This gave her a reputation for ruthlessness, but in the years when she was building the company she did not have the time to explain or justify all her decisions.

Although I have created some 15 ballets, usually when the occasion demanded it, I have never really been driven by the urge to create new ballets that marks out genuinely inventive choreographers. I certainly never felt, as Frederick Ashton once said about himself, that choreography was my whole being with more reality than life itself. During my Stuttgart days, in October 1964, in Oxford, I created *Summer's Night* for the Royal Ballet's touring company. Set to Francis Poulenc's *Sinfonietta*, two lovers and their party guests stray into a wood and, for no discernible reason, attract the interest of some ghosts. One of the leading roles was danced by Elizabeth Anderton, Betch as I always knew her. The original gipsy girl in *The Two Pigeons*, she was a dancer with passion and brilliant at conveying that in her subsequent work as a teacher. She and Rudolf Nureyev once had a row when he threw his drink in her face. She responded by giving him an almighty slap across his face. After that they became good friends.

Summer's Night was created in ghastly rehearsal rooms on tour, usually freezing cold. Betch was a joy to work with because she threw herself into the ballet, which made me feel it was rather good. The other leading roles were played by the beautiful Doreen Wells and the very handsome Richard Farley who, besides being a good dancer, was a natural actor. Partnered by Richard, Dor, as she was known, was a ravishing ghost, completely weightless and ethereal. She was in her element, beautiful and flowing, and seemed very happy in the role. Ashton came to Eastbourne to see it. He was encouraging but not excited. Madam thought it had nice style and atmosphere, but was derivative. I guess that really summed it up. *Summer's Night* was not much liked by the critics either. It was seen very much as a dutiful work rather than something I was personally desperate to create, an exceptionally good example of a middling ballet – neither a hit nor a flop. I was praised for being as smooth as silk in how I handled groups and individuals, but at the same time criticised for a complete failure of characterisation and pastel-coloured emotions. In fact I did have terrible problems with my designer, Judith Wood, a pupil of Peter Snow and Nicholas Georgiadis. Her gauzy designs were terribly fiddly and full of details that an audience could not possibly see. At least a restaging of *Quintet*, which I had made in Stuttgart the year before, went better. It was described as unpretentious and infectiously happy, and praised as triviality of the very highest quality – which I took as a compliment. Critics recognised the technical skill, acrobatic movement, confidence and humour the dancers required to make its effect.

In 1968 I was back in London from Stuttgart and trying to establish myself again there. Although I had begun to consolidate my career as a producer of classics with *Giselle* and *The Sleeping Beauty* that year, I still had to earn a living in what ways I could. Inspired by the Japanese print that Sonya and I had been given as a wedding present by Clemence Dane, we decided to collaborate on a new ballet. Clemence would write the scenario based on Endymion, the mythical moon god. Our mutual friend, the composer Dick Addinsell, would write the music and I would do the choreography. It was to be created for the BBC where I was a guest producer. Sadly, Dick, having already composed a signature theme for *Endymion*, was taken seriously ill. He had already lost confidence in his talents and this illness made things really serious. He was unable to work. In fact the illness led to his death and the end of our project. He had been the most wonderful friend, godfather to our daughter and my mentor. He taught me so much about music and its construction. He was generous to a degree, and introduced me to opera, something I had avoided until then. Thanks to Dick, I discovered it was something I grew to like.

Around the same time, in March 1968, I choreographed another ballet for Western Theatre Ballet using the first symphony by John McCabe, who many years later composed the score for David Bintley's *Edward II*. Designed by Peter Farmer, my ballet with McCabe was *Dance Macabre*. As the title suggested, it was rather gothic, depicting a supernatural seductress who lured a pair of lovers to hell. There she stabbed the man and embraced the girl in a deathly kiss. I shudder now at its lack of originality, although Elaine McDonald was very good to work with. She was very musical and did not wait to offer suggestions about the choreography, but in a good way. Prime ham and sauce diable, however, was how Clement Crisp summarised it, then writing for *The Spectator*.

I also once made a ballet with Clement. This was *El Amor Brujo* in 1975. Clement helped me with the scenario, but try as I might I could not properly get it together with the music by Manuel de Falla. It was made on Stephen Jefferies and Vyvyan Lorrayne. The designs by Stefanos Lazaridis were problematical. The gipsy skirts had about 20 layers of ruching. I was concerned the girls would develop bad backs under the weight of their costumes during the ritual fire dance which was full of violent movement. Out on tour I got all the girls together with their skirts and went at them with scissors, hacking off layers of material. The skirts still looked the same but the girls could now dance up a storm. Madam adored *El Amor Brujo* when she came to see it in Brighton, but then she adored Stephen Jefferies. I rather think she fancied him. She told him it was his best role yet. He did not look too convinced, but he did perform the gipsy lover superbly, very sexy and passionate.

New choreographers generally get into a panic at some point but you just have to get on with it. You need a deadline. There is never enough time to create a new ballet. Kenneth MacMillan always demanded more time than he needed as he knew that would give him some insurance if he was getting stuck. The speed and facility with which choreographers create varies enormously and it is not fair if you have to take time away from one choreographer to help another get finished. That is all part of the planning process. When I start to choreograph I generally know where the entrances, exits and groupings are in advance as planned with the designer. When it is finished I do try to have an objective eye as to the result. That is why personally I do not think it is a good idea to polish until you have completed the whole ballet. I rough it out so that you can see if your graph is properly shaped. On the other hand, some choreographers have to see how each part looks when perfected before moving on. However, you do have to be sufficiently disciplined so that if your dancers are not available you can continue with another section, working with whoever is free. Time is always short, not just for new ballets, but also for reviving existing repertoire. Usually I think the completed piece is pretty awful. *The Mirror Walkers*, created in Stuttgart in 1963, was one of my better pieces but there was a lot I did not like. I changed what I did not rate after the first night. A ballet does not live until it is performed in front of an audience, especially if it is a humorous work. Only then can you can judge it. I find it inconceivable that choreographers do not watch their ballets from the auditorium. Audiences' reactions can change a ballet. Their responses influence the dancers' timing. Dancers need that reaction. Dance is all about communication. To be a dancer you have to love being watched. You should want to show something of your own self and be admired.

Joe Layton was expert in knowing how to work an audience to get a response. He was a real Broadway man. Joe was somebody I particularly enjoyed working with. He was an Emmy and Tony award-winning choreographer and director who worked on many musicals. He knew all about Broadway casting, timing and showmanship. He did three ballets with the New Group. *Overture*, from 1971, was just that, an introductory piece in the style of a curtain raiser for a revue using Leonard Bernstein's overture to *Candide*, with lots of props and business. It was very well crafted and designed, with placards announcing the ballets to be performed that evening. *Overture* gave a completeness to the whole show. More serious, set to William Walton's violin concerto and with the voice of John Gielgud intoning Oscar Wilde's *De Profundis*, Joe created *O. W.* It portrayed the writer's marital and extramarital relationships beginning with a party scene where Paul Clarke as the young Wilde was depicted as a mincing butterfly. This was not a success. For once, Joe had got it wrong. Michael Somes, as the older Wilde, just could not get the rather soft, effeminate side of his persona and looked very uncomfortable. The ballet had to be advertised as unsuitable for children, which did help ticket sales, and we had the support of Susana Walton who came to the first night. Susana wore some peculiar hats. She always seemed to follow her hat into a room.

More enduring, despite its deliberately lightweight nature, *The Grand Tour* was a huge success, performed more than a hundred times over the course of four seasons. It was set on a 1930s cruise ship, where celebrities of the era encountered several fictional characters. Gary Sherwood was Noël Coward, and David Drew's impersonation of Bernard Shaw displayed the Royal Ballet's best dramatic instincts, but it was an 18-year-old Stephen Jefferies, revealing his already considerable stagecraft and humour as the ship's steward, who stole the show. Altogether *The Grand Tour* was that rare species, a humorous ballet. As with all forms of comedy, it lost its freshness the longer it stayed in the repertoire when it was played too broadly, Still, I judged it good enough to revive during my time as director in the 1980s, but more recently in 2012 its humour looked forced. Characters such as Gertrude Lawrence and Mary Pickford and that glamorous Hollywood sense of period of 80 years ago looked like a lost world.

When Sadler's Wells Ballet presented a triple-bill of recent British ballets, including Robert Helpmann's *Miracle in the Gorbals*, during its first season in New York in 1949, the programme paled into insignificance compared to the huge success that *The Sleeping Beauty*, *Swan Lake* and Ashton's new *Cinderella* had generated. The great organising force of American ballet, Lincoln Kirstein, wrote to the British critic Richard Buckle to hope that he would never have to experience another triple-bill of new British choreography again. As a director of a company, building a repertoire means you have to get hold of what choreographers you can whenever they are available. You cannot build a repertoire on untried names alone; you need to get in people who are more established and bankable. For a director, finding choreographers capable of creating inventive work that appeals to audiences and dancers alike – never mind the critics – is a never-ending occupation. When I was responsible for the New Group there was a constant need for new ballets that used small casts and minimal scenery. In 1972, when we unveiled six new ballets, the company was typically presenting a dozen different ballets during the course of a week. Even choreographers with established reputations do not always have the best ideas. Ashton made *Siesta* a sultry bedroom pas de deux for Vyvyan Lorrayne and Barry McGrath. Trying to perform on pointe on a mattress was not one of Fred's best ideas. Kenneth MacMillan's *Triad* was taken over from Covent Garden without much success. He was keen to broaden our dancers' experience by working with different choreographers to develop their range as performers. To do that, Kenneth turned to choreographers from outside the company.

Christopher Bruce was a deliberately contemporary choice with *Unfamiliar Playground* in 1974. Nadine Baylis designed a typically elegant set consisting of a framework of bars and rods. The electronic score was dismissed as bumbling and tinkering noises, and critics complained that Bruce's choreography would look better if performed by dancers trained in contemporary dance. Bruce's ballet did, however, give Marion Tait her first decidedly modern role. A year later she was the bride whose husband has been killed in Jack Carter's *Shukumei*. It drew obviously on Kabuki drama and kung-fu. Marion turned on the murderers, strangling one of them with her hair. There was drama offstage too. The ballet was designed by Carter's partner, Norman McDowell. He was wild and fought Jack constantly. In Stratford they stayed at the Hilton and managed to completely destroy everything in their bedroom. Jack also created *Lulu*, in June 1976. This gave Merle Park a rare created role. On the whole choreographers tended not to make roles for her. When they did not ask her, she asked them. Merle could be very good at crying at will. Although Jack got on well with Merle, she did not really make the most of the role. *Lulu* did not have any real spark.

Probably the most important choreographer to whom Kenneth turned was Glen Tetley. His work was more familiar in Britain with contemporary dance audiences but Glen was an important choreographer for a classically based company to acquire. He did not make steps in isolation. He thought in terms of linked movements, extended sequences and completeness. His work never fought against nature. Although contemporary, Glen did relate his choreography to classically trained dancers. It widened their range of movement beautifully. His choreography was eloquent with a contemporary bite. In one sequence in *Field Figures*, his first work for the New Group in 1970, Glen locked Deanne Bergsma and Desmond Kelly together in a sort of double yoga position which was wonderfully challenging and innovative. It was very difficult and exhausting to sustain, typical of the demands Glen made. The dancers were onstage throughout but they loved it. *Field Figures* was a departure and difficult for the staff to keep in check as the half-contemporary, half-classical style was unfamiliar. Nadine Baylis was the designer. Before she undertook the commission she insisted on telling the company's board members that she was not answerable to them. While she would be happy to receive any remarks she would only accept them via Glen, whom she regarded as her boss.

On the strength of *Field Figures*, Kenneth soon commissioned Glen to do another ballet for which he used a score by Luciano Berio. This was *Laborintus*, premiered at Covent Garden in July 1972. It again featured Deanne and Desmond, alongside Lynn Seymour and Rudolf Nureyev supported by David Wall, Vergie Derman, Julian Hosking and David Ashmole. This was part of Kenneth's focus on creating new work, essential for any company to develop. As always, some of the ballets produced were good, some bad and some indifferent – but that is the way it goes.

I asked Paul Taylor to create a ballet for the New Group. Taylor's own company was appearing at Sadler's Wells when I went to talk to him in his dressing-room after a performance. The critic John Percival – Poisonous Percy as he was known, at least to company directors – was already sitting there. It was obvious to Percy that I could not talk to Paul with him sitting there listening to every word, but he did not budge. In the end I had to ask him to leave. I wanted to acquire one of Paul's existing works and ask him to create something new. Unfortunately, due to the permanent lack of time that companies and choreographers seem to operate under, that did not happen for many years and then only in part. Twenty years later I managed to introduce Paul's *Airs* during Birmingham Royal Ballet's first year. Set to various Handel pieces, it is a joyous, sunny ballet which seems to take place in some celestial blue heaven. Taylor's style demands speed, clarity and energy. *Airs* was always very dancey and musical but did not require turn out or pointed feet. For classical dancers it is hard to do things that are more relaxed.

Hans van Manen's work fits into any company easily. It is contemporary but within a classical framework, attractive to watch. Personally I am a great admirer of Hans' works to such an extent that we managed to set up a contract with him to produce several of his works. Dancers love working with him and performing his steps. The only thing they found difficult was how to use the weight of their bodies, a characteristic needed in much of Hans' choreography. Classical training, instilled from an early age, concentrates on defying gravity. We introduced five of Hans' ballets and in addition he created *Four Schumann Pieces* for Anthony Dowell at Covent Garden. *Grosse Fugue*, set to Beethoven, was performed by the New Group only a year after it was made for Nederlands Dans Theater in 1971. It was challenging to perform, demanding great precision and attack from the dancers but was certainly an audience pleaser.

The success of *Grosse Fugue* led to the introduction of *Twilight*, a flirtation-cum-confrontation pas de deux with a score by John Cage that used a prepared piano – one with pieces of plastic, screws, rubber washers and other objects fitted between the strings. The sound of a woman's high heels attacking the floor increases as she gets angrier with her partner. Patricia Ruanne and Paul Clarke were a brilliant first cast. Another of Hans' ballets we introduced was *Tilt*, set to a Stravinsky string concerto played twice. The second time around the choreography remains the same but is performed in a purposely awkward manner when the dancers switch roles, in a deliberately amusing way. The working relationship with Hans was very rewarding. His ballets always contained interesting ideas. They were accessible with a strong personal signature but required great intensity and concentration. Both dancers and audiences loved Hans' *Five Tangos*, with its score by Astor Piazzolla. We had a big problem with the music, however. In Holland, when the ballet was new it was performed to a particular recording. Restrictions imposed by the Musicians' Union in Britain meant we were not allowed to use a recording. The score had to be played live by the orchestra and a new orchestration made. Hans was not pleased at all with the result. It did not have the impact and excitement of the original. Ultimately, we managed to strike a deal with the orchestra to allow us to use the recording but it was very expensive. Hans' ballets were always popular but it took until 2016 for David Bintley to programme *Five Tangos* again at Birmingham Royal Ballet. A shame.

The beautiful work of Jirí Kylián seems to be neglected too. He is not so much in the limelight nowadays although English National Ballet has acquired *Petite Mort*, his ballet from 1991. Twenty years before that, when working with Kenneth, we were anxious to persuade Jirí to let us have one of his ballets. After all he was a student of the Royal Ballet School, graduating in the same year as Marion Tait, Stephen Jefferies, Jeanetta Laurence and David Ashmole. I went to see Jirí in The Hague where he was director of Nederlands Dans Theater following his early career in Stuttgart with John Cranko. Unfortunately, as the Royal Ballet's plans were solid for two years ahead, I could only offer Jirí a slot with the touring company for one of his smaller ballets. He did not like that idea and said it was the Royal Opera House stage with the Royal Ballet the following season – or not at all. I was powerless. At that time Kylián was all the rage, much in demand elsewhere, and so we had to drop the matter. Another great shame. Norman Morrice programmed Jirí's *Return to the Strange Land* some years later but subsequent directors preferred other choreographers, and now the schedules are filled differently.

When I first knew John Neumeier during my days in Stuttgart he was a fine classical dancer with very good legs, feet and hands. As choreographer, he created *The Fourth Symphony* at Covent Garden in June 1977 as part of Kenneth's attempts to broaden the Royal Ballet's range. It was one of those ballets that just did not work. It had only four performances. As the only new ballet that season it carried the weight of expectation. I saw it but it was not good, boring in fact. I had seen a lot of John's work in Germany. Created a couple of years before, I saw *Third Symphony of Gustav Mahler* in rehearsal in Hamburg, and except for a ten-minute section danced in silence which lost me, it moved me very much. *Third Symphony* runs for nearly two hours with no interval and needs 30 men onstage in the opening movement, a mezzo soprano, a women's chorus and a boys' choir in addition to a symphony orchestra. At Covent Garden it was not possible to treat choreographers like that. They just have to knuckle under and get on with it.

John used another Mahler score for *The Fourth Symphony*, his song cycle *Des Knaben Wunderhorn*. The ballet showed a child's growing up. It was created on Wayne Sleep with Lynn Seymour and David Wall seemingly as his parents. The boy's journey into adolescence, his discovery of love and friendship were all implied rather than explicitly depicted. The staging was abstract and the lighting transformed dancers into silhouettes. With his own company in Hamburg, while rehearsing, John would just sit in the studio, intently watching his dancers. They would do anything for him when he raised an eyebrow or made a gesture of the hand. John really was regarded as a god there with a huge following. In London John was very dissatisfied that he could not spend the requisite amount of time needed on *The Fourth Symphony*. At Covent Garden you just have to stick to the time you have been allocated. The kindest reaction was that *The Fourth Symphony* was sincere but anonymous. I do not know whether more rehearsal would have helped, but personally I do not think so.

Which said, I rate John very highly, although in a completely different mould from the British tradition. His choreography contains a mixture of styles, incorporating action and text, and fits very much into that German approach where the director's concept is most important. Many of John's ballets are based on literary works. *Lady of the Camelias*, created in Stuttgart, is a long and literal telling of the story by Alexandre Dumas. John's more recent *Tatiana*, another work that ballerinas such as Alina Cojocaru adore, is a much more deliberate reworking of Alexander Pushkin's novel *Eugene Onegin*, seen from Tatiana's perspective.

John, and other choreographers, can speak to me when their work comes out of the classical moulding. I quite enjoyed his reworking of *The Nutcracker*. Instead of a Christmas party the action takes place at a celebration as Marie, as Clara is called in this version, celebrates her 13th birthday. Her adventures take place backstage and onstage of a theatre after she is given a pair of pointe shoes. Here again, however, John is working very much in the self-referential German tradition that demands a new conceptual approach for existing literary or theatrical titles or sources rather than creating an original work from scratch. I saw John's *Hamlet-Connotations*, to music by Aaron Copeland, in Stuttgart. There was a stepladder and a bit of drapery. I could not understand it all. The audience screamed its approval but I felt completely left out, which is the reaction I have about much new work. What am I missing, I wonder?

Many dancers aspire to be choreographers but the crossover is not an automatic one. While I was responsible for the New Group in the 1970s I gave opportunities to several dancers. Geoffrey Cauley created *In the Beginning* which, as the title hints, is set in the garden of Eden, a favourite hunting ground for choreographers. While detecting inevitable choreographic influences, particularly Ashton, which endeared Cauley to certain critics, he was seen to have an individual voice in his spare use of movements and poses. Highlighting potential puts pressure on any young choreographer. There are simply not the performance opportunities or indeed the facilities to satisfy emerging choreographers. Nevertheless I found time for Cauley to create more works. *Lazarus* attracted most attention. When revived in 1989 it still looked interesting, which is by no means guaranteed for a revival. I am glad that *Lazarus* is now fully notated so that it may be revived again, even if only for a few performances. *Lazarus* is Cauley at his best. I feel that it is vitally important that such ballets are kept alive. We should not always judge ballets by whether they sell or not.

Another Covent Garden dancer, who like Cauley had participated in Leslie Edwards' choreographic group during the 1960s and was keen to prove himself as a dance maker, was David Drew. As a performer, especially in character roles such as the gaoler in *Manon*, he was brilliant. In retrospect he was honest enough to rate his attempts at choreography on a scale ranging from most to least awful. Kenneth MacMillan pulled Drew's *Impressionists* before its first performance when David seemed to be having some sort of breakdown. His choice of music was always wide ranging and unconventional, Schubert for *Intrusion*, Alan Hovhaness for *From Walking Sleep* and Shostakovich for *Sacred Circles*. Drew's most interesting work, I thought, was *St Thomas' Wake* with a score by Peter Maxwell Davies. The stage was dominated by a huge pile of rubbish, for some reason I never understood. It was riveting to watch, however. It was not really a ballet, with little actual choreography – more a remarkable happening. I do not mind failing to understand, provided a ballet grabs you. And entertains, that is the other requisite. Drew's ballet about the Franco-Prussian war, *The Sword of Alsace*, with music by Joachim Raff, did neither. It felt nearly as long as the war itself and really rather boring. Drew learned to recognise that he was no choreographer, but those whom he taught, when he assisted

Norman Morrice with the choreographic course at the Royal Ballet School, included Christopher Wheeldon, Michael Nunn, Billy Trevitt, Will Tuckett, Christopher Hampson, Mathew Hart, Alistair Marriott, David Dawson, Paul Lightfoot, Tom Sapsford, David Fielding and Cathy Marston – among many.

A performance of new choreography at Sadler's Wells, including some attempts at imitating contemporary dance, provoked Ninette de Valois to tackle me in the interval. She was quite angry, 'This is a waste of time, Peter. Contemporary dance requires a lot of specialised training which flies in the face of classical training. Good, well-trained contemporary dancers are wonderful and it is wrong to take the work away from them. The Royal Ballet organisation is based on a tradition that draws on many influences from which it is possible to develop in all sorts of different styles.' Madam firmly believed that a young choreographer needs to produce not one isolated work but at least two productions per year – importantly – in the same environment and with the same group of artists over a considerable period of time.

David Bintley's early career with the Royal Ballet companies certainly benefited from this approach. He was not alone, but in all honesty nothing otherwise had come out of all the opportunities that I had given to many dancers within Sadler's Wells Royal Ballet. Susan Crow, Jennifer Jackson and Jonathan Thorpe all tried their hands at choreography, as did Derek Deane from the Covent Garden company. Surprisingly given his later career, Russell Maliphant did not show any interest in choreography in those days. It was only subsequently that his extraordinary talent emerged. Among many ballets Michael Corder made were *Day into Night*, *The Wand of Youth*, *Rhyme nor Reason* and *St Anthony Variations*. He was his own worst enemy, strangling himself with too many steps. I admired much of what Michael created but his ballets would mostly have benefited from what Frederick Ashton called paring down. Michael puts too many steps into too short a musical phrase. There were, however, two pieces that I really liked. One was *Varii Capricci*, using the same score by William Walton as Ashton had. This was a belated tribute to me for my 80th birthday by Michael, unveiled at the Elmhurst school in February 2007. The evening was a surprise party for me and Sonya, entitled The Wright Occasion. I imagine Michael had very little rehearsal time but it was wonderfully musical, clear and both simple and difficult, with time to appreciate the different steps and lifts. The other occasional piece of Michael's that I liked was done the same year for a celebration of John Sainsbury's 80th birthday at the Royal Opera House. Michael had the dancers on shopping trolleys. It was witty, hilariously funny, slick and very inventive.

Another member of Sadler's Wells Royal Ballet keen to try his choreographic hand was Graham Lustig. He made *Caught in Time* and *Inscape*, although *Paramour* was the most enduring. It was a witty look at a 1930s Parisian salon danced to Poulenc's much choreographed double piano concerto. The ballet was strong enough to revive and was adopted by Hartford Ballet in America where Eva Evdokimova was attracted by its central role of a society hostess of a certain age. Among others, Jonathan Burrows made *Catch* and *The Winter Play* which both drew on the traditions of folk dance but which he admits were a real struggle, and he gave up his attempts to choreograph as a result for a couple of years. Later, in Birmingham, Will Tuckett made *License my Roving Hands* to Jimmy Hendrix songs with Miyako Yoshida in skin-tight PVC. Tuckett has a wonderful sense of theatre and has been very successful when working with singers and actors in musicals.

In my retirement year Matthew Hart very affectionately choreographed a tribute to me, *Sir Peter and the Wolf,* for the Royal Ballet School at Merle Park's instigation. It was typically full of Matthew's flair and humour. The wolf was first played by Martin Harvey, a role taken by Sergei Polunin at a later revival. Matthew conceived the meadow as a line of showgirls and the pond as a group of 1920s flappers. It was all designed by Ian Spurling in his usual quirky style. Matthew's career was typical of many young choreographers. Although he is still working as a performer and teacher, his early ambitions as a choreographer were not really realised. I had wanted him as a dancer in Birmingham but he preferred to join the company at Covent Garden where he was promised opportunities to choreograph. A slot had been reserved in the scheduling in October 1993 with a new score by Brian Elias. This had been intended for a new ballet by Kenneth MacMillan, but in the event of his death the year before – and Matthew's *Street* for Birmingham Royal Ballet and *Simple Symphony* for the Royal Ballet School – the slot went to him. *Fanfare* was the result. A 21-year-old making his first ballet for the Covent Garden stage is no joke. I was 31 when I made mine and I know. It is always involved at best and often fraught. Somebody at that stage of their career needs to be pushed artistically and professionally but encouraged emotionally and mentally too. Choreographers often feel terribly insecure about their own worth.

Subsequently Matthew made a full-length *Cinderella* for London City Ballet which had some acclaim. However, his subsequent experience at Covent Garden, with *Dances with Death*, about the spread of Aids, and *Blitz*, commissioned but unperformed by English National Ballet, was discouraging. Matthew was lost to the Royal Ballet as a choreographer when he joined the Rambert company as a dancer. A choreographer needs a company, an environment in which to work regularly with a constant set of colleagues, in order to produce new works frequently. Although Matthew subsequently found opportunities to choreograph – and his *Whodunnit?* based on the game Cluedo for Ballet Central in 2009 was highly accomplished and witty – he has since worked mostly as a performer in television, film and musical theatre as well as a teacher. He is probably best known for his vivid assumption of character roles in Will Tuckett's theatrical versions of *Wind in the Willows*, *The Soldier's Tale* and *Pinocchio*, although he has choreographed a very different and highly entertaining *Nutcracker* for Sarasota Ballet based on the John Ringland Circus.

I have served on the Ninette de Valois Trust Fund committee which was founded by James Ranger. It exists to make an annual award to support emerging choreographers nominated by the directors of Britain's major classical companies. Frequently we found ourselves in the situation where the nominations were not of a sufficiently high standard to merit an award. Such is the transience of so many new works. Despite the many apprentice choreographers who I asked to produce new ballets for Sadler's Wells Royal Ballet during the 1980s nobody's work – other than that of David Bintley – has stuck. In 1976 I was on the assessment panel for when the Gulbenkian Foundation awarded grants to aspiring choreographers. We asked each applicant whether they had any ideas for new ballets. Most had a couple of things in mind, usually not suitable to be made into choreographic works. David stood out from the rest when he said he had two dozen ideas in mind. That was impressive, but more striking was that they were all so different from each other and capable of being realised.

David soon became a creative force for the company, producing an incredibly varied range. His first professional ballet in March 1978 was *The Outsider* based on *L'Étranger* by Albert Camus. It had music by Josef Bohac and was an account of prostitution and murder, which I liked. David's choice of composers for his early ballets was eclectic – Dave Brubeck, Milhaud, Lord Berners, Pafunik, Britten, Malcolm Arnold, Rossini, Aubrey Meyer, Peter McGowan, Mozart, Debussy, Simon Jeffes, Stravinsky. His choice of subjects and themes, in narrative and plotless forms, was as precocious. At the age of 24, David's first full-length ballet was *The Swan of Tuonela*, set to Sibelius and with a scenario he had constructed himself from traditional legends. His second, *The Snow Queen*, used Mussorgsky. David himself, rightly I think, regards *Hobson's Choice*, dating from 1989, more than a decade into his career as a choreographer, as his opus one, a brilliant ballet and one that I adore. His earlier works he considers as apprentice pieces, not to be revived, although '*Still Life*' *at the Penguin Café*, a strange piece but one of David's really worthwhile ones, endures, and *Allegri diversi* has resurfaced. For a ballet depicting such a complex subjects in *Edward II*, which portrays homosexuality and a cruel death, it made quite a stir when created for Stuttgart Ballet and is quite engrossing. David relocated *The Prince of the Pagodas* to Japan which for him was the key that unlocked the mysteries of the scenario first created by John Cranko. The Japanese setting gave an appropriate context for the orientalism in Britten's music. This was not a production that engaged me much when I saw it in Tokyo in 2011, performed by National Ballet of Japan. Much as I have had many enjoyable experiences of working in Japan – and of course Sonya was half-Japanese – the faux-Japanesery of the production exposed David's tendency to parody. He did find a logic for the story by presenting a court remote in its adherence to ritual, disturbed when foreign kings, including a Russian oil oligarch and gun-toting American, arrive. While that had clear resonances in Japan itself, the decision to make the principal couple long-lost brother and sister did not add to the dramatic impulse of the story. The score, Britten's homage to *The Sleeping Beauty*, prompted some of David's most appealing choreography. His own sense of his choreographic lineage was evident in how his waves and stars ebb and twinkle in homage to Petipa and Ashton. David's seahorses wittily nod to the traditions of English country dancing and the knights in *Checkmate*.

Of David's other ballets, although not that demanding technically, I like *Flowers of the Forest*, *Galanteries* and *Consort Lessons* very much. I believe David would have maintained a higher standard if he had stayed at the Royal Opera House as resident choreographer. He works quickly and tends not to refine his work to the detriment of the overall impact in my opinion. *Tombeaux* shows that he can do it. Some of his writing for the corps de ballet work in *Cinderella* is nicely arranged, particularly in the ballroom, but time will tell if it is going to last. Works such as *Carmina burana* are hugely theatrical and popular with non-ballet audiences. It was designed by Philip Prowse who felt very much on his mettle working with David, but really the ballet is mainly memorable for its staging effects. When performed at the London Coliseum in 2015, it was a great success, with the Ex Cathedra choir excelling itself.

Getting the Royal Ballet back on track after Ross Stretton's directorship and moving it forward was one of Monica Mason's ablest achievements. The decision to bring in Wayne McGregor as resident choreographer was more debatable. Dancers like working with him, although the public reaction to his works has been decidedly mixed. So far I have not found McGregor's style to be a natural extension of the way classical ballet had developed in the hands of such choreographers as MacMillan, Robbins, Cranko, Balanchine – and will continue to develop with Bintley, Christopher Wheeldon and Liam Scarlett. Is it too much to hope that some dancing should be included in McGregor's work – and by that I do not mean just pretty waltzes? He claims he wants to show classical ballet in a different way. What does that mean? Jerome Robbins did that nearly 60 years ago with his ballet *Moves*, danced in silence, and the ballet was still classical. By dispensing with a score in *Moves*, Robbins radically altered how an audience experiences ballet, with contemporary movement very much based on classical steps.

McGregor's *Woolf Works*, unveiled in May 2015 at Covent Garden, was trailed as his first full-length ballet there. The suggestion, left implicit, was that McGregor would be working in narrative form for the first time, a genre central to the Royal Ballet's identity which had been lost since the deaths in quick succession of Ashton and MacMillan as well as the subsequent resignation of David Bintley. *Woolf Works* was labelled a triptych, not in itself anything new. George Balanchine did that with *Jewels* nearly 40 years before. In comparison to McGregor's extreme physicality,

Balanchine's ballets are a stretch technically for dancers in a positive way. His bigger ballets are a challenge to stage, but during my time at Birmingham I considered it important to acquire such Balanchine ballets as *Symphony in Three Movements* which is a great work that uses most of the company and really challenges them to dance in a bold way and reach out to the audience. I find it exhilarating to watch and see another side of Balanchine's style of choreography. I revived *Divertimento No. 15* and *Theme and Variations* as both are tests of classical technique, while *Prodigal Son* is always an opportunity for a company to display its dramatic abilities. Balanchine has had mixed fortunes at both Royal Ballet companies. As Desmond Kelly, a magnificent *Apollo* in his dancing days, is now an official stager of some of Balanchine's works, I am hopeful that it will be possible to have more of his ballets in the Birmingham repertoire. The way he staged *Theme and Variations* in October 2015 was magnificent.

If any recent choreographer can be claimed to have reinvented classical ballet then it is William Forsythe. Nothing is distorted in his work, at least his earlier pieces. They can be easily encompassed by classically trained dancers. Yet even in the more straightforward ballets which Forsythe has created or remounted for other companies, such as those adopted by the Royal Ballet including *In the Middle, Somewhat Elevated*, and *The Vertiginous Thrill of the Exactitude* he takes the dancing out of its traditional alignment, with twists and unbalances, unexpected timing or placing, and a casual way of walking or standing mixed in with the formality of balletic movement. The creative procedures he has developed within his own company enable him to go further in terms of complexity, of turning sequences inside out or back to front, and of exploring minute relationships between different parts of the body. For all his technical complexity, Forsythe's works were far from the abstract or narrative styles found conventionally in ballet. Throughout his career Forsythe has always sought to explore what is possible in dance, how steps are made, how spaces and shapes are created. I saw the first pas de deux Forsythe made, in Stuttgart in 1976. It was based on classical technique, on pointe and was very beautiful and had Forsythe's stamp on it, full of sustained tension and sculptural fluidity. This was *Urlicht*. Reid Anderson, now director of Stuttgart Ballet, danced in it with Forsythe's wife Eileen Brady and he has recalled how precise Forsythe was in describing how he wanted each step to look. It is a piece that is still performed 40 years later. Over the course of his career Forsythe experimented with conventional limits of balance and flexibility, the relationship of a vertical torso and the arms, the practices of partnering and use of the pointe shoe and has often ventured far from classicism. It will be interesting to see what his latest creation for the Paris Opéra Ballet in 2016 will reveal.

Pina Bausch began studying dance with Kurt Jooss in Essen as a teenager in 1954. Jooss' form of modern dance, freed from the traditions of classical ballet, with a strong emphasis on creative expression, were formative for Pina, as were a couple of years spent in New York where her teachers included Antony Tudor, José Limón, dancers from Martha Graham's company, Alfredo Corvino and Margaret Craske. As a dancer Pina worked too with Paul Taylor. I was back with Jooss when she rejoined and I recall her as a performer who could really inhabit the different roles she was playing. One of these was the old woman, whom death takes into his arms as she dies. I had seen this danced by several wonderful artists but nobody matched the intensity that Pina displayed. She used body movement down to her last finger but no facial expressions. Although Pina had started to assist Jooss with choreography after her return from America, nobody at that time knew that she had a hidden talent as a choreographer herself until 1969 when she created a piece for the Cologne International Choreographic Workshop where I had been invited to be on the judging panel. When her piece, *Im Wind der Zeit,* or *In the Wind of Time*, which I think had eight dancers in it, was shown, I could hardly believe my eyes. It was completely individual and different from anything I had ever seen. Very strong and powerful, the dancers had become totally involved in the work. It was nothing like any of the other entries. It had extraordinary groupings which were classically inspired. I was spellbound and was determined she should be the winner. I knew I was right but I had to work very hard to persuade the rest of the judging panel. Anyhow, she got the prize and this was the beginning of the great change that took place in her life and work.

What a transformation it was. She suddenly altered from a quiet, polite dancer who everybody nonetheless respected into this amazing woman who had her own way of living and producing choreography. She created her early works in Wuppertal, *Aktionen für Tänzer,* or *Actions for*

Dancers, and *Tannhäuser Bacchanal* in the early 1970s. She soon became director of the Wuppertal Ballet, which she renamed the Tanztheater Wuppertal, where she developed her distinctive brand of dance theatre creating her own remarkable and wonderful shows. Suddenly she was a leader who did everything her way. Choreographically you cannot compare her work to anybody else. She was the most amazing power, so original in her mind. Her version of *Rite of Spring*, created in 1975, is one of the most exciting things I have ever seen. Pina covered the stage floor in earth, and phalanxes of men and women confronted each other throughout the piece. For once the choreography did not seem subsidiary to Igor Stravinsky's score, which is frequently the case with other productions of this ballet. Rare for me, I stood up, shouting my admiration when it was performed at Sadler's Wells in 2008. I thought it was absolutely wonderful. If I say that to other people they just look baffled, but Pina's works to me are like the films of Alfred Hitchcock. I like the fact that Pina's ballets are strange. In *Arien* the cast is clad in evening clothes, lying ankle-deep in water. In *Nelken* women prowl round a carnation-covered stage watched over by guard dogs, for example. Why? Hitchcock would have perhaps said, as he did about his films, that he does not worry how and why things happen but he wants the audience to be fascinated by them. That is what I find in Pina's work. Our paths crossed quite frequently, which was always a pleasure. Pina had a great sense of humour. I still regret her loss in 2009. Rather like Martha Graham, she created a new way of movement and performance. There is a beautiful 3D film, *Pina*, which Wim Wenders, her dancers and collaborators made in 2011, which gives an insight into her passion for life. She was like no one else, and no one else will ever be like her, completely surprising – a one-off. Her work, very theatrical and often incorporating spoken text, did not necessarily appeal to dance audiences and does not necessarily need to be performed by dancers, but Pina was unique in showing different ways of moving.

To describe Kurt Jooss as modern dance is to apply the wrong label, but Ninette de Valois was always concerned Jooss' style of dance making might be a threat, particularly in those towns and cities where classical ballet was not performed. We need classical ballet. It is the grounding for other forms of dance, for choreographers and dancers alike, as well as for audiences. The way in which classical ballet started, with its own language expressed in different styles around the world, was built on very strong foundations.

Having seen Christopher Wheeldon's full-length *The Winter's Tale*, I think that he is on the right track, with choreography that is based on our classical heritage, something similar in essence to the many ballets by Jerome Robbins that we no longer see these days. Wheeldon was trained as a classical dancer so the movements he creates, particularly in *The Winter's Tale*, use the dancers' innate classicism but in a very contemporary way. Dancers respond to that. But when I look to the future I think classical ballet will pull through although it is temporarily being pulled off track. I want classical ballet to be contemporary – meaning that I want it to be up to date, but I do not want it to become completely different.

Nearly 50 years ago, in 1970, Kenneth MacMillan was roundly criticised when he created his short-lived *Checkpoint*. It was Kenneth at his most provocative in its dissonant modern score and in its subject matter – illicit love in an oppressive, totalitarian state, the inclusion of film amid a complicated staging. Whatever the trappings, the critics were clear in their assessment of Kenneth's work: ballets by important choreographers should not rely on effects. The choreography must express what the choreographer is attempting to say without extra embellishments. That is a lesson that all choreographers must learn.

CHAPTER 13

International relations

I WAS NOT IN A very good state when I rejoined Sadler's Wells Theatre Ballet in 1951 after the Ballets Jooss went bankrupt. In retrospect it was probably the best thing that could have happened to me. I knew the repertoire and could go straight back into all the ballets that were going on the tour. It was a major undertaking, seven months visiting 72 cities, starting from Euston on 25 September. The tour involved 30 tons of scenery, 4,000 pairs of ballet shoes, over 500 costumes, 15 crates of props and 600lbs of music scores. For a young man of 26 in post-war Britain still subject to rationing, this was an exciting opportunity, even though for the Atlantic crossing on the *Empress of France* we travelled third class. We enjoyed all the wonderful food during the week-long crossing. Madam made a tour of inspection of our onboard quarters. 'Hmm. Be careful of the air conditioning. It can be really dangerous,' she advised as she peered into my cabin, which she evidently regarded as insalubrious compared to her own, first-class, accommodation.

Princess Elizabeth and Prince Philip had been due to sail on the same boat en route to their first visit to Canada, but George VI's recent lung surgery meant as heir apparent, the then princess was detained in London and so flew to Canada instead. She and Philip arrived in Montreal, our second venue, as we opened at the St Denis theatre but did not attend any of our performances. Over the years I was to learn that the queen is always a polite but only ever a dutiful attender of ballet. 'Very nice,' is what she said to me after my production of *The Nutcracker* was premiered at Covent Garden, years later in 1984.

The death of George VI, which we heard about when we were in New Orleans, prompted a debate as to whether or not we should wear black armbands. We decided not. In the 1950s ballet companies were used as walking advertisements for British fashions and fabrics. Our offstage attire was sponsored by different manufacturers. The men stepped out in shoes by Crockett and Jones, ties by Liberty, and our hats were provided by the British Felt Hat Manufacturers' Association. Compared to the relaxed attire of tracksuits sported by dancers nowadays on long-haul international flights, we were the epitome of smart!

In 1951 our conductors for the tour were John – known as Jack – Lanchbery and Robert Zeller. The company was led by Svetlana Beriosova, Elaine Fifield, Maryon Lane, Patricia Miller, Sheilah O'Reilly, David Blair, Donald Britton, Stanley Holden, David Poole and Pirmin Trecu – so I was among friends. The corps de ballet was only listed on the penultimate page of the programme, 16 girls and eight boys, of which I was the last named. Always a W!

Doris Thellusson, whose daughter went to my school, Bedales, came along as social secretary. She had nothing to do with the ballet officially but was a great disciple of Madam. She was engaged by her as a sort of chaperone to protect the young girls on the tour, some of them students from the school, from randy Yanks. Doris, or Dodo as she was called herself, was very fond of Pirmin Trecu, a Spanish refugee who used to tease her frequently. She arranged activities and receptions for us when we were not performing, something that was particularly appreciated when we arrived in yet another town without knowing anybody. The stage director was Richard Eastham who later became my agent. He was married to Jane Edgeworth, Madam's secretary, who not so long before had relished informing me that I was not good enough to join the company. She enjoyed speaking on behalf of de Valois but she was a gossip and could be quite nasty.

Jane was close to the dancer David Poole who lived with her and Richard, her husband. But David, short and gay, and Jane, decidedly tall, made an odd pair. The stage manager for that tour was Val West who is my agent today. Barbara Fewster, who became principal of the Royal Ballet School, was assistant ballet mistress and married to the master carpenter Alan Wilkinson, a nice man and very good at how the scenery should be hung. There were some jealousies but that will always be the case. It was a tough tour but we were a happy company overall, although Peggy van Praagh, our ballet mistress and essentially Madam's deputy, could sometimes get hysterical. There was one occasion when we were travelling to a venue in two buses when the leading bus lurched off the highway, balancing on its side wheels before fortunately coming to a halt in some wasteland. Peggy was in the rear bus and watched, absolutely horrified. She was violently sick as she saw half her company near death.

For the benefit of American audiences the theatre programme included articles about the history – and geography – of Sadler's Wells. Apparently, its location in Islington away from major transport links has always been the complaint of audiences, but James Agate joked, I think, that an excursion to Sadler's Wells was comparable to a journey to Asia Minor or Darkest Africa. Arnold Haskell described the faith and drive of those master-women – Ninette de Valois and Lillian Baylis – in establishing British ballet, comparing their importance to the brilliant actor Edmund Kean and famous clown Grimaldi. Our repertoire included the second act of *Swan Lake* and *The Nutcracker*, minus the first Christmas party scene, produced by Frederick Ashton as a classical divertissement, as well as his *Façade*, *Capriol Suite* and *Les Rendezvous*. John Cranko was represented by *Harlequin in April* which was well constructed, interesting choreographically and had superb designs by John Piper. Other Cranko ballets included were *Pineapple Poll*, *Beauty and the Beast*, *Tritsch-Tratsch Polka* and *Pastorale*, a rather good, pure dance ballet set to Mozart, almost an extended divertissement which I featured in with Michel Hogan. I was also second cast for the role created by David Blair, full of beaten steps and double tours which were a struggle for me. Also in our repertory were de Valois' powerful *Haunted Ballroom* which was practically the first English classical ballet, very clever in how she choreographed the ghosts, as well as her comedy ballet, *The Prospect Before Us*. *Jota Toledana* was a Spanish divertissement by Angelo Andes. It used to bring the house down. I did it at occasional matinees with Jane Shore – now Nicholas – but without the same brilliance.

The repertoire also included Andrée Howard's *Assembly Ball*, which was made for the company's first all-ballet evening and *Khadra*, set to Sibelius by Celia Franca, in which I sometimes danced as the prince. The ballet was like a fragment of a Persian sculptural frieze coming to life. I had to lift a girl from a shoulder-height rostrum and carry her around the stage as she sat on my upraised hands above my head. That was quite a test of my partnering skills at the time. On a tour a couple of years before, Celia discovered that there were no permanent professional ballet companies in Canada, which prompted her move to Toronto where she was well known. With no money she had to get various jobs in a department store and at a telephone exchange, at the same time sussing out the local dance schools and arts organisations to plant the idea of a national Canadian ballet company. She founded a school with Betty Oliphant which was the beginning of today's National Ballet of Canada with its big school and worldwide reputation. Celia was a truly remarkable woman and a great director. She modelled her company on Sadler's Wells Ballet, performing the classics but maintaining a strong English core in its repertoire and style, and invited major international performers and artists to work there. In 1970 she invited me to Toronto to stage *Giselle* with Lynn Seymour and Egon Madsen, and *The Mirror Walkers* for Karen Kain, who is now the company's director.

Coppélia was the only three-act ballet we presented on that tour. It was produced by Peggy van Praagh using the choreography by Nikolai Sergeyev and designed by Loudon Sainthill in pastel greys and greens. As it transpired, during our first performance in Montreal, our next venue, we soon discovered that the audience at the city's Capitol theatre was quite uncritical. There was spontaneous applause during the set of brisés, a forward diagonal of beaten jumps which Swanilda performs in the first act. Audiences were evidently very unfamiliar with three-act ballets. Critics were equally enthusiastic on the whole. One described us as ragged and pretty-pretty but mostly we were triumphant according to one, zestful said another. In the French-language papers it sounded even better: we were a troupe that was jeune, ardente, douée d'une technique sure. It was our ballerinas – Svetlana Beriosova, Maryon Lane and Elaine Fifield, fresh from her huge success as Cranko's original *Pineapple Poll* – who got most of the press attention, with articles on their training, London fashions and what they ate for breakfast. Stanley Holden and Stella Farrance had recently married so they featured in stories about their honeymoon tour to America. There was great excitement in the press – and among the company – when Jack Lanchbery announced that he and Elaine were going to be married. He was gay and very busy with the boys. She had no idea and seemed to be in a state of shock when she found out. She thought it was a big joke but they were duly married by a municipal judge at our hotel. Ashton always adored Elaine with her beautiful feet and fantastic pirouettes. She was later one of the seven ballerinas in *Birthday Offering*, created for the company's 25th anniversary when the company acquired its royal title. He used to say that if ever there was going to be another Fonteyn, it would be Elaine, or Fi-Fi as she was known in the company. She could perform the fiendishly difficult series of pirouettes in *Les Rendezvous* effortlessly. Fi-Fi could be very funny. She once did a performance of the ballet in a red wig she had found and, for fun, performed the pirouettes to the left, which meant that when the boys appeared at the corners of the stage to acknowledge her, they were on the wrong side. Fi-Fi used to drink crème de menthe from her thermos flask. Her marriage to Jack was disastrous. After it broke up Fi-Fi married an Australian sheep farmer. Nothing but miles and miles of sheep broke her.

After Quebec and Montreal we moved on to Toronto – where I managed an occasional mention in the press, offering good support as the prince's friend in *Swan Lake* – before crossing into America to visit Buffalo, taking in the Niagara Falls and Rochester NY before we worked westwards right across the country. In Seattle we played in a venue holding 5,000 people. Then it was along the western seaboard, Portland, Vancouver, San Francisco then on to Sacramento and San Diego before arriving in Los Angeles for Christmas. That was probably one of our hardest dates on the whole tour. We opened there on Christmas Day itself at the Philharmonic auditorium with a matinée of *Coppélia*. We were checked into the Ambassador hotel, famous as the home of the Coconut Grove nightclub, where great stars and groups appeared in cabaret. Unfortunately, as we started with a week's holiday and none of us knew anybody in Los Angeles, the most spread-out city in the world with virtually no public transport, we were pretty miserable. We had to take taxis which we could not afford if we wanted to buy our Christmas presents. The hotel did have a lot of boutiques which were horrendously expensive. The weather seemed to be getting hotter and heavier every day. Apparently California was going through a freak heatwave. Instead of the white Christmas with snow that Brits always long for but never actually get, instead there was an earthquake which the heatwave had been a precursor of. It was not huge but enough to unnerve us all, and it did cause the chandeliers in the hotel to rattle. In fact one of the girls, Karen Bliss – daughter of Arthur Bliss, composer of the music for *Checkmate*, *Adam Zero* and *Miracle in the Gorbals*, which after many years of neglect was restaged by Birmingham Royal Ballet in 2014 – ran down to the desk saying, 'I am awfully concerned about the noise that is shaking our room', only to be told that it was quite a common occurrence, just an earthquake. Despite all the excitement, we felt even more homesick.

After the performance, Sol Hurok gave us a Christmas party with a huge swan made of ice, about ten feet tall, in the middle of a vast ballroom. Rather like us, it seemed, the swan began to melt and droop. Eventually its head fell off. But thanks to the efforts of Hurok and Doris Thellusson, at last we met some people and the revues the next day were excellent. 'Ballet added to the gaiety of the Yule season' said one review, though another complained that in *The Nutcracker* no man, not even a fairy king, should have to wear the eye make-up seen in the production. No matter, suddenly Los Angeles sprang to life for us, with many parties, and we met quite a few stars, particularly Douglas Fairbanks, Jr, who was absolutely wonderful the way he talked to everybody and cheered us up no end. As a wedding present for Jack Lanchbery and Elaine Fifield, Hurok arranged for them to meet Charlie Chaplin on the set of *Limelight*, where they were also introduced to Claire Bloom and Buster Keaton. Others of us were invited to the film studios too. We all thought we might be discovered but I think it was only David Blair and Donald Britton who were asked back to have screen tests. Nothing came of them, however.

We watched Zsa Zsa Gabor being filmed in a cabaret scene. She was positioned on a type of raised dais, sitting in a corner with a few other people but surrounded by hundreds of extras at tables. The camera moved in and focused on her as she stood up, waved to somebody and said something like, 'Hello darling, isn't this fun', beckoning for the person to join her. It took five takes before she could get it right. Each took time to set up as the camera had to track among tables, and Gabor's line had to hit a certain spot exactly on the sound playback. She just could not get it right. She was, however, absolutely delightful with all the make-up people, hairdressers, speech coaches and assistant directors fussing round her between takes trying to help her – enough to make anyone forget their lines I should think.

Next was a long trek, three days and two nights, across the Arizona desert on board a 13-car train to San Antonio in Texas. This was pretty eventful! Back in London but aware of the itinerary, Madam worried about the rather randy American orchestra that was travelling with us. We were not allowed our own musicians because of union restrictions. The orchestra travelled in separate coaches but Madam was very concerned about our young girls. She insisted that the connecting door between the dancers' section and the orchestra was to be kept locked, presumably to prevent her girls being deflowered. Anyway, within half an hour out of Los Angeles the lock was picked and life became more interesting. We had a fancy dress party on the first evening which was hilarious. Inspired by her visit to the film studios, I remember Elaine Fifield doing a brilliant impersonation of Chaplin. Things quietened down a bit until after supper when the seats were folded back to become sleeping bunks. It felt as though we were in the films *42nd Street* or *Some Like it Hot* with Marilyn Monroe, Tony Curtis, Jack Lemmon and all that activity behind the curtained sleeping berths. I think we outdid those scenes. The next morning there may have been quite a few tears but many more smiling faces. The tour manager read the riot act, rather difficult to do on a train in fact. All that did was make the dancers more stealthy and careful as they switched bunks.

After San Antonio we were in Waco, Houston, Dallas and Little Rock. We reached Miami where we had a few days off, spending a lot of time on the beach. Dancers look fabulous in their swimwear, and the less they wear the better they look. We did not know, however, that the law in Florida in those days stated that bikinis are prohibited for women, and men must wear proper swimming shorts that suitably covered their nether regions, buttocks included. As a result, the police descended on us and about five of the company were arrested, being carted off to a local police station. The British consul was called, and somebody from the British Council rushed along and pleaded with the authorities. As a result the dancers were released with a warning. The good thing was the press got hold of the incident and the publicity boosted bookings considerably. A whole series of one-night stands followed, places like Indianapolis, Troy, White Plains, Columbus City. It was an amazing trip, the only drawback being that in many places we saw only the station and theatre before getting back on the train and heading on to the next place. Once we did 15 nights on the trot where our special train would arrive somewhere early in the morning, usually around 5am. We would be turfed off at 8.30am and bussed to the theatre, usually unable to get into the dressing-rooms until about 4pm.

A common sight wherever we played was dancers wandering along streets after another overnight train journey, trying to kill time before a performance. After a few of these horrendous journeys we complained to the manager of the tour and reluctantly we were provided with a couple of day rooms at a hotel – one for the girls and another for the boys. Just imagine about 30 girls with their day luggage in one room. The boys were better off as there were only 20 of us, but that was bad enough. Another problem was that Hurok had billed the company as the Sadler's Wells Ballet in huge letters, with FABULOUS in big italics diagonally across the posters. We were in fact Sadler's Wells Theatre Ballet, but Hurok used small italics for the Theatre part of our name, hidden between the Wells and Ballet, so that the ticket-buying public could scarcely see it. They thought they were coming to see the Covent Garden company – with Margot Fonteyn – which had undertaken hugely successful visits to America during the previous few years. Hurok had first billed the Covent Garden company as fabulous the previous year in Los Angeles. There were complaints, but all told the company was a big, big success. Young and vibrant, we may not have been quite so polished as the other company but we gave audiences their money's worth in terms of performance, enthusiasm and spirit.

Our New York season, the culmination of the tour, was quite a success but not world shattering, as that initial visit in 1949 had been for the Sadler's Wells Ballet, the Covent Garden company. We danced *The Nutcracker* in which Svetlana Beriosova was full of grandeur as the snow queen, an adorable ballerina. As designed by Cecil Beaton, the snowflakes scene was painted entirely in black and white which then fantastically transformed into a rather bilious shade of green for the magical kingdom of sweets where Elaine Fifield was revealed as the glittering and crystalline Sugar Plum fairy which earned her a lovely success. In the triple-bill Pirmin Trecu got rave notices as the young boy in Andrée Howard's *La Fête étrange*, designed by Sophie Fedorovitch. *Pineapple Poll* was liked but the humour was perhaps too British to go down really well but audiences loved David Blair's dashing Captain

Belaye. They adored *Les Rendezvous* and Elaine brought the house down in her solo.

During the season six of the principals appeared on a big TV spectacular broadcast nationwide and the whole company was paid very nice fees as well for doing nothing. This meant we could have a lovely shopping spree before we returned home by plane. We were very tired but we had all benefited from the tour and matured considerably. From my own perspective, I had gained in confidence and strength. I do believe a certain amount of touring is an essential part of the development of a good performing artist. On the other hand, everyone is different. Some dancers like Alexander Grant never did class. He did not seem to need the daily discipline of classes to keep in trim but had his own routine of a few warm-up exercises. Nonetheless Alexander became famous for his character dancing and comedy roles. After all the excitements of America it was quite a let-down to be back performing at Sadler's Wells immediately on our return. Then it was on to Edinburgh, Oxford, Leeds, Sheffield, part of the staple touring pattern.

We were soon on our international travels again. In April the following year, 1953, we went to Holland and Belgium as well as to several cities in Germany – Munich, Nürnberg, Frankfurt and Cologne among them – though not to Stuttgart which was to play such an important part of my life. In July we were off to Bulawayo, in modern-day Zimbabwe, what was then still known as Rhodesia, for the Central Africa Rhodes Centenary Festival that celebrated the birth of the country's founder, Cecil Rhodes. Happily Sonya had joined the company by then.

The Rhodes centenary celebration included an exhibition covering 50 acres – something in the style of an international expo or the Festival of Britain in 1951 in London – and showcased 18 southern African countries. They each had their own pavilion. There was a Court of Rhodes, a Hall of Africa and the Rhodesia Ideal Home Exhibit. The structural engineering firm of Samuel Patchett had converted an aircraft hangar into a temporary Theatre Royal holding 3,000, complete with a royal box, home to the cultural programme and where we were to perform. Flown in from London on BOAC's new Comet jets were 20 tonnes of scenery and costumes and 450 performers.

The trip seemed to be planned so that we would be crossing the Sahara just as the heat was at its fiercest in the afternoon, which sent the entire plane into a dizzy switch-back that had us all spewing into our sick bags. Not a pleasant sight. We had to change planes in Khartoum onto a rather ropey old plane. We did not know at the time but the ballet company had been insured for £500,000 each flight, out and back, while the opera company was insured for £935,000, each way.

Once finally in Bulawayo the programme was a mixed bill of everything British. John Gielgud, who staged and starred in a production of *Richard II*, complained the stage was so wide it took five minutes to cross from one side to the other but, shortly after his arrest in London for importuning, he evidently preferred to be out of the metropolitan spotlight among the anonymity of Bulawayo. Avoiding the taxman, George Formby did a show. The Hallé orchestra under John Barbirolli, whose instruments alone had been insured for £1 million, gave 14 concerts in as many days to audiences totalling 30,000 people. Along with umpiring a cricket match and visiting Rhodes' grave, Barbirolli also inaugurated a music school. The printed programmes for each performance advertised rival steam laundries, the Matabele and the Rhodesian, as well as the Warnborough Night Spot, apparently the place for nightly dancing, with a late licence.

The Covent Garden Opera, as it was still called, presented *La bohème*, *Aida* and, in coronation year, Benjamin Britten's new opera celebrating Elizabeth I, *Gloriana*, with choreography by John Cranko, fresh from its distinctly tepid reception at Covent Garden that June. The response was no warmer in Rhodesia. Britten and his partner, Peter Pears, who had created the role of Essex, were absent. Reginald Goodall replaced Britten as conductor. In an early role, Joan Sutherland was new among the cast as Lady Rich. Later she was famously indifferent to Britten's music – perhaps this experience was the cause of her aversion. A very white-faced Princess Margaret – looking very sad following her enforced separation from Peter Townsend, her would-be fiancé, front-page news around the world just then – attended with her mother.

The festival was officially opened when the royals witnessed an anniversary gala featuring more than 300 performers. Some of us followed behind them as they were taken through a display of brilliant woodwork and handicrafts by the local community. The queen mother was absolutely charming, desperately trying to cover for her sulky daughter. There was drama the next day when we were wandering through the exhibition grounds. A tea crate was opened from which out shot a large snake. It disappeared through the crowd, not to be recaptured.

Our repertory included *Les Sylphides* which I never danced, but I got to perform Kenneth MacMillan's usual role in *Valses nobles et sentimentales*. I was one of the magical unicorns who surround Harlequin and Columbine in *Harlequin in April*, choreographed by Cranko. I did the yodelling song in *Façade* along with David Gill and Maurice Metliss as the other mountaineers and Yvonne Cartier as the milkmaid. Our repertoire also included *The Haunted Ballroom* by de Valois in which Sonya and I were both ghosts, and *Ile des Sirènes* by Alfred Rodrigues. Sonya was one of the girls in yellow in Andrée Howard's *Assembly Ball*. We did duty among the corps in the second act of *Swan Lake* in which Sonya was a cygnet; how she hated that pas de quatre. I was usually cast as Benno but also did Rothbart in performances with Elaine Fifield and David Poole. The season was heralded in *The Sunday News* as a fortnight's treat of the most attractive modern and classical ballet. According to another report we held the audience enthralled. In one interview Peggy van Praagh said the whole company was in fine fettle, though in fact Sheilah O'Reilly slipped on the first night and sustained a bad sprain. Sonya and I were pictured with her in one of the newspapers.

In early 1954 our tour dates had taken us to Stratford, Morecambe, Stockton-on-Tees, Oxford, Wolverhampton, Bradford, Derby and Norwich, so the prospect of three months in South Africa that spring was exciting. We started off early one morning by train from Waterloo station to catch the boat from Southampton. Madam, who was not accompanying the tour, came to Waterloo to see us off. I remember she was wearing the most unflattering pair of red, wedge-heeled shoes with ankle straps. I cannot imagine where she had got them. She must just have pulled on the first pair that came to hand early that morning. We sailed on the *Edinburgh Castle*, a two-week voyage. The weather was appalling during the first week, which resulted in serious illness for some of the company. Once things improved we all started to eat too much and we got fatter and fatter as life on board was boring, being so long at sea. There was not much else to do. Also on a long sea voyage like that you begin to dread getting off the ship and facing reality. At one point Peggy van Praagh tried to get us all on deck to do class. Just a slight tilt of the boat pushes you right off balance and it soon becomes impossible, so that was soon abandoned. As we went around the Cape of Good Hope the ship seemed to tip from end to end, then side to side.

We performed first in Johannesburg before going on to Durban. We immediately came face to face with the realities of apartheid. As some of us were walking from our bus to the hotel an old man, probably in his eighties who was walking on the shaded side of the street, was kicked across the pavement into the gutter where he fell badly. He tried to protest but just got shouted at. Needless to say he was black and not allowed on the pavement, unlike his attackers. As part of a plan to make us welcome, I was invited out by a very rich, white couple for dinner at their sumptuous home in the suburbs of Johannesburg. The meal was served on a gorgeous balcony that overlooked a beautiful garden. As we were eating I noticed a very large kennel with a chain attached to it. I asked what sort of dog they had that needed such a huge kennel, to be told by the wife that the chain was to secure their houseboy at night. I was shocked but managed to ask how could they keep a human being in such conditions? I was told that blacks were not real human beings and could not be trusted. I got up and left. Horrible.

None of us liked Johannesburg, it was a hard and unfriendly city, but they certainly liked us. Overall the tour was a success, well sold. Ballet Rambert also toured there in those days and there was always a demand for their visits too. Only whites were allowed into theatres but in Durban we were allowed to do one open-air performance to a black audience. It was the best audience we had on the tour. Durban itself was lovely by the sea and we all loved the beaches there best, although they could be dangerous with sharks and strong currents that could pull you under. David Shields, one of the soloists in the company, was a very strong swimmer. He dived into an incoming wave but by the time he landed it had receded. He landed on his head in what was now an empty gorge. His neck was broken.

But it was Cape Town that we all loved and where apartheid was less evident. People of mixed blood were accepted if they were intelligent or had money. David Poole, from Cape Town, was accepted. Johaar Mosaval, from Malaysia, was not. Quite a number of Cape coloureds came to our classes and some of us went with David, to see the University of Cape Town Ballet rehearse. The company had been established by Dulcie Howes in the 1930s and it is where John Cranko started his career in the 1940s. When David left Sadler's Wells Theatre Ballet he taught briefly at Kurt Jooss' school in Essen before ultimately becoming director of the Cape Town company, then renamed CAPAB Ballet and now Cape Town City Ballet. He was a great teacher but died tragically in 1991 from the effects of the anaesthetic while undergoing a minor operation. A charity established by David to support educational development and dance programmes for children in disadvantaged areas of Cape Town still exists.

Due to his ethnicity, we were not allowed to include Johaar Mosaval on the tour. Apartheid had prevented him from pursuing a dance career in South Africa but he had managed to gain a place at the Sadler's Wells school in London and had graduated into the company. He went on to create the role of Bootface in Cranko's *Lady and the Fool* opposite Kenneth MacMillan as Moondog. In Cape Town some of us went to see Johaar's parents. They were absolutely charming in their welcome. Generally we found people there to be friendlier than elsewhere in the country and they were mad about the ballet. The Mosavals put on a show for us and brought in some native dancers who put themselves into trances before proceeding to do the most amazing feats. This all happened in a specially prepared room with the central area covered in burning coals. The entertainers walked barefoot across the coals, put swords through their thigh muscles, skewers through their tongues, pulling them out several minutes later without a mark or any hint of blood. Only occasionally, with somebody new to these acts of display, you might see a few drops of blood. Some of us felt really nauseous and had to go outside every so often – but once seen, never forgotten.

On the way back I shared a cabin with Pirmin Trecu. He was a marvellous performer who went to join the Covent Garden company where he created the role of the fool in John Cranko's *The Prince of the Pagodas*. Pirmin was Spanish, a child refugee from the civil war. He was a very classical dancer and a natural artist. He was perfect as the miller in Léonide Massine's *Le Tricorne*. After an injury that forced him to give up dancing he started a ballet school in Porto in Portugal. It was very successful but it never had enough funding. I arranged to have rehearsal floors that we no longer had use for to be sent to his school. Onboard during our return from South Africa, Pirmin and I chatted with some Indian dance students who were very good company. They were well trained but coming

to the UK as there was very little employment for Indians then in South
Africa. The Indians were quartered in the bowels of the ship and we tried
to organise with the steward for them to swap with our rooms. That was
unheard of. With great difficulty, however, we managed to get permission for them to sit with us in the dining room.

You never know what you are going to experience when you tour internationally. En route to South America in April 1973 the plane developed
a mechanical fault and had to come down at Freetown in Sierra Leone.
The airport was small, nothing more than a set of corrugated iron huts,
and had never seen a big plane before. We were stranded there for a
whole day while we waited for a new part to be flown in to repair the
plane. It was blisteringly hot. We were a source of curiosity for a group
of local boys who appeared out of nowhere. They all worshipped Wayne
Sleep who improvised an entertainment for them like some Pied Piper
character and led them in a long line through the shallow sea while he
made gestures that they had to copy. Joyce Wells, the wardrobe super-
visor who never went anywhere without her equipment to make a cup of
tea to keep her staff happy, found her primus stove and with the help of
the cabin crew got enough supplies of tea to keep a good proportion of
the 200 or so dancers, staff, stage crew and electricians reasonably calm.
But it was difficult and fairly dangerous to be in the blazing sun for the
whole day. There was very little shade to be found. What a relief it was
when the plane carrying the new part came in to land. It was not long
before we were airborne, leaving behind a bunch of kids sadly waving
goodbye. I doubt they will ever forget that day and their hero Wayne
Sleep.

There was, however, worse to come. Because Pepsi-Cola had at a late
stage withdrawn from sponsoring a week of performances at the Colón
theatre in Buenos Aries instead of starting the tour in Argentina we had
to switch to beginning in Brazil. Dalal Achcar, who masterminded the
tour, managed hastily to rearrange the schedule so that we had an extra
date, in Pôrto Alegre. Due to the speed with which Dalal had organised the change it had not been possible to send out the usual advance
group to check the theatre. So what did we find? An unfinished building. Seating in the auditorium was reasonable but the stage had virtually
nothing – no stage lamps, no hanging bars for scenery, no communication system, no proper dance flooring, no doors to the dressing-room

doors, no chairs or dressing tables for the dancers, just an empty room for the wardrobe and no access for the huge transport lorries just arrived from Rio where they had been to collect all the sets, costumes, electrics and props that had just arrived be sea from the UK. To get them to the theatre's loading area five big trees had to be cut down. The way the whole company pulled together was fantastic. There was immense good will among the stage crew and great support from the local theatre staff. Stage management were fantastic in organising the whole of the finishing of the stage and dressing-rooms and getting hold of the necessary equipment to hang the scenery, get music stands, chairs for the dressing-rooms and a few doors too. It was a complete miracle that we opened. Everything was in place and the curtain went up to cheers from a packed house. The actual performance of *La Fille mal gardée* was rapturously received in true Brazilian style.

Dalal Achcar was amazing. Through her passionate love of dance I have spent many wonderful months in Brazil. I love it there, the people and all its beauty, mystery and passion. Dalal has two dance schools in Rio, was a great friend of Margot Fonteyn, was responsible for building up the ballet company at Rio's Teatro Municipal where she was from time to time also director not only of the company but the theatre itself. Many years ago she asked me to put on *Giselle* for the company, with the designs by Peter Farmer, which I did willingly. The whole visit was wonderful despite the fact that the men in the company were unaware of the word discipline. They certainly were by the time the production went on! Dalal was so enthusiastic, even when things were going wrong. *Giselle* was a huge success and now 30 years later it is still being performed. Her great wish had always been to bring the Royal Ballet to Brazil and the visit in 1973 was the result of many months of negotiations, so when Pepsi-Cola withdrew from their participation of the Argentine part of the plan Dalal was pretty desperate. What she achieved in about three weeks, finding four other dates in Belo Horizonte, Brasilia and São Paulo as well as Pôrto Alegre to fill the gap left by Pepsi's withdrawal was fantastic. Although it was one of my first foreign tours as associate director to Kenneth it was all quite a success, but I have a lot to thank both Dalal and her husband, formerly the mayor of Rio, for looking after the company so beautifully. The parties she arranged and hospitality were of the highest standard although the last night of the tour, in a new sports stadium, the Giñasio de Esportes, was not without incident. The stadium was not finished and the whole experience was a nightmare, terrifying. A stage had been erected in the middle of a huge arena that had the seats behind it but with no view of the performance as a large curtain was hung in the way to provide a background for the performance. That in itself was bad enough, but the stadium had been double-sold as the promoter was certain that only half the audience would turn up. Wrong. People outside were chanting, 'We want Fonteyn.' Everybody had come to see her, even though she was not dancing that night, as she was well known from the many concert tours she had undertaken in Brazil.

Nobody seemed to have any idea who or what the Royal Ballet was. The performance was attended by the president Emílio Garrastazu Médici whose regime was essentially a military dictatorship. There were groups of protesters chanting anti-government threats. The first ballet of the evening was the shades' scene from *La Bayadère* staged by Rudolf Nureyev. Things never get finished in Brazil and the loudspeakers in the stadium had not been tested. The dancers could not hear the orchestra. The corps de ballet, practically naked in their tutus, were terrified because all they could see and hear were gangs of men shaking their fists and shouting in altercations that were going on in the stalls. In the interval John Tooley, director of the Royal Opera House, went to the president and told him that unless the protesters were removed he would have no alternative but to cancel the rest of the performance and the company would go straight to the airport where a plane was waiting to fly them home. The president called somebody and gave instructions. Within ten minutes all the trouble-makers were cleared. Apparently hosepipes were turned on the protesters outside the stadium but there was no more trouble after that – but we all felt that the whole place might erupt. The entire company behaved magnificently even though they felt unprotected on the stage. Though terrified, the dancers performed superbly. Everybody was glad to board the plane home for a return flight that passed without incident.

I was so delighted when Dalal was awarded the CBE as a result of this tour and the great contribution she had made to dance. During all my visits in connection with *Giselle* I had the most superb help from Dalal's assistant, Maria Luisa Naronah, known throughout the dance world as LuLu. A more charming, energetic, determined and kind person would be hard to find – if not impossible. She is an excellent teacher, marvellous with children of all ages, she makes you laugh by just being in her presence. Nothing is too much trouble. Ask for help, especially transport, and she always insists on driving you everywhere. The thing is that she loves the ballet, classical of course, and being involved really brings her joy.

For a visit to Israel in August 1973, when the New Group performed in Jerusalem, Tel Aviv and the ancient amphitheatre at Caesarea, Rudolf Nureyev appeared as a guest in George Balanchine's *Prodigal Son*. It was a strong choice for his histrionic abilities. The first-night audience at Caesarea of over 2,500 people included 200 security guards who surrounded prime minister Golda Meir. She did not look much taken with the siren's seduction of the prodigal, as Deanne Bergsma ensnared Rudi in a coiled embrace with her legs, and there were mutterings that the scene, choreographed nearly 50 years previously, was as explicit as something out of the film *Last Tango in Paris*, then causing controversy internationally. More to the audience's taste were the *Corsaire* pas de deux, again with Rudi, and extracts from *Romeo and Juliet* and *The Sleeping Beauty*.

On a subsequent visit to Israel in 1986, when Sadler's Wells Royal Ballet performed *Swan Lake* at the huge open-air arena at Caesarea in a season presented by Victor and Lilian Hochhauser, sand blowing off the neighbouring beach onto the stage in the evening breezes caused problems and some of the dancers took a tumble. In fact stages on tour, particularly in venues not familiar with presenting ballet, are frequently a nightmare and often polished to an alarming degree of slipperiness. 'We thought you would like shiny,' is a frequent refrain. One of our worst experiences in the open air was in 1976 near Cannes, on Île Sainte Marguerite where the man in the iron mask had been imprisoned. It was famous too for the early dew which meant we could not start at the normal time of 8pm and had to wait until it was dark and the stage lights were having some effect in drying the stage surface. The first piece went well, but by the time the last work started, the final act of *The Sleeping Beauty*, the dew was making its presence felt. By the time that the grand pas de deux started, the stage was awash with a generous coating of glistening dew. Poor Doreen Wells as Aurora. She rightly always had to have the stage just perfect to dance this fiendishly difficult number and she just fell about. She had a terrible time and the audience began to laugh as they were not aware of the dampness from where they were sitting in the auditorium. We had to stop as it was becoming really dangerous.

The real problem in Caesarea, however, was getting started. On the Saturday night not all members of the – local – orchestra had arrived after the end of the Shabbat religious observance. The audience was all assembled. The company was all ready. All set for overture and beginners. Except we could not begin. The principal cellist was missing. So we all waited. And waited. At last we saw him making his way into the orchestra pit, carrying his cello case over his head. He had come by public transport which, because of Shabbat, had restarted too late to get him there on time. Everybody applauded good naturedly and we began, 45 minutes late. The good thing was that it was really dark by then. I thought *Swan Lake* looked rather wonderful in that setting.

The problem in Athens in June 1975 was the heat. It was impossible to rehearse until after dark when it had cooled down in the huge open-air theatre, the Herodes Atticus. Margot Fonteyn had agreed to perform with us at the request of Pia Hadjinikos-Angelini, a somewhat crazy Greek impresario, but great fun and considered to be a high priestess of Greek culture, who was presenting us there. Margot no longer danced *Giselle* but she did still do *Raymonda*, so this was added to the end of the programme. Not ideal, but you cannot put on a big name at the beginning. As always, she worked beautifully with the dancers, never behaving like a big star. So everybody would have a break after the evening's performance, the *Raymonda* rehearsal with Margot started at about 1am, when it was still quite warm. All went well until it came to the very difficult, travelling diagonal step which ends her solo, which is always difficult to synchronise with the orchestra. The step is not so difficult in itself but musically it starts very slowly with a clap on the first beat. Gradually the tempo increases. It is vital to get the acceleration absolutely together between ballerina and orchestra. It is up to the conductor to take the opening speed from the ballerina, bringing in the orchestra as she starts. It was clearly not working. By this time it was also clear that Margot was beginning to tire and so was Barry Wordsworth, the conductor. After several attempts she and Barry had a further discussion and then tried again. And again. No good. Margot sat down on the floor, legs splayed out in front of her, nearly in tears. 'Oh dear, not again. I'm exhausted,' she said. She assured me that she and Barry would sort it out before the show the next night. We all went off into the Grecian night, upset of course. But the next evening it all worked beautifully and the performance was a triumph – especially for Margot.

In October 1977, when cultural and commercial exchanges were stronger, as part of a week celebrating British commerce and culture organised by the British Council, the largest that the country had staged overseas at the time, we travelled to Iran. Prospect Theatre Company brought their production of *Hamlet* starring Derek Jacobi and there were many musical events, films, exhibitions and seminars celebrating the arts of Britain. The week culminated in a display of the massed military bands by four British regiments followed by a football match between Manchester United and an Iranian national team in the presence of Iranian royalty. Having a national ballet, comparable to companies in the west, was important to the monarch, Mohamed Reza Pahlavi.

During a state visit to London in the 1950s he had asked Ninette de Valois to advise on the creation of a company in Iran. In 1958 she extended a visit to Turkey, where she had founded a ballet school, to visit Iran's ballet academy and company, the Iranian National Ballet which had by then been established. This led to a succession of people, including Ann Cox, Miro Zolan, Nicholas Beriozov, Marion English-Delanian, Richard Brown and Robert de Warren being sent by Madam to teach in Iran. The company acquired Cranko's *The Lady and the Fool* and *Romeo and Juliet*. Guest producers included Jack Carter as well as Anne Heaton who staged a version of *Schéhérazade* after Mikhail Fokine's original. In the years preceding the visit by Sadler's Wells Royal Ballet, *Giselle* and *Swan Lake* were in the Iranians' repertoire. Birgit Culberg had staged her production of *Miss Julie*, and Maurice Béjart and Alvin Ailey had mounted works there too. The company had links too with the Royal Academy of Dance in London, then run by John Field. The Kirov, Rambert and Stuttgart companies were among many that included Iran in their touring schedules.

Tehran in October 1977 was a difficult date, not comfortable at all. We sensed that trouble was brewing and protests against the shah had already started to build. As it turned out, this was only two years before he was deposed. On the first night, the empress, Shahbanu Farah, landed by helicopter on top of the Roudaki opera house, recently inaugurated and considered one of the most modern in the world. Her presence meant lots of security guards. The theatre was full of them. They stank too, as I discovered when I ended up sitting next to one of them in the gallery as there was nowhere else to sit as the huge number of security men were sitting in the best seats. In the interval, along with Lord Drogheda, chairman of the Royal Opera House, I was presented to the empress. Somehow, in bowing to acknowledge her, I managed to upset my champagne, almost spilling it over her. The empress laughed it off with great charm.

The evening was memorable for other reasons. There were no white Shetland ponies to be found in Iran, so in place of the usual pony in *La Fille mal gardée* that we were performing that night, a beautiful but fiery miniature horse had been found for us from the shah's stables. It needed professional handling and fortunately the company secretary, Alison Palmer, was a fully trained equestrian. She agreed to take charge of the horse and gamely dressed up as the groom and went on. As the horse was so frisky it had been given a pill to sedate it, but I could see from my seat high up in the gallery that waiting for their cue to go on with the horse and trap, Alison was clearly having difficulties with the horse. It was very dozy and unresponsive. It was only with a great deal of effort that Alison managed to make the first entrance and lead the horse and trap around the stage. It came to a standstill centre stage as it should. It then proceeded to void its bowels, but that is not unknown in *Fille*, and there is always a dustpan and brush in the trap. A groom duly cleaned up. Then, to the considerable merriment of the cast onstage, the horse's priapic part became particularly priapic, practically touching the floor. Alison only just managed to get the horse and cart off at the end of the scene without further embarrassment.

Giselle had its challenges too. Lynn Seymour was appearing with us. She was in a bad state emotionally following the breakdown of a relationship with a member of a major banking dynasty. That day I had taken the stage rehearsal and I knew that Lynn was already pretty wobbly, but I thought she would be able to do the performance. One of the pleasures of international touring is the chance to see new sites and places, but the time to do that is always limited. I wanted to visit Isfahan and so after the rehearsal Sonya and I caught a plane there. It was a wonderful place and I was very glad we went. From what I was told later, I was glad too that I had missed the performance in Tehran. Sporting a rather peculiar hairdo,

Lynn had struggled through the first act. In the second, when *Giselle* should start her big solo alone and be in command of the stage, she was clearly nervous and could not balance. She hissed at David Ashmole, her Albrecht that evening, to support her throughout her solo. I have to admit I was relieved not to have been there to see her suffer. I adore Lynn, such a wonderful artist with real allure, and cannot bear to see any artist in trouble. Perhaps I should have not let her dance that night, but then she was a big name and the public were paying a lot of money to see her. I am still not sure if it was the right or wrong decision to let her dance. John Auld, my deputy, told me that although it would have been easy to fault Lynn from a technical point of view, nevertheless she gave a performance that was unique and which was, at times, very riveting. Lynn won the audience over and the reception at the end was rapturous.

Regular international touring became a fixture for Sadler's Wells Royal Ballet from 1980 thanks to a six-year funding agreement that Paul Findlay, assistant director of the Royal Opera House, secured from the British Council. They were intent on building stronger cultural ties in emerging economies. Sponsors underwrote the seasons against loss, but for them the chance to be associated with a major British cultural institution in countries where they wanted to develop their commercial profile was an attractive proposition. For the company too it was an education. Dancers had to adapt to performing on all sorts of stages and to different audiences whose traditions and expectations varied considerably.

International travel always broadens a person's perspective but dancers too had to represent the company at official receptions. That tested their abilities to socialise and communicate, and the experience also fed back into how they performed onstage. International touring was a formative experience individually, and for the company as a whole it was a way of consolidating its profile. The tours were always well planned thanks to Paul's involvement and his attention to detail. If anything, he was sometimes too meticulous in organising as many performances as possible during a foreign tour. I had known Paul since I was first involved with the Royal Opera House when he was in the press office. It was Paul who championed my name for the directorship of the Royal Ballet when he was the right-hand man to John Tooley. In many ways Paul himself was the ideal candidate to have succeeded John as general director at Covent Garden in 1988, although he in fact went on to become chief executive of the London Symphony Orchestra. He and his wife Françoise have become two of my closest friends.

Thanks to the new funding regime, in 1980 Sadler's Wells Royal Ballet undertook its most substantial tour in many years performing in the Philippines, Singapore, Malaysia, Thailand, Hong Kong and Korea; altogether six destinations in a month. The Covent Garden companies had visited south-east Asia in recent seasons but for us this was a major undertaking and the first time that Barclays Bank had sponsored the Royal Opera House. The little red book, the guide book that detailed the itinerary and schedules for everybody on the tour, warned that while in Korea any photography taken in a northerly direction was prohibited. We were advised too that it is also considered an insult if you show the soles of your feet. During the Korean part of the tour we were taken to visit a beautiful old Buddhist temple in the countryside. The friendly priest who organised the trip sat us down in a corner of the temple and gave us a fascinating talk about the building. Now I find it uncomfortable to sit cross-legged on the floor and I am afraid I caused offence when I surreptitiously tried to stretch my legs forward and revealed the soles of my feet to our friendly priest. As we were being shown the beautiful wooden building the priest was standing in a corner while he explained things to us, sitting on the floor facing him. He suddenly caught sight of my feet and was quite horrified. All was forgiven, however, as the priest had developed an absolute fascination with our press officer, Josie Phillips' nose. It really was very cute and the priest wanted to touch it, which she allowed.

On foreign tours the company is always desperately busy; usually you never stay anywhere longer than a couple of days or so, hence such excursions are a delight, although some of the sights that you come across are disturbing. In Korea we saw an extraordinary grass mound covered with what appeared to be sentry boxes. In fact the structures contained disciples of Buddha who had decided to die. They were sitting inside in constant meditation, waiting in a trance-like state until they died. Such glimpses of other cultures are fascinating, but performing overseas does have its perils. In Seoul the stage of the Sejong cultural centre was 100 feet wide – or it certainly felt like that. Certainly the auditorium held 3,000 people and the stage felt miles away from the audience. It was like looking down the wrong end of a telescope with the little sets of *Coppélia* lost in the distance. The performance was not helped by the acoustic. There seemed to be a time lag for the orchestra to be heard in the auditorium so that the dancers looked to be permanently off the music the whole time.

In the Philippines, I was so surprised by Imelda Marcos. I did like her. She was a great friend of Margot Fonteyn and loved ballet for which she gave a lot of support. After the last performance of the season she invited the entire company to dinner at her palace. Marcos had seen to it that our dinner was kept for us and she organised a cabaret, which included a fashion show. She also sang, beautifully. When I thanked her she insisted that we did not leave and invited us all up to the top floor to her disco. A huge table was piled with food, far too much for us to eat, just having had dinner. The excess was deliberate. The untouched food was distributed to children's hospitals. Marcos frequently used to stage shows in America, the proceeds from which supported her charities in the Philippines. She also employed many men to cut the extensive lawns around the palace with hand shears as a means of job creation. The disco was really good and all the men in the company were expected to dance with her. It got later and later and I explained to Marcos that our plane was waiting at the airport and we had to leave. 'Not a problem. You can stay a little longer,' she said as she picked up the phone to the airport. Some double doors into the room were opened and a whole parade of staff entered carrying large gift bags that contained local handicrafts. Some were lovely, some kitsch, but they were another example of social philanthropy and job creation. I worried about what we were going to do with the bags we had been given. They were about two feet square and we were allowed only one item of onboard luggage on the flight. 'Not a problem,' said Marcos as she picked up the phone again.

During what turned out to be the last years of communism, in 1981 Sadler's Wells Royal Ballet undertook a two-week tour to what was still Yugoslavia. Before then I had not really seen much of life behind the Iron Curtain. About a decade or so before, in 1971 I think, I did manage to get to Leningrad for the first time. One of our daughter's teachers, Jo Carruthers, who also taught maths at the Royal Ballet School, was a good friend of ours. She also happened to speak Russian fluently which somehow led to us visiting the Soviet Union with her. We had a terrible time with the bureaucracy. Our arrival into Moscow was delayed and we had to rush to another terminal for the connecting flight to Leningrad. In my haste I managed to surrender the wrong documents and so I ended up without a pass to claim my room key or any meals at the hotel. No paperwork, no meals.

I recall huge blocks of ice on the river Neva and in front of the Admiralty, very like how it is seen in the market square in *Petrushka*. I can remember the ice cream in the interval of the ballet but not much of the production we saw at the Mariinsky theatre, one of Oleg Vinogradov's I think. The ice cream had to be weighed on an antiquated machine which took for ever. It was runny and warm by the time we got our ration. We watched classes given by Natalia Dudinskaya, a leading Soviet ballerina who was partnered by Rudolf Nureyev on his debut at the Kirov. Dudinskaya also taught Natalia Makarova among many stars. I had been charged by Frederick Ashton to give her a pot of Ponds cold cream. Dudinskaya was lovely but she complained that the students of the day, although they looked absolutely beautiful and unspoiled, all lacked discipline and were stroppy. I noticed a girl from the senior school who looked very talented, with lovely legs and feet. As she walked by, I mentioned to Dudinskaya that I liked the look of that girl. 'An absolute cow! No brain,' Dudinskaya said crushingly. It was inspiring to see young, beautifully trained boys and girls working in the junior classes in an inspired and disciplined way, but very depressing seeing how that had all disappeared when they became seniors, although I have heard since that things are now much better.

For our Yugoslav visit, unusually we went with our own orchestra. Skopje, Belgrade, Novi Sad and Zagreb were our venues. In Skopje a stage was built at one end of a theatre-in-the-round while in Zagreb we performed in a lovely fin du régime Austro-Hungarian opera house, very beautiful, but the stage crews kept changing, causing much confusion. In Belgrade they and the van loaders did not consider the final get-out to be part of their responsibilities so the scenery had to be dismantled and loaded by ourselves. Quite a few of the dancers came to the rescue and helped out. I even joined in as I was so incensed with rage.

In 1987 we were again in central Europe, close to home but still another world. Interflug, the East German airline, and Balkan Airlines give some clue as to our destinations and the era. We went to Warsaw, Łodz, Gdynia and Wroclaw in Poland, Brno and Prague in what was still Czechoslovakia, Dresden, Leipzig and East Berlin, as well as to Sofia and Stara Zagora in Bulgaria. Our red book for the tour warned that after Poland the onward travel schedule had not been confirmed. It is nice to be reassured and would have been nicer to know where we were going next.

Xerox, the document technology company, who at that time was intent on opening up a presence in the region, was our sponsor. In their publicity they wished Sadlers Wells Ballet, wrong on two counts, every success – but their own brand name proved problematic too. In the region the term 'to xerox' was the generic dictionary definition to copy, and Xerox the company had to go to court to gain brand protection for its own name. The repertoire for that tour included *The Snow Queen*, but it was *Checkmate* in a triple-bill with *Flowers of the Forest* and *Elite Syncopations* that caused most reaction. They just loved it. Poland can trace its dance history back to the court ballets of the 16th century and in Warsaw is one of the largest in the world, even bigger, I think, than the Bolshoi, though we had to wade through floods outside our hotel to reach it. The stage in Gdynia was the worst I have ever known, which was something. When Paul Findlay undertook his advance visit ahead of the tour he had discovered that the stage there was full of holes and knots as well as being slippery. He was assured that something would be done about it. Nothing was. Paul threatened to halt our performance mid-way as the dancers were having so much difficulty with it.

In Czechoslovakia, I had a great friend in Victoria Riley and through her got to see the Prague Chamber Ballet. They were a company of all shapes and sizes but dramatically quite strong. Several months later, in January 1988, I was able to arrange for them to perform in London as part of a mixed bill with Sadler's Wells Royal Ballet when they danced *Kreutzer Sonata* by Pavel Smok. The idea was one of my wrongs. It just did not work, and plans for Smok to choreograph something for us in London did not materialise.

East Berlin was quite an adventure. We stayed at the Hotel Unter der Linden, near the Berlin Wall. During our visit David Bowie was giving a concert on the other side of the wall outside the reichstag, in the western part of the city. East Berliners congregated by the wall to listen. We were horrified to see them forcibly attacked and removed by the police. While Sonya was in Berlin she wanted to get some salami. As she was walking along, not really paying much attention to where she was, through a gap in a wall she saw some people. She went through the gap and asked, 'Wo kann ich ein salami, kauffen bitte?' In reply, these people, who happened to be soldiers, turned their guns on Sonya shouting, 'Raus!' Poor Sonya. She could be a bit dizzy sometimes. She had only wandered into Checkpoint Charlie.

CHAPTER 14

Playing away from home

W HAT SORT OF COMPANY director manages to lose his leading ballerina in a rafting accident? The Wright sort. I really should have been more awake when I agreed to a white-water rafting trip that had been suggested while we were in New Zealand. I was unaware that it was going to be a stunt designed to publicise our visit. I was on one of three rafts which each held ten people including Galina Samsova and Sherilyn Kennedy, accompanied by an instructor. He fell out first while we were leaving the first rapid, not the most auspicious of starts. As we approached the second it seemed to roar as fiercely as Niagara and our raft overturned. We all got separated in the swirling waters of this huge rapid. I was trapped underneath the raft with Sherilyn. Somehow we got to the edge of the water, and with the help of those in the preceding raft which had somehow moored at a small landing ledge, we managed to pull ourselves out. Apparently I looked like a beached whale as I was dragged out of the turbulent water. I felt ghastly, the victim of some beastly New Zealand germ, and did not feel at all well. It was a scary experience. I looked around and saw that Galina was missing. I was struck with horror. Where was she? Imagine my relief when we finally found her further downstream standing on a rock, in the middle of the roaring river, coolly calling out, 'I am here!' I was only surprised that she had not managed to find her cigarette and usual glass of white wine!

It was a tour not without incident. We were also taken on jet boats that criss-crossed each other in close proximity at great speed. We were fortunate that there were no collisions, but unfortunately the next day there was a crash which caused a fatality, thankfully not any of us. New Zealand was part of an 11-week tour that also took in Australia, Singapore and Bangkok, and filled the autumn of 1982. It was hard and not a great success. Our new *Swan Lake* had earned us invitations to Singapore and Bangkok, but in Australia the promoter had insisted on *The Two Pigeons* although it had never been popular when Australian Ballet performed it. Reviews were incredibly mixed. We were criticised by one newspaper for bringing the dullest repertoire and least exciting performing style of any visiting company. Most dancers do not read or care what critics have to say as they usually reveal more about the writer's personal opinions than what they have seen. A few dancers do get upset but generally get over it pretty quickly if they have a bad notice.

Think of Sydney and you automatically picture the opera house, although in fact it has a very small stage. We performed in the far less spectacular Regent theatre, a vastly shabby 3,000-seater. Paint was peeling off the walls of the auditorium. In Brisbane, the theatre we performed in, Her Majesty's, was scheduled for demolition. In Melbourne the Palais was equally dingy and squalid. In Adelaide we had the relative luxury of a modern theatre but one with an alarmingly slippery floor. One of the sponsors in Australia was Benson & Hedges, so our visit attracted much picketing by anti-smoking activists, which was at least helpful for the box office. While in Australia we caught up with Danny La Rue whom Sonya knew from her days at the Players' theatre. He had a fabulous apartment, white carpets, white décor, everything white. Danny himself was very colourful, commenting about the drag scene in Australia. There were lots of transvestites there but Danny could not understand why men went in for surgery. 'I've earned a bob or two without it,' he said. Fortunately the New Zealand leg of the tour was much more warmly received, but *Swan Lake* looked cramped and far too big on some of the small stages that we played.

We were back in New Zealand in 1985 and again in 1990 for the country's 150th anniversary celebrations. In 1985 our repertoire included the new *Sleeping Beauty* which opened doors for us internationally. The scale of the production meant that it was tough to tour and often looked constrained on smaller stages. The tour was underwritten by the British Council and at one reception my memory deserted me as I completely forgot to thank the council's director. It was very unfortunate as they had done so much to help us. When a local official pointed this out to me as I was returning to my seat I immediately returned to the podium and apologised – too late, the damage had been done.

On that tour we performed *Five Tangos* as a curtain-raiser to *Giselle* which we also took to India. In Mumbai, still known as Bombay then, we were promised the city's chamber orchestra. What we got was a police band, some music students, a few professionals and a couple of children – who were much the best of everybody. Audiences there, in a venue with only 800 seats, had never seen a full-length ballet before and the stage crew was not familiar with working with a company like ours. They were dreadful, shouting to each other across the stage during performances, usually during the quiet bits. We had been warned not to drink the local tap water or to swallow anything in the swimming pool but we were nearly all ill. In *Giselle* we were down to five wilis on each side instead of the usual eight or more. Anybody well enough just had to go on. It took me four months to recover fully once I was back in Britain, but I did love India. Of course the country was a tremendous culture shock on a first visit, unbearably hot with streets of temporary tented homes, terrible crossroads, crowds of people, buses, taxis and cars. And sacred cows. Sonya and I wandered into a jeweller's shop followed by a white, sacred cow. It proceeded to do what sacred cows, holy or not, do, and pooped on the white carpeted floor of the shop. The cow was shooed away and we took the opportunity to disappear too, embarrassed for having let the cow in.

What was good during our visit was how one performance of *Giselle* was televised live without any camera rehearsals. Our performance even interrupted that evening's television news broadcast. Before each performance somebody came out in front of the curtain to explain about the wilis, the concept of ghosts and an afterlife, so important in *Giselle*, and alien to the central Hindu belief of an eternal Brahman. Local reviewers reported that they had seen no death-defying leaps or grand pirouettes, to their relief as they had gone to see a ballet, not a display of circus tricks.

In Kuala Lumpur *Giselle* did not have the benefit of the introductory explanation and the performance provoked laughter from the audience, which was rather unnerving for the dancers. We learned later that audiences there had never seen a full-length ballet before and *Paquita* and *Elite Syncopations* were much more popular in Malaysia. There we danced in an open-air venue. The audience was covered but the stage and orchestra were not. It was very difficult, particularly when some of the instruments began to crack in the heat. In Kuala Lumpur, when the royal family attend a performance they sit in the front row of the stalls. Nobody is allowed to cross in front of them, which caused a hiatus when I brought Margaret Barbieri and David Ashmole to shake hands during an interval. They could reach the king, but as they were forbidden to stand in front of the royals they could not reach far enough to greet the queen. It was laughed off, but the next night when I brought the dancers out again they approached from separate sides and they each made do with shaking the hand of one royal each.

The royal party also included Chesterina Sim Zecha. She was from Java and appeared in *Flower Drum Song* with Sonya and me some 20 years earlier in London where she danced like an angel. I cast her in *The Trial*, a ballet I did for the Sunday Ballet Club in 1961 where she was a girl who, after being raped, mistakenly accuses the wrong man of being her attacker, resulting in his murder by a group of villagers. It was designed by Yolanda Sonnabend and the scenery was painted in a garage in Notting Hill. When I was in Stuttgart I persuaded John Cranko to take Chesterina into the company. Tiny but plump, she scored a big success as the rather confused two of diamonds in the premiere of *Card Game*. From Stuttgart she went to Munich and became a TV personality; she had a lovely face. She attracted the attention of a Malaysian prince and businessman called Tunku Abdullah, more formally Tunku Panglima Besar Tunku Tan Sri Abdullah ibni Tuanku Abdul Rahman – but known as Charlie – and she became the fourth of his six wives in 1973. When we were in Kuala Lumpur in 1980 she gave a party for us at a palace on the edge of the city. It was lovely to catch up with her. Sadly Charlie turned out to be a womaniser and although Chesterina got a good deal when she divorced him, things turned rather nasty. I still hear from her, now living in Australia.

Belle Shenkman was exactly the sort of person you needed when you were organising international tours. She really was a cultural ambassador for the arts in Canada, organising European tours by National Ballet of Canada and Royal Winnipeg Ballet. Always elegantly attired, Belle could effortlessly charm senior executives to open their corporate purses when she was promoting such tours or when she was underwriting overseas companies to visit Canada. The way that Belle generated a sense of occasion, as we were to discover when Sadler's Wells Royal Ballet visited

Canada in 1983, for such tours was impeccable. That is particularly appreciated when a company is miles from home. The impact on morale cannot be overestimated. Belle was tireless in seeing to all the practical and social aspects which she organised with Paul Findlay. She was expert in organising galas and making arrangements for VIP guests, and she was not above selling blocks of tickets herself. Belle normally travelled everywhere first class. Horror of horrors, on one transatlantic flight to Canada to publicise the tour with Belle, we had to travel business. Belle was upset at the prospect but composed enough to arrive on board the plane with her own supply of caviar and sturgeon which she insisted the crew serve us with, along with the menu and champagne from first class. Conspicuous but nice.

Belle was mad about my *Swan Lake* and we took it everywhere on that Canadian tour. We went from Kitchener, Ontario to Ottawa, Winnipeg, Regina in Saskatoon, Edmonton, Calgary and Vancouver. In Winnipeg we gave the hundredth performance of *Swan Lake* and I appeared as the Italian ambassador to mark the occasion. Arnold Spohr was director of Royal Winnipeg Ballet and we participated in a gala to celebrate his 25th anniversary there. The Winnipeg company had been preparing for it for months. We just had to turn up and do what we could from our tour repertoire. It was there that I came across Evelyn Hart, the company's assoluta. Really everything was arranged around her, casting, rehearsal schedules, performances – everything. She even had a private coach with whom she rehearsed every day. I was impressed by her in many ways, but such behaviour was a nightmare for everybody else. I suggested that Evelyn should spend three months on tour with us in the UK to toughen her up, something which would make her much stronger as a performer. She was very excited at the prospect and came over the following season to perform with us. She could not cope with life on tour. She rehearsed extensively, every look, every finger, everything – but she ran out of one rehearsal the day before a performance. We rushed after her and found her at the railway station. I managed to persuade her to return and get her on to do the performance which she did, but she did not stay the course with us. It was so sad as Evelyn could do anything technically. She was amazing in a pas de deux created for her by Norbert Vesak.

As a friend of Belle, Clement Crisp had been invited to join part of our Canadian tour. With Belle you always had big parties. At one venue a special lunch was organised for Belle's husband Desmond Smith, a retired major general from the Canadian army, to celebrate his birthday and to publicise the tour. During lunch I thought I had better say a few words to toast Desmond, whom I knew. When I suggested this quietly to Belle, I did not pick up on the hesitation in her response. Undeterred I got to my feet. Another of my wrongs. It was only when I sat down and Belle announced, 'And Clement, I think you wanted to say something . . .' that I realised my mistake. Clement had previously been asked to make the speech and I completely stepped in ahead of him. It is not often that Clement is lost for the mot juste.

Nevertheless it was a successful if hard tour that took us right across the country. The only criticism that we really encountered was that the girls in the corps de ballet were not particularly tall, which was something of a visual shock for Canadian audiences. I think it more important that a good corps moves as one. What does not work with a corps is when dancers are of different heights. That is something that I had to agree to disagree on when I took Monica Mason to task for the different sized girls in the Royal Ballet corps. It was not a major concern for her, although it can be for audiences, as we found in Canada. On that tour many of us bought fur coats. I got a mink for Sonya and a nutria coat for myself that came down to my ankles. I have it still somewhere – if the moths have not had it.

In 1986 Sadler's Wells Royal Ballet undertook a major transcontinental American tour. This was in no way the seven-month odyssey undertaken by Sadler's Wells Theatre Ballet in the 1950s, but we were on the road for two months that February and March, the first time that we had performed in America for 35 years. The itinerary took in New York, Boston, Cleveland, Miami, Sarasota, Mexico City, Caracas and Rio de Janeiro. Barclays Bank was principal sponsor. They were still a big champion of the arts at the time. We were certainly glad to have their support – unlike the Royal Shakespeare Company which the same year found itself forced to decline Barclays' sponsorship of a production of *Macbeth*, when Jonathan Pryce, who was contracted to perform the title role, refused to appear because of Barclays' involvement in the apartheid regime in South Africa. The reception in America to *The Sleeping Beauty* was hostile. Reviews in Boston were incredibly savage and overly personal. In New York it was my turn to be on the receiving end from Arlene Croce. She was a longstanding critic of the Royal Ballet. We had never seen eye to eye. She had a fundamental objection to produc- ers – invariably British ones – who, in her view, sought to impose an interpretation on classical ballets and worried more about non-dance values such as design. She had seen my *Nutcracker* at Covent Garden and considered it wrongly conceived and that I would carry on being wrong about the Tchaikovsky ballets. So it was no surprise that she now called me Mr Wrong. It was not the first time she had used the phrase. I was similarly dubbed when she saw my production of *Sleeping Beauty* at Covent Garden in 1968, a staging she called Arthurian with that typic- ally approximate way that Americans have with English culture. You learn never to mind bad reviews, but what hurt was Croce's insistence that the company itself was decorous, genteel, restrained, untheatrical and without personality. Apparently shabby schooling compromised the dancers' range and expressiveness. They were, however, considered uniform. Uniformly bad that is. No matter that more than a dozen dancers had gastroenteritis and I had rearranged the casting so many times that I had completely lost track of which dancer was going to come on next. I was not well myself for three days. Perhaps eating oysters had been the wrong thing to do. In New York particularly we were dancing not only against the ghosts of the Royal Ballet from the heady days of 40 years previously but also in a dance capital built on a very different aesthetic, where physical force and modernity were paramount. In such situations you just have to get on with it. What else can you do? It is not as though you can suddenly import guest dancers to recast the produc- tion, and we already had Derek Deane guesting from the Royal Ballet, not that he was the role model I would have hoped for.

For our performances in Miami, things were a bit more relaxed and the fact that Margot Fonteyn, then in her mid-sixties, would be appearing with us lifted the company's spirits no end. In fact it was Prince Charles who was meant to be with us, as guest of honour at a big charity gala. He had been taken ill and had to cancel. The promoter, Doris Decker, phoned me in despair. The performance was completely sold out, at highly inflated prices. She asked whether I might be able to tempt Fonteyn out of retirement in Panama to attend. For once I had the right idea. I sug- gested that I might be able to persuade Margot to take the role as the queen in *The Sleeping Beauty* which was scheduled for the gala. Doris agreed at once, although it would be expensive. I put the phone down after our conversation. Picking it up again I dialled Margot. I heard her voice as she answered the call. I explained what we wanted her to do. A rather long silence followed, then I heard Margot say, 'Yes I will do it – and I don't want a fee.' She explained, however, that she would need to bring Tito, her paralysed husband with her, as well as his nursing staff. Then there was another pause before she said, 'But this will be a one-off. Please don't ask me again.' In the event it all proved a huge success.

I had known Margot for years and had even partnered her on television. She had never played the queen in *Sleeping Beauty* before, so we had to have a couple of days' rehearsal which she handled beautifully. There is an extra scene in my production where the queen nearly collapses in anguish when she believes Aurora to be dead. Margot was the most professional artist that I have ever worked with. She was really quite funny when she was fitted for the costume. She never had a large bosom but it was essential to fill this voluminous costume. She spent a lot of time in front of the mirror with a box of tissues to pad herself out, not in a vain way, and ended up looking gorgeous, and she performed with enormous grace. Margot was tired after the performance and wanted to slip away from the theatre unobtrusively. As we were leaving through a side door to avoid the dozens of people waiting for Margot outside the stage door, a child caught sight of her before she could reach the car. She ran towards Margot, wanting her autograph. I could hear her groan inwardly as everybody else followed, but she signed every autograph and responded with enormous charm. I wanted Margot to do other performances with us on subsequent occasions but she was right to refuse. Such appearances only work because of their rarity. Whatever their reputation, dancers cannot have a second career of positively last appearances – although many try. There is no credibility in that.

After Miami that tour took us to Mexico shortly after the earthquake that had caused so much devastation. The mess was still evident everywhere around. The pollution was terrible and a lot of the company ended up in hospital. Fortunately our performances of *Coppélia* went ahead and were much appreciated. Our repertory in Venezuela included *The Sleeping Beauty*. The new opera house in Caracas where we were to play was the most sophisticated and technically advanced I have ever come across, anywhere in the world. Every seat in the auditorium had a perfect view, the acoustics were superb and the stage floor moved in sections to facilitate the changing of sets. The first night went wonderfully well. The second night was one of those occasions when everything seemed to go wrong. Technology is fine when it works, and this night, during the transformation scene as Aurora is put to sleep, the computer operating all the systems broke down. There was no manual back-up. The technical designer was away in Los Angeles and nobody else knew how to put them right. He declined to offer any advice by phone as to how to correct the malfunction. It was his system – and nobody was going to interfere with it. And so we had to perform the rest of the ballet with the scenery half up and half down, in front of a sold-out house. We still had to do two performances of *Beauty* and had to get a triple-bill set and lit for the rest of the season. Eventually, in time for the last *Sleeping Beauty*, the technical tyrant turned up. He simply pressed a few buttons on the console and hey presto! Everything was magically put to rights within seconds. Aurora slept no more.

Our other experiences in South America also had their dramas. In Brazil it was always touch and go. The stage crew operated in their own time and the orchestra was on the verge of going on strike over pay. Although we did not fully realise it at the time, the security services learned of a plot to kidnap Princess Anne, whose four-day visit to the country included attending a performance. We knew nothing of this; such was the discretion of those responsible for royal security. Her itinerary was changed and the princess was hidden away under guard on a farm outside Rio. When she attended the gala she was met with an audience dressed to the nines in designer bling which made our sequins and tiaras for *Paquita* pale into insignificance. We came face to face with the other side of Rio when we discovered that somebody had been shot outside the stage door during our opening performance. 'That's Rio,' we were told. The Ballet Nacional de Brasil is another of the companies for whom I have staged *Giselle*. They have been performing it for nearly 35 years, so long that the sets and costumes, by Peter Farmer, are falling apart. I have forbidden them from doing it again – but that means nothing there. Still, Brazil manages to produce some very good dancers.

I have worked too in Argentina at the Teatro Colón. It is a major venue for ballet as well as opera, and Buenos Aires is where Vaslav Nijinsky married Romola de Pulszky during a Ballets Russes' tour in 1913. In more recent years Argentina has produced several dancers of international calibre, Julio Bocca, Paloma Herra and Marianela Núñez among then. The Colón is also known for producing more than its fair share of strikes and trouble. When I first staged *The Sleeping Beauty* there I was greatly assisted by Louise Lester. She studied at the Royal Ballet School and started her career in the corps de ballet of Bavarian State Ballet in Munich when I staged *The Sleeping Beauty*. She became a principal, dancing Aurora, before becoming ballet mistress there. After that, Louise worked as a guest teacher for many companies including La Scala, Milan, and Royal Danish Ballet in Copenhagen. She was invaluable to me in Buenos Aries. Performances may start on time, absolutely on the dot, but that is the only evidence of discipline among the dancers or stage crew. They are all very erratic and changeable. In fact most of the performances were cancelled as a strike, protesting about new working conditions, was engulfing the theatre. The sets and costumes had been shipped from Birmingham on loan. Nobody was available to unpack them. They finally made it onstage for only the last performance of the run. All the others were cancelled because of the strike. It was danced well thanks to Louise, but the company forgot to reserve a seat for me for the performance. They put a chair in a corner of the stalls for me. I have never felt so unappreciated. When the production was revived some three years later in 2011, we were allowed one stage rehearsal without the orchestra or lighting. 'It's all on the computer. It will work,' I was told. The first night was an absolute disaster, the worst performance I have ever seen. Some of the cast had never worn their costumes before and Philip Prowse's costumes take some wearing. It was all very difficult, shocking. I can only say thank goodness for Desmond Kelly and Denis Bonner who later put on *Swan Lake* for me there without me having to be present.

When I was in Chile in November 2003, to stage *The Sleeping Beauty* at the Teatro Municipal in Santiago, again with the help of Louise Lester, I arrived just after a special day celebrating nakedness. Everybody in the streets and squares of a certain area near the theatre removes their clothes for a day, keeping on only their socks and shoes and handbags. Everybody, all shapes and sizes, disrobed. And what was more, there were huge photos of this mass unrobing posted up around the neighbourhood.

Without exception everybody looked awful. Everything was drooping everywhere.

As for *The Sleeping Beauty*, it had lavish new designs by Pablo Núñez, somewhat in the style of those designed for me by Philip Prowse previously. It had a huge success and won a theatre award there, but it was not a production that lasted for long. When Marcia Haydée arrived as director of the company in 2004, she, as new directors tend to do, wanted to make her own mark. She re-used some of the sets and costumes but replaced my production with her own. Marcia expanded the role of Carabosse for her former partner Richard Cragun so much that the company called the ballet *Carabosse*. Chile was also memorable for a horse-riding excursion. It was through my love of riding that I first came across Wendy Toye, the director and choreographer. When I was a young teenager, my father had taken me and my sisters riding with a business associate of his who was there with Wendy and her new husband, Selwyn Sharp, a flashy socialiser who talked incessantly. Because of my own interest in dancing I knew all about Wendy. She had been a member of the Vic-Wells Ballet under Ninette de Valois and was already a successful dancer and director. Wendy looked sulky – her husband was something of a monster and very self-obsessed – and I did not dare speak to her. Years later, Sonya and I went riding with her at Kenwood in Hampstead. Riding was always something I kept up when I could on tour, and so was looking forward to the visit to Chile, along with my sister Brenda, as I thought there would be a lot of opportunities to ride. In fact there turned out to be only one occasion, and Sonya, wisely as it happened, decided to stay in a café and sketch. The ride took us up, and up, along a cliff edge in the Andes. I am sure our mounts, more ponies than horses, were trained to trip and stumble to make the whole experience all the more exciting. I could hear Brenda singing her prayers. 'I thought I would get through to God quicker that way,' she said to me afterwards, admitting she had been absolutely terrified. It really felt as though we were heading for the end of the world. Santiago was home to many of the Kurt Jooss company during the 1939–45 war. Ernst Uthoff and Lola Botka left the company in due course and set up a ballet school in Santiago. This laid the foundations for what was to become the Chilean National Ballet. Although Ernst and Lola pre-dated my own involvement with the Jooss company, it was fascinating to meet them while in Santiago and share memories of our Jooss' days.

The production of *Swan Lake* that I produced with Galina Samsova in 1981 for Sadler's Wells Royal Ballet led to invitations for me to stage it in Munich, Stockholm and Vienna, as well as Buenos Aries. It is a *Swan Lake* built to last, but I would still like to change the look of it and some of the content, although not as much as some directors might like. When I staged it in Munich in January 1984 Edmund Gleede was director of the ballet company, the latest in the continual flux of short-term directors there. A former student of August Everding, the intendant at Munich, Gleede considered himself an actor, director and dramaturg. Whatever he was, Gleede was very tall himself – and liked very tall men. It was no exaggeration to say that only tall men were offered contracts to join the company. Really I think he was mad, but he did get on well with Philip Prowse who is always good company after a show. On the other hand I myself had constant tussles with Gleede, who had his own ideas about *Swan Lake* and wanted to impose them on me. He wanted *Swan Lake* to be all about men – and this was a decade before Matthew Bourne made his version with male swans – and was constantly pestering me with his ideas. That was not my conception of the ballet, and never will be. My production replaced John Cranko's version which he made in 1970 when he was combining the Stuttgart and Munich directorships. It was highly popular with audiences but needed to be replaced as the sets had been damaged, something that caused much upset for Jürgen Rose whose work they were. Somehow we got the production on, but Munich judged it rather controversial. It was revived when Ronald Hynd became director again there after Gleede but it stayed in the repertoire for only four years. I should perhaps be thankful for small mercies. And when Constanze Vernon took over as director, Munich had yet another *Swan Lake*, this time produced by Ray Barra with designs by John Macfarlane. Ray was not an experienced producer and you have to know how to harness John's ideas. I did not see this production but I understand John had too much influence. It was all quite a rough ride. During our own preparations, Philip Prowse happened to ask the wardrobe director's wife how things were at the opera house. 'Flop after flop after flop,' was her reply.

In Vienna, in March 1995, when he arrived at the wardrobe department there, Philip discovered they had started making costumes without his involvement or authorisation. When he protested, she insisted that this was how they always worked, 'This is our job.' As Philip tossed the, actually beautifully made, costumes off their hangers and onto the floor, he snarled back, 'Not with me, honey!' Philip could be awful. When one wardrobe mistress queried the length of tutus that he had designed, Philip snapped back, 'I don't want to see their pussies.' He could be blunt. He once said about a Princess Florine in Vienna, 'Who is that blue-arsed baboon doing bluebird?' Another problem working in Vienna, as in theatres in Germany which schedule performances in the same way, is that although you get ample time to stage a new production, for a revival the time allocated to the technical aspects such as the lighting and stage rehearsals is extremely limited, even if a complex production has been out of the repertoire for a number of years. You get only one stage rehearsal, without the orchestra. You really need five. Things have changed over the years. I am pleased to say that people are willing to fight more – and the bureaucrats who control such matters are more willing to listen.

My visit to Stockholm in November 2001 when I mounted *Swan Lake* for Royal Swedish Ballet was not my first visit to the city. I had toured there in 1946 with Ballets Jooss when the midnight sun was a revelation. The opera house in Stockholm had been established in 1791 by Gustav III who was a noted social and cultural patron. The ballet company is one of the oldest classical troupes there is, designed to replace foreign troupes at court. Gustav is portrayed in Giuseppe Verdi's opera *Un ballo in maschera*, in which he is shot dead at the masked ball of the title, by a Captain Anckarström following a conspiracy of nobles, an actual incident. As I was to discover, there was much intrigue swirling around the opera house when I went there with Galina and Philip for our *Swan Lake*. I had only agreed to do the production as Petter Jacobsson, previously a principal with Sadler's Wells Royal Ballet, was now director there and I wanted to support him. Stockholm had a reputation among the company itself and with audiences alike to hang on to their productions, but Petter had decided to replace their existing *Swan Lake* – long, boring and old-fashioned. It had been in the repertoire there since 1964 and used choreography by Natalia Conus drawn from the St Petersburg production of 1895. It was designed by Henry Bardon and David Walker, both disciples of Lila de Nobili, who were revered by the wardrobe mistresses and technical departments in Stockholm, as Philip was to discover.

The opera house in Stockholm was not large, but for some reason Philip made his sets, particularly the columns, bigger than before. It was all a matter of proportion, he insisted. They were made, but they were hellish to get onto the stage. The columns at the rear of the set were designed to rotate and open to reveal the lake, a marvellous idea but one unfortunately that did not work in practice. Nor were Philip's trees in the lakeside acts particularly successful, I thought. He was in something of a minimalist phase at the time and his trees looked more like giant twigs or impractically stylised pitchforks. Altogether Philip was at his most demanding. The wardrobe department was used to making lightweight costumes, an approach quite at odds with this *Swan Lake* and the heavy fabrics that Philip specified. There were other currents in the air, however. I should have detected that something was amiss when Bengt Hall, director of the opera house, did not greet Galina, Philip nor me, as a director normally does when visitors arrive to work with a company. It transpired that many people there, including Madeleine Onne, the company's former director and principal dancer, were hostile to Petter Jacobsson. Madeleine wanted him removed in favour of herself. I was told she even wrote letters to the papers damning Petter before he had taken up his position. Madeleine, now director of Hong Kong Ballet, was one of those who did not like the idea of a new *Swan Lake*. Although it was evident that she was out for trouble, she was niceness itself to my face. But I knew she could not be trusted.

Stockholm has very strong union regulations that protect dancers' working conditions and hours, leaves of absence and salary levels. The amount of time allowed for rehearsals is actually very small, about which I had to complain. There were endless problems with casting, rehearsal hours, materials in the production wardrobe, maternity leave, and it was very hard to get started. Somehow Denis Bonner, who is a brilliant notator and répétiteur, managed to teach the ballet and I went over whenever I could. There was a lot of opposition from the principals who were all hoping to be first cast. I actually chose one – the newest, Nathalie Nordquist, just promoted – but even she was not passionate or classical enough. Try as we might, she was never able to reach her potential. However, it finally got on. The premiere went well and was well received by a very conservative public. When the production was televised, a joint production between Sveriges Television and the BBC by Bob Lockyer and Ross MacGibbon, we had a nightmare getting ready for the recording when the lighting man vanished. It turned out that he had gone home for his two-hour lunch break. He claimed that nobody had told him that he was required to relight the ballet for television. We had wasted those two already limited hours. I cannot say the ballet was terribly well danced in that broadcast, but it did look impressive and was popular. What was good in Stockholm was that the company was large enough to have a full bevy of swans. When I had first made this production for Sadler's Wells Royal Ballet, the company was actually too small. I had to settle for 16 swans including the cygnets, whereas there should actually be 24 of them with four cygnets and a further two big swans. The corps in Stockholm was sufficiently large to have the full number although the overall standard was not great as they rarely, if ever, danced the big classics.

I only learned that Petter was not to have his contract renewed when I was back in London. I was concerned for him but worried too about the future of the production. I was scarcely impressed by Bengt Hall's reassurances. Although admittedly he had experienced a family bereavement, he had been nowhere near any of the rehearsals during the weeks we were in Stockholm. The production did remain in the repertoire for a while after Madeleine Onne forced Petter out and wangled herself in as director. She proved to be difficult when the production was revived, willing to indulge dancers who wanted to alter their costumes and change any choreography with which they were having difficulties or when they wanted to introduce their own favourite steps. My policy on this sort of thing has always been clear. Guest artists may perform their own choreographic changes if they fit with the rest of the production, but company members should stick to the steps as produced and costumes as designed. Madeleine replaced our *Swan Lake* as soon as she possibly could, bringing back the previous staging by Natalia Conus which really exposed how tired it was. It really did not work any more. The company now dance a version by Mats Ek. I am pleased, however, that in recent years Petter Jacobsson has enjoyed success as director of Ballet de Lorraine. Much as I love Stockholm I will never work there again. I find their way of working, supported by the union restrictions there, too comfortable and counter-productive. Dancers need to be pushed and made to feel that they can achieve so much more than they thought possible.

I did not know what to expect when Birgit Keil invited me to produce *Giselle* in Karlsruhe in 2004. I had a ghastly journey when I first went there. I got very confused about which train I should be catching from the airport and finally arrived at the theatre in the middle of a dreadful thunderstorm after everybody had left. I was relatively nervous about working with the company. It had a long tradition which had gone down and down, becoming a contemporary ensemble of about a dozen dancers, until Birgit picked it up and reinvigorated it as a classically based company able to do justice to Christopher Wheeldon's *Swan Lake*, Ashton's *La Fille mal gardée* and Kenneth MacMillan's *Romeo and Juliet*, provocative programming as Karlsruhe is a mere tram-ride down the road from Stuttgart.

Birgit was not popular with Reid Anderson, Stuttgart's director, when she started in Karlsruhe, but what she has achieved with the company has not detracted from Stuttgart. Audiences in Karlsruhe are happy to have their own distinctive company. Birgit really wanted to have my Birmingham *Nutcracker* for them but that was just too big and expensive a production. For *Giselle* she was insistent that I worked with their resident designer, which I was not happy about but I coped. Birgit had to cope with my request for 24 wilis as the Karlsruhe stage is one of the largest in Germany, second in size only to Munich I think. She said yes to that request, knowing full well she had only 15 women in the company, but she found the rest from her dance academy in Mannheim. I soon fell in love with the company. They were very young and there were some technical difficulties but generally did very well. They were all very happy working for Birgit and her husband Vladimir. I was not able to demonstrate much during rehearsals but the wonderful ballet masters there, Matthias Deckert and Alexandre Kalibabchuk, were a great help. Horst Koegler, never my favourite critic, praised the mime particularly, saying that for the first time in his long experience it fitted into the ballet perfectly as performed by Anaïs Chalendard in the title role, with Flavio Salamanca as Albrecht and Emmanuelle Heyer as Myrtha. All credit to Denis Bonner for teaching it. On the strength of that *Giselle* I was asked back to do *Coppélia* and this time I insisted that Birgit rented my production from Birmingham with the designs by Peter Farmer. Paloma

Souza and Diego de Paula danced up a storm with Matthias Deckert as Coppélius. They were just perfect and had a big success.

I first visited Japan during my time as associate director of the Royal Ballet in May 1975. The month-long tour, including *The Sleeping Beauty*, *La Fille mal gardée* and *The Dream*, took in not only Tokyo but also Yokohama, Nagoya, Kyoto, Osaka, Kobe, Fukuoka, Chiba and Hiroshima – which all provided a fascinating window on the country, although always on tour I was used to being so busy with practical matters that it was frequently difficult to get much idea of the country. Most stages in Japan are very wide and not so high as in Britain. This does present problems with setting the dancers' placing, mostly for the corps de ballet. There is invariably very little time available, particularly when you have only one performance at a venue, which was the case at Yokohama. There is always so much to get done, including the orchestra having a sound balance and seating call to make sure they have room to actually play their instruments and are able to see the conductor.

Before that first visit in 1975 I had not been to Japan with Sonya before. Indeed she had not been there herself although her father was Japanese. He was the head of Tokyo Food Products and he used to visit England frequently in the 1920s for business. This is how he met Sonya's mother Sydna Scott, who became his partner. Sydna – Scottie – had a life and half. She had a Belgian lover during the 1939–45 war, a period when in Hyde Park she defiantly put up her umbrella to shield herself and Sonya from flying shrapnel. That Sonya's parents were not married caused her many difficulties during her upbringing and she was stigmatised at school. Sonya could not speak Japanese but on that first visit the company assumed she could and would ask her to translate. Embarrassingly too the Japanese whom we were introduced to, talked to her in their language. Later on, Sonya did study Japanese but she gave it up as too difficult and time-consuming, especially when it came to writing the characters.

On our first visit, Sonya had an introduction from Bernard Leach, one of the most influential potters of the 20th century, to meet Shōji Hamada, an equally celebrated Japanese studio potter. We visited Hamada at Matshiko. It was an amazing place. Pottery was sold everywhere. Hamada fired pots only twice per year and had a kiln that followed the slope of a hill. Runners would lie waiting when the kiln was opened to take pots all over Japan. Hamada had a big English garden with roses and herbaceous borders. Sonya gave him a bottle of whisky which amazed and delighted him. He gave her a footed slipware plate, a fantastic present as his work sold for incredibly high prices. Alexander Grant, who was also interested in ceramics and whose brother Garry used to have a pottery shop near Sadler's Wells, was with us and he intimated that he might like a gift too. Hamada twigged and gave Alexander a little pot. Alexander was very adventurous and loved making discoveries. And being given them. During that tour, Kenneth MacMillan wanted to see some Noh dancing. At the time he was working on *Rituals*, inspired by traditional Japanese forms of theatre. We were taken to an empty theatre and never discovered whether we were watching a man or woman. Initially it was hard to feel involved in the slow, measured movements punctuated by sudden gestures when the performer felt a certain resonance through the wooden floor. It was all very different. Kenneth was impressed and the experience certainly helped shape *Rituals* which was unveiled the following December.

Tadatsugu Sasaki, director of the Japan Performing Arts Foundation who was presenting the company and founder of Tokyo Ballet, took us to an authentic Japanese lunch where every dish was decorated and beautifully presented. It was a wonderful experience despite the trial of having to sit cross-legged on the floor. Japanese food I love, particularly sushi, sashimi and tempura. I like all the ceremony with which a meal is served, but I do find it strange that European women married to Japanese men were required, when clearing dishes from a table, to open the door and leave the room on their knees. We were also taken to a tea ceremony, full of ritual, though the tea itself was quite unpleasant. There is much etiquette to master in Japan. Try to avoid sneezing in public but whatever you do, do not blow your nose as this was considered exceedingly rude.

We were invited to too many receptions and parties, and the women of the company always looked wonderful except for one thing. Everyone had to discard their shoes and wear soft, unflattering slippers that were provided so as not to damage the beautiful polished floors. Their outfits were ruined by losing their high heels. Smart dinner suits do not look particularly good if you have to wear bedroom slippers; but taken altogether, Japan made a big impression on us. We were struck particularly on the formalities we observed. Audiences then were very quiet. It took them some time to really laugh at something like *Fille* but their appreciation was genuine. You felt there was an understanding of what they were seeing but it was considered impolite to exaggerate their reaction.

You could not accuse Madame Oya of any lack of exaggeration. She somehow attached herself to every ballet company that performed in Japan and appeared to give all the receptions held in their honour. She wore diamond jewellery pinned all over her kimonos. She would point at the brooches and say, 'Tiffany's . . . Cartier . . .' Madame Oya was a nightclub singer who became the mistress of a rich industrialist who owned a chain of Japanese restaurants in London. She liked to give the impression that it was she who had the money, although in reality it was her partner who did. Apparently he left her penniless when he died. Madame Oya was incredibly kind, giving the principal women strings of pearls and dress lengths. The men did not get much, other than the chance to lift her, usually wearing fish-nets – and she was quite a big woman. I do wish I could find the photo of Rudolf Nureyev lifting her! Madame Oya was very dominant. She had an extraordinary house in London, whole rooms filled with silver for example, too full of everything. Once at a performance at Covent Garden attended by Princess Margaret, Madame Oya was determined to be presented but was not on the list. As the princess was leaving, Madame Oya rushed up behind her and pulled at her sleeve, 'I Madame Oya, I meet you.'

In 1988, I took Sadler's Wells Royal Ballet on a nine-week tour to Thailand, Korea, China, Hong Kong and Japan, sponsored by Glaxo. It was the company's first visit to China and Japan and followed a visit by Central Ballet of China to Britain the previous year. Our visit to Thailand was part of the celebrations for the 60th birthday of King Bhumibol Adulyadej. Such occasions are always a minefield of protocol, not so much among the members of royal families themselves but with their officials. The king sat on a raised dais in the auditorium. Anybody taken to meet him had to keep their head lower than his, which meant practically having to lie down on the dais when shaking hands. That was something I really could not do with my bad back so I was excused. At that venue there was nowhere to put the orchestra as there was no pit. Positioning the players in front of the stage would have meant obscuring the dancers. Fortunately, as I prowled round the theatre I discovered another deep recess where we could place the players, which meant the sound was very muffled.

In China, while in Shanghai we watched ballet classes there. They were Russian in influence but so strict. The teacher had a stick and the dancers hardly dared to move their heads out of line. There were some very good dancers. They were given incredible stretching exercises and were also taught to use their eyes, eyebrows and smiles. Everything was very come-hither and flirtatious. I loved it.

As in Japan, it took Chinese audiences time to warm to the humour of *Fille* but *Elite Syncopations*, on a triple bill with *Flowers of the Forest* and *Checkmate*, was the biggest success. Houses were full and the triple bill proved much more popular than in Japan where Tadatsugu Sasaki, but other promoters too, were reluctant to programme anything but full-length ballets. That makes for conservative audiences, nervous of appreciating one-act ballets. This was something that David Bintley encountered when he was director of National Ballet of Japan. The conservatism in Japan he put down to the fact that audiences there were not familiar with the Diaghilev tradition for one-act ballets as we are in Europe.

In May 1989, when we returned to Japan, performing in Tokyo, Yokohama, Nagoya, Osaka, Takamatsu and Kurashiki we performed only *The Sleeping Beauty* and *Swan Lake*. This was heavy going, particularly for the stage crew but also for the orchestra and dancers. Miyako Yoshida had difficulties there. She was not known in Japan at the time, but when another dancer scheduled for *Swan Lake* was injured, Tadatsugu Sasaki did not want Miyako to step in. For him, and for audiences, our selling point was that we were a Western company. I thought he was wrong so I got uppity with him. In the end we compromised by sharing the black and white acts between Miyako and another ballerina. In later performances Miyako was much appreciated and she built up a big following in Japan and has continued to perform in galas since her retirement.

In Japan too, I produced *Giselle* for Star Dancers Ballet in October 1989, making it nearly as long-lived in Japan as at Covent Garden. It was revived most recently in 2015 at the start of their 50th year, with my staging of *Coppélia* following in January 2016 at the conclusion of their anniversary season. The Star Dancers company was established in 1965 by Ruriko Tachikawa after inheriting a large legacy. She saw establishing a company as a means of providing regular employment for her three nieces. She invited Antony Tudor to stage some of his ballets there.

Madame Tachikawa was practically the first person to perform classical ballet in Japan. She was a ballerina who could perform the black swan fouettés until the cows came home – but every dancer is like that in Japan, which is not to detract from Madame Tachikawa. She is an amazing woman. She and Sakiko Arai had seen my production of *Giselle* in London when it was new and were keen to acquire it. Before marrying an Indian prince, Sakiko had been a very beautiful dancer. After his death she wanted to dance and she sought me out when I was in India with Sadler's Wells Royal Ballet in 1985 for my advice on how to proceed. She had earlier trained at the Royal Ballet School in London and had danced with the Komaki Ballet in Japan, appearing in Tudor's *Lilac Garden* produced by Madame Tachikawa. Eventually she became a principal dancer and later ballet mistress with Star Dancers Ballet.

I went to see the company, who were all shapes and sizes. The boys particularly were very mixed and the girls were very different in height. Overall the standard was fairly low and getting *Giselle* on in 1987 was something of a struggle. Although companies undertake a lot of educational work, a season in Japan amounts to only five or six performances of each ballet, three times per year. The orchestra and stage crew are employed and paid by the performance, not as a permanent ensemble. Sets and costumes are often made to last only for the few performances they receive, not for twenty or thirty years as in Britain.

I have always enjoyed going to Japan. There are many beautifully trained dancers there. For Star Dancers Ballet I have staged also my Peter Farmer-designed *Coppélia* and my Birmingham *Nutcracker*, productions that have often been revived there. Christmas is a strange experience in Japan. 'Jingle Bells' blares out relentlessly from loudspeakers in the main shopping streets. The Japanese seem to love it, but they do not know why. The lighting designer at Star Dancers at the Bunka Kaikan theatre is a marvel. He appears to carry an entire lighting board in his brain. He walks around apparently talking to himself but somehow in communication with his staff. He is brilliant in how he arranges the lighting. Somehow it is all still in his head the next time you go back to revive a production, but really all the staff and orchestra are exceptionally easy to work with. The company also has a large training academy too, the Showa Akamedia, where I have acted as an adviser. The long distances involved have meant that I have not been as involved as I would like,

but I have worked with the teachers there and assisted in rehearsals for
Giselle. It is a ballet that Japanese dancers find difficult. They tend to be
too restrained facially and need to be helped with the mime. It is most
unnerving to be following around with a cameraman and sound record-
ist intent on capturing your every word when you are in the middle of
coaching somebody.

I love Japan – in moderation, two weeks at a time at most. First and
foremost everybody is very polite. The bowing and insistence on courtesy may seem tiresome, but everybody insists on doing the best for
you that they possibly can, with tremendous attention to detail. It is
considered insulting to tip as they say they always do their best anyway.
I enjoy the small carvings and paper birds that you find in Japan and
the beautiful way in which parcels are wrapped with a special technique.
What remains of old Japan is very interesting. I love the colourfulness
and traditions that you see, particularly at weddings, where the women
are immaculately made up and dressed in kimonos. Of course modern-
day Japan is almost as American as America. Hotels in Japan are the
same international boxes as the world over, although with Sonya I did
once stay with friends in a traditional house in the hills. We slept on the
floor on a thin mattress and there was no heating so it was freezing at
night. What is absolutely brilliant is how the trains are always fast and
dead on time, I believe centrally controlled somehow. They absolutely
have to be punctual. This caused problems for the station master during
a visit by the queen who was in Tokyo just after us in 1975. You cannot
take anything more than hand baggage on board and she had more
luggage than could be loaded during the brief, two-minute halt that the
train was stationary on the platform. It was impossible to delay it. The
station master had to organise a battalion of people to literally throw
the queen's luggage onto the train during the brief instant when the
doors were open. He really was distressed about it, but if they would
not change the rules for the queen's visit, you can imagine the horrors
attempting to get an entire ballet company with all their paraphernalia
boarded during that brief time. Not one of my responsibilities thank
goodness, but who would want to be the director of an international
touring ballet company?

CHAPTER 15

Heroes, heroines – and others

O F ALL THE MANY companies that I have been involved with, there is one thing that they have in common: they all work together very closely. There is a strong bond between dancers, staff and stage crew that verges between love and hate but which keeps them all together. For any ballet company too, the orchestra is vitally important, but when I made a speech at the close of the last performance at the old Sadler's Wells theatre before the bulldozers moved in in June 1996, I completely forgot to mention their important role in my appreciation of what made the company special. This was a serious wrong. The orchestra demanded an apology, which I made, standing on the podium in front of them in the pit. The trouble with orchestras is that players come and go. They tend to follow where the pay is better, though there are some who remain faithful for many years. Nowadays the standard has improved enormously.

The relationship between the stage and pit is so important, and considering the small amount of time that is given to rehearse and the constant change of conductors, I am amazed that it is as good as it is. The question of tempi is always a problem, but what I believe most dancers want when they complain about speed is not so much that as the lack of rhythmic beat that they get from some conductors. From my experience of working with a variety of them – as a dancer, choreographer and coach – I have good reason to be depressed by the fact that so few performances are as good as they are in the studio because performers and conductor just have not had more time together and then only hurried conversations about tempi with each other before the show. That really is not satisfactory and there is always a problem that conductors can rarely come to rehearsals. For me, as it is the music that is the main inspiration for choreography and the actual dancing, it seems strange that a dancer's training rarely uses music as little more than a background for their steps. There are so few dancers who really are a conduit for the music capable of performing it without ego. The good thing now is that most of the pupils at White Lodge, the Royal Ballet's junior school, learn to play an instrument.

Although I worked with several conductors before Ashley Lawrence, he was the one whom I have admired and respected most. He was conductor of the Royal Ballet touring company in the 1960s before moving to Berlin Opera Ballet during Kenneth MacMillan's directorship. Then, after a spell in Stuttgart, Ashley came back to London as music director of the Royal Ballet in 1973. My admiration for Ashley does not mean others including John Lanchbery, Barry Wordsworth and Paul Murphy are not also at the top of the list – they certainly are. Barry has a really good beat, eminently danceable and exciting, but he is not always too sympathetic to dancers' requirements, which is not unusual. Dancers frequently want something unmusical. Monica Mason's relationship with Barry was very good as she understood his point of view and both wanted to create the right musical support for the company.

There is always a tension about music for dance. It is hell for the dancer if they do not have the right speed. A ballet is not a concert, but I have witnessed quite a few rows about tempi. Barry once walked out of a rehearsal after he refused to play at the tempo Michael Corder wanted. Jack Lanchbery was probably a better conductor than arranger of scores, which tended to be heavy handed, but he could be known for doing the opposite of what dancers wanted when he grew tired of their endless, unmusical requests. Ashley, if asked to rearrange a score or make cuts for a choreographer, including myself, would always ensure that any changes were musical and would spend time explaining anything that was not possible. He would suggest what would be practical musically, as his suggestions always were. But he was always firm and understanding. Ashley was the same with dancers when they wanted a sequence faster or slower. He would be very accommodating but very firm. Then of course the next cast would ask for the same thing but the other way round. As far as the orchestra was concerned, Ashley was very different. He was always in total command and a real disciplinarian. The orchestra loved him for that because he made the music so danceable and expressive, which was no small achievement given how bad orchestras on tour used to be in those days. As a way of disguising their faults, Ashley, as many conductors do, had the violins bow in different timings. John Tooley turned up at one performance unexpectedly and took Ashley to task afterwards, 'I think it's awful that you allow the strings to play anyhow and don't get them to bow together.' This infuriated Ashley. He was only 55 when he died in 1990. It took a long time to fill the gap he left behind. I loved Ashley dearly, despite the occasion in New Zealand when he insisted that I should have some oysters at dinner one evening, something to which I am allergic. Ashley assured me they were absolutely perfect but I had the grimmest night as a consequence, feeling very ill and up at all hours being violently sick. I was still feeling decidedly liverish when Ashley bounced into the lobby of the hotel the next morning. 'All all right today?' he beamed, then as he saw how miserable I looked, he said, 'What's wrong with you?!'

Orchestras and conductors may well feel overlooked, but at least they are visible to at least part of the audience during performances. There are many others absolutely vital for a performance whose contribution is scarcely ever given a thought by audiences. One such person is Lili Sobieralska, for many years head of wardrobe for Birmingham Royal Ballet, although she had worked at the Royal Opera House since 1969. Now that Lili has retired, Birmingham Royal Ballet, for me at least, has become quite different, though certainly not worse as it continues to be extremely well run. Lili has an incredibly strong personality, could be very bossy, very funny, very passionate and loving – and sometimes infuriating. I think the fact that she is Polish had much to do with it, but there was something more, I believe. If a disagreement occurred about something, Lili would always ensure the wound was healed before it was forgotten. Heaven help any dancers she caught sitting down in costume, especially a tutu. She was generous and friendly, incredibly organised, strict with her staff and much loved by everyone. Lili is pretty sturdy, incredibly strong and was often seen hauling large costume skips onto waiting lorries. Because Lili enjoys everything in life, including food, she had quite a problem refusing goodies to eat. When she overdid a diet once, she got really thin and nearly died. Luckily she was discovered, collapsed on the floor, by Doug Nicholson, the company's head of scenic presentation, and Lili was taken to hospital where she stayed for several months. Although she recovered, she felt she really had to retire. The company gave her a wonderful send-off with a fat volume of appreciations, presents galore and the company's gold medal in appreciation of her contribution over the years. Lili has wonderfully bold handwriting and usually ends letters 'with Lily love'. I have quite a collection and I regard her as one of my dearest friends.

John Hart – Dolly – was brought up in the theatre and was for many years master carpenter of Sadler's Wells Royal Ballet. He was completely unknown to the public but he made the sets look right onstage. He was very conscientious and knew how to get columns to stand upright on a raked stage. Dolly was excellent company, a good storyteller and had very strong likes and dislikes among choreographers and dancers. If any dancer made the mistake of using a piece of scenery as an impromptu barre, Dolly would growl at them, 'Don't mess with my scenery.' When one choreographer complained to Dolly about how much floor space the scenery and floor lights were occupying, he snapped back, 'Fuck your choreography. What about my scenery?' but then gave the choreographer a big hug. He was the sort of person who could get on with everybody. Dolly could frequently cry when things were not right. I had a constant battle with Liz Dalton's designs for *Summertide*. They were full of drapery with lots of poppies that intruded into the dancing area. 'Dolly, will you get those drapes off,' I used to complain, to which he would reply, 'They're on the plan. I have to do what's on the plan.' I had to insist, 'Just get them OFF.' Dolly was part of the big touring family. He loved a drink or two. It is forbidden to drink backstage now, but in Dolly's touring days he and the other heads of department would have boozy sessions which would end with them sleeping in the theatre overnight.

In more recent years, Doug Nicholson started out as assistant carpenter. Stage carpenter really means you are in charge of the scenery and Doug is now responsible for how all the sets look onstage at Birmingham Royal Ballet. We rely on him a lot when he oversees my productions abroad, organising contracts and rental agreements, getting everything in place for how sets and costumes are made. Doug is an interesting man, somebody I like very much, and he always makes our shows look the best they possibly can.

When I was associate director of the Royal Ballet in the early 1970s, at the same time as being responsible for the touring company I needed to be in contact with both companies most of the day, as did my secretary Barbara Booroff. She was wonderfully efficient, always ready to run errands round the building at Covent Garden. I knew nobody as able and willing to help, stay late, find things and be so totally reliable and dedicated. When we later moved to Birmingham and I no longer had an office at the Royal Opera House, Barbara stayed in London and became secretary to Peter Brownlee, the general manager. He felt exactly the same way about her – perfection. He too was an unsung hero. He started as a dancer in the Covent Garden opera-ballet, joined London Festival Ballet before joining the Royal Ballet, first as a dancer and then manager. He was brilliant, kind, and the best organiser in the world. To see him in action coping with a crisis in the middle of a Japanese tour when the buses required to transport 200 people to the airport did not turn up was a lesson in patience, tact and determination. Peter could get really angry and would not accept unpunctuality from anyone. He was nicknamed Testy but he never lost his temper. Although retired now and back in his homeland, Australia, he is still loved, very highly thought of and much missed.

Somebody else who meant an enormous amount to me was John Auld. He was an Australian dancer with the Borovansky Ballet who appeared in several big musicals in London in the 1950s before joining London Festival Ballet in the days when Alicia Markova and Anton Dolin ran it. John was one of my closest and dearest friends, from 1970 until his death in 2015. I met him first when Kenneth MacMillan asked him to come and look after the New Group while I had to be away so much from the company helping Kenneth cope at Covent Garden. Although I had not met John before that day in 1970 when we had a lovely English tea party near Battersea Park with Sonya and John's partner, Manolita de Bogaerde, I knew of him from his reputation as a superb character artist, someone whose wide experience made him ideal to cope with this new group of dancers. He had served as assistant director to John Gilpin at Festival Ballet and took over the directorship of the company for a spell. He became director of Gulbenkian Ballet in Portugal, which is where Kenneth got to know him.

John had a wicked sense of humour, was a great raconteur and stood no nonsense from anyone, having the highest possible standards.

'You've had your chance and muffed it,' he said if an artist did not make the most of a chance in a new role. The company loved him though and he made a huge contribution to the Royal Ballet organisation. He really was a hero. John too was a wonderful example to the company as a performer, the best Dr Coppélius ever, who brought humour, mystery and sadness to the role. Absolutely unique. His other roles included Drosselmeyer in *The Nutcracker*, the duke in *Giselle*, Thomas the farmer in *La File mal gardée* and especially the father in *Prodigal Son*, which was his favourite role for its emotional rewards. When the son returns stripped and battered, and drags himself to his father's feet, who then gathers him up in his arms, John would be in tears as the curtain fell.

John made a huge and unforgettable contribution to the standard and depth of our productions as he had at Festival Ballet where he was hilarious as the headmistress in *Graduation Ball* and very scary as the witch, Madge, in *La Sylphide*. John and I shared similar tragedies. When his partner Manolita died he was completely shattered. I hope Sonya and I were able to help him through his grief, but then I lost Sonya seven months later. We each lost a sister too within a few months of each other but my friendship with John endured. We were very close. We met regularly for meals and went to performances together. One of our last excursions was to *Woolf Works* and John was always forthright about what he saw. As far as Birmingham Royal Ballet was concerned, John was much loved and respected, but he had his enemies because he always gave you the truth. Some people found that hard to take. He had countless tales to tell about his time with the Borovansky company in Australia, Alicia Markova, and his days with Gulbenkian Ballet in Portugal which could fill a book, but I learned not to raise the subject of British politics, no one survived censure. Although John's great contribution to dance was not publicly recognised, he will always be remembered.

Marion Tait has devoted her heart and soul to Birmingham Royal Ballet, having graduated into the Royal Ballet touring company in September 1968. She was for many seasons a principal, awarded an OBE in 1992 and the CBE in 2003 for her services to dance. Her range as a ballerina has been amazing, including all the great full-length classics as well as countless one-act works, including many created for her. When

Kenneth MacMillan mounted *Romeo and Juliet* in Birmingham in 1992 he cast Marion as Juliet, which she danced opposite Kevin O'Hare, now director of the Royal Ballet. This was probably Marion's greatest role. But like Margot Fonteyn, Marion faced certain technical difficulties, particularly her fear of pirouettes, which always made *Swan Lake* a trial for them both when it came to Odile's famous sequence of 32 fouettés. Marion also suffered from bunions on both feet due to bad early training before she went to the Royal Ballet School. Once, while guesting in Munich in *La Fille mal gardée* as Lise, a role that displayed her character to perfection, one bunion became very swollen and inflamed, full of pus. In great pain, Marion struggled until the last exit. The bunion then burst and left a trail of blood. She received an ovation from the audience and managed to take a call before collapsing in agony. Marion is a true artist who, unless seriously sick or badly injured, never gives in. When she recognised it was time to stop performing leading roles, she became the company's ballet mistress. Like Desmond Kelly before her, it was not long before David Bintley made her assistant director, a position that carries huge responsibilities, and where Marion is able to display authority, knowing as she does every step and gesture of the repertoire. What is more, Marion – and Desmond – can demonstrate this knowledge. Marion continues to perform many character roles. Having been the first Aurora in my Birmingham production of *The Sleeping Beauty* she is now brilliant as Carabosse. Her terrifying performance is much helped by her huge eyes and incredible energy that penetrates to the back of the gallery.

I adored Margot Fonteyn. She could make the simplest of things, like when Aurora pricks her finger in *The Sleeping Beauty*, really telling and special. She really knew how to project to the back of the amphitheatre at Covent Garden, in which she was helped by Frederick Ashton who went all over the auditorium to gauge how her performance was registering. I remember though during the war years, in the second act of *Swan Lake* at the Prince's theatre, Margot was rather dull. That was the way she had been taught. Then she did not project, but later she completely changed and communicated beautifully. I had one amazing experience working with her when I was associate director on tour in America. She had one performance scheduled in New York when we heard of a plane crash in which all the principals from the Colón theatre in Buenos Aries were killed. Margot asked me to organise a benefit performance at the

Colón to raise money for their families. It sold out within two hours and altogether three performances were arranged featuring dancers from the Royal Ballet, New York City Ballet and American Ballet Theatre. Margot was brilliant in programming the sequence of dances and including some younger dancers like David Ashmole. She was happy to perform anywhere in the programme except at the end of the show, the usual star spot. Richard Ahearne, a vice president of Pepsi-Cola, financed the trip. Margot performed with a dancer from the Colón as Rudolf Nureyev was not available, just as well as the usual hysteria he caused would have detracted from the purpose of the visit. He could at times be unbearably rude to Margot but she would just shrug her shoulders. She was cool, calm, clear and often self-effacing. I partnered her as one of the princes in Margaret Dale's TV film of *The Sleeping Beauty* in 1959 and as the cavalier to her Sugar Plum fairy in *The Nutcracker*. Like most of us, I was in awe of her. Partnering her I was too gentle with her, she said. She told me to hold her firmly, 'I'm a dancer like you and I need to feel you there supporting me. And please tell me if you see anything that I'm doing that's not right. I need to be told. People won't tell me and I cannot put my faults to rights.'

Rudi always had to be held in check. I met him first in Stuttgart soon after his defection in 1962, when he was having an affair with Erik Bruhn, who was rehearsing John Cranko's new *Daphnis and Chloë*. Erik could not bear to have Nureyev around while rehearsing as it always led to endless comparisons between the two great stars. After Rudi arrived, Erik only danced the first night and withdrew, apparently with back problems but really due to a crisis of confidence. Nureyev stayed on in Stuttgart as John asked him to appear in the gala during the annual festival. Nureyev said he would dance *Grand pas classique* with Yvette Chauviré. He did not bother to learn it properly and refused to wear the costume as it did not show his bum. 'Get me another,' he commanded. I tried to pacify him, but when he saw the man's costume for the *Giselle* peasant pas de deux hanging on a rail he insisted he would wear that. I protested that was another dancer's costume and already required. He prevailed and he wore the costume. He looked terrible dressed as a peasant alongside Chauviré in a beautiful, aristocratic white tutu. Because he had not learned the choreography he was on the wrong side of the stage when Chauviré needed him to support her pirouettes. She gestured to him but he ignored her. Nureyev finished his own variation 16 bars too soon while the orchestra played on. He just shrugged and walked off. The audience screamed in delight.

All the time Nureyev pushed people, behaving appallingly, testing his power. When I was a guest teacher with the Royal Ballet he arrived late for class. He made a dancer move from his place at the barre. I went over to him and told him to move to a space that was empty. Utterly amazed that anyone would dare to make such a request, he actually did as I told him. He then proceeded to do his own exercises at the barre. I told him that what he was doing was distracting to everybody else in the room and if he wished to do his own barre he should use the studio next door which was empty. From then on he behaved. I never had any further trouble from him. We got on well together. I liked him in some things, as Albrecht and Romeo for example. But he did mess around, and I can understand why. He had this extraordinary animal quality which the public loved and which Rudi played up to. Erik was a far better dancer. He had technical ability and a beautiful classical line but not Rudolf's animal attraction

I had to plan Rudi's appearances with his agent Sandor Gorlinsky but everything was always very last minute. Rudi's work rate was prodigious as he circled the globe. He used to complain that the management of the Royal Ballet was not interested in him and that he was only invited to partner Margot who was of course now dancing less at the end of her career. I had the chance to tell Rudi how difficult he was, only confirming his availability late in the day and making so many demands. When I tried to explain that in scheduling the ballet company Kenneth MacMillan and I had to take into account the opera, who always programmed longer in advance than the ballet was able, Rudi just said, 'Fuck the opera.'

Later, when Rudolf was staging his full-length *Raymonda* in Zurich in 1972, he said to Kenneth that he really must come over and see it. He had already staged it complete for the Royal Ballet's touring company at Spoleto in 1964. This staging was based on Rudi having only ever danced the all-male pas de quatre four times early in his career in Leningrad, in choreography by Vasili Vainonen. He had seen the complete ballet only on a handful of occasions too. Nureyev could not remember all the choreography, so he had his former teacher in Leningrad, Alexander

Pushkin, smuggle out the notation in an empty thermos flask which was part of the luggage carried by a young Canadian dancer who happened to be on a scholarship in the Soviet Union.

The following year he staged *Raymonda* complete again, for Australian Ballet, a production that came to Britain but did not really impress anybody very much. The plot, what there was of it, was as thin as for *Don Quixote*. Only the last act divertissement was taken into the regular repertoire of the Royal Ballet's touring company. Rudi persisted with his fascination with the ballet and also staged the last act for Norwegian National Ballet in 1968 before at last persuading Frederick Ashton as far as taking it into the repertory at Covent Garden a year later. It is still performed there and is a production that has been adopted by English National Ballet, Birmingham Royal Ballet and San Francisco Ballet.

Back in the 1960s, Rudi still hoped that he could persuade the Royal Ballet to stage the ballet in full. Kenneth deputed me and Michael Somes, who really hated Rudi for displacing him as Margot's partner, to go to Zurich to see whether the production was suitable for Covent Garden. We said a quick hello to Rudi before the performance and he invited us to have dinner with him after the show. The production really was not good enough. By now in Zurich Rudi had rearranged the music, story and choreography, largely to give himself more to do as Jean de Brienne. There was a distinct lack of genuine classical choreography and distinctly too much jousting and pantomime. Somes could not wait to tell Rudi what he thought. When we went round to Rudi's dressing-room to congratulate him, he was anxious to know our reaction, 'What you think? You like?' Somes was unusually silent, leaving me to tell Rudi that we would discuss everything later at dinner, expecting a quiet tête-à-tête with him. When we got to the restaurant we discovered it was very smart, and a table for a dozen people was set for us on a raised level in the corner, visible to the whole room. It was all pretty grand and Zurich was gripped with Rudimania, thrilled that he was performing in the city. Finally Rudi entered and the whole restaurant applauded him. For once he was not interested in basking in the adulation and made straight for us: 'What you think? You like?' When I heard Somes reply, I could hear the delight in his voice. His words were full of icy satisfaction when he told Rudi that the production was not nearly good enough for Covent Garden. Rudi and Somes practically came to blows. Rudi had to be restrained from thumping Somes. The diners in the restaurant were riveted by this unexpected floorshow. *Raymonda* was a ballet that Rudi never gave up on, however. Although the full-length version was never staged at Covent Garden, he did mount productions of it for American Ballet Theatre, in Paris and Vienna.

Somes' nickname at Covent Garden was Gladys, not because he was gay, he was not, but because the company had the same silly custom of giving women's names to the men and vice versa, as at Stuttgart. Compared to the training Michael had received in those early days which was very weak, training for men has changed so much and male dancers nowadays get excellent male teachers from Russia and America. Michael's feet were not good, his legs were ugly by today's standards and his arms were untrained. He had dreadful pirouettes but Ashton's *Scènes de ballet* showed he could do double tours en l'air extremely well. But Michael was very good looking, with a strong masculine body, and was one of Margot Fonteyn's favourite partners, the cause of his resentment about Nureyev. I loved the passion and anger that Michael put into his roles that he both created and assumed, as well as the compassion he could express through the way he used the weight and power of his whole body.

Within the company, Michael was the king-pin. Many women fell for him. After all, he was straight and had the ear of the director, Ashton, who was in love with him. When I staged *The Sleeping Beauty* at Covent Garden in 1968 Somes displayed his vile temper and really pushed Fred around. He even shouted at him in rehearsals, but then he shouted at everybody, even Ashley Lawrence, the best conductor the company ever had. Michael adored Antoinette Sibley, his second wife to whom he was married for nearly ten years. She was a very nervous performer who liked to be totally prepared for a performance. Michael would spend hours rehearsing her to the exact point of perfection. This was certainly the case with *Sleeping Beauty*. The first night, Aurora was meant to be Svetlana Beriosova. She arrived at the first stage rehearsal feeling decidedly unwell. She told me she would mark it and proceeded to walk through everything. Fred was there and was furious. He called Svetlana down to the stalls. He of course understood why Svetlana was below par. 'Unforgiveable!' he said to her. 'You have the whole stage and the orchestra and you are not doing it properly. Consider that you have missed this rehearsal. Antoinette will do the first performance,' which she did. During the interval after the first act, Michael went to Antoinette's dressing-room and tore into her for everything she had done wrong. He could be heard shouting at her right along the corridor. Antoinette's performance that night was not her best, but you cannot expect that on an important first night after being treated like that. She was in a terrible state, with two more acts to perform, but that was typical of Michael's sadistic nature, building people up only to demolish them.

With the likes of me, Michael could be very difficult. Actually he could be difficult with everyone, particularly at full moon. I had worked with him often, when he choreographed his one and only ballet, *Summer Interlude*, in 1950 for Sadler's Wells Theatre Ballet. Madam was concerned about Michael at the time. His dancing days were coming to an end, he had not shown any real talent for teaching, and his temperament was quite unsuitable to make him a good director, so she told him to try his hand at choreography. Dutifully, with her help and that of Ashton and Sophie Fedorovitch the designer, he got *Summer Interlude* together. The ballet was set on a beach and used music by Ottorino Respighi. Though Michael hated doing it, he did produce a charming little ballet. He had a pretty good vocabulary of steps and lifts from all the ballets he had danced in. I never saw it from the front as I was one of the four supporting bathers in the first cast and was second cast to David Blair's role as the sexy leading bather who tries to break up various loving couples. The ballet lasted only for a couple of seasons and Somes had no desire to do another one.

Michael never had much time for the touring company or John Field. He was very anti-Sadler's Wells. Mainly because of the new management in 1970, when Kenneth MacMillan replaced Ashton, he considered there was now nobody at Sadler's Wells who knew who he was or respected the fact that he was once a member of the company there, dancing with the great names of Fonteyn, Moira Shearer, Pamela May, Robert Helpmann and Alexis Rassine, before moving to Covent Garden in 1946. As a former member of Sadler's Wells Theatre Ballet I was, in Michael's eyes, almost beneath contempt. He really believed that it was he who had made the Wells' company into the Royal Ballet – or so he thought. When he came to rehearse many of Ashton's ballets he expected all the admin staff at Sadler's Wells to recognise him and treat him as some sort of god. I remember an awful scene at the box office once when I had arranged some seats for him which he was to collect. The foyer was crowded and I hovered in the background to make sure there was no trouble. There was. Michael strode up to the box office. 'I want my seats please.' The assistant replied, 'Yes sir. Your name please?' The exchange continued, 'You mean you don't know?' Unfazed, the assistant countered with, 'I'm afraid not sir. What is it?' This was too much for Michael. 'You really mean you bloody well don't know who I am?' he screamed. When Michael finally got his hands on the tickets, he threw them on the ground saying, 'You can keep your bloody seats', and left the theatre.

Things for Michael changed for the worse when the big intermingling of the companies happened in 1970. Everything, but everything, upset him. The fact that the New Group was rehearsing a ballet by Glen Tetley with electronic music by Stockhausen at Donmar studios and another work by Joe Layton using Nöel Coward's music made him fly into a rage. He burst into the studio one day and shouted at us all, 'This is rubbish. You are ruining the reputation of the Royal Ballet.' Poor Sheilah Humphreys got the worst of it, as Glen and Joe were not there. Somes railed at her that she was a bloody amateur. In fact she was probably just about the most professional artist and ballet mistress of anyone I knew. I managed to guide Michael out of the room.

Things were better when he actually put on several ballets for us in Birmingham. When he staged Ashton's *Jazz Calendar* he made the company look great. He was friendly and relaxed. Finally, not so long before he died in November 1994 from a brain tumour, he mounted Ashton's *Enigma Variations* absolutely beautifully. Something had changed in him. In retrospect we thought it might have been the awareness that he was soon going to die from the cancer. At that time Pat Neary, also well known as a tough coach, was putting on Balanchine's *Theme and Variations* for us. Michael came to some of the rehearsals and performances. Miyako Yoshida and Petter Jacobsson were the leads and the whole company had been whipped into a state of great excitement and gave 100 percent even in rehearsal. Michael was hugely excited by the ballet, one that he had not seen before, and actually said, 'I think the company is marvellous. Congratulations.' I got quite a lump in my throat. Though I hate to say it, Michael was not the best role model. As a character artist he was marvellous, with great power and presence. Over the years I did learn a lot from him that was positive, especially as a répetiteur. I made the eulogy at his funeral, and his widow, Wendy Ellis, gave me a most beautiful pair of cufflinks that she said Michael had wanted me to have that had been given to him by Fred. During his last weeks he was very kind to me when, suffering as I was from myasthenia gravis, he used to send me jars of the most wonderful, very expensive, honey every week.

Another dancer associated with *Enigma Variations* was Svetlana Beriosova, who was the original Lady Alice when the ballet was new in 1968. Svetlana was adored by audiences when she was with Sadler's Wells Theatre Ballet and later when she moved to Covent Garden. When in the late 1960s Frederick Ashton first considered making his ballet *A Month in the Country* it was his intention that Svetlana would play the leading role. By the time the ballet came to fruition in 1976, sadly Svetlana had retired from dancing. She had studied with Olga Preobrajenska, Anatol Vilzak, Ludmilla Schollar and Vera Volkova. Early in her career Svetlana was with Metropolitan Ballet where she was seen in *Designs with Strings* which John Taras, then an emerging American choreographer, had created for her using a Tchaikovsky piano trio arranged for strings. Absolutely beautiful. Her father, Nicholas Beriosov, a well-known producer of many of the old classics, really wanted her to be with the Covent Garden company. De Valois was keen to have her in the organisation but felt she should spend time with us on tour to make sure she could stand up to any comparisons with other ballerinas, including Fonteyn, Beryl Grey, Pamela May, Moira Shearer and Nadia Nerina.

The first we got to know of Beriosova was when this beautiful and serene young woman came and watched our rehearsals. She sat in a corner with a prayer book in her hands. We were told later that she would be joining us as a principal. She was very tall and one of the first roles she was to undertake was John Cranko's *Beauty and the Beast* in which I was to partner her. It was an extended pas de deux, complete in itself and used Ravel's *Ma Mère l'oye*, his suite for *Mother Goose*. The theme, music and movement all melded together very harmoniously. Well, I am not so tall but had already danced the role of the prince who is transformed into a beast, with Patricia Miller, a small dancer, light as a feather and easy to lift. With the exception of David Blair, who had created other roles for Cranko including *Harlequin in April*, the other men in the company were quite short and Cranko did not consider Blair suitable for this role – so it had come to me. Svetlana was only 18 at the time, quite well rounded and so beautiful. In rehearsals she hardly spoke to me. I was really struggling with the lifts, especially the magical one when she kisses him. Beauty literally kneels on the beast's chest, and as she is lifted bends over him and gently kisses him on the lips. Meanwhile, with his back to the audience, the beast has surreptitiously pulled off his face-mask and gloves and placed them in a hidden pocket in his sleeve. Then she stretches upwards as she is turned in his arms and she slides down his body to the floor as he is transformed into the prince. In rehearsals Svetlana would never kiss me. Our lips never touched. But wow! In the actual performance she bestowed on me the most passionate tongue sandwich of my life. My knees buckled, I staggered, just managed to keep hold of her as she stretched upwards in ecstasy. As I let her slip though my arms to the ground I am sure I must have looked the most dazed and cross-eyed prince ever. Svetlana was a very surprising lady, but I adored her and she became a great ballerina.

I do, however, recall one ghastly evening with Svetlana in July 1971, the second performance of the three-act version of Kenneth MacMillan's *Anastasia*. I got to the theatre about 7pm, and as I went through the stage door I could hear the tannoy announcer requesting that I go at once to Svetlana's dressing-room. There I discovered Gerd Larsen who was due to play a lady-in-waiting to the tsarina of Svetlana. That night Gerd's responsibilities went way beyond what she was expected to do onstage. She was desperately trying to help Svetlana, who was in a very inebriated state, get ready for the performance. Looking at Svetlana, who was smearing make-up across her face, I decided that our only alternative was to phone Georgina Parkinson, the second cast tsarina, and get her to the theatre to go on. I managed to get through to her, only to be told by her that she did not know the role yet. As this was only the second performance of a new ballet, she was not expecting anybody to go off so soon and so had not learned the part. No matter, I told Georgina to get to the theatre, and quick. Meanwhile Gerd had managed to get Svetlana's make-up tidied up and into her costume, ready to go on.

In that production, with its very evocative set of silver birch trees by Barry Kay, the tsarina had a beautiful first entrance as she appears from upstage on the arm of the tsar, played by Derek Rencher, as if walking through an allée of trees, before she acknowledged other members of the court. He propelled Svetlana onto the stage and watched as she did, more or less, what she was supposed to do. Then she fell flat on her face, right at the front of the stage. Behind the scenes we were all shocked. In character, Derek ordered some attendants to manoeuvre poor Svetlana into the wings. As only one costume for the tsarina had been made, we managed to get Svetlana out of it, and Georgina, who by now had arrived, into it. Svetlana was much taller than Georgina who was swamped by the tsarina's full-length skirt. Derek was gamely trying to tuck up all the extra fabric around Georgina's waist. She was still protesting she did not know the part when we pushed her onto the stage. Derek tried to indicate what she should do while members of the cast raced up and down the wings whispering instructions to her.

Svetlana had a long but desperately unhappy marriage to Masud Khan, a psychoanalyst who had trained under Anna Freud. Because of his background and character, Masud would not allow anybody else to embrace or kiss Svetlana. I made this mistake during our season at Henley in 1952 when Svetlana came to see the show at Sonya's invitation. I embraced her and was very embarrassed as Masud was there, glaring at me. During that season we were all out driving near Henley one day. I was at the wheel, Masud was navigating. As I was passing a turning, he suddenly told me to turn right. As instinctively I started to turn the car which swerved as we were travelling at speed, I shouted at Masud for giving me the instruction too late. He just laughed and said he was only interested in seeing my reactions. I know from his first wife, Jane Nicholas, who happened to be one of my first girlfriends, before his marriage to Svetlana that Masud did not allow women to express any form of sexual pleasure. This had a devastating effect on her and led to their divorce. Svetlana never had anything to do with me after that awful night with *Anastasia*. Years later, with Pamela May, I visited Svetlana at the hospice of St Charles's hospital in London where she was being cared for by nuns when dying of cancer. She claimed not to know who I was, but wanted me to find a cigarette for her, which was strictly forbidden. As I tried to reason with her, she carried on the conversation with Pamela, but all the while maintained she had no idea who I was. I was desperately upset as she died a few days later.

I was never included in any of the classes given by Winifred Edwards but I watched a lot. She had trained with Enrico Cecchetti and danced with Anna Pavlova's company before teaching in America. Back in London she was known as a disciplinarian but she had a wonderful way of communicating with all levels of dancers. I remember Antoinette Sibley and Anthony Dowell telling me how Miss Edward's guidance had helped them in their early days. Her creation of the role of Titania in Ashton's *The Dream* partnered by Anthony Dowell deserved a special gold bar to be added to her medal as Dame of the British Empire. She was truly magical. The fact that I had been brought up to expect dames to be big lumpy pantomime characters, often men in drag, loud and vulgar, made it hard to find that title to be suitable for a petite fairylike but passionate ballerina like Antoinette. It is a great honour that she has really earned not only as a dancer but also for her years of tireless work as president of the Royal Academy of Dance.

I remember Antoinette as a student at the Royal Ballet School when she was already being coached for the bluebird pas de deux in *The Sleeping Beauty*. She was already brilliant. I have another memory of her when she visited Stuttgart to dance in the annual festival. She came with her husband Michael Somes who bullied her in rehearsals of a divertissement from *Napoli* but her performances were scintillating and earned her an ovation. Antoinette was a true ballerina and since retiring she has continued to pass on her knowledge and understanding of the Ashton repertoire to new interpreters with wonderful results, especially with Birmingham Royal Ballet.

When I first started teaching in 1956, at the request of Ninette de Valois, it was the young White Lodge boys who had to suffer my first efforts. Poor Anthony Dowell was one of them. He and the rest of the class would be bussed up to the senior school for their classical lesson at 8.50am with me. There was just not enough space at White Lodge, in Richmond Park, for the juniors to get their daily classical class in the mornings. I was never given any indication of the considered potential of the boys and they all had to be treated as equals, but of course you could tell at once, even at that age, that Anthony, who was 13 at the time, stood out a mile, not because of any flashy virtuosity or high elevation but because he was so damn cool and calm. Nothing fazed him. He had a perfect arabesque. His head and arms seemed to fall into the right place to complement the rest of his body. He seemed to be able to do any of the exercises and steps that I set. He was very hard to teach as a result, but it was too early to start on expression, bravura or presenta-tion. I just hoped that somehow I could help him come to life. In fact that did soon start to happen, but at the end of the year he was moved up to the upper school and I lost track of him. The next thing I heard was that he was in the Covent Garden company, and after a very short time, in 1962, he had been singled out by Erik Bruhn no less to dance the boy's famous variation from August Bournonville's *Napoli*. I was there, and it seemed the whole house held its breath as this new lad walked forward glistening with youth and promise. Although I had seen the solo on many occasions before, it was as if I was seeing it for the first time. Anthony was so fresh and alive. He was truly classical. The rest is history. Frederick Ashton once said of Anthony that he had hidden strength that you cannot imagine where it comes from. He looked ready and able but never over-confident, Fred said that Oberon in *The Dream* and Troyte in *Enigma Variations* displayed how powerful Anthony could be. In casting Anthony as the naive boy in *Shadowplay*, Antony Tudor pulled some-thing different out of him.

It was some years before I worked with Anthony again, but I did so with both the new productions of *Giselle* and *The Nutcracker* in the mid-1980s, a long time since his White Lodge days as he was coming to the end of his dancing days. It was wonderful to observe in rehearsals for *The Nutcracker*, where Anthony partnered the Sugar Plum fairy, that before I had opened my mouth he would start to correct himself or make any alterations needed. This was all the more amazing because at that time Anthony was having to work very hard to maintain his technique.

Later, when Anthony was director of the company, he decided to revive that *Nutcracker* when the Royal Opera House reopened in December 1999. When we discussed this, I asked if I could make some alterations to the staging and told Anthony I would be pleased if he would play Drosselmeyer. He agreed. That for me was a wonderful expe-rience because the whole recreation of the role was not just me dictating but Drosselmeyer's character grew out of us both, and Anthony rightly needed to be absolutely sure of every move and gesture. One reviewer noted, however, that Anthony's debut performance was unusually tenta-tive. The truth was that, during the transformation scene, he was doing his utmost to prevent the worst and most frightening disaster. As the Christmas tree grows, Drosselmeyer commands the room to get bigger and bigger. As the tree begins to get taller, the floor surrounding it starts to sink downwards. A toy fort, which has now grown in size to hold 16 young boys from the Royal Ballet School playing the soldiers, is pushed on by several stagehands. At the first performance they were not aware that they were pushing the fort, containing the boys, towards a 40-foot-deep hole. The stage floor had not returned to position after the tree had finished growing. Anthony could see what was happening as he ran round the stage, desperately shouting over the music into the wings for the stage hands to stop pushing. There are usually three stage managers on *The Nutcracker*. They are all desperately busy. Some of the cues they give are visual, some musical, but the stage manager positioned in the prompt corner cannot see the tree coming up because of the scenery. Nobody could tell that the lift had stopped half-way up. Disaster, and certain injury, was only just averted thanks to Anthony. Later we discovered that an emergency switch had been demobilised, how or why I never discovered. Anthony has had an amazing career, but there is a side to his character that most people never see. He is actually rather shy but once onstage or in an important committee meeting he is a changed man. Although he never loses his temper he never hesitates to speak his mind. He speaks with great authority and clarity. He also has a fantastic sense of humour which you certainly need in this profession.

Stage managers are vitally important – a team, in control of all. In my fairly wide experience, I have found that women are usually the best stage managers. Birmingham Royal Ballet and the Royal Ballet are particularly well served by Diana Childs and Johanna Adams Farley. I am constantly amazed by the enormous duties they have to cope with. Against that, very little is known by the public about what they do and even by most employees of the theatres in which they work. In fact, as they do not qualify for overtime, they sometimes work practically around the clock unbeknown to the powers that be, and rarely get a pat on the back for completing the smooth running of some of the complicated shows, with difficult scores to follow, as well as coping with all the elements of sets and props that have to be set up in rehearsal rooms, and then taken down again. Their list of responsibilities is seemingly endless. Organising flying and the use of trapdoors. Giving lighting cues. Masterminding the preparation of scenery, props and costumes for tours. Packing and transportation. Then after shows there is always the job of writing up the report about the performance, something which can be very detailed, particularly when accidents occur. The difficulties at Covent Garden, where the theatre is shared by the opera and ballet companies, are enormous. They each have their own stage managers but the stage staff change all the time. Besides being used for performances the stage is also used for rehearsals, although most of them take place in the studios which means the stage managers have to set up furniture and props there, attend all the rehearsals to learn the production and then take them all back again. That sounds nothing but it involves going up five floors at Covent Garden and endless swing-doors. The Birmingham company has different problems as it is a touring company for most of the year when it is away from its home city. Diana and her team are well organised, but the constant packing and unpacking, loading and unloading, setting up and striking of shows, adapting lighting plots, all require great strength, stamina and patience. Without people like Diana and Johanna, the curtain would not go up.

When I first staged *Giselle* in 1966 in Stuttgart it was with Marcia Haydée in the title role. She had never danced it before although she knew it quite well from dancing in the corps de ballet with the de Cuevas company. We got on well. Marcia was John Cranko's new ballerina. It was typical of his great gift of seeing something in a dancer that they were not aware of themselves. With *The Taming of the Shrew* it was difficult to believe that she had not really played comedy before. The role fitted her perfectly, full of vital energy, with elbows back, shoulders forward, knees bent, and ready to attack whatever Petruchio – or the world – may throw at her.

Later on, much as I loved her, I found a great deal in Marcia's behaviour that was difficult. During a season at the London Coliseum in 1975 by Stuttgart Ballet, when Marcia was director of the company, I went to her dressing-room following a performance of *Romeo and Juliet* to congratulate her. During the course of our conversation I said that, although I realised it was still too soon after John's death for her to consider letting other companies dance his *Onegin*, I would like Sadler's Wells Royal Ballet to be the first to do so. Amazingly, she agreed. For the company at that time, *Onegin* would be an important and distinctive addition to the repertoire. Later on, Marcia told me she had changed her mind. She told me that she was not ready to let another company other than

Stuttgart perform the ballet. Perfectly understandable, or so I thought until three weeks later I read in the paper that London Festival Ballet, run by Peter Schaufuss, was all set to acquire the ballet. Again, just before my retirement from Birmingham Royal Ballet, as part of an exchange visit between our two companies that I had organised, the company was invited to perform in Stuttgart. Marcia, who was still director there, completely upstaged our first night. She used the occasion to announce her own retirement from the stage during the curtain calls. She really could be uncaring about others, or so it seemed. This news, of course, took all the space in the following day's reviews. I realised, in retrospect, that Marcia was one of those dancers who have worked hard to make it to the top and live entirely for the moment.

Marcia was always prima ballerina in Stuttgart, but John's promotion of Birgit Keil to principal put paid to the criticism that he did not like German dancers. Listening to Birgit interviewed by Michael Broderick at the London Ballet Circle in September 2015 made me remember first working with her over 50 years before. She is now professor of the Mannheim Akademie des Tanzes and director of the Badisches Staatstheater in Karlsruhe. I recall when Birgit first joined the Stuttgart company. She stood out as a young starlet with long, long legs and bright shining eyes. John was fascinated by her to such an extent that he sent her off to the Royal Ballet School to sort out some faults in her training and give her some finishing touches. This proved to be beneficial, but before she had completed her time in London she was hoiked back to Stuttgart as Kenneth MacMillan wanted her for the role of the young girl in his new ballet, *Las Hermanas*. Birgit had the most wonderful, open personality, but having to go straight into learning a principal role brought out the fact that she had a really good brain which always seemed to be driven by the music. She also had staying power and determination which helped her stand up to the unpopularity caused by her jumping ahead of others. She clearly had the makings of a ballerina, and it was not long before she was made a principal. John now had a new German ballerina who came from Stuttgart, a real feather in his cap. Birgit had a wonderful career and she gained an international reputation. She was unfortunately plagued with injuries and illness to such an extent that she had to stop performing the big, tough roles slightly earlier than anticipated, but I had a long and very happy association with her. It continued when she, with great support of her husband Vladimir Klos, transformed the ballet company in Karlsruhe from a failing small, contemporary group into a successful classically based company with a very contemporary outlook in the choice of repertoire. She richly deserved the Deutscher Tanzpreis and her many other awards.

Somebody else I knew from Stuttgart was John Neumeier who was then a dancer. I got to know him better when he and Ray Barra, who was by then John's ballet master in Hamburg, came to Munich to see my new production of *The Sleeping Beauty*. I have been to John's amazing house in Hamburg where he lives on one floor. The rest of the building is really a museum, an amazing collection celebrating Marie Taglioni, Anna Pavlova and Vaslav Nijinsky. John showed me around the priceless objects and artworks and then offered me a champagne tea. John loaned some of his collection to the Ballets Russes' exhibition organised by Jane Pritchard at the Victoria and Albert Museum, London, in 2010. That is where, after a long gap, I came across him next. I was sitting on a settee at a private view pondering what exhibits to concentrate on. 'Is that you, Peter?' I heard a voice ask. It was John, who was wondering how to tackle the exhibition too. We reminisced for 30 minutes at least and had a few laughs about my ballet *Namouna* in Stuttgart. John reminded me of the corrections I used to give him about learning the music counts before we remembered we had an exhibition to see. We agreed it would be useless to go round together as we would both laugh and chat all the way round, so we went our separate ways.

Hansi Johnson emerged into my life as a friend of Louise Browne. They were neighbours in York who got to know each other because of Hansi's interest in ballet. Louise had been a brilliant dancer in West End musicals. She could do all the fireworks, getting Frederick Ashton to choreograph her solos. I knew her later when she was director of the Royal Academy of Dancing, as it was still called. Hansi was married to a publisher, and because of her friendship with Louise, supported many projects at the RAD. They both hosted very nice parties whenever Sadler's Wells Theatre Ballet played in York. Hansi really loved the ballet. After her husband's death, she ran the publishing firm for a while before dividing her time between London and Rorschach on Lake Constance in Switzerland, although she was herself Austrian. She had a lot of theatre friends and was a marvellous hostess, very generous. She accompanied the foreign tours that Sadler's Wells Royal Ballet undertook, hosting dinners and generally making the tours brighter and better by her presence. Hansi was always keen to offer help, not as a major sponsor of productions, but in quieter, more subtle ways. I took her to meet Ninette de Valois with a view to Hansi sponsoring the publication of a volume of Madam's poetry. The two got on extremely well. The volume was published thanks to Hansi and went to a second edition. I was promised two valuable antique maps by Hansi to come to me after her death, but you know how it is with millionaires' wills. Absent relatives descended and insisted they had the right to them. But I have happy memories of Hansi. She was very good company and Sonya was very fond of her.

Hansi became a great friend of Galina Samsova. Galina was one-time principal of the Kiev Ballet, National Ballet of Canada, London Festival Ballet and Sadler's Wells Royal Ballet, was the most wonderful company member and a great example of a true ballerina. She was very strong and much loved by the company. Galina was also artistic director of Scottish Ballet where she staged *The Sleeping Beauty*. For Sadler's Wells Royal Ballet, she mounted a beautiful production of the last act of *Paquita* and helped me with *Swan Lake* with choreography that she knew from her days in Kiev, productions that are still in the repertoire. Later, Galina went on to teach. Sadly this was something she had to give up when she lost the sight of one eye, the result of having smoked too much. Through Galina's own training in Russia, which included a lot of character dancing, she developed the most beautifully expressive arms. She danced many ballerina roles in classic and new ballets. While married to André Prokovsky, I choreographed a pas de deux for them when they were principals with London Festival Ballet. It was not hugely successful but Galina had a big personal success in it. She has a lovely sense of humour and is somebody with whom I used to enjoy having a glass or two of wine, though sadly no more owing to the state of her health. She is still very good company.

Natalia Makarova – Natasha – first arrived in England in 1970 after defecting from the Soviet Union. I was detailed to go and meet her. Her arrival had aroused a certain amount of interest from the press, but I think she was hoping for more. She was well prepared, ready with answers and posed for the cameras. I could tell at once she wanted stardom. Actually I got on with her very well. She knew already that she would be dancing in my production of *Giselle* and she made it clear that she was quite happy to make changes in her established portrayal to fit in with my conception. That is why she was here, she said, to find new ways of performing these old ballets. I remember Margot Fonteyn speaking about Natasha most generously, 'I hear that dear young Makarova is going to dance *Giselle*. Please look after her, she is so sweet and lovely and will be quite overwhelmed being all on her own.' Well, she certainly did not give that impression to me – and I soon discovered that she did not need much looking after. But I loved the rehearsals with her and Anthony Dowell. Certain different things, particularly in the second act, she did so beautifully that it would have been wrong to make her change. The only problem I had with her was concerning the music. Musicality is so important in a ballerina's performance. It is not being dead on the beat but being as one with the music. That demands a total understanding of the music, not just using it as an accompaniment. In some ways Natasha was musical – she was good at feeling – but she tended always to be behind the beat. Michael Somes, who was always insistent that dancers were dead on the beat, got fed up with her when she went her own way, but as Kenneth MacMillan used to say, with such amazing talent you can overlook that because she was such a wonderful artist. Natasha was not the greatest black queen in *Checkmate*, but Madam wanted her to do it. She was probably disappointed at the result. Although Natasha was quite dramatic she did not project evil so much as the black queen should. Natasha was not physically well at the time but she ensured she was able to perform the role. In general, Madam liked stars as guest artists even if they were sometimes wrong in a role. Generally they were good for box office and hopefully an example to members of the company.

Victor Stiebel, a great couturier during the 1950s, described Peter Farmer as having the greatest understanding of line and proportion for the female shape in period costume. Peter always brings a marvellous sense of atmosphere to his sets, one of those great designers that always create a world for you to work in. He paints beautifully. He has a sense of humour too, but also a sense of sad beauty in his work that is very compelling. He now lives alone in Littlehampton and has Alzheimer's. He is very sensitive and still manages to see the humour in people. He is a wonderful, wonderful artist who has probably designed more ballets than anybody. He has certainly designed all but two of my many productions of *Giselle*. He uses the most beautiful colour combinations and the final results are absolutely ravishing, always so sensitively painted. His set and costumes for Samsova's *Paquita* are perfection, with beautiful drapery in gold and black seen in subtle perspective. The tutus were all in rich ochres and golds that complement the dance and music perfectly. He has impeccable taste, with a strong personal style which actually does not mix with anyone else's work.

He designed the sets for *The Nutcracker* for English National Ballet which had a bumpy ride when it first went on but has become a success and must be earning some money for the company. It is such a pity that designers in Britain do not get royalties, particularly for something like *Nutcracker* or *The Sleeping Beauty* where design plays such an important part. Before he became ill he was desperately hoping to have a retrospective exhibition. Although known most for his stage work, he dearly wanted to be regarded as a leading easel artist and have an exhibition at a major venue in recognition of that. At an exhibition of his work at the Southbank centre in 1983 Peter discovered the smashed and blood-covered frame of one of his pictures on the floor. The painting had been stripped from the mount and had been stolen. Peter was quite touched that somebody would go to such lengths to acquire his work. It would be wonderful if a retrospective could happen in his lifetime.

Frederick Ashton always thought *Les Sylphides* dragged along, 'It's too slow,' he used to complain. One day at the Wells when Alicia Markova happened to be in another studio rehearsing something else, she popped in and sat next to Fred. 'Oh, it's too fast,' she said. 'Alicia, I prefer the music like that,' Fred replied. 'Oh no, that's much too fast, it must be played more slowly.' After she had left the studio the dancers asked Fred who they should follow. He said, 'We'll do it her way today and we can change it back tomorrow.' She was the same with *Les Rendezvous* in which admittedly she had created the principal role. She arrived at one rehearsal, again uninvited, and proceeded to complain about a step where the arm is held behind the back. 'Oh Fred, that's not right,' she told him about his own choreography. 'I really rather like the way I have it,' Fred told her deadpan. 'That's not right,' Markova insisted. 'I am really going to have to show you.' She got up and changed the step to something much less interesting, saying, 'It's my ballet. We must have it right.' As soon as she was gone, Fred promptly changed it back to what he knew was correct. After all, it was his ballet. I was much moved by Alicia Markova's portrayal of Giselle. It was all done with body language rather than facial acting, which is why she was able to project so well even in bad lighting which in those days was never great. For her 90th birthday in 2000 Alicia asked to see my production of *Giselle* at Covent Garden. She insisted on a chauffeur-driven limousine to convey her and her sister to the Royal Opera House. Around the corner from the theatre she instructed the driver to stop and told Doris to walk the rest of the way. Nobody must detract from a star's arrival.

Somebody who knew how to present his ballerina was Markova's great partner, Anton Dolin. I learned a lot from him. He was not much of a dancer compared to today's generation, nor was he as good an actor as Robert Helpmann, but Dolin was a showman. In the second act of *Giselle*, after she has jumped diagonally across the stage she throws flowers to Albrecht, which Dolin tried to catch. Nobody bothers to now. As Giselle moves away, Dolin followed her and posed in arabesque on full pointe without the benefit of pointe shoes, with his toes knuckled under, as he did in his own version of *Bolero*. All rather embarrassing!

Dolin used to come to Sadler's Wells Theatre Ballet to give us pas de deux classes. These were mostly about how we men showcased our partners, how to stand and present ourselves. There was much less about the technique of lifting, finding a girl's centre of balance or supporting her in pirouettes. He was very inspiring because I had never considered any of those things. They are important. Dolin had seen me as Eusebius in *Carnaval*, one of my better roles I thought. He offered to give me some private coaching, about which I was flattered at his interest. After all, I was only 23 or 24 and he was considered as the first British male ballet star. After several failed phone arrangements to meet, finally Dolin rang me and suggested I should come to a party in Chelsea, coincidentally in the same street where I now live. I duly appeared at the party but it dragged on and there was no mention of any coaching. Finally Dolin said to me, 'Oh dear boy. Come back with me to Dick Addinsell's house in Launceston Place. It will be ideal, there's lots of room. I've got a car arranged.' I knew Dick of course and knew the house. I knew too where this encounter was leading, but I was determined to take advantage of his coaching. En route in the chauffeur-driven car it soon became clear what Dolin was interested in. I made it clear I was not. We carried on to the house and Dolin invited me in, saying he would just talk me through the role. We sat on a settee – and he pounced on me. I stood up, furious, and told him again this was not why I had come. I left. Needless to say, there was no sign of the chauffeured car and I had to find my own way home. Dolin was not, I think, surprised by my reaction. It must have happened a lot. On future occasions we never referred to it and he was always friendly towards me.

Much later, during the 1970s, it was Anton Dolin who introduced me to Kevin O'Hare, then aged 14, at Sadler's Wells. 'This young man is our great hope for the future,' Dolin said. Kevin and his brother will be remembered for making a huge difference to the development and success of both Royal Ballet companies. They hail from Hull and their early training was with Louise Browne, star of the Ziegfeld Follies, who in the 1930s held the world record for fouettés, with over 80 consecutive turns credited to her. Frederick Ashton choreographed much of her material for her appearances im musicals and shows. I was lucky to recruit both O'Hare boys to Sadler's Wells Royal Ballet. They both became principals. Michael progressed to ballet master, a position he still holds. He had a brilliant classical technique and was a strong actor, most noted as Will Mossop in *Hobson's Choice*, a character role David Bintley made for him. He was sensational. He still performs such roles as Widow Simone and Dr Coppélius. Kevin, on the other hand, danced all the major classical roles, including Romeo when Birmingham Royal Ballet first acquired Kenneth MacMillan's production. Bintley cast him in leading roles in *Edward II*, *Far from the Madding Crowd* and *Carmina Burana*. Sadly, Kevin's knees began to give serious problems and after various operations he had very little cartilage left. He did various courses in company management, briefly joining the Royal Shakespeare Company before returning to Birmingham Royal Ballet as company manager, subsequently becoming administrative director of the Royal Ballet before ultimately becoming director.

At an earlier time in the Royal Ballet's development, in 1999, the company appeared at Sadler's Wells during the redevelopment of the Royal Opera House, Sylvie Guillem and Laurent Hilaire were due to perform *Giselle*. I was nervous as Sylvie had not attended the rehearsal beforehand and I was never certain which version she was going to do – not that it was for her to choose. I had got myself to the theatre early as there had been a lot of problems fitting the sets designed for Covent Garden onto the smaller Wells' stage. I had invited Beryl Grey to the performance and had arranged to meet her for a drink before curtain up. But first I thought I had better make sure all was well with Sylvie, especially as she was being difficult about the mad scene and whether or not she would kill herself. I knocked on her dressing-room door. 'Allo?' came the reply. I was thankful at least that she had arrived at the theatre. The door opened slightly and a head appeared with a large yellow chrysanthemum plonked on top of it, with hair – long enough for her to sit on – left loose. 'I trust all well?' I asked, rather thrown by this apparition. 'OK,' was all she said. I asked if she had decided to kill herself or not. 'I will not kill me.' I went on to remind Sylvie that Carlotta Grisi, the original Giselle, did kill herself. 'I don't care.' I also pointed out that the synopsis in the programme also indicated that Giselle commits suicide. 'Too bad.' With that, Sylvie shut the door. It was impossible to argue and quite evident that Sylvie was intent on doing what she wanted. After the performance I took Beryl round to see her. They shook hands and I remember Beryl's words, 'Congratulations on a very interesting performance. I just found the head-dress in the first act a little odd.' Sylvie replied in an instant, 'I am a modern Giselle.' I struggle to understand how anybody could say that about a ballet from the 19th century which has its own style, but it is extraordinary how Guillem convinces audiences that getting her leg up so high beyond six o'clock that her skirt slipped down the leg is anything at all to do with classical ballet. But then Sylvie's name sold out theatres the world over, which is, of course, important.

Beryl Grey was a remarkable artist, and being exceptionally tall she always made the most of her height. She really had perfect proportions, with great strength and energy to complement her long limbs. She could turn really fast both to the right and left and once did the 32 fouettés in *Swan Lake* to the left as her left shoe had collapsed. Her performances in that ballet were strongly interpreted, more so as Odile, as her height worked against her as Odette. The men in the company in those days were not so strong, and John Field, her partner, really was not forceful enough as a character to perform opposite Beryl. I did always think that she was too tall for Giselle herself from the moment she first stepped out of the cottage. She was very tall and the cottage door was very low. In my opinion, Beryl tended to exaggerate her facial expressions and arm movements, which meant, for me, that Myrtha was a more natural role for her as she could dominate the stage in a terrifying manner. I liked her best as the black queen in *Checkmate*. She was very successful as a scarlet-clad figure of death in Léonide Massine's less than successful Scottish ballet for Covent Garden, *Donald of the Burthens*, where Massine displayed Beryl's technical skills to great effect with double pirouettes en dehors, without any preparation, and divided by a double tour en l'air, all at great speed.

When I was in *Finian's Rainbow* in the West End in 1947 I sometimes used to see Beryl at Lena's café in Soho – a place that dancers used to frequent. It was popular with Henry Danton too, the sort of place where you would always run into somebody you knew. It was owned by a large Bavarian woman, but the main attraction was an outrageous Italian waitress, called Lena, who used always to deliberately swear like a trooper, at which we all used to pretend to be shocked. But we all loved the cakes and treats which were still in short supply after the war.

Gradually I got to know Beryl better. She became interested in teaching while still quite young and worked frequently with the Arts Educational School, founded by Grace Cone and Olive Ripman. I recall Beryl once giving a talk and being so impressed by the musicality of her voice. It struck me that dancers, male and female, would be taken much more seriously as number one citizens if they learned to speak properly. Thanks to her articulate manner, Beryl has been a marvellous ambassador for dance. When she became director of London Festival Ballet and I was in charge of the New Group, Beryl and I would meet every so often to discuss our mutual plans for repertoire. She was very charming, but I could see she had an iron hand at work inside a velvet glove. Since the huge cut in funding that the Arts Council imposed in 1970, the Royal Ballet touring company had lost its status on the number one touring circuit and I felt powerless in face of Beryl as the New Group was unable to perform the big, popular ballets. Large casts, expensive sets and costumes were now the province of Festival Ballet. Quite frankly, we were struggling. I longed to be able to tell Beryl that my plans would include the classics again. Nowadays, although both companies – now English National Ballet and Birmingham Royal Ballet – are doing well, it is depressing that because of further funding cuts, they are relying heavily on popular classics to fill the houses when on tour.

Beryl, although officially retired, will never stop working. She continues to be involved and speaks her mind fairly and squarely, especially at the moment when classical ballet is seen by some as being lured away from its traditional development by various contemporary influences. If this is really the case, with people around like Beryl and the depth of our roots, classical ballet will pull through stronger than ever. Beryl and I always got on well. We generally had the same ideas about classical ballet. We applaud together and sometimes get upset together about what we see. She is very knowledgeable and very good on committees. Beryl knows everybody, by which I mean she really takes an interest in the people she knows. When Sonya died, Beryl spoke at her funeral very beautifully. She and Sonya had both taken class with Audrey de Vos in Notting Hill.

I never knew Moira Shearer during my dancing days, and she really only paid attention to me once I had become a director. She was well versed in being a star. At the stage door she always looked a million dollars with her fabulous red hair. I admired her, and her films *The Red Shoes* and *The Tales of Hoffmann* really made me appreciate what a wonderful dancer she was. Filming seemed to highlight her quick, beaten steps, so on the music. Onstage she brought out the glamour of Cinderella if not the pathos of the role. Margot Fonteyn brought out a different, less artificial dimension of that character. I believe that Moira's marriage to Ludovic Kennedy helped them both. *The Red Shoes* reveals that she was not the greatest actress, and at the time there was the prejudice that dancers could not act, but later in her career I saw her perform the title role in Bernard Shaw's play *Major Barbara* at the Bristol Old Vic, where you really did believe in her.

Doreen Wells – the Marchioness of Londonderry – dear Dor, the most beautiful, delicate, gentle, dizzy, caring, dedicated, hardworking, glamorous, incredibly kind and generous ballerina. She was born to be a star and had to feel right and properly prepared for every role she danced. She had a big problem with her pointe shoes. They were never a perfect fit and usually she would have about five pairs for a short ballet and ten or so for a three-acter, all ready and prepared. Often during the performance she would change one shoe, only to find that it did not match the other, so at the next opportunity she would change that too – and so it went on. She would never abandon a pair because they might just fit for another work. As a result, every cupboard in her house was cram full of shoes, including those in the kitchen, bedrooms and dining-room. Dor had a famous partnership with David Wall though they were not paired in all ballets. I liked them particularly in *The Two Pigeons*. She was divine in Ashton's works, though he did say to me once that he thought Dor would be perfection if she was an inch taller. Since Dor stopped dancing she has taken a big interest in the quality of teaching and the use of breath in dance including phrasing and really listening to the music. She really does talk a lot of sense and seems to bring another much-needed dimension to dance. Dor is the perfect hostess and gives the most wonderful parties. She is also a superb tap-dancer. You should see her and Wayne Sleep together, absolutely brilliant.

I have known Wayne since he joined the Royal Ballet in 1965. He is a great populariser. He is a survivor who has made his mark and gets people interested in dance. Wayne was known in the company as a naughty boy, up to tricks the whole time. He was gifted with his amazing jumps, turns and pirouettes. The extraordinary thing about Wayne seemed to be the way he had a classical technique before he was trained. It all came so naturally to him. Madam thought he was the greatest virtuoso the company ever had, but Jill Gregory, the ballet mistress, used to urge him to take his work more seriously. The company thought Wayne would be with them for ever but he had bigger ideas when he realised he could never have starring roles because of his height. He did the blue boy in *Les Patineurs* with the New Group, behaving very grandly in front of the other dancers. They did not like that at all from little Wayne, but he was always good value. I will always remember him as Kolya in Ashton's *A Month in the Country* when he executed the most spellbinding series of turns while bouncing a large rubber ball. He made it look so easy and it did not look out of place at all in that Russian country house. Wayne's version of *Cinderella* for the National Youth Ballet rather misfired but he does these productions for good causes and does not receive a penny from them for himself. When you look at his achievements both as a brilliant classical dancer and an entertainer in the commercial theatre, it really is some sort of miracle how Wayne maintains his amazing virtuosity and manages his school. He has become famous in the world of commercial entertainment, and his support for the Dance Teachers Benevolent Fund is phenomenal and helps an area of the dance profession that is usually forgotten.

Patricia Neary joined National Ballet of Canada aged 14, at the time the only American in the company. Three years later she moved to New York City Ballet where her height, speed and attack singled her out. George Balanchine created two roles on her, in *Raymonda Variations* and the *Rubies* act from *Jewels*. With Balanchine's encouragement she started to stage his ballets when she was a ballerina with Geneva Ballet. She later became director of that company and has also been assistant director in Berlin and director of the Zurich and La Scala companies. You do not succeed with a career like that without being a bit of a monster! The various stagers from the Balanchine Trust tend to have their own versions of a particular ballet. There are not huge differences, but I think Pat is the best they have. The reason why she is so successful – she has mounted over 30 different Balanchine works including *Ballet Imperial*, *Serenade*, *Apollo*, *Agon*, *Prodigal Son*, *The Four Temperaments* and *Symphony in C* – for 60 companies around the world is that she does anything but flatter dancers. She certainly knows how to make a company work. When she staged *Theme and Variations* for us, still in our days as Sadler's Wells Royal Ballet, she was a revelation. Such energy. Her legs seemed to stretch up to her chin and her ravishing smile took in the whole studio. For the ten days she was with us she screamed, shouted, laughed and danced up a storm. 'Mr B wouldn't like that', or 'For Gawd's sake listen to the music', or 'Are you deaf dear?' or 'Fantaaaastic' and 'Let's go for gold', she would say – it was Olympics time. 'Miyako, you are deeeevine' was another comment, as was 'I'm the one who should be crying, not you. That was awful.'

There were good days and bad – but mostly good. The company loved her. Pat loved to be the centre of attention and would still do class every day and, what was more, would throw in an occasional pirouette on pointe. I never dared ask Pat how old she was! She seemed to be ageless. I just adored her enthusiasm, her honesty, passionate love of every ballet that Balanchine had created, her fury if a dancer did not give their maximum and her incredible determination to get things perfect. Apparently she went to St James' Palace with some members of the Royal Ballet for a special rehearsal for Prince Charles. Pat gave the performance of her life there. She had the prince in stitches, showing off like mad in how she explained things to him. Pat once told me I was the greatest ballet director ever. It is nice to be flattered! Pat and I form a mutual admiration society and she sends me the largest poinsettia she can find every December. The card she sends at Christmas is usually a photograph of her and her husband, Bob, a male model, both semi-naked. Pat is absolutely unshockable and her wicked adventures are blissfully shocking. I do not know of anyone who has lived their life more fully. Pat is a real fighter. When she gets worked up, she turns into a divine monster.

Pat would talk about anything when she used to have lunch with me and Denis Bonner, Birmingham Royal Ballet's notator extraordinaire. She would even talk about her sex life. Denis would encourage her. He liked Pat as she was so direct and got on with things, which is Denis' approach too. He gets fed up with me when I want to change things. 'Oh no, not again. That worked last time,' he grumbles to me. I just want my productions to be as perfect as they can be. Since Denis joined Sadler's Wells Royal Ballet in 1976 he has played a huge part in my life, as a good friend and notator, not only setting and rehearsing my productions in Birmingham, but around the world. He stages many of David Bintley's ballets too, and those by other choreographers. Together with Patricia Tierney he has recorded in Benesh notation the whole of Birmingham Royal Ballet's repertoire and keeps the scores up to date. Benesh notation has become a vital part of the company's existence thanks to Denis. It is a huge help to have a notator working with you. You may be working on creating a solo one day, getting mid-way through before you are able to go back to it, by which time you may well have forgotten the details because you have been involved with other parts of the ballet. Miraculously the notator will be able to demonstrate from the movement score which runs in parallel directly under the music stave. Benesh notation records not only legs and feet but arms, hands direction, co-ordination with the music, as well as patterns, speed and dynamics too. One important advantage is that choreographers can have their works registered for copyright. Previously it had been impossible to make a claim without written evidence.

Denis is good looking, highly intelligent, with a wicked sense of humour and is very good company. If Denis had been a bit taller and less stocky he would probably have had a good career as a classical dancer. He was once cast in a short-lived, new ballet where he had to wear all-over yellow tights. It was not a good look on Denis. He looked so fed-up and unhappy but he did it. I expect the memory of it still fills him with horror. As it was, the opportunities for good solo work were few and far between. He was very good as Jasper the pot boy in *Pineapple Poll* and he had the personality to be a very good Dr Coppélius in *Coppélia*. Wisely, Denis has done much better for himself by switching to dance notation. Benesh notation, invented by Rudolf and Joan Benesh, has made a huge difference to the dance world, and exponents such as Denis are much in demand. He is much loved by all those who have worked with him. He works extremely quickly and demands attention at all times. I believe notators of his quality deserve more recognition publicly. As it is they are unsung heroes.

Over the years Monica Mason has been a loyal friend, someone to laugh with, someone to protest with and someone to trust. We have worked together in various capacities and she always made me feel that I knew what I was talking about. We have always remained good friends in spite of frequently not agreeing with each other. I seem to have known Monica for ever. When she arrived from South Africa in 1955 I was teaching at the Royal Ballet School. I was detailed to teach her and a few others John Cranko's choreographic studies which were to be used in a course. I remember Mon so well. She seemed to enjoy everything. The way she looked and moved marked her out as different from the others. She was a powerful dancer even as a student. You could not help looking at her. This is of course before Kenneth MacMillan noticed her strength when he cast her in his angular, violent *Rite of Spring*. That is a role I have never seen bettered since, danced either by a woman or man. She astounded everybody when she created the role. It is fiendishly difficult technically and musically, very primitive and contemporary for those days. Monica first danced the role in 1962 and she continued to perform it for 20 years. I thought that between them, Kenneth and Mon had created a huge step forward in choreography which nobody has yet caught up with. I think this opened people's eyes to her potential and she was soon given more roles. She had such range and could completely immerse herself in every part she performed, from Petipa's sublime, crystal-like dances in the great classics to one of the original three harlots in Kenneth's *Romeo and Juliet*. She was the dancer in apricot when the Royal Ballet first danced Jerome Robbins' *Dances at a Gathering*. In subsequent years I must have seen Mon in dozens of roles, existing and new. She was good as the cigarette-twirling hostess in *Les Biches* and as Lescaut's mistress in *Manon* with David Wall. That was a role that showed her gift for comedy, as did her fantastic created solo in *Elite Syncopations* the same year. What I have always loved about Monica is her lovely sense of humour. She loves a good joke and tells a few too. The bossy maid Webster in *A Wedding Bouquet* also suited another aspect of Monica's character. Not all roles came her way. She would have loved to have done Natalia Petrovna in *A Month in the Country* but she was a memorable Lady Alice in *Enigma Variations*. She could be so gentle, warm and loving. Not every role suited Monica's gifts. Odette in *Swan Lake* was difficult for her, as her build and legs were so strong. A long time ago I rehearsed her with Anthony Dowell and she overpowered him dramatically. It is not that Monica was more masculine, and she could certainly dance Odette from a technical point of view, but the role was just not right for her. Odile suited her perfectly.

When Mon first joined the staff of the Royal Ballet, as well as teaching and rehearsing, realising that so many injured needed guidance in getting back into shape again, she started to help them. As a result, support for the injured became an official part of the company's daily call sheet and has been invaluable in getting dancers back on the boards. When Monica became director she handed the programme over to Lesley Collier. How Monica managed to sustain a decade as director of the Royal Ballet I will never know, considering that she never wanted the job in the first place. She tells me that when Ross Stretton was asked to resign in 2002 when the company had reached its lowest ebb, she agreed to be acting director only until a new replacement was found. Accordingly she declined the use of the director's office suite and remained in her rather pokey assistant director's office, the position she then held. Stretton had left the company in a dreadful state, and Monica, with the help of Jeanetta Laurence, set about getting it back to its former standards. It was not long before things started to improve. When a board member suggested that she should move into the director's office with all its facilities, Monica agreed but still insisted on keeping her position as acting director. Before long she realised, however, that she was beginning to enjoy her new surroundings which gave her more authority. She found she really wanted to be director after all. What a fantastic life Mon has had. She is a brilliant organiser, kind, patient, willing to cope with so much of the admin herself. For me personally, she helped enormously when my productions were on. She was one of the greatest exponents of Myrtha in *Giselle*, an incredibly demanding role that requires the power to dominate the other wilis. In her mime scenes Myrtha must possess evil authority. It is something that even in retirement Mon is happy to coach today's casts in the part. She appears regularly at rehearsals and performances, and her involvement is always positive and encouraging, never too intrusive.

Leanne Benjamin first attracted attention in *Metamorphosis* by David Bintley in April 1984. She played the young sister of Gregor Samsa, the transformed title figure. It was a rather good piece, but it was Leanne who was outstanding. This was nothing to do with her great technical facility and lovely feet but her outstanding dramatic intensity which was quite incredible. I felt that here was a ballerina in the making. Leanne had a short body, long arms and very long legs which she did not yet have proper control over. As a result, her arabesque, though high, was rather distorted. In another early role, as one of the Lilac fairy's six attendants, who all have to stand in arabesque before moving into a deep penché arabesque, where the raised leg is held at an angle higher than 90 degrees and where the dancer leans forward to counterbalance the raised leg, the eye always went to Leanne but always because she looked wrong. Over the years Leanne learned to manage her turnout and control her arabesques, and certainly when she became a principal it did not matter that she looked different. Leanne was, though, the most difficult ballerina when it came to rehearsals, demanding time in the studio and onstage, and upsetting everybody. Should something be wrong, Leanne would just stop. In some ways that is good, but when you have a stage rehearsal, for which time is always at a premium, it is understood that you have just to get on with it and sort problems out later. This Leanne refused to do unless it was a solo rehearsal for her alone. However, becoming a mother changed her, I observed. She developed as an artist and became much more involved with the whole company. She retained her dramatic intensity but it was more controlled, and importantly her powers of projection became much stronger and more focused. I thought Leanne would go on much longer, but she made a good decision to retire at the very height of her powers and still have time to take on a new profession in the worlds of architecture and interior design.

The choreographer and showman Matthew Bourne has claimed that Darcey Bussell is known by the majority of the British population for her second career in television, as a judge on *Strictly Come Dancing*, not for what she achieved as a ballerina. I suppose this is true given how small the ballet-going public is in Britain, although Darcey was also a near permanent guest in New York where her great athleticism, rather than her interpretive skills, fitted well with George Balanchine's ballets. *Strictly* is only a part of what keeps Darcey active since her retirement as a dancer. Knowing what the role of president of the Royal Academy of Dance involves, I am delighted at the manner in which Darcey has undertaken it. Her outgoing personality suits the role brilliantly. Speaking to over a hundred students at RAD graduation ceremonies, Darcey spoke to each one individually. She has a natural way of communicating with everybody, an appealing presence, which really benefits the charity and fundraising work she undertakes. When I first saw Darcey at the Royal Ballet School, I immediately noticed her because she seemed to have all the assets – lovely legs and feet, beautiful hands and arms, and personality. When she joined Sadler's Wells Royal Ballet in 1987 she had a lot of confidence, though I knew that her family were disappointed that she was not joining the Covent Garden company. I could not have been more pleased, as I had nobody else of the same calibre in the company. It was not long before Darcey did one of the solo princesses in *Swan Lake*. She did it well, but she was somewhat out of control, something of which she was aware. Darcey had no delusions of grandeur, though in those days she was a giggler. She was pleased if I talked about various aspects of her great talent with her, though she was not too convinced about changing her name when I suggested that. In fact it has turned out to be the perfect name for a ballerina. I had a lot of roles on my list for Darcey but you cannot rush people too quickly. Before we could really start preparing Darcey for a big future as a ballerina, I lost her. I did not expect it to happen so suddenly, though I knew the time would come. Then Kenneth MacMillan rang and informed me that he would be taking Darcey into the big company. He was not asking me. He was telling me. He did explain that he wanted her for his new ballet *The Prince of the Pagodas* in which Darcey danced Belle Rose. Although she became a star, and having seen her rehearse dramatic roles like *Manon*, I think Darcey had much more to offer interpretatively than she was given. I need not have worried about losing her, for soon Miyako Yoshida appeared on the scene and became a truly great ballerina.

Like most ballerinas, Miyako had certain minor physical problems which she soon overcame and stemmed from a slightly stiff upper back. Unfortunately, while completing her training at the Royal Ballet School, a guest Russian teacher made her force her turn-out that resulted in a foot injury. This came after I had seen Miyako at a demonstration class where the senior girls had to execute the 32 fouettés from *Swan Lake*. Madam was present, and after she had seen Miyako perform the series, she stopped the class, praising her for making an extremely difficult trick sequence look like poetry. 'This young artist will go far,' she said. I was delighted when she joined Sadler's Wells Royal Ballet in 1984 despite suffering the foot injury which meant for three months she could only do walk-on parts, followed by a further month doing corps de ballet work. I was in desperate need of a classical ballerina. Thank goodness I took the risk of recruiting her and she did not then go to the other company at Covent Garden. She always gave the impression that classical ballet came easily to her, as she made it look so effortless. In fact she worked incredibly hard to give that impression. She had the most astonishing light jump when she seemed to literally soar through the air.

Surprisingly for a Japanese dancer, she was absolutely the embodiment of the English style for me. Her lightness, musicality and effortlessness are wonderful. One of the great things about the English style, embodied by Miyako in such ballets as *La Fille mal gardée* and *The Two Pigeons*, was her beautiful use of her feet, sharp and pointed, quick with lovely beats. That is something we generally do not see so much of these days. Miyako really used her feet. She was a lovely Aurora, brilliant in *Theme and Variations*, exquisite in *Paquita* and divine in *The Nutcracker*. After ten years of touring, and having made the move to Birmingham, she felt it was time to move to Covent Garden. She loved being corrected, but it had taken her some time to break her natural, Japanese instinct not to show emotion; but once that was achieved, she became one of the Royal Ballet's most expressive dancers, standing up to the competition of the Royal Ballet's top stars. She was made a CBE in 2007 and has received many awards in Japan. She is happily married to Takashi Endo, a football agent, lucky man. I have always adored Miyako as the embodiment of a true ballerina.

Epilogue – the future

LOOKING BACK over the training that I mustered for myself during my early years and comparing it with the sort of training methods and systems that are available today – which have helped improve technical standards enormously – I do not think I did too badly for a late starter with no money and certain major setbacks – injuries, parental disapproval and military service.

Certainly the dance element was very strong in Vera Volkova's classes, and Peggy van Praagh's Cecchetti-based teaching was extremely well balanced between technique and dance quality for both males and females. I owe them both a huge debt of gratitude for all they did for me. What I did miss out on, however, was all that wonderful character work that most schools now provide. Galina Samsova, the great ballerina from Kiev, who had the most wonderful arms, always said that having to learn so many character dances utilising her upper body made her arms flow in the big classical roles in such a natural and stylish way. All those wonderful mazurkas, czardas and other national dances, which are now so beautifully taught at the Royal Ballet School by Tania Fairbairn, help give such style, carriage and musicality to the students. Character dancing helps so much with the co-ordination of the arms, body, legs and feet with the music. However, even then in the 1940s, George Balanchine's influence was creeping in, with very high legs for the girls. Épaulement – the use of the shoulders and arms independently from the rest of the body – so stylishly taught by van Praagh, was also on the way out. Petit batterie – the small quick steps beating the feet and calves together close to the floor at great speed – was already beginning to disappear in the same way.

However, I did have the advantage of working with Kurt Jooss, which did give me more dynamic body movement and a strong feeling for dance. I think I had a big advantage in my early, rather muddled training as an apprentice: I was constantly surrounded by the company dancers, stage designers, lighting experts, musicians, wardrobe and watching rehearsals. Also I was always involved with performances, both watching and actually appearing. For me, a late starter, with a limited future as a dancer, it was ideal and gave me great focus and confidence. I had got off to a good start and thought I was ready to face the challenges of Sadler's Wells Theatre Ballet. However, I soon found that I had a long way to go and that dancers' training continues until the day you hang up your shoes.

Given the challenges I faced in getting a training without attending a full-time ballet school, I have always been interested in the work of dance schools. I am happy to be a vice president of the Elmhurst School of Dance along with Carlos Acosta, Maina Gielgud and Merle Park. Because of its close association with Birmingham Royal Ballet – its current artistic director is Robert Parker, a former principal with the company and its artistic advisers are David Bintley and Desmond Kelly – people tend to think of Elmhurst as a fairly recently established school. In fact it is Britain's oldest vocational ballet school, having been established in 1923 at Camberley in Surrey. It became the associate school of Birmingham Royal Ballet in 2002 and relocated to its present five-acre campus at Edgbaston a couple of years later. Although students may end up working in all areas of dance, as is the case with graduates from many schools, under Robert Parker classical ballet is at the heart of the teaching. Robert rightly recognises that without ballet technique many doors will remain closed to young dancers. He is keen for me to be further involved with the school's work, which I am more than happy to support. I was delighted to open Elmhurst's new building along with Merle, and I have donated funding to help staff and students with their training programmes. It takes many years for a new school to settle in and it is truly remarkable how firmly its roots have taken. With Elmhurst School in place, the future of Birmingham Royal Ballet is much more secure.

It is striking how the standards of technique and virtuosity in classical ballet in Britain have improved, particularly during the last 20 years. This has been greatly helped by the Royal Academy of Dance spreading the gospel about good teaching to ballet schools all over the United

Kingdom and in fact all over the world including Australia, New Zealand, Japan and India. In addition, the Royal Ballet School's junior and senior associates' scheme, which has centres all over Britain, gives young talent opportunities to work with teachers from the Royal Ballet School who keep an eye on them. It is those early years that make such a difference to their future when early faults become magnified.

Although there are mime sequences used in many – though by no means every – company productions of the classics, they no longer have the power and impact that Tamara Karsavina gave them in a series of lectures in the 1950s, which they need. Ursula Moreton, a former assistant director of the Royal Ballet School, was a great expert on mime. Not only did she know the exact gestures but also how the weight of the body and the positioning of the arms and fingers were placed. For me, as much as I admired her accuracy, I found it all too academic. Barbara Fewster, former principal of the Royal Ballet School, is also a great expert, but she has retired and mime really needs a champion who is young and passionate. Barbara was an excellent teacher – who called me Pimpernel as she said I always cropped up everywhere! A dear friend.

With less reliance on mime, and the creation of fewer narrative ballets over the years, choreography has become far more athletic, with the way the arms are used becoming generally less dynamic, either over-stretched or too relaxed. Virtuosity is much improved, but fast pirouettes, which I love, seem to have become a rarity. Controlled turns, which I also love, are much better. In years gone by, however, I think we used to actually dance much more, but much of that stemmed from the fact that we were trying to hide the fact that technically we were not so hot and our legs were lower. Everything that Jooss did was directed towards performance and there was a proper theatre in his school, whereas in other ballet schools in those days the approach was much stricter. As you hardly ever had a performance, you did often wonder why you were training.

It is marvellous today that student dancers receive a proper academic classical training and learn about other dance techniques. With Christopher Powney recently appointed director, the Royal Ballet School has produced some really interesting dancers much better equipped and ready to take their places in companies. The relationship between company and school staff is now very good, but that has not always been the case. This augurs well for the future. I also think that reading notation should be part of dancers' training: in the same way that a musician learns to read music, so should a dancer be able to read dance, especially soloists and principals. The staff spend hours teaching solos, explaining the musical timing of each step, whereas it is all there in the notation and available at any time, so a newcomer to a role could come to the first rehearsal already step perfect. The young dancers that to me display the greatest maturity while at the same time maintaining their youthfulness are graduates from the Rambert School of Ballet and Contemporary Dance, led by Amanda Britton. They move, dance and perform like young adult men and women.

Companies such as the Bolshoi, the Mariinsky, Paris Opéra Ballet, the Royal Danish and New York City Ballet still have a recognisable style of moving. Whether or not style can be taught is a much discussed topic. I know that Samira Saidi, director of dance at English National Ballet School, believes that style can be taught – rather than it being something that a dancer acquires through performance – but that is a belief that is not shared by everyone. Style – which I believe in its widest sense includes the alignment of the arms and legs co-ordinated with the head and eyes, dancing and feeling the music, proper understanding of épaulement – is fundamental in ballet in the same way that teaching music is not just about technique but also phrasing, feeling and expression are vitally important. There is an amazing difference – in any profession – in the difference that a teacher can make in how a student follows what they have learned. The thing that I have observed with the teaching of ballet is that even if somebody works with an uninspired teacher, natural talent will still come through. Dance training still requires a lot of work which is not just about being musical or about physique or placing. But if you have talent you can overcome an enormous amount through hard work, concentration and determination.

I often go to the assessment classes and showcase presentations that Samira organises at English National Ballet School. She danced several principal roles with Sadler's Wells Royal Ballet. David Bintley created *The Snow Queen* on her which highlighted her wonderful quality as a dancer, although she did not have a particularly strong technique. She was fabulous too in the second movement of Léonide Massine's *Choreartium*. After retiring from dancing she qualified as a teacher, working at the Royal Ballet School, before joining Elmhurst School for Dance tutoring graduate girls. She became director at English National Ballet School in 2012. Since then I always notice a development in the way the students work both in terms of technique and style. I believe it is important that schools complement each other rather than detract from each other. The better all schools are, the better companies will become. Under Samira's leadership it has been transformed and several of her students have been taken into that company as well as other major companies.

David Gayle, a former soloist with the Royal Ballet, was founder of the Yorkshire Ballet Summer School, a very successful annual event which originally took place in Ilkley before becoming firmly established in York. As a result of this, many young dancers were discovered and won scholarships to the Royal Ballet School or English National Ballet School and also had the benefit of taking class with some great teachers from Europe and America. One of the scholarships is named after me and is funded by the Friends of Birmingham Royal Ballet. When David retired, the seminars were taken over by Marguerite Porter, a former ballerina at Covent Garden. She has continued the admirable work that David started, and with her allure, powers of communication and wide experience she is playing a big part in the future of classical ballet in this country.

The transition from training to establishing a career as a professional dancer or choreographer has always been a challenging one. The National Youth Ballet was founded in 1988 by that marvellous woman, Jill Tookey. Her commitment to the company was full-time and voluntary. She really was remarkable, fully deserving her CBE, and I am more than happy to be a patron of the company. It exists to give young people from all over the United Kingdom the opportunity to perform in new ballets, often working with new music, from conception to performance at a professional level. The level of creativity that the company exhibits is impressive, as when the emerging choreographer, the 18-year-old Andrew McNichol, choreographed *Chocolat*, based on the novel by Joanne Harris and using the music by Rachel Portman from the film. I feel that Andrew really is someone to watch.

The company's show at Sadler's Wells in September 2015 included several really worthwhile pieces. Jo Meredith's *The Sighting*, depicting a sylph-like woman carried by a large group of soldiers, was outstanding. *Rock 'n' Roll* by Jenna Lee and Arielle Smith's *Athena* also impressed me. One wonders what will be the next step for these choreographers. I suspect it will have to be another opportunity to work with National Youth Ballet. However, after a choreographer has proved him – or herself

– it strikes me that in a country which has now established a great dance tradition, talented young choreographers should be able to work at choreography where it would be a priority, with its own place in the timetable and proper attention given to creating scenarios, understanding musical construction, art appreciation and the other creative aspects that contribute to a choreographer's development. It really is time that we accept that probably the most important part of classical ballet is the choreography and at the moment this is the weakest. It is the same in most other countries and is caused by the fact that technique and virtuosity are given priority, hence that side of our art form has improved enormously. This has led companies to produce so-called abstract works, very few narrative ballets, plenty of athletic, even acrobatic works, with less and less expressive pieces with an idea, theme or story.

We need a place for choreographic talent to be developed after people have had their initial chance to create. There is no college anywhere that teaches choreography in the same way that if you want to study composition you can go to the Royal College of Music or other conservatoires. If it were possible to have such a thing it would be marvellous. For young choreographers, even those associated with a major company, finding enough opportunities to develop your work and for it to be seen is problematic. Over the years, from the 1960s onwards until its closure in 1994, London Contemporary Dance showcased the work of many modern choreographers including Alvin Ailey, Martha Graham, Paul Taylor and Jerome Robbins. Importantly too the company was a stepping-stone for many emerging choreographers when they could not sustain full evenings of exclusively their own work. It is this situation that faces many young choreographers today, as they are forced to establish their own companies as a way of getting their work seen. This is hugely exposing for novice choreographers and rarely flatters even the most accomplished ones.

Kevin O'Hare has talked about being more forward looking with the genre of narrative ballets created by the Royal Ballet. He is on record as saying that by the end of 2020 he would like every full-length ballet presented by the company to have been created in the previous ten years, believing that directors have been too averse to risk. Kevin is experienced enough to recognise that not everything that is attempted will work. That is the nature of a live art form. The excitement of attending the theatre is not knowing what you are about to see, argues Kevin. I championed his appointment as director of the company in the face of strong support from senior figures at the Royal Opera House for other candidates. Taking risks is an intrinsic aspect of any director's remit. Kevin believes strongly that the appeal of narrative ballets particularly is that they involve audiences in a story over an extended period so that viewers are carried away in how dance can explore subjects really quite deeply.

But why, apart from David Bintley, is nobody producing new full-length ballets with a theme? I do not mean fairytales or works drawn from existing literary sources but full-length ballets about contemporary subjects. It is 50 years since Peter Darrell, working with the contemporary playwright David Rudkin, made *Sun into Darkness*, a three-act ballet about a present-day Cornish fishing village. Yet consider the familiar territory of the so-called story ballets created in recent years: Christopher Wheeldon's *Alice's Adventures in Wonderland* at Covent Garden and his version of *Cinderella* for Dutch National Ballet. However theatrical these productions may be in their presentation, they do not strike new ground for ballet in terms of subject matter. Think too of *Carmen, Hansel and Gretel* and *Frankenstein* at Covent Garden, all well-trodden paths for ballets. David Bintley ventured further afield with his earlier choice of subjects with *The Swan of Tuonela, Far from the Madding Crowd* and *Edward II*, but more recently with *Beauty and the Beast, Aladdin* and *Cinderella* he has been on the more familiar terrain of recognisable titles.

When Frederick Ashton and Kenneth MacMillan were creating work it was unique to the Royal Ballet. Nowadays, for newly created ballets, the company usually holds the sole performing rights for five years. Beyond that, the licence needs to be renewed if the company wants to continue to perform the ballet in question, which the Royal Ballet usually does not do. Otherwise the choreographer is free to take the ballet for performance by other companies elsewhere, a commercial arrangement that favours choreographers. These days choreographers frequently insist on a non-exclusivity clause which means they are free to mount the same ballet for as many companies that want it at the same time. Think how familiar Wayne McGregor's *Chroma* became with companies around the world after its premiere by the Royal Ballet. Kevin O'Hare considers it a strength that choreographers supposedly resident with the company, Wayne McGregor, Christopher Wheeldon and Liam Scarlett, are equally, if not more, busy with other companies around the world. The work of other choreographers with a particular association with Covent Garden, Kim Brandstrup and Ashley Page for example, is as widely seen elsewhere around the world. Cinema broadcasts, popular with non-theatre-going audiences, may well broaden the reach of ballet, but they also break down the exclusivity, in the sense of uniqueness, of companies' repertoires. That, and the real shortage of really distinctive, top rank choreographers working at an international level, means that the repertoire of companies worldwide is becoming less distinctive, more homogenised.

Following McGregor's huge success with *Chroma* in 2006, which premiered along with the first performance of Wheeldon's *DGV*, Monica Mason, as then director, wanted to ensure that the Royal Ballet continued to move with the times. She wanted a choreographer who would feel part of the company, not just a guest. Her concern was for how dancers moved physically and performed. Having seen a lot of McGregor's work and talked to him, Monica felt he would be a good choice as he communicated well with the dancers, made them feel involved and could make them understand why their movements were sometimes distorted and why their costumes were different from what they were used to. The company's music director, Barry Wordsworth, thought that a triumvirate – himself, Wayne and Monica – would be a strong and unified force in planning for the future. The company's administrative director Anthony Russell Roberts and Monica's associate director Jeanetta Laurence supported the idea. McGregor would not accept anything less than being resident choreographer as a title. As Monica recognised the need for the company to make an impact, she agreed to that. McGregor became the first contemporary choreographer to hold the position in the company's then 75-year history. He is a man full of ideas which he seems to find hard to express through his choreography – if you can really call it that. I really detect a minimal amount of choreographic imagination in terms of dance composition, musicality, variety, contrast and human expression in his work compared to such genuinely mould-breaking and progressive choreographers as Mikhail Fokine, Bronislava Nijinska, Martha Graham, Merce Cunningham, Kurt Jooss or Pina Bausch – not that I want McGregor to imitate or copy these great creators, but surely our development depends a little on the past.

As much as I like Wayne, and he is a very likeable man with an infectious smile and eyes that are very friendly, I do have certain problems when watching his ballets, both abstract and narrative. I find the movements very ugly, unnatural and inexpressive with very little variety and no steps. He is full of good ideas but actually they are, for me, never understandable unless you refer to his programme notes – but then the same can be said of classical steps and mime. But to me, theatre is about communication, and in Wayne's pieces the lighting is usually so dim that facial expression does not exist, and the feet and hands, which can be very expressive – Frederick Ashton would often speak about talking feet – never seem to be used to much effect. And then the music, from which the inspiration comes and plays such a vital part in dance, serves only as a background in Wayne's work, which has so little to do with dance. I know that other choreographers have done the same. Glen Tetley would often add the music after he had composed the choreography. I must admit that part the problem comes from my way of watching his ballets although I do try to keep an open mind.

Of course classical dancers tend to like the extreme physical demands that McGregor places on them because his work is something different. He is precise and knows what he wants to achieve, but there is too a limit to what joints and the human frame can achieve. So far McGregor's works seem to me a dangerous distortion of classical ballet. In my opinion, and with the prospect of more of his works entering the Royal Ballet repertoire, I feel that some contemporary training needs to be introduced to protect the company's strong and beautiful classical line and technique – as hopefully the company will still remain a classical one, albeit with the ability to dance more contemporary choreography better. Currently there is no proper training for it. Martha Graham created a whole new syllabus for her form of dance training at her school to prepare students to dance her type and style of dance which apparently combines well with classical ballet. Maybe Wayne is planning to do the same.

While today's continent-hopping world may give young choreographers more chances of becoming more fluent and efficient in the art of setting their choreography on different companies who dance in a different way, I do not think it does much to help them find their own distinctive language. Without that, they will find it difficult to become well known for their particular style and exciting for their own choreography. In an ideal world, young choreographers should be able to work with the same dancers on each project with a deadline that does not pressurise them, allowing them to polish and pare down their creations, eliminating anything that does not fit the choreographic pattern, Frederick Ashton always advised this. In doing that, choreographers would find it hugely beneficial to work in rehearsal studios that can be adapted to match the dimensions of different sized stages, complete with wings and orchestra pit as well as seating for the audience. This is something that many international opera houses have, and they are used to huge advantage. As there seem to be so many new ballets and workshops these days requiring much stage time, fully equipped studios would make it less painful, even having unofficial dress rehearsals before a new ballet faces the acid test of being performed onstage. Studios that match stage dimensions and conditions would benefit students too ahead of their graduation performance, as they make that all-important transition from school and the stage.

I am a great supporter of the Royal Ballet School, however reluctant I was to attend when Ninette de Valois insisted in 1948, although I was only there very briefly. Having come away from watching a recent rehearsal at the school I was feeling quite elated, not because the dancers had done particularly well, which they had, but because there was such a good feeling of achievement and sense of purpose around the place. This must surely be something to do with the fact that the current director, Christopher Powney, is now fully established. The focus of the students' hard work is to learn to dance. Technique and style and time are still as important, but the Royal Ballet School now has a direction that has been missing for some time. Dance quality and the feeling of elation that dance should bring to the performer and the onlooker, rather than high legs and technique for their own sakes, are now firmly in focus. It is the ability to communicate and project the music and all the emotions. That is what it is all about now. In the 1940s, when Madam was still struggling to set the company on a firm financial basis, she would say that the school should be the most important part of the whole organisation, providing the companies with physically sound and well-trained dancers in a style that can be used in the creation of new works and the classics. That is harder and harder now that dancers are expected to execute such contortions and acrobatic movements in some present-day new works. De Valois based her ethos very much on that of the great classical companies of Russia, France and Denmark, though sadly no longer Italy where classical ballet began under Catherine de Medici.

I do have more confidence in the future of the Royal Ballet, now that things seem better at the school in London. Similarly Elmhurst in Birmingham, where Robert Parker is producing much more usable company material. However, until Birmingham Royal Ballet raises its image and hugely increases awareness of its work in London with big publicity, it cannot expect to keep Elmhurst's best recruits, who are being tempted into companies based in the capital, or even get more talent from Birmingham itself. Parents seem more concerned about the ultimate future of their offspring and see the image of the Royal Ballet as the Royal Opera House rather than Birmingham Royal Ballet at the Hippodrome. However, what is encouraging is that there are some excellent men in the company who are doing extremely well. And consider the fact that at the season of *Swan Lake* at Sadler's Wells in October 2015 the company was able to present four new swan queens, all brilliantly danced and who received high praise from critics and the public alike.

As standards are so high at the moment in classical ballet and its popularity has increased, and although the Arts Council always gets more of a battering from the government compared to other funding organisations, I believe that the future for development of dance in this country is looking better. But I do also believe that it is important that classical ballet and contemporary dance keep their own particular styles of presenting dance. I go back again to our founder Ninette de Valois' words, 'Contemporary dance is very strong at the moment with some wonderful dancers. Don't try and copy them – they will always do a better job and we must never be seen to detract from their successes. You must learn to live with each other but keep your own identity. They have already learned from us by incorporating classical training to strengthen their dancers but not to use it in their performances. We should surely be able to use some of their training to give our dancers more dynamics in their work which they badly need in order to enhance classical ballet's range of movement and expression.'

I think one of the most important organisations that has been established recently is the Frederick Ashton Foundation. For this I am very much aware of the huge contribution that its chairman, Tony Dyson, as well as the other trustees have made in order to perpetuate Ashton's huge contribution to classical ballet. I am very appreciative of Cranko and MacMillan, as well as Fokine and Nijinska, Balanchine and Robbins, whose influence and style have also made a huge difference. But as I see it, it is Ashton who has left the most important legacy: a completely unique and influential choreographic style. Tony was one of Fred's really good friends and although as an architect and non-dancer he cannot perform Ashton's choreography himself he recognises and appreciates the real thing. The Ashton heritage is now being jealously guarded by the foundation's trustees whose aim is to ensure that Ashton's ballets are performed accurately and with great effect, as he always demanded. Everything must be done to ensure that his heritage will live on in perpetuity, ensuring its survival for the future.

To finish, I would like to say that, having seen Christopher Wheeldon's triple-bill performed by the Royal Ballet in February 2016, I feel very positive about choreography in this country. I am so pleased, with *Strapless*, that he has created another narrative work that, although not wholly successful, showed that Wheeldon has good ideas about bringing these sorts of narrative works back into the running. What really excited me were the two other works, *After the Rain* and *Within the Golden Hour*, so wonderfully musical and brilliant danced. I felt I was right there with the dancers on the stage. Having watched Wheeldon's development with some concern it was heartening to see abstract ballets that had so much content and humour. They were comparable but different to Ashton's style full of lightness, defying gravity and I feel that Wheeldon will come to have as big an impact on the company as Ashton did. Wheeldon's work is all based on his contemporary understanding of classicism and I now feel really feel confident about him. With Kevin O'Hare at the helm of the Royal Ballet, Wheeldon creating such works and Christopher Powney's leadership of the Royal Ballet School, the way ahead looks good and exciting. I also congratulate Tamara Rojo for the brilliant way she has transformed English National Ballet into such a strong and exciting company. At the same time Birmingham Royal Ballet has scored a major success in Ashton's *A Month in the Country* and David Bintley is well into his new three-acter, *The Tempest*, based on Shakespeare. The Elmhurst School in Birmingham is producing some really interesting dancers under Robert Parker's strong leadership. Also in Birmingham, William Bracewell has won outstanding classical performance for *The King Dances* in the Critics' Circle awards for 2015. There are also two dancers, Francesca Hayward at the Royal Ballet and Brandon Lawrence with Birmingham Royal Ballet, whose performances have been consistently of an incredibly high standard which for me represent the future of the Royal Ballet organisation.

APPENDIX

❧ ❦

My dancing steps

I danced in many ballets. I was never Siegfried in *Swan Lake* but usually Benno when not a huntsman or occasionally Rothbart, but a company is not just about the principals. I do not claim that this list of ballets in which I danced mainly supporting roles is exhaustive, but I performed in a wide variety of ballets, TV and commercial theatre including *The Green Table*, *Big City*, *Prodigal Son*, *Night Train*, *Columbinade*, *Weg im Nebel*, *Pandora*, *Ball in Old Vienna*, *Company at the Manor* and *Die Thyrambus*, all by Kurt Jooss, as well as *Fantasie* and *Le Bosquet* by Hans Zullig and *Sailor's Fancy* by Sigurd Leeder. Although I never fulfilled my ambition to dance in *Les Sylphides* I did dance in Mikhail Fokine's *Carnaval*; Victor Gsovsky's *Dances from Galanta* and *Pygmalion*; Letty Littlewood's *Marchaund's Tale*; and *The Picnic* by Pauline Grant. Among Frederick Ashton's ballets, I have appeared in *Capriol Suite*, *Les Patineurs*, *Les Rendezvous*, *Façade*, *Valses nobles et sentimentales* and his version of *The Nutcracker*. I performed in *Coppélia*. Of ballets by Ninette de Valois, I danced in *The Haunted Ballroom*, *The Rake's Progress*, *The Prospect Before Us* and *The Gods Go a'Begging*. I have also performed in Nancy McNaught's *Étude*, Angelo Andes' *El Destino* and *Jota Toledana*, Celia Franca's *Khadra*, *La Fête étrange*, *Selina* and *La Belle dame sans merci* by Andree Howard, *The Vagabonds* by Anthony Burke, *The Catch* by Alan Carter, *Blood Wedding* by Alfred Rodrigues and *Summer Interlude* by Michael Somes. I danced in Kenneth MacMillan's *Solitaire*. For John Cranko I was in *School for Nightingales*, *Tritsch-Tratsch*, *Pastorale*, *Beauty and the Beast*, *Antigone*, *Romeo and Juliet*, *Lady and the Fool*, *Harlequin in April*, *Sea Change*, *Paso Doble*, *Pineapple Poll* and *The Forgotten Room*,

Aside from apprentice pieces, my choreography for musicals and the occasional pas de deux for galas, below is a mostly complete list of my original choreography for new one or two-act ballets.

1957
December 26   *A Blue Rose*
                     Royal Ballet Touring Company
                     Royal Opera House Covent Garden
                     Music: Samuel Barber, *Souvenirs*
                     Designs: Yolanda Sonnabend
                     Cast included: Anne Heaton, Donald MacLeary

1958
September 18   *The Great Peacock*
                     Edinburgh International Ballet
                     Empire theatre, Edinburgh
                     Music: Humphrey Searle
                     Designs: Yolanda Sonnabend
                     Cast included: Claudia Algeranova, David Poole

1960
February 18   *Musical Chairs*
                     Western Theatre Ballet
                     Theatre Royal, Hanley
                     Music: Sergei Prokofiev, *Musiques d'enfants*
                     Designs: Kenneth Rowell
                     Cast included: Laverne Meyer, Hazel Merry, Brenda Last

1961
April 23   *The Trial*
                     Sunday Ballet Club
                     Lyric theatre, London
                     Music: Heitor Villa-Lobos, *Lliraportt*
                     Designs: Yolanda Sonnabend
                     Cast included: Chesterina Sim Zecha, William Martin,
                     John McDonald

1963
April 27   *The Mirror Walkers*
                     Stuttgarter Ballett
                     Würtembergische Staatstheater, Stuttgart
                     Music: Piotr llyich Tchaikovsky, *Suite no. 1*
                     Designs: Wilfried Gronwald
                     Cast included: Marcia Haydée, Ray Barra

July 13   *Quintet*
Stuttgarter Ballett
Würtembergische Staatstheater, Stuttgart
Music: Jacques Ibert, *Trois pièces brèves, Deux mouvements*
Designs: Walter Gayer
Cast included: Helga Heinrich, Ray Barra
British premiere: BBC TV, May 14, 1964 with Georgina Parkinson, Christopher Gable, Anthony Dowell, Bryan Lawrence and Laurence Ruffell
First stage performance in the UK, Royal Ballet touring company, New theatre, Oxford, October 29, 1964.
Designs: Judith Wood
Cast: Brenda Last, Ronald Emblem, Johaar Mosaval, Piers Beaumont and David Wall

1964
May 20   *Entwürfe für Tänzer* (*Designs for Dancers*)
Stuttgarter Ballett
Würtembergische Staatstheater, Stuttgart
Music: Béla Bartók, *Music for strings, percussion and celesta*
Designs: Yolanda Sonnabend
Cast included: Ana Cardus, Egon Madsen

October 29   *Summer's Night*
Royal Ballet Touring Company
New theatre, Oxford
Music: Francis Poulenc, *Sinfonietta*
Designs: Judith Wood
Cast included: Elizabeth Anderton, Richard Farley, Doreen Wells, Gary Sherwood

1965
May 21   *A Ballet to this Music*
Western Theatre Ballet
Kansallisooppera, Helsinki, Finland
Music: Joseph Haydn, Symphony no. 55
Designs: Peter Cazalet
Cast included: Simon Mottram, Donna Day Washington
British premiere, August 9, 1965, Nottingham Playhouse

1967
June 2   *Namouna*
                         Stuttgarter Ballett
                         Wurtembergische Staatstheater, Stuttgart
                         Music: Édouard Lalo arranged Kurt-Heinz Stolze
                         Designs: Peter Farmer
                         Cast included: Birgit Keil, Richard Cragun

1968
March 7   *Dance Macabre*
                         Western Theatre Ballet
                         Sadler's Wells theatre, London
                         Music: John McCabe, Symphony no. 1
                         Designs: Peter Farmer
                         Cast included: Elaine McDonald

1969
September 21   *Concerto*
                         Bat-Dor Company,
                         Tel-Aviv, Israel
                         Music: George Frideric Handel
                         Designs: Era Lev
                         Cast included: Miriam Zamir, Igal Berdichevsky, Ole
                         Derek

September 21   *Variations*
                         Bat-Dor Company
                         Tel Aviv, Israel
                         Music: Antonio Vivaldi, *La Stravaganza* concerto no 1
                         Designs: Peter Farmer
                         Cast included: Miriam Zamir, Shimon Hofenung, Ole
                         Derek, Lazar Dano, Igal Berdichevsky

1975
February 14   *Arpège*
                         Royal Ballet Touring Company
                         Royal Shakespeare theatre, Stratford-upon-Avon
                         Music: François Boïeldieu
                         Designs: Peter Farmer
                         Cast included: Brenda Last, Alain Dubreuil
                         Originally created for the Royal Ballet School, June 29,
                         1974 with a cast that included Michael Batchelor.

September 5   *El Amor Brujo*
                Royal Ballet Touring Company
                King's theatre, Edinburgh
                Music: Manuel de Falla
                Designs: Stefanos Lazaridis
                Cast included: Stephen Jefferies, Vyvyan Lorraine

1976
October 12   *Summertide*
                Sadler's Wells Royal Ballet
                Music: Felix Mendelssohn
                Designs: Elisabeth Dalton
                Cast included: Margaret Barbieri, David Ashmole
                Revised and revived version, designed by Dick Bird,
                staged by Margaret Barbieri and performed by Sarasota
                Ballet, November 20, 2015.

I have staged the following productions of full-length ballets:

Giselle
Designed by Peter Farmer:
Stuttgarter Ballett, 1966; Cologne Opera Ballet, 1967; Royal Ballet Touring Company, 1968; Royal Ballet, 1971; Bayerisches Staatsballett Munich, 1976; Het Nationale Ballet Amsterdam 1977; Houston Ballet, 1979; Ballett Frankfurt, 1980; Ballet Nacional do Bracil Rio de Janiero, 1982; Royal Winnipeg Ballet, 1982; Star Dancers Ballet Tokyo, 1987 and Sarasota Ballet, 2009.

Designed by Desmond Heeley:
National Ballet of Canada, 1970.

Designed by John Macfarlane:
Royal Ballet, 1985.

Designed by Michael Scott:
Badisches Staatstheater Karlsruhre, 2004.

The Sleeping Beauty
Designed by Peter Farmer:
Cologne Opera Ballet, 1968; Bayerisches Staatsballett Munich, 1976 and Wiener Staatsballett, 1995.

Designed by Lila de Nobili, Henry Bardon and Rostislav Doboujinsky:
Royal Ballet, 1968.

Designed by Philip Prowse:
Het Nationale Ballet Amsterdam, 1981; Sadler's Wells Royal Ballet, 1984;
Teatro Colón Buenos Aries, 2008 and Hungarian National Ballet, 2016.

Designed by Pablo Núñez:
Teatro Municipal Santiago, 2003.

Coppélia
Designed by Osbert Lancaster:
Royal Ballet Touring Company, 1975.

Designed by Peter Snow:
Sadler's Wells Royal Ballet, 1979 and Scottish Ballet, 1992.

Designed by Peter Farmer:
Birmingham Royal Ballet, 1995, Star Dancers Ballet Tokyo, 1997 and
Badisches Staatstheater Karlsruhre, 2005.

Swan Lake
Designed by Philip Prowse:
Sadler's Wells Royal Ballet, 1981; Bayerisches Staatsballett Munich, 1984;
Royal Swedish Ballet Stockholm, 2001 and Teatro Colón Buenos Aries, 2013.

The Nutcracker
Designed by Julia Trevelyan Oman:
Royal Ballet, 1984, revised 1999.

Designed by John Macfarlane:
Birmingham Royal Ballet, 1990; Star Dancers Ballet Tokyo, 1998 and
Australian Ballet 2007.

Acknowledgments

F IRST AND FOREMOST I want to thank Paul Arrowsmith for all his patience and understanding in helping me write this book. He has worked tirelessly on researching my long career, given me wise counsel at all times and coped with my often illegible writings.

It was never my intention to become a producer of classic ballets. I certainly do not want to be remembered just for *The Nutcracker*. Everything I did in my career led to Birmingham Royal Ballet. In compiling this book my always erratic memory has been principally prompted by many friends and colleagues: Ray Barra, Desmond Kelly, Henry Danton, Monica Mason, Derek Purnell, Claudia Algeranova, Jeanetta Laurence, Stephen Wicks, Christopher Carr, Jay Jolley, Johanna Adams Farley and Diana Childs.

I particularly want to thank my beloved daughter Poppy for her calming influence as she coped with me and looked after me during the writing of this book. 'Oh stop fussing,' she told me. 'It's only a book!'

Peter Wright, London, March 2016

Peter Wright – the man of theatre – I discovered in November 1976. My first excursion to the ballet in this country was a performance in Manchester of Peter's production of *Coppélia* performed by Sadler's Wells Royal Ballet. Petal Miller and Murray Kilgour were Swanilda and Franz – and a 19-year-old David Bintley was Coppélius.

Peter Wright – the man – I discovered thanks to an introduction from David Drew, for 56 years a member of the Royal Ballet, noted raconteur and near neighbour. I got to know him after I first interviewed him for *The Dancing Times*. Sadly David is no longer here to read the finished book but he was with us every step of the way, trying to look over our shoulders as it came together.

My thanks to Simon Harper and Claire Lishman, PR managers past and present at Birmingham Royal Ballet and Lee Armstrong there. For sharing personal memories of working with Peter my thanks go to Christopher Nourse, Ross MacGibbon and Anthony Sargent. Thanks to Julia Creed at the Royal Opera House for organising access to files within its 30-year rule normally still closed. For unlocking other sources, thanks to Jonathan Gray, editor of *The Dancing Times*; the staff of the Islington Local History Centre; archivists Jane Fowler at Trinity Laban Conservatoire of Music and Dance, Arike Oke at Rambert ,Victoria Khodorkovsky at the Israeli Dance Archive and Caitlin Dyer at National Ballet of Canada. Wolfgang Oberender at Bayerisches Staatsballett, Ariane Rindle and Birgit Keil at Badisches Staatsballett Karlsruhe, Kumi Oyama at Star Dancers Ballet, Vivien Arnold at Stuttgart Ballet and Richard Heideman at Het Nationale Ballet could not have been more helpful. Thanks to David Thompson, whose experience of television production prevented a mistake. Any other lacunae or divergences from existing biographies or histories, particularly those by Sarah Woodcock about the development of the Royal Ballet companies, are our own.

Paul Arrowsmith, London, March 2016

Index